THE ORIGINS OF THE
MARSHALL PLAN

JOHN GIMBEL

THE ORIGINS OF THE MARSHALL PLAN

STANFORD UNIVERSITY PRESS

1976  STANFORD, CALIFORNIA

Stanford University Press
Stanford, California
© 1976 by the Board of Trustees of the
Leland Stanford Junior University
Printed in the United States of America
ISBN 0-8047-0903-3   LC 75-39334

Published with the assistance of
The Andrew W. Mellon Foundation

For Gisela, Monika, Karen, and John

Acknowledgments

A GREAT MANY people helped to make this book possible. Humboldt State University gave me a research leave for one quarter in 1968, and the Humboldt State University Foundation gave me travel grants to do research in Washington, D.C.; Independence, Missouri; Clemson, South Carolina; and Tucson, Arizona, in the summers of 1972 and 1973. A grant-in-aid from the Harry S. Truman Library Institute supported a full summer of research in the Truman Library in 1969. An American Council of Learned Societies summer fellowship in 1970 made possible a research visit to the Truman Library and a full summer of research in the National Archives, Washington, D.C. The Institute of German Studies at Indiana University gave me a most generous fellowship from its Stiftung Volkswagenwerk funds and afforded me the opportunity of a full year of residence and research in Bloomington, Indiana, in 1970–71. A sabbatical leave from Humboldt State University and a fellowship and travel grant from the Stiftung Volkswagenwerk of Germany enabled me to do research in 1973–74 at the Seminar für Politische Wissenschaft, Bonn University, and in Hamburg, Munich, and Koblenz. The sabbatical leave and the fellowship gave me free time from teaching to write the manuscript.

The Department of the Army gave me virtually unrestricted access to the records of the Army and the Office of Military Government for Germany. The Army also gave me access to the Papers of Lucius D. Clay, a decision Clay himself recommended. The custodians of the Modern Military Records in the National Archives—particularly Thomas Hohmann, William Cunliffe, and Elizabeth Ward—helped me into and guided me through the military records each time I went there over the years. Philip Lagerquist helped in the same way during my visits to the Truman Library. Erich Schimps, of the Humboldt State University Library, was often a great help when I needed him.

The members of my family to whom the book is dedicated come last, but they are not the least. Gisela translated my English into proper German when I needed it done. She proofread the manuscript, as she did my previous two book manuscripts and other writings. She also worked for my living when I did not. Monika accepted without protest the disruptions of her education that my research, writing, and travels imposed upon her, and she made the best of it in the end—by enjoying herself in Bloomington, by learning the German language, by skiing in Norway, by hiking through the Odenwald, and by visiting Berlin, Munich, Freiburg, and other places. Karen, doing me no small favor, held things together at home in Arcata when the rest of us were away.

The conclusions and judgments expressed in this study are my own. They are not to be identified with or attributed to the Department of the Army, to the individuals who helped me, or to the agencies, foundations, archives, and repositories that so generously made records and funds available to me.

J.G.

Arcata, California, 1975

Contents

Abbreviations

NA National Archives

OMGUS Office of Military Government for Germany (U.S.)

PPS Policy Planning Staff (U.S. Department of State)

RFC Reconstruction Finance Corporation

RG Record Group

RGCO Regional Government Coordinating Office

SED Socialist Unity Party (Sozialistische Einheitspartei Deutschlands)

SPD Social Democratic Party (Sozialdemokratische Partei Deutschlands)

SWNCC State-War-Navy Coordinating Committee

TIIC Technical Industrial Intelligence Commission

UNRRA United Nations Relief and Rehabilitation Administration

USFET United States Forces, European Theater

US Group CC United States Group, Control Council

USPOLAD United States Political Adviser (to ACC)

THE ORIGINS OF THE
MARSHALL PLAN

Occupied Germany, 1945–49

CHAPTER ONE

Introduction

THE REASONS for the Marshall Plan for European economic recovery appear to be almost endless. It was a humanitarian program to aid Europe's postwar recovery and to extend a helping hand to those in need. It was a political program to preserve a civilization out of which the American way of life had developed. It was a program to promote peace, freedom, and prosperity. It was an economic program to promote Europe's financial, fiscal, and political stability; to stimulate world trade; to expand American markets; to forestall an American depression; to maintain the open-door policy; to create a multilateral trade world which could be dominated by American capitalists; and to maintain a capitalist hegemony over the regions later to be called the Third World. The Marshall Plan has been referred to as a corollary to the Truman Doctrine: a program to stop communism, to frustrate socialists and leftists, to attract the Soviet Union's satellites, and to contain or roll back the Russians. It was a program that promised future reductions in direct military expenditures, but it also provided Americans with opportunities to stockpile strategic materials and maintain friendly access to military bases abroad. It was a program to promote economic integration in Europe: to reduce nationalism, to further European federation, perhaps even to achieve European union.

Historians who have analyzed and commented on the reasons for the Marshall Plan may be divided into two major groups: the traditionalists or orthodox cold warriors and the revisionists or New Left. Each of the groups is, of course, subject to further subdivision based on the emphases, the self-imposed topical limitations, and the objectives of the various authors. The authors also differ greatly in the skill and thoroughness of their research, the subtleties of their arguments, and the refinements of their exposition. Many of them were limited by the unavailability of sources at the time they wrote.

The traditionalists, of whom Herbert Feis, John W. Spanier, and Arthur

Schlesinger, Jr., are examples, see the Marshall Plan as one of a series of responses to Soviet initiatives in the postwar world: The Russians had taken liberties in Poland and Eastern Europe. They had first refused to withdraw from Iran, and then they did so only under strong American pressure. They inspired revolutionary movements in Eastern Europe, in Greece, and elsewhere in the world. They supported Communist parties in Italy and France and in the Soviet occupation zone of Germany. In Germany they caused the failure of four-power control: they would not agree to establish central German administrations, to treat Germany as an economic unit, and to adopt a common export-import program for the four zones. Furthermore, they removed reparations unilaterally and pushed radical land reforms, socialization, and one-party rule in their zone.

The traditionalists argue that Americans (and their allies) responded to the various Russian initiatives—first hesitatingly, then piecemeal, and finally with a program of containment. The accounts follow a pattern: Franklin D. Roosevelt had hoped to cooperate with the Russians after the war. Some cold warriors think he made unreasonable concessions at Teheran and Yalta. Others defend him for doing what was historically necessary and morally proper, but note that he had become disillusioned with the Russians at the time of his death in April 1945. Traditionalists all agree that Harry S. Truman took a firm stand. He listened to hard-liners, such as W. Averell Harriman, James V. Forrestal, Henry L. Stimson, and William D. Leahy. Following their advice, he lectured Soviet Foreign Minister V. M. Molotov on Poland eleven days after taking office. He told Secretary of State James F. Byrnes in January 1946 that he was "through babying the Soviets." In March 1946 he accompanied Winston S. Churchill to Fulton, Missouri, where the latter gave the iron-curtain speech. Following Truman's lead in Washington and George F. Kennan's advice on the sources of Soviet conduct from Moscow, Americans got tough in Germany: General Lucius D. Clay stopped reparations from the American zone in May 1946. Byrnes pushed for a revival of western Germany in the summer and fall. On September 6, 1946, he made a policy speech in Stuttgart, Germany, and set forth an American program for German recovery and rehabilitation. Byrnes's speech foreshadowed the policy of containment: a policy described and justified publicly by Kennan in his famous Mr. X article in *Foreign Affairs* in July 1947; a policy implemented by the Truman Doctrine, a new directive on Germany, the Marshall Plan, and many other things.

The cold war revisionists, of whom William A. Williams, Gar Alperovitz,

Gabriel Kolko, Lloyd C. Gardner, and Bruce Kuklick are examples, see things differently. For the most part they use the same events that the traditionalists do, but they assign primary responsibility for the collapse of the wartime coalition to the United States rather than to the Soviet Union. They argue that the United States wanted to deny to Russia its legitimate security requirements in Eastern Europe. Americans wanted to dictate a postwar settlement in Eastern Europe and elsewhere, and they used economic warfare and the implied threat of their atomic monopoly as leverage. Americans wanted a world economy characterized by the open door and multilateral trade, an economy that the United States could easily dominate by virtue of its advanced industrial plant, which had not suffered from wartime destruction. In the long run, the United States wanted to undo the Russian Revolution and bring communism into eclipse.

Revisionist historians assign importance to Truman's personality; to his sense of righteousness; to his small-town, country-judge mentality; and to his lack of experience in foreign affairs. They judge him to have been at the mercy of his hard-line advisers (Harriman, Leahy, Stimson, Forrestal), many of whom had failed to get through to his more experienced and sophisticated predecessor. Revisionists focus on Truman's tongue-lashing of Molotov on April 23, 1945; on his abrupt cancellation of lend-lease shipments in May; on his decision to drop the atomic bomb; on American intentions regarding Eastern Europe; on the failure of the United States to advance a $6 billion postwar reconstruction credit to the Soviet Union; on Byrnes's and Clay's initiatives in Germany in the summer and fall of 1946; on the American opposition to socialism in Germany; on the Truman Doctrine; on the Marshall Plan.

Although they differ sharply in their analyses, traditionalist and revisionist historians generally treat the occupation of Germany as a key element in the global cold war. They describe such things as the American suspension of reparations deliveries, the American invitation that led to the British-American Bizone, Byrnes's German-policy speech in Stuttgart, and the origins and purposes of the American draft-treaty for German disarmament as though they were aspects of a Soviet-American cold war. They describe the failure of four-power control in Germany as though it was caused by the Russians and the Americans. But none of this is accurate. Historians who have conceptualized the occupation of Germany as an aspect of the cold war between the United States and the Soviet Union are wrong in their understanding of these and other events that occurred in Germany, and they have consequently failed to see or understand the context out of which the Marshall Plan grew.

My study shows that there is little basis for the myth that the Russians caused the breakdown of the Allied Control Authority in Berlin or for the belief that the Americans abandoned four-power control to frustrate the Russians. There is considerable evidence that the lines of battle were not *clearly* drawn until July 1947, after Molotov left the Paris three-power talks on how the European governments might respond to Marshall's invitation of June 5, 1947. There is, on the other hand, much evidence that France was the major obstacle to four-power cooperation in Berlin. France blocked the implementation of the Potsdam Agreement. France vetoed the proposals for central German economic administrations in Berlin. France refused to agree to all-German political parties, to national trade unions, or to a central German statistical agency. Long before the Russians walked out of an Allied Control Council meeting in 1948, France had stymied the Allied Control Authority by exercising its veto power and by sending observers rather than working delegates into the committees and directorates of the four-power administration in Berlin.

The idea that the Marshall Plan originated as an American initiative in the cold war with Russia is apparently much clearer in the minds of historians in search of grand plans and historical systems than it was in the minds of those who fashioned the Plan. Historians in search of the cold war have, in fact, discovered a Marshall Plan that never existed. The thesis of this book is that the Marshall Plan originated as a crash program to dovetail German economic recovery with a general European recovery program in order to make German economic recovery politically acceptable in Europe and in the United States. It was not a plan conceived by long-range planners as a response to the Soviet Union or as an element in the cold war. The Marshall Plan was a series of decisions that grew out of a continuing bureaucratic struggle between the Army and the State Department over the costs of the German occupation, over reparations, over German exports and imports, over the purposes of the American presence in Germany and Europe, and over contrasting conceptions of the roles being played by Russia and France. The Marshall Plan was hammered out piecemeal by bureaucrats under extreme pressure; by bureaucrats who had neither the time nor the inclination to make long-range plans based on grand conceptions of what the future should be like. They went from issue to issue and from problem to problem, and they compromised, resolved, and reconciled their differences and conflicts as best they could. They followed their instincts and met their deadlines, and as bureaucrats will, they dredged up whatever explanations and rationalizations they thought they needed for their actions, decisions, and compromises. In the process the Marshall Plan mushroomed into a program with so many stated objectives, purposes, and motives as to make these virtually meaningless as a list of reasons for its origins. The contradictions alone are enough to boggle the mind in search of rationality. What the plan eventually did is deceptively simple, however. It provided direct American economic aid to the nations that had expected to use German reparations and cheap German exports for their postwar recovery and rehabilitation programs. It reduced Germany's reparations payments and substituted American grants and loans for them.

CHAPTER TWO

A Mysterious Phenomenon

S PEAKING IN the House of Representatives on the Marshall Plan for European economic recovery, Congressman Thomas A. Jenkins of Ohio asked, "Who knows exactly what it is?... It seems to be something one day and something else the next day. Its origin, apparently, was accidental and it now seems to have no definite purpose or direction."[1] Six months earlier a State Department functionary wrote to a colleague that "the 'Marshall Plan' has been compared to a flying saucer—nobody knows what it looks like, how big it is, in what direction it is moving, or whether it really exists." It was, he said, a "mysterious phenomenon," with which he and his colleagues were trying to cope.[2]

Current mythology on the Marshall Plan notwithstanding, records now available show conclusively that there was no plan when Secretary of State George C. Marshall spoke at Harvard University on June 5, 1947. Marshall said as much later, and the speech he made is remarkably short on details. Marshall talked at Harvard about European economic dislocations, the "breakdown of the business structure of Europe," and the inability of European nations to pay for food and essential products. He asserted that "the remedy lies in breaking the vicious circle and restoring the confidence of the European people in the economic future of their own countries and of Europe as a whole." He thought the United States should do what it could "to assist in the return of normal economic health in the world, without which there can be no political stability and no assured peace." Whatever assistance the United States might give, he said, "must not be on a piece-meal basis as various crises develop." It should be designed to "provide a cure rather than a mere palliative." But, he concluded, "the initiative ... must come from Europe." The European countries would have to agree among themselves "as to the requirements of the situation and the part those countries themselves will take in order to give proper effect to whatever action might be undertaken by this Government. It would be neither fitting nor efficacious for this Government to undertake to draw up unilaterally a program designed to place Europe on its feet economically. This is the business of Europeans."[3]

A State Department message of June 12, 1947, to Jefferson Caffery, the American ambassador in France, asked for information upon which a recovery plan might be based and said the scope and nature of the program were not yet foreseeable. It speculated on whether the program should concentrate on a few vitally important items, such as food, coal, and transport, or whether it might become a regional program "somewhat along the lines" of France's Monnet Plan for postwar economic recovery and growth, but on a "much larger scale involving several countries."[4] The State Department's instructions for Under Secretary of State William L. Clayton's consultations in Europe after the Harvard speech also show the tentative nature of things. The instructions were drafted on June 5, revised on June 9, and apparently changed again before Clayton left for Europe on June 24.[5] When they were completed, Clayton's instructions called for a European initiative and contained nothing that could be construed as a plan. In fact, Clayton told his British counterparts that there had been little discussion on the subject in Washington and that the State Department's considerations had been "meager indeed." He said "most of his views came out of his own head," and he had talked with Marshall only once, chiefly about coal.[6] Back in Washington, Under Secretary of State Robert A. Lovett reviewed Clayton's reports of his discussions in London and observed that Clayton had "developed some points further than we have taken them." Though he thought Clayton and the State Department were thinking along parallel lines, Lovett nevertheless identified a number of issues and questions on which no policy, program, or plan existed as yet.[7]

While Clayton developed policy ad hoc in London—nearly three weeks after the Harvard speech—George F. Kennan, the Director of the State Department's Policy Planning Staff (PPS), scratched for data in Washington. He asked Willard L. Thorp, the Assistant Secretary of State for Economic Affairs, to have staff studies prepared on a European recovery program. He submitted some suggestions and said he needed the studies in a hurry to get a European reconstruction proposal into Marshall's hands. He thought his suggestions "may look so naively broad as to horrify the scholarly economist," but he urged Thorp to tell his people "to disregard their consciences, take a deep breath, and let us have their best guess." A month later Kennan advised Marshall that "we have no plan."[8]

THE STATE DEPARTMENT'S STUDIES TO JUNE 5, 1947

There is no substance to the myth that Marshall announced his plan after thorough, careful, and rational study in the Department of State. The accepted version of the origins of the Marshall Plan may be found in the works of Joseph M. Jones, Harry B. Price, William C. Mallalieu, Max Beloff, Ellen Clayton Garwood, and others.[9] Its essence is that Marshall became convinced, especially during the Moscow Council of Foreign Ministers (CFM), that action on European recovery was urgent. His private talks with Stalin led him to believe that the Russians wanted to delay European recovery— perhaps for the political advantage that economic chaos would provide to Communists. He was disillusioned by his experiences in Moscow: "The patient is sinking while the doctors deliberate."[10] Upon his return to Washington late in April 1947, Marshall recalled Kennan from the National War College and instructed him to activate the Policy Planning Staff and to begin work immediately. He thus initiated the studies that were to play such a significant and compelling role in his decision to speak out at Harvard.

Earlier, the current version continues, while Marshall familiarized himself with his new assignment as Secretary of State and prepared for the Moscow Conference, Under Secretary of State Dean G. Acheson had acted on his own initiative. He talked informally with Kennan in January and again in February 1947, about a possible planning unit in the State Department. Then, on March 5, shortly after discussions on aid to Greece and Turkey had begun, he asked the State-War-Navy Coordinating Committee (SWNCC) to prepare a broad study on possible future American foreign-aid programs and requests. The ideas Acheson generated and the thoughts he had expressed ad hoc before various Congressional committees formed the basis for a preview of the Marshall Plan which he gave to the Delta Council in Cleveland, Mississippi, on May 8, 1947, after he had used the same ideas in a "preliminary canter" at a League of Women Voters luncheon on May 1.

Kennan's and Acheson's initiatives and studies were complemented by Clayton's. As American negotiator for the General Agreement on Tariffs and Trade (GATT) in the International Trade Organization in Geneva, and as United States delegate to the Economic Commission for Europe,

Clayton gathered first-hand information on Europe's economic and financial problems early in 1947. Busy though he was with GATT, ITO, and ECE, with testifying before Congress on a wool tariff bill, with visiting "every major European capital,"[11] and with doing such other things as an Under Secretary of State for Economic Affairs does, Clayton managed to write two memoranda—one on March 5 and the other sometime in May—on Europe's financial and economic plight. The two memoranda have assured him a place in the literature as father of the Marshall Plan (if one reads Ellen Clayton Garwood and Ross J. Pritchard); as stepfather (if one reads Acheson); as artificial donor (if one reads Kennan).[12]

But the picture of the State Department engaged in beehive-like activity, producing studies of Europe's problems and providing a rational, long-range policy that Marshall used for his Harvard address, is out of focus. It is out of harmony with Marshall's frequent protests that he had no plan at the time and it does not reflect the contemporary statements and judgments of Clayton, Kennan, Lovett, and others who participated closely in the development of the Marshall Plan. Furthermore, it conflicts with the evidence now available on the studies Marshall supposedly used to make his decision and his address of June 5, 1947.

The SWNCC Study

Acheson initiated the SWNCC study on March 5, 1947. He wrote to Secretary of War Robert P. Patterson and Secretary of Navy James V. Forrestal that the discussions of aid to Greece and Turkey had convinced him of the need for a study of "situations elsewhere in the world which may require analogous financial, technical and military aid on our part." On March 11 SWNCC appointed an ad hoc committee to conduct the studies. The committee received instructions jointly from SWNCC's parent departments to identify other countries that might need American assistance and to study such things as American objectives; possible financial, technical, and military aid programs; national security; domestic United States resources; and the consequences of the failure to extend aid or of a failure of programs that might be undertaken.[13]

One can hardly quarrel with Joseph M. Jones's description of the committee's structure and its work, especially not with his observation that "the scope of the committee's terms of reference was breathtaking." One can, however, quarrel seriously with his conclusions about the committee's contributions to the Marshall Plan. Jones noted that SWNCC was neither a policy committee nor a research organization. Referring to the ad hoc committee's study, he said "the whole effort was awkwardly organized, jurisdictions were not clear, and the machinery creaked and groaned." The committee's members lacked "rank and prestige," they got little support from senior officials in their departments, and they finally formed "several expert groups" consisting of men of "modest rank." His evidence and his discussion to the contrary, Jones concluded that "the work got done expeditiously," and that "the early studies of the committee . . . contributed directly and powerfully to the launching of the Marshall Plan."[14]

The SWNCC committee's own judgments were more modest, as were its contributions. It described its initial report on April 21, 1947—apparently the only one it made before Marshall's Harvard address—as "highly tentative in nature," and as a "hasty analysis" prepared "from information presently at hand." The report was, in fact, a hodgepodge of observations, recommendations, suggestions, and conclusions that the committee itself considered to be lacking in thorough analysis. It listed eight nations that needed aid within a few months. Three of them were never included in the European recovery program. It listed eight nations that had no urgent needs for aid. Five of them were eventually included in the Marshall Plan. The report itself stated that it was "based upon fragmentary data," that it was an "interim report," and that it would "be revised as better data is assembled." It said further studies were underway, and that a more analytical and refined report would probably be ready in three months. But not even that was to be. The committee completed its final report on October 3, 1947. It observed, then, that the "rapid progress of events has made obsolete much of the data on which the report is based," and that its report was no longer current. It noted that the Marshall Plan had been initiated after the committee had received its terms of reference and that therefore the "report relates only indirectly to the Plan."[15]

The Policy Planning Staff Study

The State Department's newly formed Policy Planning Staff (PPS) had hardly begun to function *as such* before Marshall's Harvard address. Jones says it had met three times.[16] The PPS report of May 23, 1947, which Kennan drafted,[17] said "it is only a few days since the Planning Staff, with an incomplete and provisional complement of personnel, was able to begin to give attention to the substance of its work." Kennan thought the time had been too short, but he was obviously under pressure to produce a paper that could be used as a "basis of further planning."[18]

Kennan had discussed the PPS's plans and tentative working principles with Acheson on May 19. He said the PPS had decided to concentrate on Western Europe. It wanted to leave detailed planning to the SWNCC committee, which "is completing an interim report and is beginning work on a final report scheduled for completion in mid-July." The PPS had prepared a tentative list of principles for "a master plan for US assistance to western Europe," which it hoped to have ready by midsummer. In the meantime, the PPS thought an immediate program was needed for psychological effect: "some energetic and incisive American action to be undertaken at once in order to create in Europe the impression that the United States has stopped talking and has begun to act." It was searching for a "suitable field" for such immediate action, and it was considering a "Coal for Europe" program that would concentrate on restoration of coal production in the Rhine Valley as a most likely scheme.[19] Acheson apparently stressed the urgency of an early recommendation and Kennan drafted the PPS's first report without further formal staff consideration, and certainly without systematic basic research of any kind. He had it ready four days later. Kennan remembered that "the paper had been hastily produced,"[20] and he might have remembered that a month later he was asking his colleagues to "disregard their consciences, take a deep breath," and guess.[21] He said the PPS worked steadily for another two months and produced a second version by July 23, 1947. This one, he remembered, examined in detail the American interest in European recovery, the requirements of the program's success, and the like. The documents show, however, that in 1947 the PPS still regarded its July 23 paper as a preliminary report; a working paper for discussion only. It said the factual material was still incomplete and that the second paper would be revised as facts were developed in Europe and America.[22]

The May 23 PPS report recommended that Western Europe be rehabilitated in two stages or phases: by a short-term action to eliminate bottlenecks and a long-term program for European economic recovery. The United States should seize the offensive and inspire confidence in Europe and America with a short-term program designed to increase production of coal in the Rhine Valley and assure its distribution "to the places of consumption in Europe." The PPS said it attached great importance to the short-term project, and it proposed "to come up with more detailed suggestions in the near future." The long-term program, it said, was enormously complex and difficult, and would require careful study over "a period of at least several weeks." It insisted that "this is the business of the Europeans.

The formal initiative must come from Europe; the program must be evolved in Europe; and the Europeans must bear the basic responsibility for it." The PPS had concentrated on principles, but it obviously had produced nothing that could be construed as a plan or a program. It expressed concern about the delicate and difficult problem of inspiring a European initiative without making it appear to be an American initiative, and it thought the project might possibly be advanced in the Economic Commission for Europe (ECE). It forecast difficulties there—possible Russian opposition—but it remained firm in its recommendation that the initiative should come from Europeans and that the United States should "be careful not to seek unduly to influence their decision." In the meantime, SWNCC should continue its studies, with the State Department representative on the SWNCC ad hoc committee coordinating its findings with the work of the PPS. The Chiefs of Mission in several Western and Central European countries should be asked to present their views on various problems relating to European rehabilitation, and they should be requested to send qualified officers to Washington when they were needed for discussions and planning. Furthermore, the "overall approach" should be "informally and secretly discussed with British leaders."[23] With few exceptions, the report's recommendations were soft, spongy, and tentative. For a policy statement the report is remarkably vague. It was a preliminary paper for discussion, as the PPS admitted its report of two months later was. It was not a plan, except as it was a plan to develop a plan.

The Clayton Memoranda

Clayton's memorandum of March 5, 1947, which was written on the same day that Acheson initiated the SWNCC study on foreign aid, has been used as evidence to support the claim of Clayton's fatherhood of the Marshall Plan. Garwood saw it as a springboard for the May memorandum, which focused directly on the ideas Marshall used at Harvard. Pritchard saw it as evidence of a basic plan evolving in Clayton's mind. But the memorandum was addressed to no one, and there appears to be no evidence that Clayton used it, except perhaps as a prop to write the second memorandum. Clayton wrote it by hand on a plane to Tucson, or while vacationing in Sasabe, Arizona.[24] Normally burdened and perhaps bored with the seemingly endless routine of committee meetings, consultations, and discussions so frustrating to the imagination and so characteristic of the bureaucratic life, Clayton was freed of all that for a fleeting moment by the consequences of a foot infection. He let his ideas flow freely, his thoughts soar, and his pen skip from problems to solutions—as if there were no checkmates. He was disturbed. Britain was slipping as a world power. Either Russia or the United States would fill the vacuum. If Russia did, there would be war in a decade. The United States would have to assume world leadership. That would be impossible unless the American people were shocked into supporting this role. The President could shock them by telling the truth from the cables arriving in the State Department daily. Russia was boring from within. If Greece and Turkey succumbed, the Middle East would be lost, France might capitulate to the Communists, and, as France went, all of Western Europe and North Africa would go. The President and the Secretary of State should inspire the American people and the Congress to struggle for world peace. The United States should extend financial, technical, and administrative aid to gravely threatened nations. Congress should appropriate $5 billion and create a Council of National Defense to disburse the funds as the vital interests of the United States required.[25]

Such an exercise in self-expression by the Under Secretary of State for Economic Affairs is not without significance. It suggests the climate that prevailed in the State Department during the early days of the Greece-Turkey "crisis." Furthermore, it shows that Clayton had already formed some of the ideas that he supposedly gathered later in his meetings in Geneva and in his visits to every major European capital. It shows the strength of Clayton's conviction that the United States had to assume the initiative and to provide financial, technical, and administrative aid abroad, and that the United States should exercise considerable control over the funds and the assistance thus provided. It shows, further, that Clayton would oppose the PPS recommendation calling for a European initiative. That opposition is at the heart of his second memorandum and it is crucial to an understanding of the Marshall Plan.

Clayton's second memorandum surfaced in May. There is considerable confusion as to when. The copy in *Foreign Relations* is dated May 27, 1947. The one in the Truman Library is dated May 31. Garwood, Pritchard, and Jones have said that Clayton wrote the memorandum on the plane from Geneva on May 19, and Robert H. Ferrell has gathered information that it circulated in the State Department before May 27.* The memorandum

* *FRUS*, 1947, III, 230–32; Clayton, "The European Crisis," Clayton Papers (Confidential Marshall Plan Memos, General File), Truman Library; Ellen Clayton Garwood, *Will Clayton: A Short Biography* (Austin, Tex., 1958), pp. 147–48; Ross J. Pritchard, "Will Clayton: A Study

may have been based on notes Clayton made on the plane on May 19, as Clayton said in 1963. It could have been formally written from those notes on May 27 or 31. In any case, there is a strong basis for believing that the memorandum took its final form only after Clayton saw the PPS report of May 23, or after he had learned of its recommendations. There is intrinsic evidence that he wrote it as an alternative to the PPS recommendation or as a counterproposal. A comparison of Clayton's memorandum and the PPS report reveals fundamental differences between Kennan's and Clayton's approaches to European recovery at the time. Those differences, which were not resolved when Marshall spoke at Harvard, show conclusively that no agreed plan or policy existed in Washington on June 5, 1947.

Kennan and the PPS had recommended a "Coal for Europe" program, consisting of technological assistance, special grants of money, special drives by the occupation forces in Germany to recruit labor and to supply materials, a campaign to increase food supplies ("breadless days, etc." in the United States), and various activities to dramatize the program and gain popular support for it. Clayton, on the other hand, wanted the United States to take over the management of Ruhr coal production. Kennan and the PPS recommended minimum American influence on the long-term program: "It would be neither fitting nor efficacious for this Government to undertake to draw up unilaterally and to promulgate formally on its own initiative a program designed to place western Europe on its feet economically. This is the business of the Europeans." According to the PPS the initiative should come from Europeans, "and we should be careful not to seek unduly to influence their decision." Clayton, on the other hand, wanted the United States to save Europe. He wanted the President and the Secretary of State "to make a strong spiritual appeal to the American people to sacrifice a little

---

of Business-Statesmanship in the Formulation of United States Economic Foreign Policy" (Ph.D. dissertation, The Fletcher School of Law and Diplomacy, 1956), p. 286; Joseph M. Jones, *The Fifteen Weeks (February 21–June 5, 1947)* (New York, 1955), p. 246; Robert H. Ferrell, *George C. Marshall*, in Ferrell, ed., *The American Secretaries of State and Their Diplomacy*, vol. XV (New York, 1966), pp. 280–81. In 1950 Clayton seems to have thought the May 31 date was correct, but in 1963 he said he handed the memorandum to Marshall on the 27th. See William L. Clayton, "GATT, The Marshall Plan, and OECD," *Political Science Quarterly*, LXXVIII (Dec. 1963), 496. In a letter of Jan. 7, 1950, to his daughter, enclosing the copy (dated May 31) now in the Truman Library, Clayton said: "This was the basis of the Marshall Plan." Garwood (see p. 13) was apparently determined to have Clayton's memorandum dated early enough to have been considered at the meeting in Marshall's office on May 27 (Jones, p. 249, had already dated the meeting on May 27 or 28), and was also determined to use Clayton's own words as proof that his memorandum was the basis of the Marshall Plan.

themselves, to draw in their own belts just a little in order to save Europe from starvation and chaos." Kennan and the PPS wanted studies in Europe and America to determine needs, conditions, and forms of assistance. Clayton said "the facts are all well known." Europe must have a grant of $6 to $7 billion over the next three years. The grant should be in commodities: coal, food, cotton, tobacco, shipping services, "and similar things." According to Clayton, all were produced in surplus in the United States except cotton. Kennan and the PPS suggested the Economic Commission for Europe as a possible agency to advance a project for European recovery. Clayton thought the ECE was "completely unusable as a forum, even to make a beginning," and he said, "we must avoid getting into another UNRRA. *The United States must run this show.*"*

MARSHALL'S DECISION

Marshall had no developed plan when he spoke at Harvard on June 5, 1947. His speech was, in fact, a mixture of ideas taken from the PPS report of May 23, 1947, Clayton's memorandum of May 27 (31), and Acheson's Delta Council speech of May 8, 1947. At the time, the SWNCC study was tentative and incomplete. The PPS report had been "hastily produced," and it was little more than a plan to develop a plan. Clayton wanted an American program, and he had introduced enough new and divergent recommendations to require the four to six months that Acheson thought might be needed to work out an agreement within the United States government. As late as August 22, 1947, both Clayton's divergent views and the lack of a clear policy on the Marshall Plan were discussed formally within the State Department.[26]

If Marshall had no plan, if he had no complete, systematic studies upon which to base a policy on European recovery, if he had achieved no agreement within his own department, one might ask what prompted him to go to Harvard and say what he did. Marshall's own explanations always took him back to the Moscow Conference, where the foreign ministers had failed to reach agreement on Germany and Austria. He told Harry B. Price in 1952 that the Marshall Plan grew out of his disillusionment in

---

* Kennan to Acheson, May 23, 1947, *FRUS*, 1947, III, 223–30; Clayton, "The European Crisis," *ibid.*, 230–32; Summary of Discussion on Problems of Relief, Rehabilitation and Reconstruction of Europe, May 29, 1947, *ibid.*, 236. It is interesting and, I think, highly significant that Clayton deleted the sentence "The United States must run this show" when he reproduced the memorandum "almost in full" in the *Political Science Quarterly*, LXXVIII (Dec. 1963), 496–98. He had *underlined* it in the original.

Moscow, where the Soviets proved they did not want to negotiate in good faith. He said some thought had been given to developing the plan at the end of the Moscow Conference, but he had vetoed that because he did not want it to appear that the Western allies had come to Moscow with a pre-conceived plan. Besides, he said, there had been difficulties with the British on reparations and on other details.[27] These observations, as well as Marshall's other brief statements, remarks, and comments on the subject, are limited in scope, selective in their information, and cryptic at best. For example, he failed to reconcile his repeated protests that he had had no plan with the inference that "something" already existed in Moscow. Or what was it that he had vetoed? A thought? He named the Russians as the troublemakers, but he failed to mention either the problems created by France or his discussions with the French on coal and other things before and during the Moscow Conference. Perhaps Marshall's explanations were conditioned by his conviction that "it is very difficult to reduce the problems to a simplicity of statement that is understandable to our citizens generally." His early experience as Secretary of State, so he told an audience of state governors in Salt Lake City in 1947, had taught him that lesson, and he said "that experience . . . has guided my language to a considerable extent in the various public statements I have had to make."[28]

Marshall's speech before the Pittsburgh Chamber of Commerce in January 1948 is typical of his caution and of the nature and content of his public statements on the origins of the Marshall Plan. He said one must go back to the Moscow Conference for perspective on the European recovery program. The failure of the CFM in Moscow to reach four-power agreement on the German and Austrian settlement—because of unacceptable Soviet conditions, he said—required the United States to make a major policy decision. Either the United States would have to quit Europe altogether or it would have to complete the task of European recovery. Having decided not to quit, "the United States put into effect certain measures susceptible of immediate application. These concerned Germany, where we have major responsibilities as an occupying power." Although Marshall passed over them lightly with a remark that "this is a rather technical matter which is not readily understood," the "measures susceptible of immediate application," *which had already been put into effect in Germany*, are basic to the origins of the Marshall Plan of 1947.[29]

The Marshall Plan originated out of the failure of the Moscow CFM to solve the German problem. A discussion of that problem leads one to give attention to the experience and frustrations of four-power control in the Allied Control Council in Berlin (ACC); to the causes for and the consequences of the failure of the ACC; to the disagreements and disputes between the Army and the State Department regarding German policy and the future of Europe; to the Army's impatience with the State Department's French priority and its Western European orientation; to the Army's (and Britain's) initiatives regarding the German problem; and to the crisis that developed and the battle that raged after the Army, the British, and the Congress forced the issue at the time of the Moscow CFM early in 1947.

AMERICAN VIEWS ON GERMANY

CHAPTER THREE

Occupiers and Missionaries

THE OCCUPATION of Germany had hardly begun when the earlier American interdepartmental differences on German policy resurfaced as administrative problems. They had never disappeared. Paul Y. Hammond has written that even as the May 11, 1945, version of the Joint Chiefs of Staff (JCS) directive 1067 was being cleared, "the lines of dispute could be seen reforming."[1] The process may be illustrated from the discussion in Washington on the recommendations of the June 7, 1945, Potter-Hyndley coal report.[2]

The Potter-Hyndley report had predicted a drastic coal famine in Northwestern Europe and in the Mediterranean unless emergency measures were taken. The report called for extraordinary steps to increase German coal production. It recommended that the military commanders in Germany be directed to assign top priority to German coal production and to export 10 million tons of coal during 1945 and another 15 million tons by the end of April 1946. They were to deliver the exports irrespective of the consequences in Germany.

The consequences of excessive coal exports from Germany worried the Army, which was responsible for security and order in the defeated country. The Potter-Hyndley recommendation seemed to be a "too hasty" listing of reparations, about which General Lucius D. Clay, the Deputy Military Governor, had warned Assistant Secretary of War John J. McCloy in April. It called for removal of a basic commodity which Secretary of War Henry L. Stimson thought the Army needed to build up "a contented Germany interested in following non-militaristic methods of civilization." It seemed certain to aggravate conditions that Clay already considered "extremely difficult." Clay thought the coal export program would increase cold, hunger, and human distress in excess of that apparently "necessary to make the German people realize the consequences of the war which they caused."[3] Furthermore, implementation of the Potter-Hyndley recommendations promised to cost money—appropriated money, the expenditure of which the Army had to (and would have to) justify to Congress.

The Army's unwillingness to implement the Potter-Hyndley coal recommendations aroused the State Department. H. Freeman Matthews, the Director of the Office of European Affairs, reminded McCloy on June 15, 1945, that "you will remember that at this afternoon's CCAC [Combined Civil Affairs Committee] meeting we were all in agreement that the most persistent efforts must be made in all quarters to offset the natural human tendency of all our high-powered people in Germany to use the German economy to make that country run and to disregard completely in practice the vital needs of the liberated areas of northwest Europe."[4] Three days later Under Secretary of State Clayton wrote to McCloy to complain about the "narrow view" taken by War Department people during the coal talks. The Army was willing to assume responsibility for German imports related to military needs, he said, but not for procuring supplies to increase German production for other purposes. According to Clayton, the State Department believed the Army should procure and finance supplies not only for the occupation forces and to prevent disease and unrest in Germany, but also to provide relief for countries devastated by Nazi aggression. In short, the State Department wanted the Army to be responsible for "all imports which serve the purposes of the United States government in Germany."[5]

The Army disagreed. It was anomalous, McCloy thought, for the Army to determine and finance the rehabilitation programs of foreign countries, for the Army to conduct American economic foreign-policy operations in Europe from its occupation bases in Germany. The Army's occupation forces could see to it that Germans produced what was required of them, but financing that production was another matter. It would be an expense of European rehabilitation, not an expense chargeable to the occupation of Germany.[6]

Clayton would not be put off, and he replied that the State Department would seek a policy decision "at the highest level," to make the Army "responsible for all imports which serve the purpose of the United States in Germany." He said the State Department hoped for an early four-power agreement in the ACC on a four-power German supply program, and he stated that such a program would include interzonal distribution of supplies and imports into Germany based on the principle that "the sum necessary to pay for imports into Germany should be a first charge on all German exports from current production or stocks on hand." If the latter were insufficient, Clayton said, arrangements would have to be made for interim financial advances to Germany by the allies. Reimbursement for net outlays thus advanced was to be sought from subsequent German exports, and "claims for reimbursement of this type should rank above reparations." Clayton had reminded McCloy in an earlier letter that it was established United States policy to "seek to make the reimbursement of all expenses incurred by it in importing supplies into Germany as a first charge on German ability to make foreign payments."[7] But that was not enough (perhaps it was too much) for the Army, and Secretary of War Stimson took over the issue personally.

Stimson explained to James F. Byrnes, the newly appointed Secretary of State, that although it was indeed United States policy, the first-charge principle had not yet been agreed to by the allies. Even if an agreement were to be achieved, he wrote, it would be some time until German exports would balance out the initial advances. In the meantime, German imports would be needed to protect and maintain American troops, to implement American political objectives, and possibly to protect troops and implement American political objectives in the other occupation zones as well. If the War Department were to finance supplies and imports into Germany for these purposes, "it should do so only pursuant to policy established on a governmental basis and approved by the President." Stimson wanted a decision on what areas in Germany were involved, on the purposes for which supplies would be imported (for British and Russian military needs, reparations, relief for Europe, and/or for what?), and on whether the supplies should come from the United States or from non–United States sources. Furthermore, Stimson wanted to know to what agency of government Congress would be asked to appropriate the necessary funds. That was another way of asking who would go to the Congress and its committees and defend United States policies and operations in Germany.*

Byrnes referred the issue to President Harry S. Truman on July 5, 1945, and said the War Department would act only under specific instructions from the President.[8] Truman resolved the interdepartmental dispute in two

---

* Stimson to SecState, July 4, 1945, *FRUS*, 1945, Potsdam I, 479–81. On the same day Stimson wrote to Under Secretary of State Joseph Grew to question whether the State Department's request that the Army speed restitutions from Germany to the liberated countries was consistent with reparations policy. He said: "If the State Department will transmit to the War Department a definite policy to be followed in the administration of Germany with respect to reparations pending action by the Reparations Commission, the War Department will gladly endeavor to carry out such a policy." Stimson to Grew, July 4, 1945, *FRUS*, 1945, Potsdam I, 524–26.

significant decisions at Potsdam. On July 16, 1945, he agreed to a proposal that the Department of State be the primary policy-making agency for the treatment of Germany and Austria, and that the War Department's function be primarily executive and administrative.* Then, pressed by the State Department for a clear directive on the Army's responsibility for finances, imports, and initial outlays in Germany, Truman issued orders to Stimson on July 29, 1945.[9]

Truman's orders listed the Army's economic responsibilities in Germany. The Army would finance and procure German imports that would contribute to certain objectives already approved by the foreign ministers at Potsdam,[10] specifically: (1) the programs of industrial disarmament, demilitarization, reparations, and approved exports and imports; (2) the production of goods and services for the occupying forces, displaced persons, and the German economy to maintain a standard of living not to exceed the average standard of living of European countries (excluding Russia and Britain); (3) the development of interzonal trade, a balanced economy, and the reduction of imports, to the extent that the Control Council could agree; and (4) the control of "German industry and all economic and financial international transactions, including exports and imports, with the aim of preventing Germany from developing a war potential and of achieving the other objectives named herein." Truman's orders required the Army to finance and procure all imports for which the United States "assumes responsibility . . . whether or not an agreed program is formulated and carried out in the Control Council," and to assume responsibility for the entire United States share of any combined financing that might be undertaken by the occupying powers.[11] In summary, Truman's orders directed the Army to implement a wide range of potentially expensive and unpopular policies which would be made by the State Department.

After Potsdam the State Department would make United States policy in Germany; the Army would (in addition to its police function as an army of occupation) administer and execute United States policy in Germany, seek funds from Congress for its implementation, and—in effect—bear the burden of defending that policy to the Congress and thus to the American

---

* The documents suggest that Truman's decision may have been hastily taken and verbally expressed during his busy schedule. Apparently the State Department had no formal record of Truman's approval of its memorandum of July 16. Byrnes submitted it to him again on Aug. 30, 1945, indicated that Truman had approved it at Potsdam, and asked him for "a formal indication of your approval," which Truman gave. See Byrnes to Truman, Aug. 30, 1945, *FRUS*, 1945, III, 958.

public. The practical, day-by-day problems and difficulties inherent in that arrangement have long since been recognized, and they have been discussed often. But the practical, administrative, and jurisdictional problems were mere reflections of a fundamental disagreement between the State Department and the Army regarding the occupation of Germany and its relation to liberated Europe.

THE ARMY'S APPROACH

The Army assumed that its major task in Europe had been completed on May 8, 1945, and that the rest was epilogue. The Army's position in the wartime debates on German policy had reflected that assumption. No matter how the personal views of Army representatives may have differed on details, no matter how Stimson and McCloy rationalized the Army's position to their State and Treasury Department colleagues during the long negotiations that led to the JCS directive 1067, the Army consistently opposed the hard-line approach (the Morgenthau Plan, for instance) because it did not want the occupation to become a long, potentially explosive, and unpopular assignment; an impossible task. Abused by Henry Morgenthau and those who sympathized with his plan to pastoralize the German economy, the Army debated the issues in terms of the hard versus the soft peace for Germany. In the process, the Army's institutional interests remained in the background, and they have apparently never been considered to have been as fundamental as they actually were at the time.

The Army's position was essentially that Germany must be disarmed, demilitarized, denazified, democratized, and made incapable of renewing its domination over Europe, but that these things must not be accomplished at excessive expense to the army of occupation. The Army did not want to administer a failure; to preside over hunger, cold, chaos, confusion, and possible revolution in Germany. Its leaders worried that the Army's recently acquired public image as an efficient, well-managed, successful, and respectable institution would suffer; that the American public would eventually lose interest in vilifying Germans and punishing Germany; and that when that occurred the Army would become the scapegoat for "the failure."* As Stimson expressed it to Clay and General Dwight D. Eisenhower,

---

* See, for example, Clay to McCloy, June 29, 1945, OMGUS Papers, Box 410/3, NA, for the admission that "I am just as apprehensive over possible impatience and lack of understanding at home of our failure to obtain rapid progress, as I am of our ability in the long run" to reach agreement in the Control Council.

the American people would in the long run approve only a decent and humane occupation.[12] Drawing on his experience in the Philippines, he said little could be gained from an occupation that repeated the mistakes of the occupations of the American South, of Cuba, of the Philippines, and of the Rhineland after World War I.

The Army's approach can, perhaps, be illuminated better by illustration than by discussion and assertion. As noted above, the Army resisted the State Department's attempt to define the Army's functions in Germany to include broad political and financial responsibilities, and it refused flatly to accept such responsibilities unless ordered to do so by the President. When Truman assigned it even broader functions than it originally feared, the Army maneuvered speedily and effectively to get out of the occupation business altogether. It sought means, methods, and arguments to accomplish the early transfer of its political, financial, and administrative responsibilities in Germany to the Department of State.

The Army's program to get out of the occupation business assumed many facets. Eisenhower and Clay began to replace military personnel in Germany with civilians, and they made plans for drastic reductions in American field-staff. Clay planned to reduce his staff from 12,000 to 6,000 by February 1, 1946, and he expected to have a completely civilian organization by July 1, 1946. To replace the American staff, Germans in the towns, the counties, and the states would elect their own officials, and the Council of Minister-Presidents of the American zone (*Länderrat*) would assume increased responsibilities. Neither Washington's officialdom nor the Germans affected seem to have understood the full significance of these developments at the time, and it has also escaped historians. Washington expressed concern at Clay's rapid personnel reductions. German politicians and Clay's own advisers, including the political scientist James K. Pollock, thought Clay was moving too fast on German elections. Clay explained and justified his actions by referring to the wishes of Congressional visitors, to certain features of the Potsdam Agreement, to the American democratization objectives in Germany, and to the pragmatic value of teaching people to swim by throwing them into the water. But the speed and deliberation with which the various programs were implemented make most sense in the context of the Army's drive to convert military government in such a way as to make a case for relief from the political functions and economic responsibilities that Truman had assigned to the Army on July 29, 1945. Clay remembered telling Pollock

that his actions were those of a hard-boiled soldier running a military occupation.[18] His actions were in accord with those of the War Department in
Washington.

As the costs of the occupation under Truman's orders of July 29, 1945, and
under the tenuous, incomplete, and contradictory decisions of the Potsdam
Conference became clear to the Army; as the ACC floundered as a result
of France's vetoes, and as the State Department's approach to the occupation of Germany and to postwar Europe emerged, the Army conducted a
campaign to get a government-level decision to transfer its political functions in Germany to the Department of State. Eisenhower summarized the
arguments for Chief of Staff George C. Marshall on October 13, 1945. German governmental agencies would begin to function soon, he said. Except
for police functions, which the Army would continue to perform, the American presence in Germany would be essentially for the purpose of control
and supervision of German officials and agencies. That was a civil function.
"The Government of Germany should, at the very earliest practicable moment, pass to a civilian organization," and the State Department should
assume United States functions in the Control Council.[14]

On October 23, 1945, claiming to have tried unsuccessfully "for some
months" to get the State Department to establish an organization to recruit
personnel for the occupation when military responsibility would terminate,
Secretary of War Patterson took up the issue with the Secretaries of State
and Navy in the so-called Committee of Three. Patterson argued the Army's
case from reason, from the historical perspective of the occupation of North
Africa, and from the practical standpoint of administrative unity and jurisdictional clarity. If the State Department assumed control, Patterson said
the Army would agree to transfer to it some of the Army's best men, including Clay and General John H. Hilldring, the Director of the War Department's Civil Affairs Division.[15] Three days later, clearly showing that
this was more than a routine matter so far as the Army was concerned,
Eisenhower sought the intervention of Truman. He reminded Truman that
they had discussed the question in Frankfurt in July, during Truman's visit
while in Germany for the Potsdam Conference, and recalled that Truman
had agreed in principle to civilianization of the occupation. Eisenhower
said organizational steps were already underway. He thought a reasonable
date for the turnover of the Army's responsibilities to a civilian agency
would be June 1, 1946. The turnover, he argued, was in conformity with

"the American principle of keeping the Army as such out of the civil government field."[16] Truman released Eisenhower's letter to the press and commented on it in a press conference on October 31, 1945. He seemed to agree.

Two days after Truman's press conference, Patterson sent Byrnes a proposal suggesting that the transfer be accomplished in a series of steps to be completed "no later than June 1st."[17] After that the issue simmered for more than a month, until the Army brought it to a boil on December 18, apparently after having estimated the costs in Germany of the State Department's December 12, 1945, statement of policy on "The Reparation Settlement and the Peacetime Economy of Germany," a policy to which we shall return. Patterson met with Acheson and other State Department officials on December 18 (Byrnes was in Moscow), told them the Army was preparing to withdraw from Germany, and left his hearers with the definite impression that the Army was prepared to abandon even the steps-and-stages proposal that had been under discussion since November 2, 1945.[18] But Patterson seems to have underestimated both the State Department's determination to resist and Dean Acheson's maneuverability. He apparently overestimated the strength of Truman's commitment in principle as well.

Byrnes had objected to the transfer when Patterson brought the issue to the Committee of Three on October 23. He said the Army had a better organization for the job and that it would be a mistake to change over now. He referred to the issue as "bad news," and hoped a decision could be postponed for about eight or nine months.[19] A week earlier, Donald S. Russell, the Assistant Secretary of State for Administration, had warned Robert D. Murphy, the United States Political Adviser in Berlin, to be ready to plead the State Department's case with the so-called Kilgore Committee (the U.S. Senate Special Committee Investigating the National Defense Program) when it arrived in Berlin. Russell was sure the committee would get into the Army-State dispute over control in Germany and he said Murphy should present the State Department's side of the story: State is a policy agency, not an operating agency. It does not have the operational experience or the operational agencies that the Army has. The Army has organizations to deal functionally with transportation, industry, production, procurement, and the like. Murphy could counter the Army's argument for a single policy-and-administrative agency by emphasizing the coordination that would occur in Washington and by arguing that Clay, an Army regular, was the best military governor available. "If you are half the diplomat I believe you are," Russell concluded, the committee "should be convinced before they return that our position—and not Army's—is the correct solution of this problem."[20]

Acheson went to Truman on December 19, 1945, the day after Patterson's meeting with him and others. He apparently convinced Truman that it was impractical and impossible for the State Department to take over the occupation of Germany, and Truman discussed the question in the cabinet on December 21. According to Patterson, he and Acheson presented their views, and Truman directed the Secretaries of War and State to confer further on the matter when Byrnes returned from Moscow. Patterson also said that it was evident that Acheson had taken up the matter with Truman before the cabinet meeting. According to State Department records, Truman agreed with Acheson in the cabinet meeting and "this provoked a loud protest from Secretary Patterson."[21] In any case, Patterson restated the Army's position in a letter to Acheson on December 22. He remained opposed to an intermediate stage which would have assigned both policy determination and administration to a separate agency under SWNCC, and he said, "If you should decide to lay before the President the question of this responsibility, I should appreciate the opportunity of accompanying you."[22] But Truman had already decided in favor of the State Department.

Patterson wrote to Byrnes on December 29, 1945, after the latter's return from Moscow. He reviewed the history of the issue in some detail, mentioned the Byron Price report, which had also called for civilian control, and reviewed the Army's arguments. Later Eisenhower saw Byrnes personally, but Byrnes was "adamant and unbending" in his opposition to the State Department taking over the administration of military government. Byrnes told Eisenhower he would be willing to make it clear to the President, to the Congress, and to the American people that the State Department could not handle the job. He also said he would be willing to support actively the Army's requests for funds from Congress, since the funds were to be used for political rather than military purposes.[23] Attempts to resume the negotiations after that never got off the ground. An internal State Department memorandum summarized the entire episode as follows: "The plain fact is that the Army became panicky over the idea that military government in Germany was becoming a liability. This is the basis for the War Department's desire to unload the job on the State Department—and not the various rationalizations which have been offered."[24] The War Department's panic was, in fact, caused by its knowledge of the State Department's objectives, purposes, and policies.

THE STATE DEPARTMENT'S APPROACH

Within the State Department there was a strong inclination to regard the end of the war as the beginning of an opportunity. It was an opportunity to use the American presence in Germany to undo the mistakes of the 1920's and 1930's; to do what Woodrow Wilson et al. had failed to do. It was an opportunity to root out Nazis, Fascists, and others who had led their people to war, to restore liberated Europe, to experiment with programs designed to correct the basic evils that had caused the war, to reduce political and economic nationalism, to further the principles of free trade, to strengthen the forces of liberalism—in short, to do missionary work.

There having been no departmental philosophers, the State Department's approach—like the Army's—can perhaps be illustrated best from cases and incidents that called forth actions and responses. The implementation of the Potter-Hyndley coal report is such a case. The State Department's efforts to have Truman issue a coal directive, to have him assign exclusive authority to the State Department for making policy on Germany, and to have him order the Army to assume responsibility for financing and procuring supplies and imports to serve the purposes of the United States government all point clearly to the prevailing view in the State Department that the American presence in Germany should be used as a base of operations from which to promote recovery and rehabilitation of the liberated areas, to further a general European political program.

The early discussions of the Potter-Hyndley report and a possible Presidential coal directive are instructive, indeed. They called forth the significant observation from H. Freeman Matthews that liberated Europe would have to be protected from the Army's high-powered people, who would restore the German economy.[25] Similar considerations caused Clayton to upbraid the War Department for its "narrow view" of its responsibilities in Germany, and furnished the reasons for the State Department's determination to get Truman to order the Army to procure and finance supplies to provide, among other things, for reparations, restitutions, and relief to allied nations.[26]

The State Department, assisted by Secretary of Interior Harold Ickes,[27] got Truman to issue the coal directive recommended by the Potter-Hyndley report. In the process, it ignored Ambassador Edwin W. Pauley's warning about the implications of the directive for reparations and German exports. Pauley, who was Truman's representative on the Moscow Reparations Commission, wrote on July 7, 1945, that countries receiving coal from Germany should be "given definite notice" that the costs would be charged to them either as reparations or as exports to be paid in acceptable currency. But a contrary decision had already been made in Washington: "the questions of whether these exports shall be charged to the receiving countries on reparations or commercial account will remain in suspense and supplies necessary for production as well as exports will move forward without reference to solution of this problem."[28] More than a month later, and after the Potsdam Conference, Pauley could only report his frustration and distress. He did not know if the coal would be paid for by the consignees, whether it was to be lend-lease, or on what terms it was being shipped. He said it was "impossible for me to intelligently carry on this job without being properly notified of our intentions regarding foreign countries before their happening."* The British, who were co-sponsors of the Potter-Hyndley report, also objected to the State Department's approach.

The British agreed in principle to Truman's draft coal-directive, but asked for certain changes.[29] They wanted prior consultation and coordination with the Russians and the French, in the interests of treating Germany as an economic unit. They agreed that Eisenhower and Field Marshal Sir Bernard L. Montgomery might implement the directive in their own zones as an emergency measure, but they thought the two military governors should also try to reach a four-power agreement in the Control Council, particularly since the Russians had made clear that they wanted coal as reparations.[30] Furthermore, they thought the directive's effects would be excessive hardship and they wanted to leave greater flexibility and discretion in the field regarding the amount of coal to be exported. In reply the State Department advised the British that it had revised the draft to meet some of the British objections, that Charles de Gaulle had agreed to the directive, and that Truman would inform Stalin and ask him to instruct the Russian commander in chief in Germany "to concert ... in the Control Council with a view to the formulation of a coal production and export program for Germany as a whole and the adoption of measures required to carry out

---

* Pauley to SecState, Aug. 10, 1945, RG 59, file 740.00119 EW, Box C-241, NA. Three days later Pauley recommended that no gold or securities restitutions be made until the issue was settled and asked for information "as to whether any arrangement has been made for payment of coal which is being shipped out of Germany and for food and coal from the United States to Western Europe." Pauley to SecState, Aug. 13, 1945, *FRUS*, 1945, III, 1254–55.

this program." Anthony Eden advised Byrnes at Potsdam on July 23, 1945, that the British would issue an interim directive to Montgomery and that they understood Truman would discuss it with Stalin at Potsdam.[31]

Truman sent Stalin a copy of the directive on July 27, 1945, on the same day that it arrived in Eisenhower's headquarters from the Joint Chiefs of Staff. Truman commented on the seriousness of the coal problem and told Stalin he had issued the directive to avoid delay. He said he understood that Britain and France had issued similar directives and trusted that the Soviets would be able to join in the policy. Stalin promised to study the directive, but he expressed concern about its effects in Germany. The directive had, in fact, stated that its effect would be to create "unemployment, unrest, and dissatisfaction among Germans," and it recommended "firm and rigorous response."[32] France's response is apparently not subject to documentation, but there are vague American references to De Gaulle's similar directive and to France's approval.

Noteworthy in the entire episode is the fact that there were no four-power consultations to speak of, on perhaps the most vital issue affecting German reparations, the level of German production, and German exports and imports. There had been no consultations with the French, and there certainly were none with the Russians. With the British there was an exchange of memoranda, but the final decision on what to include and what to leave out was made in Washington. Neither were the military governments asked, despite their great interest in the matter. Clay, writing to McCloy in September on the problems of coal production in the Ruhr and the Saar, said that "neither our own experts here nor the British experts were consulted in establishing the 25,000,000 tons export figure."[33] After he received the directive, Montgomery demanded greater flexibility than the directive permitted and he induced the British government to reopen the issue. He said Germany needed coal to manufacture durable building materials and to meet other basic needs. He thought the suspension of German industry that would result from implementation of the coal directive, "a complete stoppage of this kind," was neither feasible nor with precedent.[34] The British passed Montgomery's reservations and objections to Washington, but Byrnes rejected them out of hand. Even if the goal of 25 million tons in exports could not be reached, he wrote, the coal directive should not be changed, either by formal action or by interpretation. Byrnes observed that there would be distress and unemployment all over Europe and reported that the considerations Montgomery raised had been anticipated, discussed, and rejected (in Washington) in favor of a program to benefit the liberated areas over Germany.*

The political significance of Truman's coal directive has apparently been lost to historians. The reason for that is revealed by what occurred when the so-called Meader Committee of the Senate tried to investigate the United States military government in Germany late in 1946.† Once the State Department realized the scope of the Meader Committee's inquiries, it held up reports and refused to supply information to the committee and its staff. It induced Truman to intervene with the committee's acting chairman, Senator Harley M. Kilgore, and the latter apparently agreed that the committee would not investigate the international aspects of the German occupation.[35] But George Meader made inquiries of Byrnes in Paris and of military government personnel in Germany nevertheless. He asked about the problems of four-power cooperation in the ACC, and specifically about the reasons for the failure to agree on economic unity. Byrnes had asked Meader on October 13, 1946, not to go into that matter,[36] but he did so anyway three days later in Berlin. There he heard that the major problems in Berlin were with France, not with the Russians, even though he had asked specifically whether the Russians were responsible.[37] Later, Hilldring—who had been director of the War Department's Civil Affairs Division in 1945 and had become Assistant Secretary of State for Occupied Areas early in 1946—explained the State Department's position to a Meader Committee staff member and to Meader himself. He wrote to Meader and warned him about the "potentially undesirable effect upon our foreign policy of any inquiry" into the four-power impasse in Berlin and noted that "you will be aware of the international political problems presented by the agreement to invite France to participate in the occupation of Germany."[38] He told the Meader Committee staff member that an inquiry would quickly reveal

---

* In apparent resignation, the British simply authorized Montgomery to use his discretion, "provided always that the needs of the civil population in the liberated territories concerned have preference over the needs of the civil population of Germany and the general standard of coal consumption in Germany remains below that in those liberated territories." See F. S. V. Donnison, *Civil Affairs and Military Government: North-West Europe, 1944–1946* (London, 1961), p. 414; and Winant to SecState, Nov. 8, 1945, *FRUS*, 1945, III, 1542.

† The committee was the U.S. Senate Special Committee Investigating the National Defense Program. Its chairman in 1946 was Senator James M. Mead of New York. He resigned on Sept. 26, 1946, and Senator Harley M. Kilgore of West Virginia became acting chairman. The committee was popularly called the Meader Committee, after George Meader, its chief counsel.

that "one of the primary reasons for the present state of the German economy is that the American occupation authorities have shipped 'every extra ton of coal' mined in Germany to France. These shipments began in the summer of 1945 and have evidently continued to the present, resulting in the transfer of 'many millions of tons of coal from Germany to France.' "[39]

Byrnes and Hilldring made clear how important France had been to the coal directive of July 1945 and to the orders and directives Truman issued to the Army at the same time. The State Department's policies in Europe were in fact marked by a French priority; an almost single-minded determination to restore and accommodate France.

CHAPTER FOUR

Mission France

I N NOVEMBER 1945 John D. Hickerson, the Deputy Director of the State Department's Office of European Affairs, advised his colleagues in the State-War-Navy Coordinating Committee (SWNCC) that "it is the policy of the United States Government to assist in the reestablishment of a strong France in order that the country may serve as a bulwark of democracy on the continent of Europe and be in a position gradually to assume an increasing share of the responsibility of the occupation of Germany and in maintaining the peace."[1] The policy, which took shape when the future glory of France was still little more than a gleam in Charles de Gaulle's eye, rested on practical considerations and apparently on a deep-seated and seldom discussed American affinity for France and on an American hope for French leadership in postwar Europe. A stable, rehabilitated France was politically important to the United States because a stable France would not threaten the security, the supply depots, and the communications and supply lines of the American troops occupying Germany. A stable France would contribute to the frustration of socialists, communists, and leftists—whatever their ultimate goals for France may have been. A strong France would help to maintain a postwar balance of power in Europe. France would participate in the occupation of Germany, help to ensure against German resurgence, and help to enforce the peace treaty Germany would eventually be required to accept. A new, strong France would be able to cope with a new Hitler.

The practical, political reasons for France's rehabilitation were fortified by a pervasive American sympathy for France and the French. American officials had been educated to believe in a European heritage that had radiated from the salons of Paris in the eighteenth century; to believe that modern European history began with, and was conditioned by, the French Revolution and its impact. Americans were equipped with a historical model that depicted France as the point of origin of some of their most revered institutions, that showed many instances of Franco-American cooperation and friendship, and that showed France to have been the victim of repeated German aggressions. State Department functionaries were steeped— and trained—in the traditions and methods of diplomacy so profoundly influenced by the French language and by French practice. They were marked by an inbred, deep-seated, and highly cultivated French orientation or bias that is easier to sense than to demonstrate. Moreover, as the war came to an end, they were mystified by the New Tartars who had ridden into the heart of Central Europe on iron horses. Along with their compatriots throughout the land, they were fascinated by the Russians, but politically apprehensive of them as well. Wartime diplomatic experiences, and numerous encounters with Soviet Foreign Minister V. M. Molotov and others as the war came to an end, caused uncertainty within the State Department—uncertainty about the political and economic future of Europe, and uncertainty about the adequacy of traditional diplomacy for dealing with the Russians. Influenced by these things, State Department functionaries inclined toward conservatism. In any case, they wanted to reestablish France "as a bulwark of democracy on the continent of Europe."[2]

CREATING A BULWARK OF DEMOCRACY

Early in 1945, Secretary of State Edward R. Stettinius proposed, and President Roosevelt approved in principle, a policy that would "assist France to regain her former position in world affairs," make "concessions to French prestige," and treat "France on the basis of her potential power and influence" rather than "on the basis of her actual strength at this time." The occasion was the State Department's request for a Presidential decision on France's request, made in the European Advisory Commission in London, for French participation in the German occupation, for a change from tripartite to quadripartite agencies in the control machinery for Germany, for a French-language authentic text of the instrument of surrender, and for French participation in its eventual signing. Stettinius admitted that "the French requests are out of all proportion to France's power," and that the addition of "a fourth country on an equal basis" in the German occupation would complicate an "already complex problem." Nevertheless, he recommended that Roosevelt approve the French requests and that he do so "at an early date prior to detailed consideration with the War and Navy Departments." He said there was "every likelihood" that Britain and Russia would agree to the French requests and he argued that favorable action would help to increase France's contribution to the war and to the peace; it would recognize France's vital interests in the future of Germany; and it might "help to create a cooperative spirit among the French, who may as a consequence be less inclined to raise objections to many of the arrangements which have already been agreed to."[3]

Though France participated in neither the Yalta nor the Potsdam Conference, United States policy toward France remained consistent with Stettinius's recommendation. A briefing-book paper prepared for Yalta repeated the essentials of Stettinius's earlier statements: "The best interests of the United States require that every effort be made by this Government to assist France, morally as well as physically, to regain her strength and her influence." The French "are at present unduly preoccupied, as a result of the military defeat of 1940 and the subsequent occupation of their country by the enemy, with questions of national prestige. They have consequently from time to time put forward requests which are out of all proportion to their present strength." The United States should "take full account of this psychological factor," and "treat France in all respects on the basis of her potential power and influence rather than on the basis of her present strength."[4] Nothing changed in the months that followed, for a similar paper of June 23, 1945, prepared for the Potsdam Conference, repeated the policy almost word for word. In fact, it said: "Our policy of treating [France] on the basis of her potential power rather than on that of her present strength has been justified and should continue." According to the paper, France had "made great strides towards resuming her former position of influence in world councils." Her "somewhat intransigent attitude on ... reparations and restitution springs largely from her exclusion, at Soviet insistence, from the Reparations Commission."[5]

The policy continued at Potsdam and afterward, even though France's actions in Germany did not fulfill Stettinius's hope of creating a more cooperative French spirit. At Potsdam the policy manifested itself behind the scenes and on the fringes of the main event. As noted previously, Truman assigned exclusive policy-making authority to the State Department. He directed the Army to assume broad financial and supply responsibilities in Germany, in part to ensure reparations, restitutions, and relief to allied nations. He also issued the coal directive, which—according to one who was there—resulted in shipment to France of "every extra ton of coal" mined in Germany.[6] Truman thus laid the basis for the State Department to implement its program to reestablish France as a major power.

After the Potsdam meeting Truman and Byrnes discussed German policy in Washington with De Gaulle and Foreign Minister Georges Bidault. The gesture was symbolic, but Byrnes went beyond symbolism. He suggested a possible twenty-five-year treaty of guarantee of French security, a proposal he and State Department spokesmen later described as a revolutionary departure in American policy; as a commitment not even Clemenceau had been able to get from Wilson.[7] But the State Department's policy became increasingly difficult to maintain and defend, in part because of France's resentment and reaction at not having been invited to Potsdam, in part because of France's extreme demands regarding Germany, and in part because the Army insisted that France was jeopardizing four-power cooperation in Berlin, blocking attempts to treat Germany as an economic unit, and—in the words of one of the State Department's own—sabotaging the Potsdam Agreement.[8]

The Shape of the Bulwark

France's post-Potsdam demands regarding Germany frustrated Byrnes considerably. De Gaulle and Bidault complained bitterly in Washington about the Potsdam decisions, and they demanded the Saar for France and the detachment of the Ruhr and Rhineland from Germany. De Gaulle argued with Truman for territorial guarantees of French security, referred to the erosion of the assurances given France after World War I, and insisted that history would repeat itself, since there were no guarantees.[9] Byrnes and Bidault went over the same ground during the next two days, August 23 and 24, 1945. They discussed German reparations, European coal resources, France's disappointment with the Potsdam boundary decisions, France's insistence "that a section of territory be cut off in West Germany similar to that in East Germany," France's desire to continue occupying the Rhineland "without interference from Berlin," and the decision at Potsdam to establish central German administrations, about which Bidault "felt obliged to make the most explicit reservation."* Byrnes readily admitted his perplexity, and his floundering reveals it as well. At one point he as-

---

* The Potsdam Agreement, Section II, A9 (iv), provided that, "for the time being, no central German Government shall be established. Notwithstanding this, however, certain essential central German administrative departments, headed by State Secretaries, shall be established, particularly in the fields of finance, transport, communications, foreign trade and industry. Such departments will act under the direction of the Control Council." See U.S. Department of State, *Germany, 1947–1949: The Story in Documents,* Pub. 3556, European and British Commonwealth Series 9 (Washington, 1950), p. 49.

serted that the United States "would not advance a single dollar to Germany to permit the latter to pay reparations to other countries," contradicting flatly the decisions that had been made relative to the coal directive and that were implied in Truman's orders of July 29, 1945, to the Army. In the end, Byrnes summarized the French, American, and Russian objectives regarding the Ruhr and confessed that he saw no practical way to resolve the differences. He reportedly talked about a possible twenty-five-year treaty of guarantee, which Bidault said he would view favorably.[10] But there was more to come less than a month later.

Even though the subject of Germany was not on the agenda of the London Council of Foreign Ministers (CFM) meeting, France presented a detailed memorandum of its German demands on September 13, 1945.[11] The memorandum stated France's reservations to the Potsdam decisions on political parties and central German administrations. It noted that German territories had been separated in the East for Poland's benefit, and objected that no similar decisions had been made for France's benefit in the West. It said France wanted the Rhineland and Westphalia, including the Ruhr, separated from Germany. Meanwhile, France's representatives in Berlin had been instructed not to agree to central German administrations or to other actions that presumed or implied a settlement of Germany's western frontier.* The effect of the latter was to cause the State Department much difficulty as it tried to maintain its French policy.

On September 23, 1945, Ambassador Murphy reported on three French vetoes in the Allied Control Authority (ACA) in Berlin.[12] Following further French vetoes on October 1, Murphy reported that a French foreign-office observer at the meeting had told him privately that France's opposition to central German administrations was intended "to force consideration" of its demands for annexation of the Saar and the separation of the Ruhr and Rhineland from Germany. On October 20, in reporting on a discussion in the ACA to collect documents and recruit personnel for German central administrations, Murphy made clear how complete the impasse was: "The French member stated that his Government had submitted a memorandum as to its point of view at the London Conference. As no decision had been taken on the matter, the French Government had ordered its delegates in

---

* CFM(45)17, Sept. 13, 1945, *FRUS*, 1945, III, 871. During the debate on the French demands in the CFM on Sept. 26, 1945, Bidault reread portions of the French memorandum of Sept. 13. Two days later the CFM decided to recommend study of the French memorandum through diplomatic channels without delay. U.S. Minutes, CFM, Sept. 26, 1945, *FRUS*, 1945, II, 407–10; Record of Decisions, CFM, Sept. 28, 1945, *ibid.*, 429.

Berlin to *abstain from all discussion* of the matter. The question was accordingly adjourned."[13]

Clay and Murphy, who cabled their views to Washington regularly, consulted with Byrnes in London in September and then carried their problems to Washington early in November 1945.[14] In a full round of discussions at the War and State Departments, Clay and Murphy came down hard on France, claiming that France's refusal "to agree to the establishment of central administrative services threatens to break down the provisions of the Berlin Protocol with respect to treatment of Germany as an economic unit."[15] Secretary of War Patterson took the cues from Clay and Murphy, and on November 6, 1945, he told Byrnes and Secretary of Navy Forrestal that the French were blocking everything in Berlin. He thought France should be pressured. Byrnes, who admitted that Clay had talked with him, explained how touchy the French were at not having been invited to Potsdam, but he agreed "that some action would have to be taken."[16]

Byrnes having given him an opening, Patterson prompted the State Department often after that. He wrote to Byrnes on November 21, 1945, referred to their discussion of November 6, reviewed the problems in Berlin, and said "the very basis of the quadripartite administration in Germany might well be jeopardized" if France continued to block the creation of central German administrations. He urged the State Department to "bring to bear upon the French Government all requisite pressures in order to effectuate the mandate of the Berlin Protocol." Patterson wrote again on December 10. He referred to his November 21 request for State Department pressure on France, noted Byron Price's recommendation to Truman that the United States use the "full force and prestige of American diplomatic power" to break the deadlock in Berlin, asked again for political and economic pressure on France, and suggested "that full publicity be given to such efforts in order to mobilize the support of American and world public opinion behind such efforts." Fortified by continuing reports from Clay in Berlin, perhaps mortified by his failure to get satisfaction from the State Department, Patterson wrote once more on December 28, 1945. He repeated the essence of his two previous letters and said, "the War Department is gravely disturbed by the danger that continued refusal of the French Government to agree to the establishment of central administrative machinery in Germany may result in a breakdown of the provisions of the Berlin Protocol with respect to treatment of Germany as an economic unit."[17]

Clay and the Army changed tactics in 1946. At first they wanted to let Germans criticize France's German policy publicly. Clay reported on February 22, 1946, that France's recent reaffirmation of her position on the Ruhr and central agencies had caused vigorous political reaction in Germany. The German Communists were calling for "a unified Germany less Silesia," whereas the Socialists and Christian Democrats—in deference to allied policies prohibiting Germans from criticizing the occupation powers—had refrained from public discussion of the issue. Clay thought the situation worked in favor of the Communist Party and the Soviet Union and against the Social Democrats, the Christian Democrats, the United States, and the West. He admitted that a policy which permitted Germans to discuss German unity would aggravate France, but he said not to permit such discussion would jeopardize United States objectives.[18] Murphy reported similarly to the State Department two days later. Moving ever closer to his conclusion of April 4, 1946, that "French sabotage of the Potsdam decision" would result in the United States financing reparations, Murphy said: "There is a growing conviction here that the time is overdue when a firmer and more aggressive stand should be taken on one of the basic elements of the Potsdam decision, namely, the establishment of German central administrative agencies." While the French had remained intransigent for the past eight months, the Russians had taken advantage of the situation to consolidate their position in eastern Germany. If France could not be persuaded by discussion, Murphy concluded, "the question is asked whether it might not be desirable temporarily to withhold cooperation in other fields from the French until a more favorable attitude might develop."*

Clay recommended more active pressures in April and he subsequently turned to even more drastic and dramatic measures, but we shall return to those events in another context. Meanwhile, Patterson's and Clay's campaign (in which they were assisted by Murphy) to induce the State Department to apply pressure on France motivated the State Department. But the latter acted in accord with the priority it had assigned to France's rehabilitation rather than do what the Army asked.

Protecting the Future Bulwark of Democracy

When the Army asked for diplomatic pressure and/or economic and political sanctions against France, the State Department regularly delayed, procrastinated, and resisted; occasionally it claimed to detect signs of a

---

* Murphy to SecState, Feb. 24, 1946, *FRUS*, 1946, V, 505–7. See Murphy to SecState, March 19, 1946, *ibid.*, 527–28, for a recommendation against a policy change that would permit Germans to criticize the occupation forces and a commentary on the effect of the continued French blockage of central administrations on the ability of the Americans to influence events in the Soviet occupation zone.

change in France's position; increasingly it tried to shift responsibility for the Army's problems in Germany to the Russians. It also tried to forestall and prevent public discussion of France's resistance and the Army's complaints. In November 1945, when Clay and Murphy criticized France sharply during their visit in Washington, James W. Riddleberger, the Chief of the Division of Central European Affairs, countered Clay's argument that France had frustrated the implementation of the Potsdam Agreement by questioning whether the Russians intended to carry out the agreement's political and economic principles. He cited the inhumane and unplanned population transfers that had occurred, the restrictions on interzonal travel, the Russian failure to develop interzonal trade, the control of the press in the Soviet zone, the Russian support of favored political parties, and the unilateral land reform and nationalization programs in the Russian zone as ominous indicators of Russian intentions. Annoyed by the suggestion that Soviet intentions were as serious as French actions, Clay emphasized that until central agencies and economic unity were a fact, unilateral actions in the zones were the rule, not the exception. Restrictions in the French zone compared with those in the Soviet zone, Clay said, and every zone commander had taken unilateral action, as the United States commander had also done. He did not mention the coal directive, though it applied precisely. Riddleberger's obfuscations were, in fact, an attempt to establish a context for Matthews's admission that the State Department had put no pressure on France to cooperate in the ACC in Berlin. Clay had asked, directly, whether anything had been done.[19]

Byrnes also tried to shift responsibility from France rather than apply pressure. His reply to Patterson's request of November 6, 1945, for pressure on France was that the French were sensitive on the point of not having been invited to Potsdam. Naturally, he did not have to repeat to Forrestal and Patterson that the Russians had caused that condition. Byrnes nevertheless agreed that some action would have to be taken. His own staff preferred obfuscation, however. A memorandum prepared on November 24, in response to Truman's request for advice on whether Byron Price's report might be published, states that "the responsibility which Mr. Price places on the French for the failure to establish central administrations for the conduct of activities for Germany as a whole is not entirely accurate and the French Government and public will doubtless react unfavorably." This, despite what Clay, Murphy, Caffery, and the Army had been saying since September, and despite what the State Department knew directly from

France. Bidault had said in September that French representatives in the ACC would not be empowered to agree to central administrations until the future of the Ruhr and the Rhineland had been settled. Murphy had reported in October that French representatives in Berlin had received orders to abstain from all discussion of the matter. The French, it seems, had little basis for reacting unfavorably to Price's statements on French policy, except to their publication. In fact, the bond that unites the State Department's maneuvers and explanations is "the policy ... to assist in the reestablishment of a strong France ... as a bulwark of democracy on the continent of Europe," as Hickerson described it to his SWNCC colleagues on November 29, 1945.[20] The French would have to be treated gently, and they would have to be protected from the Army's attacks as well as from public criticism.

The impulse to protect France from the Army and from possible public wrath can be documented. H. Freeman Matthews had warned in June 1945 that "our high-powered people in Germany" would have to be prevented from restoring Germany and disregarding the needs of liberated Europe. In January 1946, in a memorandum for Acheson on a draft speech for Eisenhower, Matthews applied the theme specifically to France. He wrote that he could not go along with the draft's severe criticism of France's position. "While we are anxious to have French concurrence in the establishment of central administrative agencies in Germany, we do not feel that the way to obtain this is through public criticism put in the mouth of General Eisenhower." In justifying his objections, Matthews said that there were many instances of British and Russian obstruction in Berlin (though he gave no examples), and that the parts of the speech he objected to were not germane to its main purpose.[21]

It being the better part of wisdom to do so, Acheson admitted to the Army that there were serious problems with France. But, as his reply of December 12, 1945, to Patterson's urgent plea for "all requisite pressures" upon France shows, he apparently preferred procrastination to action. He commented on discussions in Washington with Maurice Couve de Murville, the political director of the French foreign office, and noted that France's demands regarding the Saar, the Ruhr, and the Rhineland would require reexamination and possible amendment of the Potsdam Agreement. But he said the French and Russians were discussing the matter in Moscow and that the State Department did not want "to express a definite opinion" on Germany's geographical limits in the meantime. Acheson thought that after the French-Russian discussions were completed, the War Department should instruct Clay again to urge the adoption of central administrative agencies either with or without France.[22] Then, on January 12, 1946, Acheson responded to Patterson's additional pleas and demands, particularly to his warning of December 28, 1945, that the War Department was "gravely disturbed." He wrote a rambling letter in which he reported on the indecisive conversations with the French in London, Moscow, and Washington; speculated on possible informal talks in London; reiterated the State Department's authority to Clay to establish central German agencies "by the signatories to the Potsdam protocol"; and expressed the Department's opinion that Clay should be instructed once again to urge the adoption of the Potsdam decision on central agencies. He insisted that the United States position on the matter had been made clear to France and noted that it had been "explained with force and clarity to Mr. Couve de Murville" in Washington.[23] The latter may serve to illustrate how far the State Department was actually prepared to go.

Byrnes had advised Couve de Murville on November 20, 1945, that if France would not agree to central administrations in Germany he would advise Britain and Russia that the United States would be willing to establish them in the other three zones. Later, prompted by pointed questions in a press conference on December 5—particularly by questions on France's position on central agencies, on the future of the Ruhr and the Rhineland, and on Byron Price's advice, "which seems to be to crack down on France"— Byrnes acted. On December 6, 1945, he instructed Ambassador Caffery to inform Bidault that the United States was "determined to stand by" the Potsdam Agreement on central administrations "and that if the agreement can be implemented in no other way we will, with great reluctance, agree to having the agencies in question operate in the Russian, British, and American Zones. We hope this will not be necessary." Caffery replied two days later, saying that Bidault's only response was "to manifest much distress" and to repeat previous French warnings that such action would lead to "a Soviet dominated central government in Germany."[24]

Though he tried other methods as well, Byrnes appealed directly to Bidault on February 1, 1946, asking him to review the French position on central agencies. He said he recognized France's security needs; he argued that some central administration would be needed even under a loose German federation (which is apparently what he thought France wanted); he believed that creation of central administrations would not prejudice the consideration of Germany's western frontier; he said the British and Russians agreed to central agencies; and he concluded that the issue was a test of four-power cooperation in the postwar world. He advised Caffery that in delivering the note he might "orally and discreetly inject the thought" that public French cooperation at this time "should help to create a more favorable atmosphere for the important economic and financial talks" that France planned to initiate soon.[25]

Bidault's reply, which arrived a month later, showed France's position to be as firm as ever. France wanted territorial changes in western Germany as a guarantee of French security. France "could not in any case agree to the extension of the authority of [German central] administrations to the Ruhr, Rhineland or even more to the Saar."[26] But Byrnes, responding to a message Caffery had sent him a day earlier, had already foreclosed the possibility of real sanctions. He advised Caffery that France should not be pressed so hard as to threaten the French coalition government or cause Bidault to resign.[27]

Byrnes next combined verbal pleas with a partial concession, while Acheson tried to head off possible intervention by Truman. On March 22, 1946, Byrnes advised the French ambassador, Henri Bonnet, that he had had "disturbing reports of recent developments in Germany." He commented on the "chaotic relations existing between the four zones of Germany," and he said he could not "conceal his conviction that the resolution of this problem stands as the most pressing task confronting the Occupying Powers." Then he made a partial concession: "As soon as this situation has been met," he would "actively support prompt quadripartite consideration and discussion of the proposal of the French Government" to annex the Saar permanently.[28] Four days later, referring to an article in the *New York Times*, Acheson wrote Truman that "because of the uncertain political situation in France, it has not been thought desirable to publicize" the French resistance to central agencies and United States efforts to get France to reverse her stand. "Latest indications," Acheson continued—albeit in contrast to the facts—"are that the French are now receding from their stubborn opposition and it looks as if they may give in on this point."[29]

Acheson's hopes were false in conception and in realization, and Byrnes's flabby concession on the Saar was not enough to move France. The impasse in Germany remained, and it became even more frustrating early in April 1946, right after the ACC had achieved paper agreement on a German reparations and level-of-industry plan, which will be discussed later. On April 4, 1946, Murphy reported that the French in Berlin had blocked an

American proposal for an export-import bureau, and referred to "French sabotage of the Potsdam decision" on central administrations. He offered no constructive advice and simply observed that the primary effect of the stalemate would be an increase in United States occupation costs.[30] While Murphy seems to have been dispirited, Clay demanded sanctions.

On April 11, 1946, Clay's office asked that all shipments of wheat to France and the French zone be stopped until France agreed to central administrations. He addressed the message to the War Department, to the State Department, and to Secretary of Agriculture Clinton P. Anderson, apparently hoping to draw the Department of Agriculture into the Army's dispute with the State Department. The State Department's responses were manifold, complex, and confusing, but they remained consistent with the policy not to press France too hard. Matthews reviewed the history of the State Department's efforts for Assistant Secretary of War Howard C. Petersen on April 17: "The Department of State has continuously reminded the French authorities of its determination to adhere to the Potsdam decision on this question." It had pressured Couve de Murville in November 1945, and Byrnes had sent a message to Bidault on February 1. Bidault repeated the French arguments on March 2, Matthews continued, but he said France was willing to examine the issue further. Ambassador Bonnet talked about the French concept of *services communs* on March 12, and he thought American and French views were close together. Then, indirectly admitting where things stood, Matthews said the United States would try to gain leverage from recent French requests for zonal boundary changes in Baden and for permanent annexation of the Saar. Furthermore, he said that the United States would press France during the coming economic and financial talks and that Bonnet had been advised that French requests for additional grain from the United States and for coal from Germany "were intimately linked with the problem of central German agencies." Finally, he promised, American officials—in their day-by-day contacts with the French Embassy —would continue to impress on the French the grave concern of the United States at the delay in establishing central administrations.[31]

But the Army had demanded sanctions, not explanations and promises. On April 24, 1946, Acheson wrote to Patterson and said it would be unwise to apply the kind of sanctions Clay had asked for on April 11, because "Germany was to be discussed" at the CFM meeting in Paris beginning on April 25. In the meantime, Byrnes had advised Patterson on April 10 that the State Department could not approve a policy revision that would permit Germans to criticize the occupation powers, even though it recognized the political problems created in Germany by France's policy. Byrnes assured Patterson, however, that "the Department of State has been maintaining its pressure on the French Government to recede from its stubborn opposition to the establishment of central German agencies and we have some reason to believe that the French Government is willing to modify its attitude." Byrnes said he had agreed to support France's aspirations for the Saar and that France had proposed early four-power talks to discuss boundaries and central agencies. He hoped a meeting could be arranged soon.[32]

True believers might go along with Acheson's and Byrnes's interpretation of Bidault's message of March 2, 1946, as a modification of France's rigid position. But Bidault had restated France's position categorically. The only thing he agreed to examine in four-power talks was "any other method of examination which might be presented to [the French Government]."[33] Byrnes persisted in his belief, however, and when he finally expressed it publicly, both Clay and Murphy formally and sharply denied its validity.

When Byrnes returned from Paris in July 1946, he made a radio report to the American people. He said he had proposed interzonal exchange of products, a balanced program of exports and imports, and the establishment of central administrations which were necessary for German economic unity. "The French Government, which had previously opposed the establishment of central administrative agencies, indicated their willingness to accept our proposal when we suggested that the Saar be excluded from the jurisdiction of these agencies."[34] Clay cabled the War Department and Murphy the State Department, each protesting that he did not understand the French position that way at all. Clay said that France's plan for a series of German-staffed coordinating bureaus in Berlin, subject to the ACC and the implementing directives of the zone commanders, would not resolve the impasse in Berlin. It would, however, complicate administration by putting a German coordinating agency between policymakers and policy implementers. This was not a change for the better, Clay asserted, but a step backward.[35] Murphy cabled Benjamin V. Cohen, the Counselor of the State Department and apparently the author of Byrnes's radio report, and said Bidault's statements in the CFM in Paris did not correspond with the conclusion in Byrnes's speech.[36] The published CFM records show that Bidault had in fact reiterated France's position in Paris. During the significant exchange of July 10 he had complained that France was not being heard on the issues that concerned her most. He lectured his colleagues on the lessons France had learned from World War I. He asserted that "the French Government considered it its mission and duty to prevent the process of history taking a course which had been disastrous to France." France "would certainly examine in the best spirit the various suggestions put forward," and "it had already given its agreement in principle to the appointment of special deputies." Bidault "wished to repeat, however, that the position of the French Government was maintained in its entirety." In short, as he had said in a formal statement earlier in the day, "we have not changed our position [on France's proposals for annexation of the Saar and the permanent detachment of the Ruhr and the Rhineland from Germany] and ... it does not seem possible to us to postpone examination of them any longer."[37]

Cohen's reply to Murphy explained Byrnes's purposes and tactics, but it also reiterated the State Department's policy toward France. "There may not be complete meeting of minds between Secretary and Bidault on central agencies," Cohen said, but an effort should be made to "minimize if not obviate" their differences. The names and titles of the agencies in Berlin were immaterial, so long as the agencies received authority to administer Germany as an economic unit as provided in the Potsdam Agreement. Byrnes "hopes that we may find a *modus vivendi* with the French if we avoid clash on verbal differences upon which their political situation may cause them to put exaggerated importance."[38] But Clay and Murphy had made clear that the differences were fundamental, not verbal, and Clay had judged the French position to be a step backward.

The policy not to press France too hard notwithstanding, Byrnes tried repeatedly in 1946 to bring the French around. He agreed to support French aspirations for the Saar. He pressed his twenty-five-year treaty of guarantees as a substitute for French territorial guarantees. He tried to have special deputies appointed by the CFM to study the German problem, including the Ruhr, the Rhineland, and Germany's western frontier. He finally went to Stuttgart, Germany, on September 6, 1946, and stated United States policy publicly, perhaps hoping—in the fashion of Wilson at Versailles—that the public exposure of the problems might help to make them disappear. When none of these things worked, some because of France, some because of Britain, some because of Russia, and some because of bureaucratic inertia and/or cumbersome procedures in the ACC and the CFM, Byrnes reverted to the established policy of his department. He shocked George Mcader in

Paris on October 13, 1946, when he told him that he could not "tell the people the truth," for fear that the Russians and the French Communists would use it to play on people's fears. Furthermore, he told Meader that direct pressure on France was out of the question. There was an election coming up in France in November. In the meantime "we could not talk with anybody below Bidault's level along this line, since in the present coalition government most of those people are Communists." Finally, as Assistant Secretary of State Hilldring put it precisely at about the same time, public discussion of the issues in the United States would have a "potentially undesirable effect upon our foreign policy" and would "embarrass the President and the United States Government."[39]

After the November 1946 Congressional elections in the United States, John Foster Dulles—a foreign-policy expert in the successful Republican Party and the prospective Secretary of State in a Republican administration which seemed almost certain in 1949—began to speak out publicly in favor of a Western-European, French-oriented American policy in Europe. Dulles's scheme was, in fact, based on a brilliantly conceived amalgamation of the State Department's consistent French policy and the American public's anti-Communist sentiments, which had featured so importantly in the Republican victories in November 1946.[40] Marshall's selection of Dulles as a personal adviser for the Moscow CFM was, therefore, more than a mere gesture of formal bipartisanship. Marshall's pilgrimage to Paris on March 6, 1947, is testimony to that.[41] To these events we shall return after a discussion of the impasse in Germany and its effects.

THE POST-POTSDAM IMPASSE

CHAPTER FIVE

Reparations and Restitutions

FOUR-POWER government in Berlin floundered, then failed, for many reasons. The conflict on reparations and restitutions was one of them. There are currently two explanations of the American contribution to—and responsibility for—the failure to agree on reparations. Stripped of their rich detail and the finesse, the sophistry, and the passion with which they have been argued, the theses—which often reinforce each other—are as follows.

First, the Army—a key element in what later came to be called the military-industrial complex—never wanted to disarm and demilitarize Germany by reducing its economic power. The Army received support from the industrial-financial community, from which its leaders came and to which they often returned upon retirement from the military. The Army and its collaborators pled Germany's case, publicly in the interests of saving American taxpayers' money; privately in the interests of capitalism and its imperialistic necessities, and in the interest of creating a German bulwark against Russia. Army leaders and their friends in the industrial-financial community feared socialism with a passion and they magnified the actual and potential threat from Russia. They eventually succeeded in convincing themselves and the American people that economic warfare with Russia and anticommunism in general were a natural, logical, and historical continuation of the struggle of "the free world" against Nazism and Fascism.[1] In the interest of all of these considerations, German reparations fell victim to a program to restore Germany—at least to a policy designed to prevent Germany from remaining as a political-economic vacuum in the center of Europe, as a soft spot for the infiltration of Communists and the establishment of a Soviet sphere.

Second, there is the thesis that American policymakers recoiled at the economic, financial, and foreign-trade consequences of their necessary wartime collaboration with the Soviet Union; of their own wartime propaganda and commitments. Once the Axis powers were defeated—and with Truman at the helm—American policymakers gradually returned to the mainstream of American foreign policy that had developed throughout the twentieth century. They returned to the open-door policy, to multilateralism, and to the policies needed by the economic system that had nurtured them and that they represented. American policymakers could not accept the destructive implications of a stringent German reparations program, in part because it would contribute to Russian development and strength, to socialism, to the decline and eventual fall of capitalist hegemony in the world of production, distribution, and trade.

Though each of the theses contains elements subject to demonstration, neither will survive the test of historical research and documented analysis of the reparations issue in Germany. What emerges is a complex picture that boggles the mind in search of order, system, pattern, and long-range plans. What emerges is a web of decisions, counterdecisions, conflicting interests and thrusts, compromises and feigned compromises, bureaucratic pushing and pulling, personal pushing and pulling, and a great deal of pasting, patching, muddling, and drifting.

THE POTSDAM CONFERENCE AND ITS ANTECEDENTS

Among the many issues that divided American policy planners for Germany in 1944–45, one agreement in principle stands out: the United States should avoid the mistakes it had made after World War I. One such mistake, identified again and again by the policy planners, had been to advance American dollars and credits to Germany to facilitate its reparations payments and thus its economic rehabilitation. At Yalta the United States made clear that it would "not finance the transfer of reparations either directly by extending loans or credits to Germany, or indirectly by assuming the burden of supplying at its own expense essential goods or equipment to Germany."[2] During March and April 1945, when the essential form and content of JCS 1067—the basic American policy directive for the occupation of Germany—were hammered out, Roosevelt gave firm instructions that the practice of financing German reparations indirectly through American loans would not be repeated. Accordingly, the policymakers agreed on March 23, 1945, that "the first charge on all approved exports for reparations or otherwise shall be a sum necessary to pay for imports."[3] After much additional pushing and pulling between the White House, the Treasury Department, the War Department, and the State Department, the policy remained as a key feature of the instructions approved by Truman on May 18, 1945, for the United States Representative on the Allied Commission on Reparations (Edwin W. Pauley): "This Government opposes any reparation plan based upon the assumption that the United States or any other country will finance directly or indirectly any reconstruction in Germany or reparation by Germany." Furthermore, "The Reparation Plan should not put the United States in a position where it will have to assume responsibility for sustained relief to the German people." And finally, "The first charge on all approved exports for reparation or otherwise (other than removals of existing plant and equipment) shall be a sum necessary to pay for approved imports."[4]

It might be observed, before continuing the story, that the key feature of American reparations policy in 1945 was to *avoid* the policies the United States had followed in the 1920's and 1930's; to *avoid* policies similar to those that had contributed to Germany's prewar recovery; to *avoid* policies characteristic of multilateralism and the open door. Within the larger context of JCS 1067, American reparations policies were a feature of the American determination to destroy Nazi Germany and to alter the socioeconomic foundation on which it had rested, to destroy German war potential and prevent its resurgence, to prevent rehabilitation of the industrial power with which Germany had dominated her neighbors, to reduce the German standard of living so it would in no case be higher than that of Germany's neighbors, and so on. The argument—advanced most recently by Bruce Kuklick— that the first-charge principle was conceived as a gimmick to lock postwar Germany into a multilateral trade world to be dominated by the United States neatly avoids all that evidence.[5]

The Allied Commission on Reparations

Isador Lubin, Pauley's deputy in Moscow, remembered later that the Allied Commission on Reparations (ACR) had reached agreement with little difficulty, except on the relationship of reparations and import payments. Much has been made, nevertheless, of a supposed Russian-American impasse on current-production reparations and on a $20 billion reparations total the Russians had suggested at Yalta. But neither the amount of reparations nor their source proved impossible to compromise at Moscow. The Russians referred to the Yalta figures often. Pauley did not resist officially, he said, because the Big Three had "agreed at Yalta to use this as a basis for discussion." He argued, instead, for a physical inventory of Germany's ability to pay, for consideration of the reparations demands of other countries, and for a formula based on percentages rather than dollars. He suggested proportions of 55 percent for the Soviet Union and 22½ percent each for Britain and the United States, with reductions and adjustments to meet the demands of other claimants as they would be approved.[6] The State Department advised Pauley that it did not oppose discussion of an amount of reparations, but that it considered a figure approaching $12 to $14 billion to be more realistic than the $20 billion demanded by the Russians. If the ACR decided in the end to specify proportions rather than dollars, the State Department advised Pauley that it preferred to include France in a four-power split. Then, in contrast to the assumption that Americans would have denied Russia its share, the State Department instructed Pauley that in any event "the Soviet share should be sufficiently in excess of fifty percent so that the net portion of reparation finally allocated to the Soviet Union will be approximately fifty percent after joint contributions by the four powers for the benefit of the smaller Allies." On July 6, 1945, Pauley was able to report that after weeks of negotiations in Moscow the ACR had agreed on eight principles, all of which were in accord with his instructions of May 18, 1945.[7] Significantly, the $20 billion figure was absent, and the other principles suggest that it had been abandoned as a point of departure. Current-production reparations were not ruled out, but their use was to be limited by the policy to avoid building up German industrial capacity and disturbing the long-term stability of the economies of other nations. In effect, German industry would not be built up simply to pay current-production reparations, and current-production reparations would not be in the form of goods and services that other nations would have to export in order to survive economically. In other words, Germany would not be permitted to flood the markets, either during the reparations phase or later.

The differences on a reparations figure and on current-production reparations had apparently been compromised at Moscow. Acting Secretary of State Joseph C. Grew thought Pauley's was a "considerable achievement." He had reached agreement in accord with United States instructions which had been drafted by the Informal Policy Committee on Germany, cleared by the Joint Chiefs of Staff, and approved by President Truman.[8]

But Grew's praise and gratification were premature. A week later Pauley reported that the Soviet government could not accept principle 8 of the ACR's agreement: "After payments of reparations enough resources must be left to enable the German people to subsist without external assistance.

In working out the economic balance of Germany the necessary means must be provided for payment of imports approved by the [governments] concerned before reparation deliveries are made from current production or from stocks of goods."[9] Devastated by a long war fought deep in their homeland, the Russians desperately needed anything the Germans could produce and their markets were in little danger of being flooded with German production. How they proposed to deal in the future with the power of a revived and rehabilitated German economy—after reparations had been paid —is, perhaps, contained in the essentials of Marxist-Leninist theory. In the short run, the occupation forces were guarantee enough, for the occupying powers were determined not to permit Fascists and militarists to recover and to rule or govern in Germany again. But Pauley's instructions permitted no latitude on the "first charge" issue and the ACR finally referred the disagreement to the Potsdam Conference.

Reparations at Potsdam

The tortuous reparations negotiations at Potsdam were marked by the continuing and fundamental disagreement carried over from the ACR. Should reparations or necessary imports be a first charge on the German economy? Ivan M. Maisky, the Russian expert, argued that it was politically undesirable to give imports priority over reparations. There would be much criticism of such a decision and capitalists would see their chance. The Germans would take advantage of the import priority to avoid paying reparations, as they had done after World War I. The Russians were convinced, Maisky said, that "if there is a conflict between reparations and imports, then imports must give way." Clayton responded for the United States: the "American people will not again, as they did after [the] last war, finance Germany."[10] Three days later Byrnes said flatly: "Imports must be a first charge, and not a dollar will be paid on reparations until imports are paid for." Byrnes's categorical statement, which he applied to all of Germany, had actually evolved from an earlier statement that reflected only the commitment the State Department had made to the Army, to wit, that there could be no reparations until imports into the *American zone* were paid for, and that "there can be no discussion of this matter."[11]

Unable to compromise their differences on reparations, the Potsdam conferees institutionalized them by accepting the so-called Byrnes formula. The formula emerged gradually at Potsdam, and it was heavily influenced by the bureaucratic wrangling within the American delegation on the coal directive and the Army's financial and procurement responsibilities. Pauley later reported to Truman that the zonal plan had been worked out during the course of about a week, after Americans had concluded that "the division of reparations as applied to Germany as a whole would have to be abandoned for some less controversial method of dividing what would be removed as reparations among the nations entitled to reparations."[12] The records show that the zonal plan was the creation of the same minds that produced—at the same time—the final version of Truman's coal directive and his order of July 29, 1945, outlining the Army's financial and procurement responsibilities in Germany.

American participants at Potsdam justified the zonal reparations plan as a practical method for minimizing the mistakes of the past and for reducing conflict in the future. It was unavoidable; "regrettable, but inescapable,"[13] because of Russia's unilateral transfer of portions of Germany to Poland, Russia's unilateral removals from her own zone in Germany, and Russia's broad definition of war booty. Later analysts have added to the contemporary justification and explanations the interpretation that Americans were determined to deny Russia her legitimate reparations claims, to prevent Russia from achieving rapid postwar recovery in the interests of compounding the domestic problems of Soviet leadership, and to restore Germany as a bulwark against the Soviet Union and as a functioning unit in a multilateral trade world. No one seems to have recognized, however, that the Byrnes formula accords precisely with the commitments the State Department made to the Army to get the Army to cooperate in a political and economic rehabilitation program for Western Europe and especially France. In order to get the Army to accept Truman's coal directive (issued July 26) and to concur in Truman's directive to Stimson (issued July 29), Clayton and Byrnes had clearly committed the State Department to make imports a first charge on Germany's ability to make foreign payments, *and* to rank that charge above reparations.[14] The interrelationship of these things in their conception is clearly illustrated in a memorandum written by one of the leading participants, Emilio G. Collado, on July 23: "Present thought is that four power joint programming of imports, exports and reparations and combined procurement and interim financing of imports will not be feasible. We are consequently drafting on a zonal basis with expectation of combined handling and financing for the three western zones. We are preparing with McCloy and Hilldring a draft directive to War Department on financing responsibility along lines discussed in Washington."[15]

Molotov seemed reluctant to accept the American proposal of July 23, 1945, for a zonal approach to reparations. He was not apparently impressed by Byrnes's references to the problems created by Russia's transfer of territory to Poland and by Russia's definition of war trophies. As everyone knew at Potsdam, there was no basis in reality for rejecting the Soviet definition of war trophies or war booty. Only Russia's definition would have sufficed to cover the sequestration and removal of machines, equipment, gold, securities, scientific know-how, scientists, patents, copyrights, documents, libraries, archives, art treasures, horses, cattle—and the body of Hindenburg, no less—occurring in Germany at the time. What was needed at Potsdam was negotiable: a time limit on war trophy collection, and a blanket reduction in claims to account for trophies and unilateral removals; a reduction taken as a political rather than an economic decision—something similar to Molotov's suggestion to Byrnes on July 23, 1945.[16] Russia's transfer of territories to Poland could have been the basis for reparations adjustments, similar to the adjustments eventually negotiated as a result of France's annexation of the Saarland.

Molotov's reluctance to accept Byrnes's zonal approach seems to have been conditioned also by his hope to achieve a compromise. The Russians had suggested a formula whereby German consumption, exports, and reparations would be proportionally reduced in the event that Germany's approved imports could not be paid for.* Anthony Eden was willing to explore the Russian proposal, but Byrnes—clearly reflecting his commitment to the Army—said he could not discuss "this matter." He said the United States could not agree to reparations unless payment for imports into the American zone was provided for. "Imports must be a first charge and not a dollar will be paid on reparations until imports are paid for." Molotov seemed willing to reduce Russia's claims in the interest of an overall plan for reparations, and at one point he mentioned in succession $10, $9.7, $9, $8.5, or $8 billion as acceptable totals. He argued that Byrnes's zonal plan would have the same effect as a failure to agree on reparations, because it would simply give each power a free hand in its own zone. But Byrnes

---

* Soviet Proposal, July 23, 1945, *FRUS*, 1945, Potsdam II, 810. An American analysis of the Soviet proposal (Riddleberger to Dunn, July 23, 1945, *ibid.*, 811) noted that the concept of "approved imports" in the Russian proposal was crucial. The 1944 agreement establishing the ACC gave the zone commanders supreme authority in their own zones and specified that ACC decisions would have to be unanimous. Logically, therefore, if the ACC could not agree on an "approved" minimum import program, the American zone commander (or any other zone commander for that matter) could halt reparations from his zone. He could also cut German consumption, but the memorandum did not say so.

thought that arrangements for exchanging needed products, such as food and coal, could be worked out; that in all respects other than reparations Germany should be treated as an economic unit. According to Byrnes, central administrations and common economic policies would exist, but reparations would be handled zonally.[17]

Molotov finally agreed to the new American plan in principle, but he wanted assurances on the amount of reparations Russia would get from the Ruhr. It was generally agreed that the Russian zone did not provide a sufficient base for Russia to realize at least 50 percent of the total reparations Germany would pay, a percentage to which Americans had agreed during the ACR negotiations in Moscow. Byrnes therefore proposed that Russia should get 25 percent of the capital equipment removals from the Ruhr in exchange for an equivalent value of food, coal, potash, zinc, timber, and clay and oil products, and another 15 percent without reciprocal deliveries. The percentages were changed in the final agreement to assure Russia 15 percent of the "usable and complete industrial equipment" removed from the western zones in exchange for the products mentioned, and 10 percent of the same without reciprocal deliveries. Russia would satisfy Poland's reparations claims out of Russia's share. In accepting the American plan, Stalin noted that they had agreed not to mention a definite figure, but had accepted a statement of percentages.[18] Interestingly, Molotov conveniently ignored Stalin's statement of 1945 when he brought up the $20 billion figure later, in Paris in 1946 and in Moscow in 1947.

Few understood clearly what had been wrought at Potsdam. The participants themselves were far apart in their interpretations and descriptions of what they had done. Stalin, apparently wanting to record responsibility for the plan, said the Russians "accepted the point of view of the Americans." Molotov seems to have remained puzzled throughout the plan's negotiations, for he kept asking Byrnes to interpret it for him. Byrnes tried. Pauley said the reparations formula called for zonal removals, but that it did not contemplate the division of Germany. Pauley's experts were not so sure, for they advised the American military government to plan for two contingencies: for Germany as a unit, and for the American zone independently. They said reparations would be in machines, equipment, and current production. Their explanations caused the head of the military government's reparations division to ask questions for which there were no answers, and he finally remarked that he was "worse confused than ever."

Pauley said current-production reparations had not been ruled out at Potsdam, but that a final decision on their use would depend on ACC agreements on deindustrialization and an export-import program. He said publicly that there would be reparations from current production. Sir David Waley, the British expert, thought the Americans had given up the hope of collaborating with the Russians in treating Germany as an economic unit.[19] Reflecting the view from Clayton's office in Washington late in July 1945, Willard L. Thorp thought the American plan "would go very far toward a *de facto* division of Germany," and that it threatened "uniform economic treatment in all zones of occupation."[20] When Clayton and Collado, the State Department experts at Potsdam, learned of Thorp's views, they complained about the "unfortunate tendency to interpret the reparations operating agreement as an indication of complete abandonment of four-power treatment of Germany." The Potsdam Agreement, they argued, called for common economic policies, and the reparations agreement did not contradict the general economic principles. The reparations agreement was an exception; a practical approach, designed to reduce friction.[21] Finally, nobody seemed to know whether the ACR would continue in Moscow or whether the ACC in Berlin would work up the detailed reparation plan, which was due within six months.[22] Further complicating the incomprehensible, the French—who had not been at Potsdam—thought otherwise.

Restitutions as Reparations

After discussions with the French in June 1945, Pauley observed to Truman that the concept of restitutions could be abused badly. France's proposals for restitutions in kind, he said, "are proposals for full scale reparation programs."[23] The French wanted restitution of all identifiable objects taken from France during the German occupation and insisted that, if the total taken from France could not be located, France should receive an equivalent amount of restitution to make up the difference.[24]

United States policy on restitutions proved difficult to formulate, despite the strong moral compulsion to speed the return of looted property to the liberated countries. Clay resisted Clayton's and Pauley's early attempt to draft a directive for his use in the ACC. So far as Clay was concerned, all removals of noncultural objects from Germany had similar economic effects, and he told Pauley that he wanted "to feel his way for some little time longer." Byrnes referred to the heavy pressure on the State Department from claimants and wondered whether a JCS directive or negotiations at government level were needed. Pauley sent Eisenhower a "Proposed Principle on Restitution," which had been approved by the State Department but not in the ACR in Moscow. Clay and Murphy appealed for a clearer definition, and Clay observed that Pauley's advice would have him remove things needed for a minimum German economy and thus cause pressure for increased imports or reduced reparations, or both. The result would inevitably be "calls on the U.S. for relief." Notably consistent with its views regarding coal, the State Department advised Clay that restitutions should not be delayed on the grounds that they would increase or give rise to import requirements.[25] The advice is also a remarkably clear statement that the State Department was prepared to let the Army put subsidies into Germany (by financing and procuring imports) for the ultimate benefit of restitutions recipients. Given France's determination to use restitutions as an alternative for reparations, such subsidies could have become the basis for a major French recovery and rehabilitation program ultimately financed by the United States through the German occupation.

Clay's headquarters released an interim restitutions policy for the American zone on September 24, 1945, but it had not been approved in the ACC. It also fell short of France's expectations. The French had taken their restitutions proposals to the London CFM, but the issue was delayed for future decision.[26] Ambassador John G. Winant reported, however, that informal discussions with the French in London showed that they were coordinating their restitution demands with their proposals on the Ruhr and the Rhineland. They "hope to see establishment of [a] Rhineland-Ruhr state which would be joined in some form of economic union with France and are opposed to removals from this area to USSR."[27] Seen in this light, France's instructions to its representatives in the ACC not to agree to any action prejudging the future of the Ruhr and the Rhineland take on a new and revealing dimension.

The ACC reached stalemate early on reparations and restitutions. The French, who had apparently been slow to appreciate the power they had over reparations, learned quickly with proper coaching by the Americans. Ambassador Winant wrote on October 4, 1945, that he was impressed that the French had not realized their power to influence reparations through their veto right in the ACC, but that "they now appear to have grasped the point."[28] Reviewing the lesson, Byrnes asked Ambassador Caffery on October 18, 1945, to try to get France to agree on interim, advance-reparations deliveries as a way to break the vicious circle caused by France's refusal to approve advance-reparations deliveries and Russia's refusal to agree to a restitutions policy in the ACC. Byrnes said France could agree to advance reparations and keep her veto power as insurance against delivery of those items France wanted as restitutions. Taking their cues from Byrnes, the French agreed in principle to advance reparations, but according to Caffery, "France has no intention of agreeing to actual shipments from the western zones to Poland and Russia until Soviet Union has agreed to restitution (France however is willing to have Allied Control Council proceed with allocation as long as no actual shipments take place)."[29]

Clay tried to get a policy statement from Washington on the relationship of reparations and restitutions. He said he needed a definition of priorities because France was claiming 1,200 machine tools as restitutions from a plant that the American military government (OMGUS) had declared to be available for advance reparations. If France's claims for restitutions were honored, he said, the plant would be destroyed as a usable operating unit for reparations.[30] Observing that restitutions removals from plants which would be left in Germany for its minimum economy would have a similar effect, Clay asked for a higher priority for reparations.[31] The State Department agreed to work up a position.

In the meantime, various levels of the ACC in Berlin were deadlocked on restitutions and reparations. France would not accept a British compromise that proposed to compensate for restitutable materials found in plants declared available for reparations by making restitutions from other plants not on the reparation lists. The French insisted that "the looted goods themselves must be restored to their original owners" and that looted goods included "that property apparently 'purchased' by the Germans without force," since it was "paid for with stolen money." The Russians would not agree to restitution of property sold legally to the Germans "for reasons of profit," and the French would not agree to ship "looted goods, ... even in the case of the proposed advance deliveries." Responding to Russia's criticism of the continuing delays, Clay finally proposed to withdraw an entire plant from the advance-reparations list and ship two other plants instead. The Soviet member in the ACC thanked Clay for his proposal; the British member wanted to consult his government; but the French would not agree until the ACC had defined "looted property." Clay said in that case he would have to reserve his position on looted property until France changed her views on central German administrations.[32] Murphy observed that the French member let Clay's remark pass, but there is evidence to suggest that he did not ignore it.

The French communicated frequently—through Ambassador Caffery or directly—with the State Department, apparently trying to negotiate the restitutions issue outside the ACC and to do so without the Russians if possible. According to a State Department memorandum, the French resented "the attitude which they attribute to General Clay in the Control Council, particularly on the subject of restitution."[33] When the State Department passed one of France's protests on to the War Department, Clay responded with a convenient summary of the twists and turns that the reparations-restitution issue had taken in the ACC during 1945. Clay did not understand what the French had to complain about. He had, in fact, suggested a compromise between the Russian and French definitions of restitutions, and the French deputy military governor, General Louis Koeltz, had understood it in those terms.[34] The Russians had come a long way to compromise with France, Clay asserted, but "I can not but feel that [the] French are being quite stubborn in [their] unwillingness to compromise. In point of fact, French position in quadripartite government is not understandable to me. To date, their only contribution has been insistence on adoption of their restitution policy and opposition to central administrative machinery." The French had made no constructive contribution to four-power government. The United States was on a one-way street. It had supported France and gotten nothing in return.[35]

Meanwhile, on November 29, 1945, the JCS had issued a directive for Clay's use as a basis for ACC agreement, or for exploring a possible three-power agreement. The directive was to be applied in the American zone in any case. It specified currency, cultural and art works, and a long list of machinery, equipment, and other goods and valuables as subject to restitution if they had "been looted or acquired in any way by Germans from United Nations during [the] German occupation." Claimants for goods produced during the occupation would have to submit adequate proof that the Germans had acquired the property "through an act of force." Furthermore, during the interim period an appropriate representative of the claimant's country would have to certify that the property was "urgently required for the rehabilitation and reconstruction of his country."[36]

Using the JCS directive as a basis, the ACC finally put together a restitution policy that was neither an agreed policy nor a compromise. It called for a case-by-case approach, based on a wartime declaration that the United Nations reserved the right to invalidate all property transfers occurring during the German occupation. It provided for restitution of properties and goods obtained by force, but it did not specify the nature of force. It said: "All other property removed by the enemy is eligible for restitution to the extent consistent with reparations." Clay agreed to the policy on the condition that its effect would not increase the expense of the United States occupation, and the British took a similar position. The French asked that the record show that the ACC would decide "to what extent restitution is consistent with reparations," a decision that would, of course, be subject to the veto of any of the ACC's four members.[37] France then appealed to Washington once again, asking the State Department to "intervene with the proper authorities in order that instructions be given, as soon as possible, to the American delegate to the Allied Control Council in Berlin, requesting him to withdraw" certain reservations on restitutions.[38] But a paper agreement had been achieved, and the unresolved issues were taken up during the complex negotiations that led to the reparations and level-of-industry plan of March 26, 1946. Before we turn to those negotiations, it might be noted that restitutions remained a point of contention. Clay tried several times to get authorization from Washington to suspend restitutions to France until the French agreed to uniform policies and their implementation.[39] An OMGUS message of April 15, 1947, which was repeated to the War Department on June 23, 1947, is illustrative of the issues and the continuing impasse. Perhaps as a result of discussions in Moscow with the French and the British, but perhaps for other reasons,[40] the War Department had pressed Clay to speed up restitutions, and it apparently raised questions about the validity of Clay's interpretation of ACC restitutions policy. Clay insisted that OMGUS practices were consistent with the ACC policy. OMGUS was not obligated to restitute all property regardless of the method by which it was acquired. It was removing identifiable goods that were taken by force. All other property removed by the enemy was subject to restitution only if its removal was consistent with reparations. In negotiating the level-of-industry plan, Clay continued, the United States had taken the position that it could not grant reparations to a level that would leave only a minimum German economy and then add a restitutions program of unknown extent on top of that. These were the considerations that caused him to insist that restitutions had to be "consistent with reparations." Clay argued that greater restitutions would be possible only if the level-of-industry plan were revised upward. He went on to give various reasons for his difficulties, and he raised the specter of communism, apparently realizing how effective such an argument would be in Washington. He said the United States restitutions program was as good as any other one; that his problem with the French was that they wanted hunt and seizure rights; and that communism could win in Germany if the United States continued to play its cards as it had.[41]

CHAPTER SIX

Reparations and the Level of Industry

THE REPARATIONS provided for at Potsdam were in the nature of residues. Germany's peace economy was to be fixed at a level marked by living standards not to exceed the average living standards of her European neighbors, except Britain and Russia. Existing resources, mainly plants and equipment, in excess of those needed to maintain the peace economy were to be removed as reparations. The Potsdam Protocol provided that "the determination of the amount and character of the industrial capital equipment unnecessary for the German peace economy and therefore available for reparation shall be made by the Control Council under policies fixed by the Allied Commission on Reparations, with the participation of France, subject to the final approval of the Zone Commander in the Zone from which the equipment is to be removed."[1] After a brief period of confusion (and considerable disagreement) on the division of labor between the ACR in Moscow and the ACC in Berlin, an understanding was reached to close down the Moscow operation and transfer its functions to Berlin. The ACC inherited a whirlwind.

The task of constructing common indexes and determining an average living standard of Europe's economically, culturally, and socially diverse nations was in itself forbidding. To try to do it by committee—by four-power committee—under a severe deadline, with personnel that had to be shuffled and reassigned from other duties, from data and statistics that were as variable as they were incomplete, and "without the aid of a single adding or calculating machine," seems, on reflection, to have been foolhardy. Benjamin U. Ratchford and William D. Ross, two American participants, have written an admirable account of the attempt.[2]

The difficulty of the task was matched by the ambiguity of the mandate. For example: What would Germany's boundaries be in the future and for planning purposes? Was Germany's living standard to be regarded as a maximum (ceiling) or a minimum (floor) for planning purposes? What were "peaceful domestic industries," which were to have primary emphasis? What markets would there be for the products of Germany's peaceful, domestic industries? In other words, how would Germany pay for its necessary imports of food and for ball bearings, gasoline, rubber, nitrogen fertilizers, and other things that it was to be prohibited from producing? What was an "excessive concentration of economic power," which was to be eliminated? How was the directive to treat Germany as a single economic unit to be reconciled with the zonal reparations program or with the instruction to take "varying local conditions" into account when applying it? Did the latter merely permit, or did it require, free and unrestricted interzonal trade? When would war trophy seizures end? When would exploitation of German science and scientists cease? When would restitutions cease? Would France prevail in its effort to implement an auxiliary reparations program in the guise of restitutions?

THE ARMY AND THE LEVEL-OF-INDUSTRY PLAN

The Army attacked the problem of determining a post-Potsdam reparations and level-of-industry plan on two fronts, one in Berlin and one in Washington.

The Berlin Front

In Berlin, Clay took the lead in the ACC. Encouraged by his interpretation that the Potsdam Agreement released him from the rigid financial and economic restrictions of JCS 1067, he moved rapidly to try to make four-power rule work.* Eight days after the Potsdam Conference adjourned, Clay appointed a German Standard-of-Living Board and instructed it to have a report ready for the ACC within a month. The board, headed by Calvin B. Hoover, the Duke University economist currently in the industry division of military government, prepared a study of the German peace economy under the Potsdam formula and submitted its findings to the ACC's Industry Committee on September 18, 1945. The report became the basic working document for the deliberations and negotiations that led to the ACC's Plan for Reparations and the Level of Post-War German Economy of March 26, 1946.[3]

---

* Lucius D. Clay, *Decision in Germany* (Garden City, N.Y., 1950), pp. 41–42. Ross Berkes, an American member of the Allied Secretariat in Berlin, wrote in 1947 that "Potsdam seemed to make good sense to the Americans at the time," and that they sent more proposals into the committees and directorates of the ACC than the other three powers combined. Ross Berkes, "Germany: Test Tube of Peace," *The American Scholar*, XVI (Winter, 1946–47), 46–55.

Owing mainly to Hoover's own unhappiness with its findings, the German Standard-of-Living Board's report received public attention in the United States before it was thoroughly discussed in Berlin. The public discussion in the United States was monopolized by the so-called "hard" and "soft" peace advocates. As a result, the fundamental economic questions the report raised were, for the most part, passed over in favor of the report's more spectacular political contribution to the Morgenthau/anti-Morgenthau controversy. The board had, in fact, held closely to the Potsdam mandate to reduce Germany's living standard to the level of Germany's European neighbors. It calculated Germany's 1930–38 average living standard to have been approximately one-third higher than the standards of the rest of Europe. Taking into account normal population increases and the influx of refugees from Eastern Europe, the board calculated that Germany's postwar living standard would have to be reduced to about 74 percent of the 1930–38 average. The living standard that emerged from these calculations—coincidentally, according to Ratchford and Ross—was almost exactly the living standard that prevailed in Germany during the politically explosive and crucial year of 1932.[4]

The board's calculations reflected the mandate of the Potsdam Agreement in other respects as well. The board assumed that certain German heavy and special industries (notably arms, munitions, instruments of war, ocean shipping, synthetic oils, aircraft, aluminum) would be destroyed completely; that other German industries (notably steel, electric power, automobiles, machine tools, and chemicals) would be controlled and restricted; and that agricultural and peaceful domestic industries would be emphasized. The board assumed, further, that Germany's postwar population would be about 70 million, that her boundaries in the East would be along the Oder-Neisse river line, that no productive capacity would be left in Germany to provide for current-production reparations, and that no extra capacity would be left there in the interests of speeding rehabilitation.[5]

The board's three major conclusions were that Germany's postwar living standard would be reduced to the level that existed during the politically explosive year of 1932; that under the Potsdam mandate Germany's annual balance-of-payments deficit (calculated at RM 10 to the dollar) would be about $81.8 million ($355.5 million, if occupation costs were included); and that Germany could therefore not exist without external assistance, as the Potsdam Agreement provided it should. In other words, even if the proceeds of exports from current production and stocks were to be available in the first place for payment of imports—as the Americans had insisted they be—Germany's balance of payments would still be in the red. The report's own statements, taken out of context, were as follows:

a) The resulting import-export balance . . . reflects the extreme difficulty, if not the impossibility, of carrying out a severe program of industrial disarmament while still providing for a minimum German standard of living and providing for the costs of the occupying forces as required by the Report of the Three Power Conference.

b) The German standard of living reduced to the European average of 1930–1938 would be roughly the equivalent of that which actually existed in Germany in 1932, the worst year of the economic depression.

c) The conclusion cannot be avoided that the conflict between an extreme degree of industrial disarmament spread over a number of key industries and the goal of maintaining a minimum German standard of living according to the assumed formula while providing for the costs of the occupying forces seems insoluble under the conditions such as those brought about by losses of territory.[6]

The Washington Front

The War Department and the State Department made their own studies of reparations and the level of the German peacetime economy. But the Berlin effort was far ahead, and that caused problems in Washington. When Calvin Hoover returned to the United States in September he talked with various people in Washington, and a story on the German Standard-of-Living Board's findings was published in the *New York Times* on October 8, 1945. Clay, who knew Hoover's personal views firsthand, had anticipated trouble. He cabled the War Department on September 26, 1945, that the report Hoover was discussing in Washington was not a policy statement but a paper for discussion within OMGUS and the ACC. He said, "Hoover abhors destruction and his personal views are towards leniency."* A week later Clay wrote McCloy that Hoover "was greatly distressed over the reparations program in Germany and I fear basically at heart not in sympathy with the policies agreed upon at Potsdam. The result was that he was not happy in his work."[7]

When Hoover's judgments and conclusions became public knowledge, the War and State Departments responded, in part to provide answers to journalists who were happily reporting on the Hoover report's significance

---

* Two years later, Calvin Hoover was selected to serve on the President's Committee on Foreign Aid (the Harriman Committee) to study the Marshall plan for European economic recovery, an assignment he apparently found to be more satisfying.

for the Morgenthau Plan, and in part to clarify their own positions. The latter are the more significant. The War Department followed Clay's lead and apparently saw to it that Eisenhower made a statement about the so-called Hoover report's unofficial status. General Hilldring, who prepared an analysis for Secretary of War Patterson's use in a meeting demanded by Morgenthau, detected two major shortcomings in the report: the erroneous assumption that Potsdam guaranteed Germany a living standard equal to her European neighbors, and the failure to distinguish between short-run and long-run problems. In the short run, Hilldring wrote, Germany's deficits would have to be made up by a combination of emergency-type permitted production (the facilities for which would apparently be eliminated in the long run) and Congressional appropriations. In the long run, Germany would have to subsist on her own. The first error that Hilldring detected was obviously an answer to Morgenthau and an attempt to calm public clamor—*Time* magazine grabbed the bait—while the second reflected the Army's position in the absence of a clear definition from the State Department on the scope and ultimate costs of the finance and procurement responsibilities Truman had assigned to the Army on July 29, 1945.[8]

The State Department's response was more detailed than the Army's, and, as we shall see, its implications aroused the Army. Clayton cabled Murphy on October 12, 1945, that "large industrial removals from Germany are compatible with and *required by* other U.S. objectives in Germany and *elsewhere in Europe*." Prefacing his discussion with observations that the ACC "should avoid hasty conclusions" and that much more study was needed, Clayton said Hoover's report failed to make clear that there were reparations available from the excess capacity in the steel, machine tool, and chemical industries of Germany. He seems to have missed the fact that all of these availabilities were incorporated in the Hoover Board's calculations. Furthermore, Clayton thought Hoover's people had probably estimated Germany's exports too conservatively and that they had failed to calculate food imports of "different constitution and lower value" in their balances. Ignoring the implications of Truman's coal directive as well as the reality of the impasse on economic unity and central administrations in Berlin, Clayton asserted that "the revival of the German economy over the short period appears contingent, primarily on improvements in coal and raw material supply, transport, on expansion of inter-regional and inter-zonal trade, and in general on efficient reorganization of [the] German economy." Then, significantly shifting ground, he got to the essence of the

State Department's policy to use Germany as a base for rebuilding liberated Europe. The State Department could not agree that the program of re-movals from Germany would have a marked effect on *European* economic recovery, in either the short run or the long run. In the short run, coal, transport, raw materials, and food were more important to recovery than capital equipment. As long as that condition existed, Clayton said, re-activation of industry in the allied nations must have priority over reactiva-tion of German industry. Germany could export coal, the products of ex-tractive industry, and such things as textiles to the rest of Europe. In the long run, *European* industrial capacity would not be reduced, even though centers of production and power would be shifted from Germany to the rest of Europe. According to Clayton, further study was needed on means to reduce Germany's imports, to increase Germany's exports of nonmilitary industries, and to maximize removals of "industries of military importance such as metal-fabricating and chemicals industries."[9]

Clayton's response to the German Standard-of-Living Board's report made clear some of the consequences of the State Department's approach to the occupation of Germany. That caused the Army to intensify its cam-paign to be relieved of its nonmilitary functions in Germany. Eisenhower summarized the Army's arguments for Marshall on October 13, 1945, one day after Clayton's message to Murphy. Patterson took up the matter with the Secretaries of State and Navy on October 23, 1945, a campaign described in Chapter 2. The Army also pressed the State Department for further policy clarification. It began to do so in earnest early in November, during Clay's and Murphy's visit to Washington.

On November 3, 1945, in a meeting with Clayton, Matthews, and their deputies and assistants, Clay asked the State Department for a policy on France's proposal to annex the Saar and separate the Ruhr and the Rhine-land from Germany. He argued that there was little prospect of progress in Berlin on a three-power basis unless the Russians—who favored central ad-ministrations—knew how they stood on reparations from the Ruhr and the Rhineland. Clay also wanted a policy statement on whether reparations or restitutions should have priority, and he recommended priority for repara-tions, except for cultural and artistic objects, because such a priority would favor countries that had adopted a wartime scorched-earth policy (i.e. Russia) over those that had allowed plants and equipment to fall into the hands of the Germans during the war (i.e. France, Belgium, Denmark). Finally, Clay said he needed clarification on the extent of population transfers, on the relationship between the Allied Commission on Reparations and the ACC, and on the disposition of German external assets.[10]

As he did on the central administrations issue, Patterson took his cues from Clay on the Ruhr-Rhineland issue. On November 6, 1945, he urged Byrnes to inform the War Department of the State Department's attitude on the French proposals. Two weeks later he wrote Byrnes that it was "manifestly impossible" for OMGUS to negotiate a reparations plan and the level of the German peacetime economy unless it knew what Germany's boundaries would be. If the Ruhr and the Rhineland would be lost to the German economy, OMGUS needed to be advised "immediately," since the ACC had to develop a reparations plan by February 2, 1946.[11] Acheson replied that the State Department "does not desire to express a definite opinion on" the Ruhr-Rhineland question, because the French and Russians were discussing it in Moscow. He admitted that the Americans had not stated a position to Couve de Murville during the latter's discussions in Washington from November 13 to 20, 1945, and he observed that it was "readily apparent" that the French proposals required a reexamination of the Potsdam Agreement, which the American government could not do unilaterally.[12] Patterson persisted, however, and reminded Acheson on December 28 that despite the State Department's unwillingness to express an opinion on the Ruhr and Rhineland, it had sent the Army a memorandum on November 30, 1945, defining Germany's boundaries for planning reparations and the German peacetime economy as "those of the Altreich, less the territory east of the Oder-Neisse line."[13] Patterson asked for clarification and Acheson replied on January 12, 1946, confirming the instruction of November 30, but not without implying that the issue was still unsettled: "Unless and until there has been a modification of German frontiers, this Government must necessarily base its policy on the Potsdam decisions and earlier agreements respecting the occupation of Germany."[14]

THE STATE DEPARTMENT AND THE LEVEL-OF-INDUSTRY PLAN

The following circumstances contributed to Byrnes's decision to release a United States policy statement on reparations and the German peacetime economy: the public discussion of the German Standard-of-Living Board's report; Clay's and Murphy's requests for policy clarification in Washington; the intense internal discussion following Byron Price's report of November 9, 1945, to Truman; Patterson's continuous prodding; the State Department's own studies, and SWNCC's ongoing studies on "The Determination of the Amount and Character of Reparation Removals from Germany in Relation to the German 'Peacetime' Economy."[15] Riddleberger sketched the problems and the pitfalls of the effort in a speech delivered in Kansas City, Missouri, on November 24, 1945, when the policy statement was already being drafted. One of the most difficult and pressing problems, Riddleberger said, was to restore the "German economy to a point which will enable the German people to live without endangering their neighbors." The United States' zeal to destroy Germany's war potential and reduce her as a threat, he noted, might create intolerable conditions in Germany and leave a people so desperate and embittered that future democratic development would be foreclosed. "Germany cannot be maintained indefinitely on a basis of a 'soup kitchen' economy," but if the United States proposed to leave resources in Germany it would be open to charges that sinister forces were at work to rebuild Germany. It would be accused of constructing a bulwark against the Soviet Union and of being more concerned with Germany's problems than with those of its former allies.[16] Riddleberger concluded that American policymakers would have to follow a course somewhere between the two dangerous alternatives, which was precisely what the policy statement of December 12, 1945, tried to do.

The State Department's policy statement of December 12 interpreted the Potsdam Agreement and outlined United States economic policies in Germany in such a way as neither to arouse Morgenthau and the liberal press unnecessarily, nor to bring down the wrath of the Army and OMGUS upon the State Department. In a press release accompanying the policy statement, Byrnes summarized the State Department's conception of Germany's postwar economic development. He said the Potsdam Agreement provided for Germany's return "to normal economic conditions" in three stages. During the first stage, until the spring of 1946, Germany would make a maximum contribution to the recovery of the liberated areas, mainly by exporting coal. Recovery in the liberated areas would thus be furthered "at the cost of delaying recovery in Germany." Meanwhile, the ACC would develop a reparations and disarmament program, which was due on February 2, 1946. The ACC would set up German administrative agencies to treat Germany as an economic unit and prevent mass starvation, albeit at a lower priority than for the liberated areas. In the second stage, from the spring of 1946 to the end of capital-equipment reparations removals on February 2, 1948, Germany would recover gradually. While reparations removals in plants and equipment proceeded, other plants would be designated for retention in

Germany. As fuel, transport, and raw materials became available, the plants retained in Germany would resume production. Germany's heavy coal exports would continue, but increased production would permit larger coal allocations for German domestic use. Germany's exports would gradually move to a level equal to imports, and they would eventually be sufficient also to repay the occupying powers for their outlays during the first period. During the third stage, Germany would recover to the level equal to her European neighbors (as provided at Potsdam). Germans would then resume control over their own economy, subject to such residual limitations as the occupying powers might prescribe. The United States preferred to limit only Germany's future rearmament. It did not want to restrict or reduce the German living standard indefinitely after the reparations period had ended.[17]

The policy statement of December 12, 1945, which Byrnes's press release summarized and interpreted, was a set of instructions and a guidance for OMGUS to be used in the ACC to negotiate the reparations and level-of-industry plan that was due on February 2, 1946. The policy called for the elimination of Germany's war-industries capacity (arms, ammunition, implements of war, aircraft, seagoing ships); drastic reductions in "metallurgical, machinery, and chemical industries"; and retention of "German industries of a peaceful character," sufficient to provide the living standards allowed at Potsdam. Retentions were to be sufficient to permit export production to pay for Germany's needed imports. The Potsdam reparations agreement would be adhered to strictly, even though doing so would "undoubtedly retard Germany's economic recovery." The United States and other occupation powers would have "to finance imports into Germany and possibly pay for such imports in the next few years," but that condition was caused not so much by the reparations removals agreed upon at Potsdam as by the general economic standstill occasioned by Germany's defeat. In any case, "during the next two years," the United States and others would have to finance minimum essential imports into Germany to the extent that exports from stocks and current production would not cover the cost of such imports. As long as coal and raw materials remained in short supply in Europe, United States policy was to make them available from Germany in maximum quantity to promote rehabilitation in the liberated areas. In the immediate future, therefore, coal allocations for Germany's domestic use would be insufficient to permit "a significant volume of industrial production." Coal shortages in Germany would also limit agriculture and the

repair of transport, housing, and utilities. The United States did not en-
vision permanent limitations on the German economy, however, and "the
German people under a peaceful democratic government of their own
choice" could develop and work for a higher standard of living in the
future, restricted only by the prevention of armaments production as would
be laid down by the peace settlement.[18]

Byrnes's policy statement probably helped to moderate the criticism of
United States policy in Germany occasioned by the publication of Morgenthau's *Germany Is Our Problem* in December 1945. Byrnes's thoughtful-
ness in sending personal copies of the statement to Senator Walter F. George
and others may have helped the cause.[19] In any case, the lid stayed on, and
no less a journal of opinion than *The Nation* editorialized that "No one
can say that this program deviates from Potsdam or that it dilutes the pre-
scription for a hard peace."[20] The statement proved to be less gratifying to
the Army and OMGUS.

On the positive side, Byrnes's statement settled the boundary question
temporarily by defining Germany's geographical limits for planning purposes as "those of the Altreich, less the territory east of the Oder-Neisse line."
The resources of the Saar, the Ruhr, and the Rhineland were to be used in
calculating the level of the German peacetime economy. Though United
States policy provided for periods of heavy Army financial outlays (the first
stage) and moderate Army outlays (the second stage), the State Department
nevertheless envisioned a future Germany capable of sustaining itself *and*
of redressing its earlier negative balance of payments. In any case, the December 12, 1945, statement was a public reference that the Army could use
in the future to justify its heavy occupation costs in Germany to the Congress and the American people. Furthermore, the statement made clear that
the German living standard specified at Potsdam did not have to be attained during the occupation period, and predicted that it might be un-
attainable even in 1948. In effect, this meant that the Army would not be
required by policy to finance and procure for Germany in order to attain
the German living standard provided for at Potsdam—all it needed to do
was to prevent "mass starvation," as Byrnes put it; to prevent "disease and
unrest," as the official jargon described it.

If the Army's and OMGUS's previous concerns and questions are used
as criteria, the December 12, 1945, policy statement was far from satisfactory.
For example, it did not clarify the relationship of restitutions and reparations. Furthermore, it instructed OMGUS to concentrate on repairing trans-

port, housing, essential utilities, and "the maximization of coal and agricultural production," but it admitted that "existing directives" would cause shortages and thus "limit activity" even in those fields of endeavor. The statement instructed the occupying authorities to "devote primary attention" to improving German administrative machinery, increasing interzonal production and trade, and applying "common policies in transport, agriculture, banking, currency, taxation, et cetera," but it ignored completely the stalemate in Berlin occasioned by France's instructions to its representatives in the ACC to veto everything until France's Saar, Ruhr, and Rhineland proposals had been considered. The Army's increased effort (its panic, according to a State Department official) in December 1945 and January 1946 to transfer military government to the State Department is, perhaps, adequate testimony to the Army's dissatisfaction with the December 12 policy statement. But time passed and the level-of-industry plan was due on February 2, 1946.

THE CONTROL COUNCIL PLAN

The ACC's plan for reparations and the level of the postwar German economy was finally adopted on March 26, 1946, almost two months after the deadline fixed at Potsdam.* It was a delicately balanced edifice, the foundation of which was a set of unrealistic assumptions, the roof of which was a patchwork of political compromises, and the superstructure of which was threatened by the four winds of national interest represented in the ACC. According to an American working paper, the plan's purpose was "to eliminate the base of the German war economy and to force the diversion of resources to other industries, which will become the mainstays of the new German economy."[21] It was, in fact, a program to eliminate Germany's war potential, reduce her industrial potential for rearmament, provide reparations, develop agriculture and peaceful industries, and retain in Germany sufficient capacity to maintain without external assistance a living standard no higher than the average living standards of Germany's neighbors (except Britain and Russia).

* Distressed by the delay and anxious to adhere to the Potsdam schedule, Clay had released report unilaterally in Berlin and Frankfurt on Feb. 2, 1946, listing the major disagreements that had prevented the ACC from completing the plan on schedule. See Hilldring to SecWar, through Chief of Staff, Feb. 8, 1946, RG 335, file OSW 387.6 (1946), Safe file, Box 6, NA. The Russians, apparently similarly motivated and anxious for more rapid reparations deliveries, communicated their disappointment at the delays to the State Department—and possibly to France and Britain too. See Schulgen to Matthews, March 19, 1946, War Dept. Papers, file VDSCA 014 Germany, Feb. 15, 1946–March 14, 1946, NA.

The level-of-industry plan of 1946 listed the industries that would be prohibited in Germany and those that would be restricted, specifying either absolute production figures or percentages of the 1936 base year as maximum limits for the restricted industries. It also listed the unrestricted industries for which no levels had been determined. The general effect of the plan would have been to reduce Germany's level of industry to approximately 50 to 55 percent of the 1938 level and to about 70 to 75 percent of the 1936 level. Specifically, steel production *capacity* was set for possible annual production of 7.5 million tons; *annual permitted production* was to be planned at 5.8 million tons, however. That was approximately one-third of the 1938 production. The plan projected exports and imports at RM 3 billion annually (in 1949), compared with the 1936 levels of RM 4.8 and 4.2 billion, respectively. Exports of metal products (machinery, electrical equipment, optics, precision instruments, and nonferrous metal goods) were to be 37 percent of those in 1936; chemical products, 42 percent; coal, coke, and potash, 122 percent; and consumer goods (leather, textiles, glass, ceramics, paper, etc.), 109 percent of 1936. Germany's primary imports were to be food, ball bearings, synthetic gasoline, oil, nitrogen fertilizer, and rubber.[22]

The plan rested on three basic assumptions, which were stated. None of them was realistic. The assumption that Germany's postwar population (in 1949) would be 66.5 million was based on an estimate and a political compromise, both of which were conditioned by lack of clear information on the expulsion of refugees and by doubts regarding the future of the Saar the Ruhr, and the Rhineland.[23] The plan's assumption that Germany would be treated as a single economic unit ignored the reality of the impasse in Berlin, to which we shall return in the next chapter. And last, the plan's assumption that Germany's exports would be acceptable in international markets was an expedition into economic no-man's-land. Would Germany's merchants and products be acceptable on an equal basis with those of Germany's competitors? Would potential customers buy goods they could obtain more cheaply as reparations and restitutions? Even under the best of conditions, where would Germany find markets for domestic, peaceful consumer-type production that even relatively underdeveloped nations could produce?

The negotiations that produced the level-of-industry plan show why it was so complex and fragile. Even after the ACC had agreed with great difficulty to the 7.5 million ton steel capacity and the 5.8 million ton production figures on January 10, 1946, the British had second thoughts. Pressed by the Americans to live with the compromise, Britain's negotiators accused the Americans of "going more and more in Morgenthau's direction." General Sir Brian H. Robertson, the British military governor, told Murphy the British government could not accept Clay's apparent "premise that if starvation, misery and slavery were to result from demilitarization, they would have to be accepted." The British were worried that Germany would become a financial burden on England, and Robertson insisted on 7.5 million tons as a production-planning figure.[24] Clay, Murphy, Robertson, and Sir William Strang (Murphy's British counterpart) finally took their differences to Byrnes and Foreign Secretary Bevin in London. In the end, the British accepted 5.8 million tons as a planning figure, but with the understanding that the 7.5 million ton capacity would be kept in place in Germany and that the plan would be reviewed. Britain's continuing fundamental objection to the compromise is revealed by Robertson's suggestion of March 22, 1946, that the first review of the plan be undertaken on January 1, 1947.[25]

The other delegations also stated reservations during the debates and discussions on the level-of-industry plan, and the French linked theirs with frontier claims. On February 1, 1946, France's representative in Berlin proposed that the ACC prepare an alternative study of steel capacity, to be based on the assumption that France would annex the Saar. Murphy cabled Washington, saying Clay had advised the War Department that the question of the Saar's future had to be resolved at government level. Murphy said that the British were willing to study the matter even though France's proposal went beyond the Potsdam Agreement. The Russians, on the other hand, insisted that the issue had been settled at Potsdam. According to Murphy, "State Department should be advised as a matter of urgency and should give instructions to govern future course of action. No real progress on reparations possible till then."[26] In Washington Patterson took up the issue with Byrnes, who had already received an *aide-mémoire* from France on the subject.[27] Matthews seemed willing to "agree to permanent French occupation of the Saar," but recommended that Byrnes inform France that the United States could not discuss the disposition of the Saar until there was some prospect of getting central agencies in Germany.[28]

Meanwhile, in Berlin on March 8, 1946, Clay "stressed that ... the Saar and Ruhr are an integral part of Germany," and that "if boundary or other changes" were made, "the agreed plan would have to be modified as it probably would no longer be sound."[29] Two weeks later, as the negotiations went into their final stages, Clay (this time endorsing Robertson's remarks) said he "also understood failure to operate Germany as [a] unit, either through lack of administrative apparatus or further change of frontiers, would make plan subject to revision." The Soviet representative first insisted that no revision of the plan "would be admissible unless reparations plan executed," and then only with four-power unanimity.[30] Four days later, apparently after receiving instructions from Moscow, he agreed to accept the following wording: "Plan is subject to review as may be agreed by the Control Council in the event that the fundamental assumptions of the plan are bound to be changed." France's representative wanted him to confirm that his wording meant that if Germany's western frontiers were changed the plan would be subject to revision. He replied that if some such decision were made, he presumed the ACC would be advised and instructed to take appropriate action.[31]

In the final debates on the plan, each representative in the ACC restated the conditions, assumptions, and reservations that governed his acceptance. The British accepted on condition that the plan would be reviewed periodically; that Germany would be treated as an economic unit within the boundaries specified at Potsdam; that changes in the western boundary or failure to achieve economic unity would make revision mandatory; that Germany's population did not exceed 66.5 million; and that Germany's exports would be sufficient to pay for necessary imports. Robertson, in fact, stated that Britain would reject the entire plan unless the "principle of mandatory revision on proof of changes or errors in fundamental assumptions of [the] plan" were accepted by his colleagues. The French conditions were similar to those of Britain on periodic review, on the "thesis that any partial changes of plan must be considered as to effect on whole plan," and on the need for revision if Germany's frontiers were changed. In addition, the French emphasized that Germany's food imports of RM 1.5 billion "must be a maximum to be lowered as soon as possible," regardless of population increases, and that Germany's 45 million tons of coal exports annually (34.4 percent of the planned production) be a minimum. The American conditions were that Germany would operate as a unit, that failure to establish central administrations or further boundary changes would require revision, and that the plan would be regarded as a program for reparations rather than as a permanent limitation on German industry (except as specifically stated in the plan). As noted above, the Soviet member said, "Plan is subject to review as may be agreed by the Control

Council in the event that the fundamental assumptions of the plan are bound to be changed," but he did so only after withdrawing his original condition that no changes were admissible until the reparations plan had been executed.[32]

The treatment of Germany as an economic unit having been a basic— and crucial—condition of the plan's acceptance and implementation, we may turn now to examine that impasse.

CHAPTER SEVEN

Economic Unity and Central Agencies

AMERICAN POLICYMAKERS interpreted the zonal reparation formula adopted at Potsdam in such a way as to require economic unity by administrative practice. As noted earlier, Clayton complained immediately after the Potsdam Conference about "the unfortunate tendency [in Washington] to interpret the reparations operating agreement as an ... abandonment of four power treatment of Germany." He asserted that the zonal reparations plan did not contradict the general economic principles of the Potsdam Agreement, which provided for central German administrative departments for finance, transport, communications, foreign trade, and industry. Furthermore, he argued, the agreement called for common policies on deindustrialization, import-export programs, food supplies, the German living standard, and reparations deliveries.[1] On September 6, 1945, Clayton applied his interpretation in a set of instructions to General William H. Draper, the director of OMGUS's industry division, currently in Moscow as American representative on the ACR. Clayton advised Draper that reparations removals would affect Germany's living standard and her ability to subsist without external assistance. Therefore, Clayton reasoned, reparations from the Western zones and the Soviet zone had to be based upon an agreed four-power plan that would treat each zone as part of a unified Germany. Specifically, Clayton said, the Russians would have to furnish data on removals they had taken and permit mixed commissions of industrial experts, "which Soviet would send into Western Germany, to enter eastern Germany."[2]

The Russian response to Clayton's interpretation reflected Pauley's and Byrnes's (rather than Clayton's) interpretation of the American reparations proposal at Potsdam. Byrnes had told his colleagues at Potsdam, "If the Soviets agreed to his plan they would have no interest in exports and imports from our zone. Any difficulty in regard to imports and exports would have to be settled between the British and ourselves. The Soviets would have no interest and they would get their percentage regardless of what happened to us."* In any case, Andrei Vyshinsky, speaking for the Russian team with which Draper was negotiating in Moscow, wrote on September 16, 1945, that the Potsdam decision could not be changed unilaterally and that Russia could not agree to the American proposal for a four-power reparations plan as outlined by Clayton. The Potsdam Conference had accepted the American reparations proposal, which provided not for a four-zonal reparations plan but for one collections procedure in the Soviet zone and for another in the Western zones. The Potsdam Agreement provided for a common reparations policy and for maintaining an average living standard not to exceed the average of Germany's neighbors. To achieve these objectives, Vyshinsky wrote, the Soviet government was prepared to inform the ACC and the ACR on "the presence of equipment which has been left in the Soviet Zone" and to permit mixed commissions of experts to examine the equipment "on the spot."[3]

The larger significance of the Clayton-Vyshinsky exchange is that economic unity in Germany would apparently have to be achieved not by administrative interpretation of the reparations decision but by the two methods specified in the Potsdam Agreement: the adoption of common economic policies and the establishment of central German administrative departments. General Clay had already assigned top priority to those methods.

CENTRAL GERMAN ADMINISTRATIONS

On August 10, 1945, at the second formal meeting of the ACC, the Americans proposed that the appropriate four-power directorates of the ACC make studies and recommendations on the establishment of German administrative departments for finance, transportation, communications, foreign trade, and industry. The French government having expressed formal reservations on the Potsdam Agreement three days earlier, General Marie-Pierre Koenig, the French military governor, responded to the American

---

* Dept. of State Minutes, 10th Meeting of Foreign Ministers, July 30, 1945, *FRUS*, 1945, Potsdam II, 491. Pauley wrote to Maisky on July 27, 1945 (*FRUS*, 1945, Potsdam II, 896), that "the United States has ... been placed in the position where it must deal with reparations along the same lines as have, in fact, been initiated by the Soviet Government. It was for this reason that we have submitted (two days ago) a further proposal which formally recognizes that removals will be conducted on a zonal basis. This we regard as regrettable, but inescapable, in view of the unilateral actions taken by the Soviet Government.... Our proposal need not interfere with the efforts of the Control Council to work out other economic and political problems for Germany as a unit" or with Russia's desire to obtain heavy industrial equipment from the Ruhr.

proposal by asking for deletion of all references to German administrators and by saying that he "was obliged to reserve his opinion" on central administrations "because his Government had not been a signatory to the Potsdam agreement."[4]

Less than two weeks later, Bidault warned Byrnes in Washington that German central administrations would, in effect, bring the Russians right up to the borders of France. He asserted that the central administrations decision at Potsdam encroached on France's vital interests in the border regions between France and Germany and that he therefore "felt obliged to make the most explicit reservations in the matter."[5] In September 1945, as noted earlier, the French presented their views and demands in a memorandum to the CFM meeting in London. They emphasized "the paramount importance" France attached to preventing the Rhineland and Westphalia from "ever again becoming an arsenal, corridor or base for an attack by Germany on her western neighbours." To "cover the French frontier" and to provide essential security for "Europe and the world," France wanted "final separation" of the Rhineland and Westphalia, including the Ruhr. If central German administrations were to be set up in Germany, "it should at the same time be specified that their authority should not extend to the Rhineland and Westphalia." Finally, the French memorandum noted that France's representatives in the ACC were not authorized to agree to any action that would prejudge the future of the Rhineland and Westphalia until their status had been discussed and decided by the CFM.[6]

Meanwhile American military authorities in Berlin had reported progress on a program to locate, interview, and earmark "suitable German administrative personnel for key positions in the central departments and agencies" that were to be established.[7] But there were hang-ups in the ACC. On September 22, 1945, General Koeltz, the French deputy military governor, objected to a British proposal to establish a central German statistical agency because it would be a useful tool for German mobilization. Koeltz also stated a reservation on a plan to establish a central agency for communications and posts, and he criticized a plan for a central transport agency. He objected in general to central agencies and in particular to a central administration of railways, because railways were "a crucial war potential." If such an agency would be created anyway, he said, "it should have no directing authority." Koeltz said he expected additional instructions as a result of France's discussions at government level, but General Vasili Sokolovsky, the Russian deputy military governor, protested that the issue had been studied and decided at Potsdam. Clay thought the ACC would become a negotiating rather than a governing body if the French position prevailed, and he seems to have tried to establish a precedent for majority rule. He wanted to refer the issue to the military governors, with a majority report and a French minority statement. That was done, and the issue came before the ACC on October 1, 1945.[8]

According to Ambassador Caffery, the French had "an almost panicky fear" of any action that might lead to a central German government, in part because a central German government would be dominated by the Russians and France would then "have the Soviets on their frontiers." In any case, on October 1, 1945, the French military governor blocked further ACC consideration of the plans for central administrations of transport, communications, and posts. He referred to the London CFM meeting and said he had been instructed not to agree to anything that might "prejudice or otherwise affect the settlement of the Rhine-Westphalia regions." Central administrations, he said, would affect those regions and he could not discuss the current plans. Murphy reported that the French foreign office observer who attended the meeting told him frankly afterward that France wanted an autonomous government in the Rhineland and Ruhr, that it wanted to annex the Saar, and that such action would be similar to Poland's annexations in the East. French opposition to central administrations, he said, was "based upon the intention to force consideration of this matter."[9]

Clay tried to break the impasse at his level in Berlin, but he failed. He had cabled the War Department late in September 1945, asking for authority to establish central administrations for the American, British, and Russian zones if the French refused to cooperate. He repeated his request on October 2, 1945. On October 12, before he received a reply from Washington, he used the occasion of a British-Russian wrangle over the use of the Berlin-Helmstedt railway line (which was single-track since the Russians had removed one track) to argue that a German central transport agency would reduce such problems. He then invited his colleagues individually or collectively to join with the Americans in forming a joint transport organization and a similar one for communications. Murphy reported that the British and Russians seemed sympathetic and that Koeltz said it was a good plan provided no Germans were involved. When Clay returned to his invitation at the next meeting, the British and Russians expressed disappointment at the delay in establishing central agencies, but the British objected to Clay's solution because it would set a precedent for actions outside the four-power organization. Clay withdrew the proposal on October 16, 1945. Four days later he got his authorization from Washington to "enter into any arrangement with the Russians and British" for central administrations in accordance with the Potsdam Agreement. The War Department had cleared the authorization with the State Department, and, presumably, the pushing and pulling going on there about the French priority and the future of the Ruhr and Rhineland explain the instruction that "such arrangement" be for administrative purposes only and that it not "prejudge final disposition to be made of territories within these zones."[10]

France's obstructions permeated to all levels of the Allied Control Authority and they prevented the development of common economic policies as well as the creation of central administrations. On October 18, 1945, the French member in the ACC's Political Directorate said his orders from Paris obliged him "to abstain from all discussion" of an American proposal to transfer to Berlin the documents and personnel that Americans had gathered in the Ministerial Collecting Center in Kassel for eventual use by the central administrations and a German government. Murphy said, "The question was accordingly adjourned."[11] Two days later, on October 20, 1945, the French blocked an ACC law that would have permitted German labor unions to federate or amalgamate. France wanted all political activity of unions forbidden, federal amalgamation of unions only by special consent of the ACC, and union organizations only on a zonal basis. The Russian military governor, Marshal Georgi Zhukov, pointed out that zonal unions already existed and that the primary purpose of the law was to permit them on an interzonal basis. Eisenhower, in apparent frustration, observed that the ACC's job was to run Germany as a unit and that the members were all wasting their time until that was settled. The issue went back to the CORC, the next lower level of the Allied Control Authority, from whence it had come. There the majority argued for national labor unions "as a force against the reconstitution of Nazism," but the French suggested amendments and expressed conditions that would have deprived the law of all substance. It was finally referred to government level.[12]

The story goes on and on. The official American military government report for October 1945 said France was holding up the establishment of the administrative machinery necessary to treat Germany as a single economic unit.[13] As noted earlier, Clay and Murphy reported similarly in Washington in November. On November 20, 1945, Byrnes told Couve de Murville in Washington that he "expected to" advise the British and Rus sians that the United States was willing to establish common policies and central administrations without France if necessary.[14] There is no record that he did so. But four days later, during a discussion of transport problems and policies, Clay tried the three-power approach again at his level, this time with authority from Washington. He declared the United States to be ready "to enter into tripartite agreement for the establishment of central administrations." Following the British precedent of October 16, 1945, the Russians said they could not do that, "since the Potsdam decisions called for central organs for all four zones." The transport agency proposal was therefore deferred indefinitely and a British proposal for a central statistical agency was also withdrawn from the agenda.[15] In December, when Clay suggested three-power agreement on a central administration for communications and posts, the British said they lacked authority to proceed on a tripartite basis.* Before that the French had vetoed a proposal to establish a German patent office and it was withdrawn from the ACC agenda. Murphy had also reported that a proposal for an export-import agency was stalled in the Trade and Commerce Committee and in the Economic Directorate of the ACC.[16] At the same time Byrnes advised Bidault that if there was no other way to achieve central administrations the United States would agree "with great reluctance" to have them established for the Russian, British, and American zones. According to Ambassador Caffery, Bidault's only reply was "to manifest much distress" and to repeat the De Gaulle–Bidault litany: the Soviets will dominate a central German government. Byrnes apparently had second thoughts, for there is no available record of his approach to Britain and Russia until he issued his general invitation for zonal amalgamation the following year, on July 11, 1946. The French—not unlike Senator Arthur H. Vandenberg at home—seemed worried, however, that Byrnes might strike a Christmas bargain with the Russians during his special visit in Moscow in December 1945.[17]

The new year was burdened by the legacy of the old. On January 21, 1946, the French vetoed a British proposal for a central German finance department. General Koenig explained why: the British plan called for centralization "incongruous with reiterated French policy." It proposed a German administration "whose authority extends over all Germany."

---

* Murphy to SecState, Dec. 22, 1945, RG 59, file 740.00119 Control (Germany), Box C-131, NA, also referred to in *FRUS*, 1945, III, 921, note 88. Ross Berkes, with terrible word pictures but accurate information, wrote in "Germany: Test Tube of Peace," *The American Scholar*, XVI Winter, 1946–47), 48, that "astute Soviet tact first rose up to shelve the project, and blunt British objections finally broke the bubble before it was underway."

France had consistently refused to discuss that issue "until [the] western boundary of Germany was fixed." Although an "advisory committee of German experts" would be helpful to the ACC, Koenig continued, no such committee could be created until the German states east of the Rhine had been organized. In the interest of such organization, France was negotiating with the Americans to alter zonal boundaries, particularly in Baden and Württemberg. Once the German states were formed, France would permit such states to "delegate German experts to [the] Control Council to study financial questions of common interest." The advisory committees envisioned by the French would, however, "not have representatives from [the] Pfalz, Saar and Rhineland," and they would "be incompetent to handle questions affecting those areas."[18]

Murphy considered Koenig's remarks to have been an important statement of French policy and intention. He and Clay flew to London to talk with Byrnes about France's policy, the level-of-industry plan, and the dispute with the British about steel capacity. Regarding France's vetoes, they emphasized the valuable time that had been lost and pointed out the injury that had been done to Europe's economy in the meantime. Murphy later wrote to Matthews about the talks with Byrnes and suggested that perhaps the boundary and central-agencies questions could be separated by agreeing to establish central administrations "without prejudice to whatever settlement might be made in the West." He thought the two problems were not related, "except as the French may wish to use their opposition to the central agencies as a pressure point to stimulate favorable consideration of their proposals." He asked Matthews whether he had "formulated an opinion by now regarding a possible way out of the impasse. We have exhausted every argument we know here." The military government report compiled in January 1946 stated: "It has become evident that only the solution at government level [of the western boundary issue] will permit further progress in the establishment of central German administrative agencies."[19]

Byrnes tried the government-level approach by appealing to Bidault on February 1, 1946, to review the French position on central administrations. He followed Murphy's suggestion and advised Bidault that the agreement on central administrations need "not prejudice the eventual consideration of Germany's western frontier." He reviewed some of the history of the issue and said the other three powers were agreed that central agencies were required. Without central agencies, he emphasized, "it will become impossible to administer Germany as an economic unit" and to reduce Ger many's war potential. Cooperation in the ACC was "a test of the ability of the four Allies...to work together in the post-war world." Failure there would be crucial. Byrnes went over the same ground with Henri Bonnet, the French ambassador in Washington. He objected to the French use of the veto on central agencies to force consideration of France's boundary claims and he said "it was an utterly impossible situation and should not be continued." He objected to negotiations under duress.[20]

Given its unwillingness to try the Army's recommendations for economic sanctions, for marshaling world opinion against France, and for other pressures, the State Department knew that nothing short of a resolution of France's Ruhr, Rhineland, and Saar proposals would work.[21] If there was any doubt, Bidault's reply to Byrnes's personal appeal removed that possibility. Caffery previewed what was to come. Bidault was convinced, he said, that once central administrations were set up there would "not be the slightest chance for the French views on the Ruhr, Rhineland and Saar to prevail." Unless those areas were separated politically and economically from Germany, they would "serve as a springboard for aggression against France: not German as such but from a Russian-dominated Germany."[22]

Bidault's long reply arrived in Washington on March 2, 1946, a day after Caffery's preview and a month after Byrnes's appeal. According to Bidault, the occupation provided security for France for the time being, but the occupation would end one day. The German menace would remain so long as Germany had the industrial resources to reconstitute her military power, especially if she were "favored by a relaxation of international vigilance such as occurred between the two World Wars." As for France, "the experience of the last 25 years has made it clear that territorial clauses are the last that revisionist states question." Disagreeing with Byrnes, Bidault insisted that central agencies would indeed prejudice future territorial settlements. Once they were established, central agencies would make decisions affecting the future, and their administrators would have direct access to the German population. After World War I "the most active and successful adversaries of any kind of decentralization of the Reich were precisely the local agents of the central German administration." If the occupying powers wanted to decentralize Germany, they should not begin by establishing "extended (*tentaculaires*) administrations having independent authority. The French Government could not in any case agree to the extension of the authority of such administrations to the Ruhr, Rhineland or even more to the Saar." According to Bidault, France would not object to German technical-services organizations to assist the ACC, but their functions would need to be defined by the four governments. In any case, France wanted a four-power conference to discuss the French proposals presented to the London CFM meeting in September 1945, to examine "both the question of central German administrations and that of western Germany."[23]

Byrnes's response to Bidault's reiteration of France's demands *preceded* the State Department's receipt of Bidault's message by two hours, and that is significant because he caved in before he knew Bidault's arguments in full. Replying to Caffery's preview of March 1, 1946, Byrnes cabled: "I am sure that you have done everything that could be done to persuade the French to take action regarding establishment of centralized German administrative agencies. I fully agree that they should not be pressed to a point where there is real danger of Bidault's resignation and of a split in the coalition government which could rightly or wrongly be attributed to our intervention and which would have wide political ramifications in France."[24]

THE COMMON EXPORT-IMPORT PLAN

Having achieved paper agreement on reparations, the level of industry, and the German living standard late in March 1946, Clay pushed with vigor —and with a certain amount of vengeance—for a common export-import agreement. Reflecting the continuing United States interest in having Germany's exports at a level sufficient to pay for imports, conscious of the Army's financial and procurement responsibilities in Europe, and using the Potsdam Agreement as a lever, the Americans in Berlin had—since August of 1945—been pressing for export-import control machinery "as a business of first priority." They succeeded in getting the ACC to adopt an interim export-import plan on September 20, 1945.* In October they had prepared a draft proposal for a permanent Allied export-import authority and they introduced it into the committees of the ACC. In November the JCS prepared an export-import directive for OMGUS's use in negotiating a four-power agreement and for interim use in the American zone. On December 7, 1945, Murphy reported the American proposals to be stalled in the

---

* OMGUS, Monthly Report of the Military Governor, No. 1, Aug. 20, 1945, p. 11; Murphy to SecState, Sept. 10, 1945, *FRUS*, 1945, III, 1527–28; Sept. 20, 1945, *ibid.*, 836–38. Perhaps its most significant—certainly its most overlooked—feature is that Germany's exports were to be paid for "at a rate of not less than 80 percent of provisional prices." Presumably the 20 percent would be reparations from current production, though I have nowhere found it referred to as such. It was never paid—not, for example, for the coal exported in accord with Truman's coal directive.

ACC, but he did not say why. After that they seem to have lain dormant while the export-import policy decisions necessary to the reparations and level-of-industry plan took precedence.[25] Clay brought them up again in the Coordinating Committee of the Allied Control Authority (CORC) on April 2, 1946, at the first meeting of that body after it had agreed on the reparations and level-of-industry plan.

Meanwhile a host of import-export problems had accumulated. On November 8, 1945, the State Department had sent a circular message to interested governments informing them that exports (other than capital equipment removals and restitutions) from the American zone would be payable in United States dollars unless special arrangements acceptable to the ACC were made. The letter referred to the Potsdam Agreement's provision that Germany would have to subsist without external assistance and to the ACC's interim export-import policy of September 20, 1945, and it specified that payment would normally be in full, but at no less than 80 percent of the prices established by the American zone commander.[26] But nothing happened. On November 29, 1945, the State Department asked Murphy whether the policy to require payment of exports at 80 percent was being implemented and whether the French and Russians were cooperating. It also sent a lot of advice. Murphy replied on December 7, 1945, that he knew "of no instances where exports from any of the zones have been paid off in U.S. dollars." Acheson seemed puzzled: "Are not British and French collecting for coal exports or are they simply presenting bills which are unpaid by recipient countries?" Murphy's reply is unknown to me. He had reported in September, however, that coal was being exported against quantitative receipts.[27] A statement by Clay in March 1946 is perhaps a sufficient answer. He said the United States was contemplating spending $200 million on German food imports, exclusive of loans to its allies, and that "it had received no payments for exports." On the same day General Joseph T. McNarney, the American military governor, said in the ACC that "no dollar payment had been made for coal exports."[28]

The American proposal that Clay brought to the CORC on April 2, 1946, was for an interim allied bureau to coordinate the import-export programs of the zones and to "proceed immediately to prepare and organize a central German Administrative Department for zonal trade, headed by a state secretary." The French, who had stated reservations to the proposal when it was reviewed in the Economics Directorate on March 27, 1946, objected again in the CORC on April 2. The French member of the CORC said he favored an export-import bureau, but he added that his government did not want immediate creation of a German agency and that the entire question of German central agencies was being discussed at government level. According to Murphy, "he indicated he would accept the paper provided all references to creation [of a central German administrative department] be deleted." Clay insisted that the French reservations would leave a bureau that could do nothing the ACC could not do on its own, and he withdrew the proposal from the agenda. He reported to the War Department that failure of approval of a four-power export-import plan was "largely due to our unwillingness to accept French conditions." According to Clay, the most important feature of the plan was a proposal for an allied bureau charged "in principle" with establishing a central German administration for foreign trade, as required by the Potsdam Agreement. The "French demanded that this provision be stricken and refused to accept it even in principle although we were fully willing to accept [an] Allied Bureau for an indefinite period without setting any specific date for such a department to begin operations." He said the changes proposed by France would have established not uniformity but "a Government of treaty and negotiation between four distinct and independent zones."[29]

Murphy's report on the meeting was similar to Clay's in detail, but it also contained comments on the larger significance of the event. Murphy said that "French sabotage of the Potsdam decision" on German central administrations was continuing the deadlock that was doing so much to nullify American efforts "to implement the public declarations so solemnly made by the three powers" at Potsdam. "One of the primary effects of this stalemate will certainly be, in the absence of a substantial volume of exports paid for in dollars, an augmentation of US occupation costs. We shall thus succeed in financing reparations—a proposition which as I remember it we vigorously opposed [last summer]."[30]

After Clay withdrew the export-import proposal from the CORC agenda, it went back to the Economics Directorate, where it was discussed further. On April 5, 1946, the Soviet representative (K. I. Koval) made the remarks that Clay remembered in his memoirs as having touched off the succession of events that led to his reparations suspension of May 3, 1946.[31] According to the American records of the meeting, Koval said Russia would "adhere to the principal [sic] of Zonal foreign trade and individual responsibilities of the countries for the results of the occupation of their Zone and substitute this for the collective responsibility of all the powers."[32] Clay remembered that he reacted strongly to Koval's statement three days later, on April 8, 1946, and that he commented on the Potsdam Agreement and the relationships it assumed between trade balances, German deficits, the level of industry, and reparations. The CORC minutes show that he also talked about requiring a "revision of the Reparations Plan" if a common import-export plan could not be agreed upon.[33]

Clay had told the War Department what he planned to do at the CORC meeting on April 8. He said he had always been apprehensive of the Soviet position on treating Germany as an economic unit if and when the French agreed. Nevertheless, he continued, the Soviets had always supported all papers relating to central machinery, "so that [responsibility for the] failure to operate Germany as an economic unit has rested on the French." The Soviet representative in the Economics Directorate had talked about zonal foreign trade and interzonal barter arrangements, and Clay thought that pointed to trouble ahead for a common export-import program. Clay said he planned to raise the issue in the CORC later in the day and point out that the Soviet position was not in accord with the Potsdam Agreement regarding a common export-import policy. He would say, further, that if no agreement on a common policy could be reached within the next two or three months the reparations program in the Western zones would have to be revised. "In this way it is hoped to smoke out now the Soviet position."[34]

Smoke it out he did. The Soviet response was uncanny, but only if one suspects the Russians of wanting to renege on the Potsdam Agreement. At the next meeting of the Economics Directorate Koval asked—obviously under instructions—that the following be substituted for the statement to which Clay had reacted:

The Soviet Delegate, in accordance with the decision of the Berlin conference, considers that Germany should be dealt with as an economic whole and that to this end common policies should now be determined with regard to the import-export program for Germany as a whole. At the same time, as indicated in the decision of the Berlin conference, in implementing this policy various local conditions should be taken into account when necessary. Therefore, for the immediate future, foreign trade for Germany should be conducted on a zonal basis within the net balance of each zone. Barter transactions should be permitted and the payment for allowed exports may be made by allowed imports.[35]

The Soviet position was strictly in accord with the Potsdam Agreement, and it paralleled the American position, except in details. The Russians and the Americans wanted economic unity and common export-import policies. They wanted the interrelated economic elements of the Potsdam Agreement to be implemented together. The Russians insisted that until central administrations and economic unity were a reality, they would engage in zonal foreign trade, but that was the existing practice in all the zones. The major difference between the two was that the Russians assumed that their share of reparations had been sacredly fixed at Potsdam. Subsequent events provide further evidence on the similarities and the difference.

Murphy's report on the April 26, 1946, CORC meeting shows that the British supported the American import-export proposal. A French discourse on the meager resources of the French zone and the need for pooling the assets of the four zones caused the Soviet member to ask if France had changed her views on central German administrations. According to Murphy, the "French member said emphatically No, French delegation always having favored economic unity but not central organs." The French having confirmed their previous views, the Soviet member said he would have to stand by the position expressed by Koval in his corrected statement in the Economics Directorate: "Taking Potsdam Protocol as basis and considering Germany as an economic whole, *common export-import policy must now be formulated*. However, *while implementing policy*, local conditions must receive consideration as also prescribed by Protocol." Clay regretted that "he could not do as his French colleague and accept favorable parts of Protocol, while rejecting less favorable ones," and expressed the opinion that "the cleavage of opinion was too wide to be bridged at this time." He therefore suggested that they "report to their respective governments that principles of reparation, import-export program, and central organs were so interrelated that *application of the first two must be held in suspense until [the] latter shall have been decided*."[36] The British concurred. But the Soviet member, apparently carefully instructed on Byrnes's remarks at Potsdam to the effect that British-American import-export difficulties would be settled independently and without respect to the Soviet reparations percentages,[37] objected to Clay's linkage of the export-import program with reparations. Clay then commented on "the bricks that built the house," as he reported in his memoirs. Clay's commentaries brought no response from the Soviet delegate, but, as Clay remembered, they did bring the usual French response that Clay's concerns were subjects the French government had reserved for discussion at government level.[38] The meeting closed with a statement by Clay that "U.S. authorities might now find it necessary to interrupt [the] work of some 16 to 17 thousand persons engaged in dismantling machines for reparation deliveries."[39] To that situation we now turn.

AMERICAN MANEUVERS

CHAPTER EIGHT

Reparations, Special Deputies, and Bizonia

CLAY'S REFERRAL of the reparations, import-export, and central administrations issues to government level on April 26, 1946, and his conviction that central administrations had to be established before the reparations and export-import issues could be resolved leave little room for doubt
that he saw France's resistance to central administrations as the key issue
and the major problem at the time. The Russians had responded to his
effort to smoke them out by making clear their desire to proceed with the
implementation of the Potsdam Agreement on economic unity. For a variety
of reasons, however, the Russians deferred to the Americans and the British
to apply the pressures that would be needed to bring France around. France
had been brought into the occupation as a British/American client in the
first place, and, as Robert Cecil put it, the Russians apparently "believed
they knew a satellite when they saw one."* Murphy had warned the State
Department as early as February 1946 that "it is difficult for either the Russians or the Germans to believe that France is acting independently without
the tacit or active approval of the UK and/or the US."[1] Clay remembered
that "on several occasions my Soviet colleague suggested to me that France
was receiving too much financial assistance from the United States to maintain such strong opposition unless it was with our acquiescence."[2] The Russian deference to the Americans and British was not without promise of
political advantage. Pressure from the West, combined with apparent benign
neutrality from the East, would have disturbed the "uncertain political
situation" in France and cut across the State Department's standing policy
to restore, rehabilitate, and stabilize France. In fact, Byrnes and Acheson in

* Robert Cecil, "Potsdam and Its Legends," *International Affairs*, 46 (July 1970), 460. See
also James P. Warburg, *Germany, Key to Peace* (Cambridge, Mass., 1953), p. 24, for the conclusion that, "In effect, [the Russians] said to Britain and the United States: 'If you are going
to let the French sabotage the Potsdam Agreement, we can get along very nicely without it.
We have the only zone which produces more than it needs and we can make excellent use of
the surplus. You can make up deficits in your zones just as long as you like.' "

March 1946 had each warned against pressing France too hard.[3] But Clay's patience was at an end.

THE REPARATIONS SUSPENSION

True to his earlier warnings, Clay invoked the basic assumptions of the level-of-industry plan to seek revision of the reparations plan. On May 3, 1946, he announced in the CORC that he had suspended further reparations deliveries from the American zone of Germany. In reporting his action to the War Department, Clay said the Soviet delegate had taken "the position that for the present, imports-exports must be conducted on a Zonal basis with only surpluses available for export and for the common pool. When Soviet representatives were advised that their position was inconsistent with Potsdam, their reply was a query to the French" asking whether France was "ready to establish central administrative machinery. Of course," Clay's report continued, "the French answer was their usual statement that they favored treatment of Germany as a single economic entity but still opposed central administrative machinery." Clay said he asserted that "a common import-export program definitely required central administrative machinery to be effective," and he thus revealed once again his conviction that the French resistance to central agencies was fundamental to the impasse and to his reparations suspension. He noted that the United States "regarded reparations, the import-export program and the establishment of central machinery as subjects which had to be decided concurrently in view of their effect on each other." He then went on to describe his announcement of the reparations suspension and warned Washington that it was not a bluff. He had issued appropriate orders that would stop "any further physical efforts to carry out the reparations program until major overall questions are resolved and we know what area is to compose Germany and whether or not that area will be treated as an economic unit."[4]

Clay's action was clearly an attempt to break the impasse that France had caused in Berlin. It was an attempt to force government-level decisions on Germany by jolting the State Department and forcing it to respond to his, Patterson's, and Murphy's requests, pleas, and recommendations for pressure on France. But Clay's expectations and the State Department's response were incongruous.

Byrnes was at the CFM in Paris when Clay suspended reparations in Berlin. Acheson and Hilldring sent Byrnes a plan on May 9, 1946—a plan designed to test Russian intentions rather than to get the French obstruction cleared up.[5] The Acheson-Hilldring plan was intricate enough to require a separate cable to summarize and interpret it for Byrnes. Acheson and Hilldring said the plan was "designed to avoid threatened breakup of ACC, to remove principal block to reparation program, and above all, to put Soviet protestations of loyalty to Potsdam to final test in order to gauge their willingness to live up to substance as well as letter of Potsdam and fix blame for breach of Potsdam on Soviets in case they fail to meet this test." They proposed a twofold approach: (1) four-power negotiations on the Ruhr and Rhineland, to get France to accept central German agencies and to determine whether the resources of those two areas would be available to the German economy, and (2) a 60- to 90-day resumption of reparations from the American zone, provided the Russians agreed to a complex set of common economic policies.[6]

The State Department's plan did not suggest how Byrnes might counter France's repeated objections to having Russians on the French frontier. Neither did it suggest how to cope with the Russian insistence that the reparations issue had been settled at Potsdam and that central administrations would have to be established to implement common economic policies, particularly for exports and imports. In balance, the plan was marked by its gingerly treatment of France and by its implied and stated suspicions of Russia's motives and intentions. For example, it noted the technicality that the French had not signed the Potsdam Protocol and concluded that France was therefore under no obligation to agree to central German agencies. Furthermore, it predicted that France would accept a modified form of central administrations, but failed to note either the conditions the French had expressed or Bidault's flat declaration that such agencies were to have no authority in the Ruhr, the Rhineland, and the Saar. With reference to Russia, the plan discussed long-range motives and "shifting Russian tactics" in the ACC, especially during the import-export negotiations of April 1946.

BYRNES'S SPECIAL-DEPUTIES PROPOSAL

Byrnes implemented the Acheson-Hilldring plan with its Russian test. He constructed his own questions, however, and presented them to the Paris CFM on May 15, 1946, as a proposal to appoint and instruct special deputies for Germany. Byrnes's special-deputies proposal had long-run and short-run elements. For the long run it suggested appointment of deputies who would initiate studies, make interim reports, and prepare a draft of the eventual German peace settlement. For the short run, it called for "clarification of policies and principles agreed . . . at Potsdam."[7] The proposal said the ACC had agreed on a level-of-industry and reparations plan, but that "this agreement is based on the treatment of Germany as an economic unit." Agreement to appoint the special deputies would remove the "need to delay further" the allocation of reparations already declared available. After noting that France had asked for permanent control of the Saar, Byrnes listed five questions as a basis for the work of the special deputies:

1) What will the future status of the Ruhr and Rhineland be? Will the resources of those two areas remain part of the German economy?

2) Will German resources be available to all of Germany? Will an export-import program be established so as to permit payment of essential imports as a first charge against German exports?

3) Can central administrative machinery and economic unity be established "during the next ninety days"?

4) Will zonal boundaries be eliminated as "artificial barriers to a reasonably free movement of goods in Germany"?

5) Can tentative agreement be reached on a western boundary of Germany?

The five items were all features of the Acheson-Hilldring plan of May 9, 1946. Questions 1 and 5 featured the issues on which France had demanded a decision since September 1945, the issues the French had used to justify their vetoes in the ACC; and they were thus the issues that had caused the failure of the ACC to implement the Potsdam Agreement. The presumption of Byrnes's proposal—clearly stated as such in the Acheson-Hilldring plan—was that if France could be satisfied on the Ruhr, the Rhineland, and the western boundary of Germany, it would agree to central agencies, economic unity, an import-export program, and the elimination of artificial zonal barriers to trade (questions 2, 3, and 4). The three questions France would presumably agree to were the elements of the Acheson-Hilldring plan designed to test the Soviets, "to force Soviet Union to show its real attitude toward unification of Germany."[8] Significantly, the three questions focused precisely on the issues that had been under discussion in the ACC in Berlin prior to Clay's suspension of reparations on May 3, 1946. The presumption was that the Russians had benefited indirectly from France's vetoes in the ACC; that the Russians may not have been interested in German unity, central administrations, and four-power cooperation in Germany; and that French vetoes had, in fact, made it unnecessary for them to reveal their true intentions.[9] According to the Acheson-Hilldring plan, "shifting Russian tactics [in Berlin] cast serious doubt on Russian willingness to put into effect

Potsdam provisions on treatment [of] Germany as [an] economic unit." The Russians had, nevertheless, been "cleverly seeking to reconcile their position with [the] letter of Potsdam in order to put onus for breaking with Potsdam on other powers. For this reason, we consider it important to confront Russians with a plan which will really put their protestations of loyalty to a test and place onus for failure of Potsdam on them in [the] event they do not meet the test."[10]

Byrnes introduced the special-deputies proposal in the CFM on May 15, 1946, and the discussions that followed show the fundamental disagreements on Germany in all of their complexity. They also show that this was more than a simple Soviet-American dispute. Byrnes suggested that the deputies be instructed to report to the CFM by June 15, 1946, because answers to his questions were "essential if the reparations program was to be carried out." Bidault thought the proposal "deserved study," but he first wanted a CFM decision in principle on France's demand for annexation of the Saar. Molotov said the proposal "should be studied closely," but he raised questions about France's plans for the Ruhr and the Rhineland and about Britain's policy in its zone of occupation. Foreign Secretary Ernest Bevin—easily aroused by Russia's interests in the British zone—objected to Molotov's implied criticism of Britain, and a brief exchange occurred between the two.[11]

The discussion continued throughout the next day, May 16, 1946. Bidault wanted a decision on the Saar. Molotov pressed Byrnes for a United States statement on France's claims, but Byrnes preferred a discussion on procedure to a debate on substance.[12] He finally said the United States would agree to France's proposal on the Saar, provided the French withdrew their objections to central agencies. Molotov seemed surprised at Byrnes's linkage of the two questions, but he did not object.[13] Bevin thought Byrnes's proposed mandate to the special deputies to study the Ruhr, the Rhineland, and the western boundary was too narrow. Bevin wanted a study of all German boundaries, including those in the East, "where Silesia was of great importance for the economy of Central Europe."[14] Meanwhile, he did not want to take a position on the Saar. Bevin objected specifically to questions 1 and 5, because they were too limited in scope and because they singled out the British zone. He was prepared, however, to agree to immediate study of questions 2, 3, and 4 of Byrnes's proposal (the test of Soviet intentions). In summary, Bevin favored the appointment of special deputies, provided that they received "a broad directive to study the future of Germany with priority given to" points 2, 3, and 4 of Byrnes's proposal.

Bidault protested. He remarked that his failure to receive an answer on the Saar was but another "link in the chain of disappointments which France had experienced for twenty-five years in regard to the German question." He declared that Bevin "was putting the cart before the horse," since "it was impossible to settle immediate difficulties [questions 2, 3, and 4] while fundamental decisions remained open [questions 1 and 5]." He said it was illogical to "treat secondary matters first," and he emphasized that "no directives could be given to our representatives in Berlin until there was some decision as to the future political status of Germany." Bidault had said it before, on September 14, 1945, and again on September 26, 1945, when he told the CFM in London that "the French representative on the Allied Control Commission will not be empowered to agree to any action prejudging that area's future [the Ruhr and Rhineland] until the question here raised has been discussed by the five Ministers and decided by the Council."[15]

The impasse was complete, the points of friction were clearly defined, and the disagreements were unmistakably more broadly based than cold-war theorists would have us believe was the case. Bevin wanted to discuss economic issues (questions 2, 3, and 4), but not boundaries (questions 1 and 5). Bidault wanted to discuss boundaries, but not economic questions. Meanwhile the French would do nothing in Berlin until France got her way. Molotov thought "the discussion revealed that they were dealing with a very complicated question." He also wondered "what was the purpose of [the U.S.] proposal." Byrnes characterized his effort as "a mechanism" to get things moving. Bevin objected again to Molotov's inferences regarding British policy in the Ruhr, and the discussions went round and round. Bevin would not discuss boundaries unless all of them were studied—not just those in the British zone. Molotov regarded the eastern boundaries to have been settled at Potsdam and he said "he did not believe" Britain would renege on the Berlin "decisions concerning the eastern frontiers."[16] Bevin agreed to the appointment of deputies as a procedure. Molotov said the Russians needed more time to study the American proposal.

The next session got them no further. Byrnes pressed, but Molotov wanted to study. He also reminded Byrnes that Bevin "had a reservation concerning Special Deputies." Bidault agreed "to discuss the suggested procedure," but he had "a reservation as to the terms of reference." Bevin agreed again to the appointment of deputies, but specified that "they should consider the German question as a whole—the execution of the Berlin decisions, frontiers, and any other appropriate question." Bevin having agreed to Byrnes's *procedure* and Bidault having agreed *to discuss it,* Byrnes tried to get Molotov to come along. Failing, he said, "if M. Molotov could not give an answer to the appointment of this body, it was useless to discuss terms of reference for a body that did not exist."[17] Molotov did not respond with the obvious rebuttal, perhaps because he had already said it so clearly: if it was impossible to agree on terms of reference, it was useless to appoint special deputies for whom no work had been assigned. The intriguing question in all of this is whether Byrnes was administering the Russian test or trying to get an agreement. In any case, he conveniently ignored Bevin's and Bidault's fundamental reservations and he failed to distinguish between Bidault's agreement to discuss and agreement itself. Byrnes focused instead on Molotov's procedural objections and he judged them to be the major problem.

Byrnes returned to his special-deputies proposal again on July 10, 1946, after Bidault, Bevin, and Molotov had in turn made formal statements of their German policies and proposals. Byrnes commented on reparations, the airtight compartmentalization of the zones, the limitations on the free flow of trade, the lack of an agreed export-import program, the lack of other common policies, and the promise of the Council of Minister-Presidents in the American zone. He observed that Bidault and Bevin had both agreed to the appointment of special deputies (as they had indeed done in their formal statements) and he "wondered if his friend M. Molotov would not agree."[18]

Lest his agreement on procedure be mistaken for agreement on substance, Bidault spoke before Molotov replied. He complained that France was not being heard on the matters that concerned her most. He lectured his colleagues on the lessons France had learned from World War I. He asserted that "the French Government considered it its mission and duty to prevent the process of history taking a course which had been disastrous to France." France "would certainly examine in the best spirit the various suggestions put forward," and "it had already given its agreement in principle to the appointment of special deputies." Bidault "wished to repeat, however, that the position of the French Government was maintained in its entirety." In short, as Bidault had said earlier in his formal statement, "we have not changed our position [on France's proposals for annexation of the Saar and the permanent detachment of the Ruhr and the Rhineland from Germany] and ... it does not seem possible to us to postpone examination of them any longer."[19]

Molotov pointed out that if Byrnes's special deputies on Germany were appointed they would have no terms of reference, no directives, no basis from which to work, "because agreement had not been reached in the Council of Foreign Ministers on such a basis." He suggested a compromise: a special session of the CFM to devote itself solely to German questions. He held out the hope that the passage of time and the efforts of the special session might enable the CFM to instruct deputies "in a more specific way." Byrnes, impatient for progress and perhaps anxious to test the Russians, pleaded his case further. He asked for another meeting the following day to "try to agree on a basis for the work of the deputies."[20] Molotov agreed. But Bevin, apparently sensing that Molotov's compromise was the emerging decision, raised a new point. Bevin's impatience with the post-Potsdam impasse was as evident as Clay's.

THE BRITISH INITIATIVE

Given the inaccuracies contained in the literature on what transpired in the Paris CFM, especially on July 10 and 11, 1946, it might be appropriate to fix the state of things at the point of Bevin's initiative. The CFM had begun its formal discussions of the German question on July 9, 1946, with Molotov's critique of Byrnes's draft treaty on German disarmament. On July 10 Bidault, Bevin, Molotov, and Byrnes—in that order—made formal policy statements, declarations, and proposals. The session was businesslike and there appears to have been no unusual stress or acrimony. Although Byrnes would write and say otherwise later, there is no evidence that he was put out by Molotov's previous statement. As a matter of fact, an agreement of sorts seemed to be evolving: either they would accept Molotov's recommendation for a special session of the CFM to be held later, during which instructions for the deputies might be agreed upon; or they would succeed in resolving the issues before they left Paris, as Byrnes had suggested they try to do.

Bevin's proposal was for an immediate agreement by the CFM to share equally the indigenous resources of Germany, to make surpluses in one zone available to meet deficits in other zones. Should surpluses occur in any zone and not be required in the other zones, those surpluses could be exported as reparations only if there was no deficit in the balance of payments in any other zone. Should such a deficit exist, the surpluses would have to be treated as commercial exports and be paid for in an acceptable currency and the proceeds be used to meet the deficit.[21] According to Bevin, adoption by the CFM of his proposal—which he circulated as a paper for action on the following day—would provide the basis for treating Germany as an economic whole and for an orderly taking of reparations from current production. In essence, Bevin was asking for an immediate decision on those items of Byrnes's special-deputies proposal that he had already agreed to discuss: questions 2, 3, and 4.

There is a current legend—widely repeated in the literature—that Byrnes responded on the morning of July 11, 1946, to Molotov's statement of July 10 by inviting Britain and France to join their zones with the American zone in economic unity, and thus, in effect, to divide Germany.[22] Neither the time, nor the invitation, nor the substance and flow of the negotiations accord with the legend. The record shows that Byrnes opened the July 11 session (which began at 4:00 P.M.) with a very general statement in which he reviewed American aims and objectives for Germany. He had asked, the day before, that they meet to try to instruct the deputies, and this was his opening plea. He spliced his remarks richly with pronouncements and exhortations which remind one of the daily fare in the *Congressional Record*: "It is ... the duty of the Allies to set up the machinery to work out the definite lines of the peace settlement which they expect Germany to accept and observe.... If we fail to do this, we will be confessing to the world our own lack of constructive purpose and our inability to agree and will betray the millions who died in order that freedom might live."[23] Byrnes intended his statement as an argument for the appointment and instruction of special deputies for Germany and he urged again that the CFM appoint them.

Molotov continued to argue for his compromise: a special session of the CFM to discuss German questions. Now he said it could be held later in the year, and he repeated his hope that such a session would produce sufficient agreement to instruct the deputies. He then shifted to discussing reparations, probably (though not certainly) in response to the paper Bevin had presented at the close of the July 10 session. Byrnes felt challenged by Molotov's digression, particularly by Molotov's references to the Yalta Conference and the $20 billion reparations figure. He delivered a lecture on his understanding of the reparations discussions, agreements, and nonagreements at Yalta, Moscow, and Potsdam. There followed a fruitless exchange between Bevin, Molotov, and Byrnes on the status of reparations deliveries, on the production and allocation of coal, on dismantling, disarmament, and demilitarization—a discussion that prompted Bidault to observe "that they were on a merry-go-round" and to state that he preferred "to ride his own horse and say something about coal."[24]

Byrnes finally returned the discussion to his proposal for appointment of special deputies. Molotov wondered what the deputies would do, since no agreement on directives was in sight. He repeated his desire for a special CFM session. Byrnes wanted to continue to try to work out terms of reference over the next two days. He was impatient to move ahead immediately; Molotov wanted to wait for the special session, and they repeated their respective positions several times. In the end Molotov's compromise prevailed. The CFM formally resolved to meet in special session to consider the German question in the fall, "immediately after the session of the General Assembly of the United Nations."[25] Bevin wished someone had thought of that two hours earlier.

There is a legend that Byrnes invited his colleagues, on July 11, 1946, to join their zones with the American zone in economic unity because he wanted to force a division of Germany, to force a split with the Soviet Union over Germany. But Byrnes spent the entire session of the July 11, 1946, CFM meeting trying to get some form of agreement on his special-deputies proposal, and he offered to remain in session for the next two days to continue to try. The Byrnes proposal envisioned neither a division of Germany nor a split with Russia. It called for *four-power* study for the next *four-power* CFM meeting. Throughout the entire session, Byrnes gave not the slightest hint of a direct reaction to Molotov's formal statement of the previous day. Nor did he even hint that he might offer a suggestion that the American zone cooperate with other zones to achieve economic unity in the field.

Byrnes's zonal-union invitation was, in fact, offered as an alternative to the unilateral action announced by Bevin for the British zone. As the session of July 11 was coming to a close, Molotov, who was chairman for the day, asked for and received approval of the records of previous meetings in apparent anticipation of adjournment. The record shows that Byrnes asked what action would be taken on the paper Bevin had presented on the previous day. The proposal, it will be recalled, had been offered by Bevin with some urgency, and it focused on the economic issues contained in Byrnes's special-deputies proposal—the ones designed to test Soviet intentions. Molotov, without elaborating—though clearly in conformity with Byrnes's own explanations of the Potsdam reparations plan—said the British proposal contradicted the decisions of the Berlin Conference and that its adoption would hamper the execution of the Berlin agreement on reparations. "The Soviet Delegation could not agree to any such proposals."*

Bevin thereupon announced that in the absence of an agreement among the four (and, of course, in the light of the decision just taken to delay discussion of the German question until later in the year), his government was obliged "to organize the British Zone," and "to produce for export in order to reduce the burden on the British taxpayer." According to Bevin, Britain "was unwilling to go on borrowing dollars to import food into Germany." Bevin thought the British zone (with the Ruhr) could be put on a self-supporting basis. His discussion of German coal production, allocations, and exports reflected the initial and the continuing British dissatisfaction with Truman's coal directive of 1945 and subsequent German coal export programs. Britain had, in fact, considered—then shelved—the possibility of "a complete moratorium on coal exports from the Ruhr" in June 1946.[26] Bevin's threat "to organize the British Zone" to produce for export raised the specter of a socialist solution, which the British had openly favored. Furthermore, and perhaps more significant at the moment, Bevin's implied priority for coal allocations to increase German production rather than for export threatened the State Department's industrial disarmament plans whereby German industrial capacity would be shifted to other non-German regions of Europe; it threatened the State Department's long-standing policy to rehabilitate and restore France as a first priority; and it flew in the face of that policy's most important derivative, recently expressed by Clayton: "Coal is such a critical item that it must be assumed that the French will get the coal they need."[27]

BYRNES'S INVITATION TO ZONAL UNION

Immediately following Bevin's threat to organize the British zone, Byrnes invited the other powers to join their zones with the American zone. He began with the following sentence: "I hope that we can avoid the situation outlined by Mr. Bevin." He said he still hoped the CFM could agree on central German administrations and economic unity. Indirectly identifying France as the major problem, Byrnes said the United States would agree to

---

* U.S. Delegation Record, CFM, July 11, 1946, *FRUS*, 1946, II, 896. Byrnes had explained on July 30, 1945 (Dept. of State Minutes, 10th Meeting of Foreign Ministers, July 30, 1945, *FRUS*, 1945, Potsdam II, 491), that "if the Soviets agreed to this plan they would have no interest in exports and imports from our zone. Any difficulty in regard to imports and exports would have to be settled between the British and ourselves. The Soviets would have no interest and they would get their percentage regardless of what happened to us."

exclude the Saar from the jurisdiction of the central agencies and permit France to administer the area until the western boundaries could be determined. He then repeated at government level what Clay had been authorized to do in the ACC since October 1945: "Pending agreement among the Four Powers to implement the Potsdam Agreement requiring the administration of Germany as an economic unit, the United States will join with any other occupying government or governments in Germany for the treatment of our respective zones as an ecoonmic unit." Byrnes said the union of "any two zones" would be an improvement over the airtight compartmentalization that existed. He noted that officials from the American and British zones had already met and discussed agricultural policies and that officials from the Russian and American zones had met and reached agreements on interzonal exchanges of products. His failure to cite an example of French-zone cooperation was not an oversight. There had been none. Byrnes said the United States was prepared to instruct its representatives in Berlin to begin general discussions with the representatives of any other zone willing to do so. The arrangements to be made "should at all times be open on equal terms for the participation of any government which did not elect to participate in the beginning. This proposal," Byrnes emphasized, "is not intended to divide Germany, but, on the contrary, to expedite its treatment as an economic unit."[28]

Neither the Russians nor the French responded positively to Byrnes's invitation, which was issued formally by General McNarney, the American military governor, in the ACC on July 20, 1946.[29] The Russians seemed interested at first, but they would not move toward economic unity without corresponding political measures, such as the establishment of central administrations. They said they regarded the creation of central agencies as a first step and warned that for two or more zones to proceed "on pronounced autarchy" would divide rather than unify Germany; it would divide Germany into separate economic parts and militate against political unity and German democracy. Indicating where the trouble lay, a Russian representative in Berlin said "he hoped the French would change their position."[30]

The French, who had been regarding their representatives in the ACC directorates as "observers" rather than as participants, responded to McNarney's invitation by reintroducing a proposal that Clay had already judged to be a step backward. On August 10, 1946, France submitted to the ACC a proposal for *allied* central agencies, which they said they would accept if the Saar were excluded from their jurisdiction and "immediately incorporated into [the] French economic and monetary system." Murphy's report on the French proposal found France's sudden emphasis on "maintaining coordinated action" to be "not without its amusing side," because France had in the past "disrupted allied unity" in the face of "agreement on it" by the other three powers.[31] Neither the British nor the Americans considered the French proposal to be an improvement over the existing organization in the ACC, and they rejected it on August 17, 1946. The Russians reserved initial comment, apparently awaiting instructions from Moscow. On August 28, 1946, the Russians also rejected the French proposal, saying there was no need for *allied* agencies in addition to those already existing in the ACC and that France's proposal could not be acted upon by the ACC, because it envisaged incorporation of the Saar into the French economic and financial system. That question could only be decided at government level. The British, Russian, and American delegates all agreed that "central German agencies are needed now to permit effective operation [of the] German economy as a unit."[32] Meanwhile, the British had decided to join their zone with the American zone, and the negotiations that led to the formation of the bizone were under way.[33]

Given the British acceptance of Byrnes's invitation, given the prevailing interpretations of the formation of Bizonia to be found in the literature, given the parallel American and British interests in an all-German import-export plan and its necessities, and given the striking similarity between the paper Bevin presented at Paris on July 11, 1946, and the economic questions contained in Byrnes's special-deputies proposal, one is tempted to conclude that the Americans and British had adopted a common strategy in Germany. The evidence does not support such a conclusion, however. There are no traces of joint planning, consultations, or coordination, and one can infer from existing materials that none occurred. On July 12 Bevin said Byrnes's proposal required careful consideration and that the British government would "examine it urgently and sympathetically."[34] That could be interpreted to mean that Bevin had no prior knowledge. It could also have been a ploy to cover a prior two-power understanding, except for the fact that as late as July 28 the British government was still debating the issue.[35] More significant, however, is the complete absence of American documents showing prior planning and discussion of the issue. The instructions to Generals McNarney and Clay to issue the invitation in Berlin were hastily drafted in Washington only *after* Byrnes had issued the invitation orally in Paris.[36]

The absence of American records showing prior planning for the kind of zonal union Byrnes proposed is all the more significant, because as early as May 26, 1946, Clay had suggested British-American zonal merger as a possible alternative to four-power union, if France and Russia could not be brought to agree.[37] In June Clay proposed to hold a press conference in Berlin to discuss some of the major items in his May 26 cable. The War Department advised him not to do so and, among other things, said Byrnes would probably ask Clay to come to Paris. If Clay wished, however, he might state in a press conference that he had recommended to his government that it urge the other occupation powers to adopt in their zones councils of minister-presidents similar to the one in the American zone.[38] Nowhere in these exchanges does there appear any trace of serious consideration, study, or policy-planning looking toward zonal merger, either with the British zone, as Clay had suggested on May 26, or with any or all other powers, as Byrnes was to propose on July 11, 1946. The State Department was, in fact, working on studies for a special four-power conference on Germany, such as Molotov suggested in Paris. The record of a proposed agenda, dated July 1, 1946, is significant for its emphasis on German economic unity and the implementation of the Potsdam Agreement, and for its silence on anything approaching the Byrnes invitation that was to come eleven days later in Paris.[39] An office memorandum of July 16—two days before the instructions went out to McNarney and Clay—still contains not a word about zonal amalgamation in any form. It says, in fact, that pending study of a long list of issues contained in the memorandum, the United States should not introduce important policy in the Control Council, *nor should it attempt partial solutions to the German problem*. It does not mention Byrnes's invitation of July 11, but it does refer to Molotov's speech of July 10 and to Byrnes's brief response to it.[40]

Despite the extensive historical literature to the contrary, and despite the fact that the formation of Bizonia eventually proved to be the first step in the division of Germany, Byrnes neither proposed nor apparently envisioned the division of Germany in July 1946. There is no substantial evidence that either Byrnes or the State Department had seriously considered the division of Germany *as a matter of policy* at the time. There is no evidence that Byrnes went to Paris with preconceived plans to divide Germany or that he regarded his invitation as a step in that direction. Byrnes shot from the hip in Paris in response to Bevin's threat to "organize the British Zone." His invitation was defensive against Britain rather than offensive toward Russia. It was tactical rather than strategic. It was hastily conceived rather than planned as a last resort. It reflected past failures rather than plans for the future. The failures of the past were due primarily to France's refusal to agree to central German economic administrations, and thus to economic unity, unless her other demands were satisfied first. Byrnes had tried in vain since 1945 to clear up the French obstruction to Potsdam, and he was to try once again later in the fall of 1946. To those efforts we may now turn.

CHAPTER NINE

The Treaty of Guarantees and Policy

WITHIN THE State Department's self-imposed limits on how far it would go, Byrnes tried regularly to get France to accept German central administrations, economic unity, and other features of the Potsdam Agreement. As described previously, he negotiated with Bidault in August 1945. In November he warned Couve de Murville that the United States might seek a three-power solution, and in December he converted his warning into a mild threat. In February 1946 he asked Bidault to reconsider the French position on central administrations. In March 1946 he offered American support for the French claims to the Saar as a *quid pro quo*. His major effort to bring France around, however, was the draft treaty of 1946 for the demilitarization and disarmament of Germany. That treaty has a history quite different from the one found in Byrnes's memoirs and other literature.

BYRNES'S DRAFT TREATY

President Truman had considered the possibility of proposing a military guarantee for European security at the Potsdam Conference. He asked the State Department to advise him on a proposal he might make that the United States, Russia, Britain, France, and possibly other countries enter into a twenty-five-year treaty to enforce German demilitarization.[1] A State Department brief of June 27, 1945, listed arguments for and against such a treaty and mentioned Senator Vandenberg's speech of January 10, 1945 as an indication of possible Congressional support. It concluded, however that it might be best to wait with such a proposal, because Germany con stituted no threat so long as there was a military occupation. The State Department therefore recommended to Truman "that this matter not be raised formally [at Potsdam] but that the opportunity be taken to sound out the Prime Minister and Stalin." The idea could be explored later through diplomatic channels and with the Senate.[2]

There is no evidence that Truman raised the issue at Potsdam, but Byrnes raised it during De Gaulle's and Bidault's visit in Washington in August 1945 and at the London CFM in September 1945. It will be recalled that De Gaulle and Bidault had complained bitterly to Truman and Byrnes about the Potsdam Agreement's failure to provide adequate territorial guarantees of French security. In that context Byrnes suggested a possible twenty-five-year treaty of guarantee of German disarmament and Bidault seemed "favorably inclined to such a plan."[3] Byrnes next raised the issue in a private conversation with Molotov in London. As had been the case in August, Byrnes was apparently prompted by France's demands for security, for he talked with Molotov soon after France presented its territorial demands and threatened to block progress in Berlin until they had been considered by the CFM. Byrnes told Molotov that he recalled Stalin having remarked at Yalta that Germany had attacked Russia twice through Poland and that the United States might withdraw from Europe, as it had done after World War I. Byrnes asked Molotov whether the Soviet government would be interested in a twenty- to twenty-five-year treaty of guarantee, the details of which could be worked out later. Byrnes said Truman favored the idea and that he was prepared to recommend the treaty to the American Congress. If the Russians were interested, it could be discussed with the French and the British. Molotov said he could not speak for his government, but he would report to Moscow and they could talk again. He thought it was something he could view favorably.[4]

Throughout the remainder of 1945 the French restated their territorial demands often and they carried out their threat to block progress in Berlin. The latter action caused the Army to become restive, to demand pressure and sanctions on France, and to intensify its effort to transfer responsibility for the occupation to the Department of State. Byrnes's warning to Couve de Murville in November and his mild threat to Bidault in December produced "much distress," resulted in no action, and seemed to verify the State Department's fear of the consequences of applying the kind of diplomatic, economic, and political pressures the Army had been demanding. Against this background Byrnes broached the treaty idea to Stalin in Moscow in December 1945. Perhaps he thought—as he said he implied to Stalin—that Molotov's promise in London to explore the issue in Moscow had been unfulfilled. Perhaps, however, he had decided to try the treaty-of-guarantee route to French security, and thus to French cooperation in Berlin, rather than to force the issue. In 1946 Byrnes reported that "the Generalissimo said that if the United States made such a proposal he would wholeheartedly support it." A year later he had Stalin saying: "If you decide to fight for such a treaty, you can rely on my support."[5]

Byrnes, whose published references to the draft-treaty proposal are extremely unreliable, said Bevin assured him of his personal sympathy for the treaty and that he discussed it with Vandenberg, Tom Connally, and other senators, as well as with Truman before he sent it to London, Paris, and Moscow in mid-February 1946.[6] He neglected to note, however, that American efforts to bring France around in Berlin were feverish at the time, and he remained silent on how much France's demands for territory and security had influenced him. Murphy and Clay had met with Byrnes in London late in January and complained that France's vetoes in Berlin had injured the European economy and delayed recovery. Following the conversation Murphy wrote to Matthews asking whether he had an opinion on "a possible way out of the impasse." On the same day Byrnes told a press conference that civilian control of the occupation depended on "how soon we can get France to agree to central administrative agencies." The January 1946 report of the military governor appealed for government-level settlement of the western boundary issue in the interests of securing French cooperation in Berlin. On February 1, 1946, Byrnes asked Bidault to reconsider the French position on central agencies and commented at length on the security provided by the presence of the occupation forces. On February 6 Byrnes talked with Ambassador Bonnet about the "utterly impossible situation" in Germany, which "should not be continued." He said he regarded the French vetoes in Berlin as duress. Three days later Willard L. Thorp prepared a draft letter in answer to another of Patterson's protests at French actions in Berlin and a draft telegram "to provide a temporary riposte to the French proposal with respect to the Saar." Thorp believed that nothing short of "resolution of the Ruhr, Rhineland and Saar proposals of the French" would be sufficient, however, and he predicted that France's adamance would eventually affect "the entire reparation procedure." He warned that Clay felt strongly on that point.[7]

Ambassador Caffery's efforts in March and April 1946 to follow up in Paris on the draft-treaty proposal of mid-February suggest a linkage between the treaty and the efforts to get the French obstruction cleared up.[8] Significantly, there are no records of similar follow-ups in London and Moscow. Furthermore, when Bidault finally replied on April 16, suggesting that the CFM discuss the draft treaty, central administrations, and "the status of western Germany" at its meeting scheduled to begin on April 25, Byrnes immediately alerted Bevin and Molotov that he wanted to discuss the treaty in Paris.[9]

Byrnes's later assertions to the contrary, Bidault neither favored the treaty in principle nor endorsed it. His message of April 16, 1946, said that the French government was studying the draft carefully and that he would inform Byrnes as soon as the study was completed. He said he did "not wish to anticipate the results of a more thorough study," but he nevertheless made clear France's reservations to Byrnes's approach to French security. He argued that disarmament itself was not a guarantee against German threats to the peace after the occupation ended. The experience of World War I, Bidault lectured, should constitute a warning that security could best be ensured by "territorial, military or economic clauses." Though his language was imprecise, his meaning was clear: France did not regard Byrnes's draft treaty as a substitute for her territorial, military, and economic proposals for the Saar, the Ruhr, and the Rhineland. According to Bidault, disarmament limited in time was not a "genuinely effective guarantee" of France's security. Despite his negativism, Bidault said he had no objection to "a preliminary discussion" of Byrnes's draft and he suggested the Paris meeting as an appropriate time and place.[10] It never came to that.

Molotov responded to Byrnes's request for discussion of the draft treaty in Paris by agreeing to an exchange of views and warning that the draft "arouses serious objections."[11] On April 28, 1946, in a private conversation with Byrnes and others in Paris, and on April 29, when Byrnes put the item on the CFM agenda, Molotov outlined Russia's objections to the draft treaty. He argued that the proposal was premature, and that the occupation authorities should ensure the disarmament of Germany under existing agreements rather than "postpone the question . . . until after a new treaty had been concluded."[12] In this argument Molotov was remarkably close to the State Department's analysis and advice of June 1945. But on July 9, 1946, after Clay's suspension of reparations and after the Russians had studied the draft treaty carefully, Molotov went much, much further. He found the proposed treaty to be completely inadequate to the task of disarmament. He said it was narrower in scope than the Yalta and Potsdam agreements, and that it was delinquent in its failure to provide for social and political aspects of German disarmament: land reform, elimination of monopolies and cartels, denazification, and democratization. Molotov's analysis was sharp and his language was brutal. He called portions of the draft "utterly inadequate." He said the draft "evades and disregards ... important prerequisites of ensuring lasting peace and security of nations"; "it does not achieve its purpose"; "it is in conflict with earlier joint decisions of the allies"; "it fully ignores the necessity to secure reparations deliveries"; and it "is in need of radical revision." He asserted that reparations deliveries were encountering "ever new obstacles," and he referred to Clay's "unlawful statement announcing the refusal to carry out reparation deliveries to the Soviet Union and other countries." He said "everybody knows" that the "main objectives in the matter of safeguarding Europe and the world against the danger of a new German aggression" were adopted at the Yalta and Potsdam conferences. "There is no reason for us to renounce these decisions. They must form a basis for our further steps in the maintenance of peace."[13]

Molotov insisted that the Yalta and Potsdam agreements should be the primary bases of German policy. France's positions on reparations, restitutions, political parties, trade unions, and central administrations would have required revision of the Potsdam Agreement. Acheson, it will be recalled, had written to Patterson on December 12, 1945, that France's demands for the Saar, the Ruhr, and the Rhineland would require reexamination and possible amendment of the Potsdam Agreement. Though Byrnes argued that it was not so, Molotov detected in the draft-treaty proposal an American maneuver to reexamine and amend the Yalta and Potsdam agreements and make them acceptable to France. The context in which Byrnes developed the proposal suggests that Molotov was correct. But the French—who were spectators to the Molotov-Byrnes exchanges and disputes—were never required to state publicly their own objections to the American approach. Their objections existed nevertheless.

In March 1947 Bidault told Marshall at the Moscow CFM that "Mr Byrnes, while he proposed a pact for the Four Powers, seemed a bit surprised and disappointed with our lack of enthusiasm." He went on to explain that "what we fear is that the Four Power Treaty may be considered as a sort of 'substitute' for other guarantees which we believe necessary. France wanted to "superimpose on the Treaties material guarantees of territorial and industrial character."[14] Bidault had, in fact, made clear the French demands for territorial guarantees in his message to Byrnes of April 16, 1946, and in his statement to the Paris CFM on April 25, 1946. France's demands of an "industrial character" emerged piecemeal in the CFM and in Berlin, but they are as fundamental as the territorial demands. France wanted "an adequate supply of German coal for French industry without becoming economically and politically dependent on Germany." Her proposals for the Ruhr, the Rhineland, and reparations were calculated to ensure that "the Ruhr did not unfairly compete with other areas with a similar range of production." France pressed for a restitutions program that was, in fact, a reparations program; she demanded permanent restrictions on German imports and exports, and she pushed for permanent restrictions on German industrial capacity in steel, chemicals, machine tools, and other basic production. In short, France wanted territorial, military, and economic measures that would ensure the transfer of German industrial and economic power to France or to French control; to shift political power from Germany to France permanently and thereby guarantee French security after the occupation ended.[16]

Although Byrnes and the State Department minimized and covered up France's objections to the draft treaty at the time, they were fully aware of their nature and importance. Vandenberg, in his official report to the Senate on the Paris CFM meeting, said the American offer of a long-term military guarantee against German aggression "now seems to attract relatively little interest, although it is the maximum proof of our good faith."[17] In September 1946 Byrnes told Bidault that he had never understood why Bidault "had not made more political capital at home out of the American proposal for a 25 to 40 year treaty to keep Germany disarmed; he did not see why M. Bidault had not proclaimed to the French public that he had obtained from the United States what Clemenceau had failed to get from Wilson."[18] On the same day in Washington, State Department officials complained to the Counselor of the French Embassy "that the French had not taken seriously our security offer, an offer which was revolutionary from the point of view of traditional American policy."[19] The latter two statements were made as part of an American effort to reduce France's alarm at Byrnes's German policy speech in Stuttgart on September 6, 1946—a speech he had made in part to avoid a public confrontation with Clay and the Army over the impasse in Berlin and American policy in Germany.

THE ARMY'S POLICY APPROACH

Long before Byrnes spoke at Stuttgart, Clay and the Army had tried to get the State Department to clarify and publish American policies in Germany. But after it released the policy statement of December 12, 1945, on reparations and the level of industry, the State Department seems to have been at loose ends with respect to policy. A draft memorandum of March

26, 1946, on "Future Policy Toward Germany" is little more than a description of the existing situation, a series of comments on the policies and practices of the Russians, the French, and the British, and an argument on the need for a new American policy statement that would be more long-range than JCS 1067. Its author, David Harris, the Assistant Chief of the Division of Central European Affairs, thought the memorandum suffered from "vague generalities," and Matthews sent it on to Acheson on April 3 with a notation that it was high time for some "top level decisions with regard to Germany."[20] The draft went to SWNCC and to various offices and individuals, where it accumulated comments, explanations, and notations—none of which reflect hard policy discussion and decisions. Riddleberger took a copy of it along to the Paris CFM, and on May 1 the original author noted that a general directive should be issued very soon for its propaganda effect, if for no other reason.[21] The matter stuttered and sputtered along until Clay forced the State Department's hand.

Clay's Cable of May 26, 1946

On May 23, 1946, the Army cabled Clay saying that the foreign ministers would continue their German discussions when the Paris CFM reconvened on June 15. To help the United States to prepare for those discussions the War Department wanted to submit to the State-War-Navy Coordinating Committee plans and studies on reparations, political structure, Germany as an economic unit, and the disposition of the Ruhr and Rhineland. It asked Clay for his comments and recommendations and he responded in detail on May 26, 1946.

Clay said he needed a clear definition of economic unity and argued that central German administrations for finances, food, agriculture, industry transport, and trade and commerce were essential. He also needed a decision on whether the Saar would be ceded to France. The Saar's cession would require revision of the level-of-industry plan, which Clay thought could be managed. Separation of the Ruhr and Rhineland would, however, be "a world disaster." Clay wanted the Ruhr and Rhineland to remain a part of Germany, even if they were to be internationalized in some way. He would propose a Ruhr Control Authority for steel and coal, and he thought the British would agree, the French would resist, and the Russians would accept in principle and then cause problems on details. Clay stressed that the level-of-industry and reparations plan of March 1946 assumed German economic unity and that any attempt to implement the plan without such unity would leave economic chaos and result in heavy financial outlays in the American zone. Pending agreement on economic unity, Clay continued, the suspension of dismantling for reparations should be maintained and reparations from current production should be stopped, unless they could be provided for in an agreed export-import plan for all of Germany. Clay thought a provisional German government should be planned for and he suggested the Council of Minister-Presidents of the American zone as a model for all of Germany. Should the French and Russians be unwilling to agree on unity and other issues, Clay recommended that a British-American zonal merger be considered. He thought the merger would be an improvement over the existing airtight zonal structure, even though the United States would have to provide aid to the combined zones until they became self-sustaining. Unless something was done "in the immediate future," Clay said, "we face a deteriorating German economy" and "political unrest."[22]

In June 1946 Clay's patience ran out. His request for a policy change which would have permitted Germans to discuss unity and other political issues publicly had been denied. His request for wheat delivery and restitutions sanctions against France had been vetoed by the State Department. His referral of the three basic economic issues of the level-of-industry plan to Washington for resolution had produced no results. His reparations suspension had produced the Acheson-Hilldring plan to test the Russians and to blame them for the impasse in Berlin if they flunked the test. His cable of May 26 remained unanswered. Against this background Clay proposed in June to hold a press conference to discuss the major items in his May 26 cable. The War Department, obviously under instructions from the State Department, advised Clay not to do so. It said policy positions of such importance should, perhaps, not be revealed in a press conference. Furthermore, Byrnes wanted to use the material in Clay's cable at the Paris CFM meeting and Clay's prior release would reduce its effect. Byrnes would probably ask Clay to come to Paris. Clay might, if he wished, state in a press conference that he had recommended to his government that the political plan that had been so successful in the American zone—presumably the Council of Minister-Presidents—be urged for adoption in the other occupation zones. One day later Clay cabled McNarney in Frankfurt asking for return to the United States for terminal leave and retirement. In a cable to Washington—subsequently canceled—Clay advised his former Chief of

Staff in Berlin (Oliver P. Echols) of his request for immediate return to the United States and said Echols would understand. He planned to state publicly that he was tired and needed a rest.[23]

Clay's Policy Summary of July 19, 1946

How Clay was persuaded to withdraw his resignation and who persuaded him are not revealed in the available records. Clay went to Paris, however, and he attended the crucial July 10 and 11 sessions of the CFM. His advice probably influenced Byrnes's invitation of July 11 for zonal amalgamation. Perhaps the invitation was Byrnes's and the State Department's *quid pro quo* for Clay's continuation as military governor. Clay's retirement would have been an ideal time for the Army to try once again to shift responsibility for the German occupation to the State Department, a development that Byrnes and the State Department wanted to avoid with passion. But Clay remained dissatisfied and frustrated. Immediately after his return to Berlin from Paris, he dictated a comprehensive policy summary and sent it to the War Department on July 19, 1946, asking that it be reviewed before he released it in Germany. Clay said he needed the summary urgently to distribute to the military government, the army of occupation, and possibly to the German people: "While occupied Germany is busily discussing the Molotov statement [of July 10, 1946], our own Military Government people have no ready up-to-date summarized version of our policy or objectives which they could use in discussions with our German people."[24]

Clay's policy summary caused a serious bureaucratic conflict in Washington; a conflict that reflected the differences between the Army and the State Department on the purposes of the occupation, the future of Germany, and the implementation of the Potsdam Agreement. Assistant Secretary of War Petersen advised Clay on August 5, 1946, that the Army considered Clay's paper to be excellent and agreed with him that a policy statement was needed. Clay should, however, delay its publication. The State Department believed Clay's policy summary had implications much broader than military government, and it had advised the Army that a public policy statement of such magnitude should properly be made by the Secretary of State. According to Petersen, the State Department was studying German policy for Byrnes's use at the special CFM meeting to be devoted to German problems. He said Clay's paper would be a useful source.[25] As a matter of fact, Acheson had hurriedly created a special study-committee on July 31, 1946, and instructed it "to consider and report on long-range United States

Policy for Germany," and "as a second priority" to prepare a policy summary to be issued by military government. The committee, headed by Riddleberger, was to report by September 15, 1946. Its members were relieved of all other duties and authorized to travel to Germany. Both the timing of the committee's formation and Acheson's August 7 cable to Murphy advising him of the committee's appointment, instructions, and schedules show clearly the State Department's intention to substitute its policy study and review for the summary Clay had proposed on July 19, 1946.[26]

Clay protested that he needed neither a policy study nor a policy revision. He needed a concise statement of what policy was. He said his summary was based on OMGUS operations and observed that the United States was drifting if operations could not be summarized. Unless instructed otherwise, Clay said, he would publish the statement within a week. Five days later the War Department instructed him not to do so, noting that Clay's statement referred to a provisional German government and to Germany's eventual membership in the United Nations, on both of which the United States had not determined a definite policy. Furthermore, the War Department said Clay's statement referred to policies that were under urgent consideration for revision (by whom is neither clear in the cable nor evident in the available documents): (1) the reduction of German war potential by heavy-industrial-equipment removals; (2) financial policy; (3) Germany's frontiers; and (4) internationalization of the Ruhr and Rhineland. Clay's public reference to the unresolved policy issues would tend to bind the United States. On the other hand, for him to issue a statement deleting the items under review would also be undesirable, since it would imply a possible change that might not, in fact, occur after study and review.[27]

Clay protested that his office was at sea, but he agreed to follow his instructions and told Secretary of War Patterson that he had "thrown [the paper] in the waste basket." He said he would make recommendations to Washington on policy whenever his views were requested, but he thought it was improper for him to discuss policy piecemeal with Riddleberger's committee during its scheduled visit to Berlin. More important, he went to Paris to see Byrnes, who raised his spirits considerably by agreeing to make a statement on German policy, either in Paris or in Germany, probably in mid-September.[28]

Byrnes assigned Benjamin V. Cohen to draft a German policy speech. The State Department subsequently advised Cohen that Clay's statement of July 19, 1946, was lucid and readable, in contrast to JCS 1067 and the

Potsdam Agreement, and that it was on the whole consistent with United States policy. However, Byrnes needed to approve Clay's statements regarding (1) the establishment of a provisional German government, (2) the establishment of a central German administration for agriculture, (3) United States opposition to separation of the Ruhr and the Rhineland from Germany, (4) United States support for an international coal and steel authority for the Ruhr, and (5) United States support for transfer of the territories east of the Oder-Neisse line to Poland. With respect to the Oder-Neisse boundary, the State Department advised Cohen that Riddleberger's policy-study committee was considering the possibility of *reopening* the question with a view to restoring some of the territory under Polish administration to Germany.[29] Perhaps it was looking for means to soften the blow for France, if Byrnes agreed with Clay and the Army (and the Russians) that the Ruhr and the Rhineland should not be separated from Germany. Perhaps, also, the State Department could not resist the temptation to test the Russians once more. Murphy has written that the United States "could scarcely reject outright France's proposal for ... amputations in the west" in the light of what had been conceded in the east. He remembered that he and Byrnes's advisers had studied the problem from every angle and that they "came up with an adroit scheme." Byrnes would raise "doubts about the virtual annexations of territories which had taken place in eastern Germany." In fact, Byrnes would state publicly that permanent Russian and Polish control of the areas east of the Oder and Neisse rivers "had not yet been confirmed, because the Potsdam Protocol provided that Germany's boundaries would not be finally fixed until the peace treaty was signed." "As we anticipated," Murphy concluded, "the news reports [on Byrnes's Stuttgart speech] emphasized the status of German territories in the east, and this diverted pressures for amputations in the west."[30]

BYRNES'S STUTTGART SPEECH

Byrnes's speech in Stuttgart, Germany, on September 6, 1946, was clearly an attempt to pacify Clay and the Army. Both the content of the speech—which follows Clay's July 19 summary closely—and the origins of Byrnes's decision to make the speech support that conclusion. But there is more. Byrnes cabled Truman that "our officials in Germany" and others[31] had advised him to make a statement of policy to offset the effects of Molotov's July 10 policy statement in Paris and "to enable our German officials and

editors and our administrators to know what is the American policy."
Byrnes said Russia had made political gains among Germans after Molotov's announcement that Russia opposed the separation of the Ruhr and
Rhineland from Germany. The United States could make gains of its own
by stating its determination to remain in Germany and thus end the speculations that the United States was "so disgusted with European affairs
that we will not remain in Germany."[32] Though Byrnes did not say so, an
American commitment to remain in Germany would also disarm the
French, who had always strengthened their argument for territorial, military, and economic measures by asking what guarantees of French security
would remain after the occupation had ended.[33]

Byrnes delivered his speech in Stuttgart at the seat of the Council of
Minister-Presidents of the American zone. Prior to his speech, Byrnes met
personally with the minister-presidents and thus provided Clay and his staff
with considerable leverage to promote German economic unity from the
"grass roots" by encouraging interzonal conferences and meetings of German minister-presidents and other officials.[34] Three days later Byrnes wrote
to Secretary of the Treasury John W. Snyder:

The Army officers in Germany in charge of administering our zone were de-
lighted to have the Government announce its views so that they could adjust
their own policies. For some time they have been complaining that they were
unable to answer questions of the anti-Nazi officials they have appointed in the
American zone.... The German officials appointed by our people ... felt that if
we were going to leave it was useless to rely upon any plan we had for restoring
the economy ... and establishing local government. The argument was daily
made that while the Soviets would remain, the Americans would leave. We had
to declare our views on this problem and also on the very important boundary
questions which would influence our decisions as to economic questions.*

At Stuttgart Byrnes addressed himself to the whole range of German
problems and policies. He talked about demilitarization, reparations, the
level of the postwar German economy and the need for its upward revision
in the absence of economic unity, the economic imbalance of the four occu-

---

* Byrnes to John W. Snyder, Sept. 9, 1946, Snyder Papers, Box 15 (Germany—General,
1946–51), Truman Library. Byrnes's confusing accounts and distortions on the subject of his
Stuttgart speech are, in part, due to his subsequent efforts to soften the speech's impact on the
French and to his inability to separate the event from his reaction to Wallace's Madison Square
Garden speech of Sept. 12, 1946. See my "On the Implementation of the Potsdam Agreement:
An Essay on U.S. Postwar German Policy," *Political Science Quarterly*, LXXXVII (June 1972),
esp. pp. 248–49.

pation zones and the need for uniform economic policies, the failure of the ACC to establish central German administrations, the American desire for increased German self-rule and the early establishment of a provisional government on the initiative of the German minister-presidents, the American determination to stay in Germany so long as an occupation force remained there, and Germany's future boundaries. He bore down most heavily on the level-of-industry plan and its relation to demilitarization, reparations, plant removals, imports and exports, current-production reparations, and Germany's standard of living. He followed that with a detailed discussion of the failure of the ACC to treat Germany as an economic unit, emphasizing that "the Control Council is neither governing Germany nor allowing Germany to govern itself," and continued with a list of the central administrations that were essential. He dwelt at length on the American proposals for a provisional German government composed of a national council of minister-presidents. Finally, he discussed Germany's future boundaries. He said the United States had agreed to the cession of Königsberg and adjacent areas to the Soviet Union. It was now prepared also to agree to French annexation of the Saar. At Potsdam it had agreed to Russia's prior transfer of the territories east of the Oder-Neisse rivers to Poland for administrative purposes, but it "did not agree to support at the peace settlement the cession of this particular area." The United States would, however, "support revision of these frontiers in Poland's favor," to an extent to be determined at the final peace settlement. Beyond that the United States would support no further encroachments on German territory, and it opposed the separation of the Ruhr and Rhineland from Germany, though it favored and would help to enforce such controls over the areas as were necessary for security.[35]

Responses to Byrnes's Stuttgart Speech

In Britain "there was general approval" of Byrnes's speech.[36] The Russian response was apparently routine, except that Molotov—as he had done much more dramatically and brutally with the draft treaty on German disarmament—made clear that Russia would not play pawn in the State Department's game of chess with France. Replying to a request from the Polish press agency in Paris for a Russian statement on the Oder-Neisse boundary, Molotov reviewed some of the background, repeated the Potsdam Agreement, noted that large numbers of Germans had been resettled from the areas in question, asked (rhetorically) whether the allies now wanted to return them again, and stated categorically that the historic decision taken by the Potsdam Conference on the Polish-German boundary could not be reversed.*

Although Byrnes and historians have emphasized the anti-Russian nature of Byrnes's speech, the French government and the French public reacted most immediately, sharply, and critically. *The New Statesman and Nation* concluded on September 14, 1946, that Byrnes had succeeded in unifying Frenchmen from the extreme political right to the Communists. They all agreed that Byrnes wanted a revived Germany "as a pawn in the American orbit without regard for the security or economic interests of France."[37] Three days after Byrnes's speech, Armand Bérard, the French Minister in Washington, was at the State Department with the news that France's reaction to Byrnes's speech "had been extremely adverse." Byrnes had failed to make "even a verbal" concession to French feelings on security. Bérard complained about the American unwillingness to redraw zonal boundaries in Germany and about "the abrupt rejection" of France's proposal of August 10, 1946, on central allied agencies. He warned that France could not possibly join the American-British zonal union until Bidault had "talked out the problem" with Byrnes, Bevin, and Molotov in the CFM.[38] Two weeks later Bérard renewed his complaints. The State Department had just rejected a French proposal of May 7, 1946, for zonal boundary changes that would have transferred Karlsruhe, the capital of Baden, and other areas from the American to the French zone. It had advised France that the United States was unwilling to discuss changes in zonal boundaries until central German administrations and other economic problems had been resolved. Bérard protested the recent decision and referred to Byrnes's Stuttgart speech as "a move in the direction of a centralized Germany, a move which the French had to deplore." Apparently aware of Clay's and the Army's influence on Byrnes's Stuttgart speech and on the State Department's rejection of the zonal boundary changes, "M. Bérard in conclusion spoke with considerable vigor of the way in which General Clay in Berlin allegedly dealt with his French counterpart," and he "stated unequivocally that the character of French collaboration in Berlin will be in no small

---

* V. M. Molotov, *Fragen der Aussenpolitik: Reden und Erklärungen, April 1945–Juni 1948* (Moscow, 1949), pp. 256–60. It might be observed here that the Oder-Neisse boundary issue was being discussed actively in the election campaigns occurring in the Soviet zone of Germany at the time, and that it was threatening to split the Socialist Unity Party (SED) wide open until Molotov made his statement, which was published in Moscow on Sept. 17, 1946. See Wolfgang Leonhard, *Die Revolution Entlässt Ihre Kinder* (Köln, 1955), pp. 448–49.

measure determined by the character of the relations of the two generals in question."[39]

Neither Bérard's listeners nor Byrnes seemed to understand that France's demands for security were actually demands for territory and for economic encroachments in Germany, and that they could not be satisfied by American promises and guarantees. Bérard's listeners complained "that the French had not taken seriously our security offer." On the same day in Paris Byrnes told Bidault that "he had never quite understood why [Bidault] had not made more political capital at home out of" the American draft treaty on German disarmament. He said he had not blamed France at Stuttgart "for holding up the establishment of Central Administrative Agencies though this was of course the fact." The French press had failed to emphasize his promise to keep American troops in Germany so long as there was an occupation. Furthermore, Byrnes thought the French were disturbed by alleged American intentions to establish a strong central government in Germany when, "on the contrary," he "had in mind only a loose and highly decentralized federation such as we have in our own 3 *Laender* [states] at the present time."[40]

Murphy, Clay, and the Army had long since understood the basic French demands regarding Germany, and they understood and appreciated the French responses to Byrnes's Stuttgart speech. After seeing the memorandum of the Bérard conversation in Washington, Murphy cabled on October 5, 1946:

As I see M. Bérard's effort, it is designed to confuse the issue and gloss over the fact that there is a certain fundamental difference between the French and American approach to the German problem. The French keep on saying that there is no difference but their actions and official attitude on the principal economic and political issues which have been under consideration during the past months belie their words. We need only refer to the topics of central administration, national political parties, national trade unions, economic unification, among others, to perceive quite clearly that whether the French and the United States Deputy Military Governors are fond of each other or not could hardly resolve the questions.[41]

Murphy's attempt to set the record straight did little to convince his superiors in the State Department that French obstruction had caused the collapse of four-power control in Berlin. The State Department was blaming the Russians for that.

CHAPTER TEN

The Russians Are Coming

DESPITE THE seemingly endless repetition of the idea in the literature and despite the refined arguments that it was in fact so, neither the Russians nor the Americans were primarily responsible for the breakdown of the ACC and the failure to establish German central administrations and economic unity. Eisenhower recorded his early judgment that "the cooperative and friendly spirit of the Soviet delegation was particularly marked."[1] Russian support for central administrations in the ACC's negotiations is now a matter of published record. It is true that the Russians resisted when the Americans wanted to establish a central food-and-agriculture administration in addition to the five specified at Potsdam.[2] It is true that they would not accept Under Secretary of State Clayton's effort to revise the Potsdam zonal reparations agreement by administrative interpretation, and that they resisted Clay's attempts at a tripartite approach without France. However, the British objected to a tripartite approach even more strongly than did the Russians. And it is true that Clay said on April 8, 1946, that he had always been apprehensive of the Soviet position on treating Germany as an economic unit. But he qualified that with the observation that the Russians had always supported central machinery in the ACC, and I have shown that the Russians clarified the statement that had caused Clay's immediate concern and that the clarification reflected the Potsdam Agreement and existing practices.

Evidence of Russia's willingness to abide by the Potsdam Agreement and to unify Germany is legion. Murphy reported in September 1945 that the Russians were organizing their zone and selecting personnel that would "be useful to the Russians later on in Allied negotiations for creation of central German Ministries" and for pushing forward their "own already tested candidates."[3] Clay stated flatly in November 1945, and in sharp rebuttal of James Riddleberger's speculations to the contrary, that the Russians were carrying out the Potsdam Agreement and that they favored central administrative agencies in Germany.[4] Assistant Secretary of War McCloy, in a speech before the Academy of Political Science in New York—published in January 1946—said that "the difficulty we are now encountering in our attempt to achieve a central machinery for the nation-wide services, contrary to the general conception, does not emanate from the Soviet Union but from France, one of the western democracies."[5] General Hilldring, the head of the Army's civil affairs division, told a committee of Congress, on December 11, 1945, that "there is the finest understanding between the military governor and the Russian representative, as is evidenced by the great amount of accomplishment that has occurred."[6] In May 1946 Clay reported to Washington that he thought the British would accept a proposal for Ruhr control and that the Russians would find it acceptable because it was in accord with Potsdam. He said the Russians would cause difficulties on details, however.[7] The Russians, though critical of British-American zonal union plans, were ready to move on central administrations for all of Germany in August 1946. Clay wrote James P. Warburg on September 21, 1946, that the French were the cause of the ACC's failure, and Warburg later reflected on this and his visit to Berlin in August 1946: "It was not Russian violation of the Potsdam agreement but French intransigence that first broke down the four-power plan. Soviet exploitation of the breakdown was to come later."[8] Colonel D. L. Robinson, the OMGUS Control Officer, apparently surprised and disappointed George Meader, the chief counsel of the Senate Committee Investigating the National Defense Program, on October 16, 1946, when he insisted the record showed that "the Russians have advocated the economic unity [of Germany] as much as we have."[9] Meader's questions show that he was expecting examples of Russian obstruction. David L. Glickman wrote in December 1946 that "the US, UK, and USSR are agreed that Germany should be treated as an economic whole. The French prefer to postpone action on treatment of Germany as an economic whole until after their contention that the Saar, Ruhr, and Rhineland should be separated is resolved."[10] Clay told a press conference in Berlin in November 1946 that disagreements with the Russians had been on details, not on principles. They had always favored central administrations, whereas the French had blocked them from the beginning.[11] The Russians, in fact, prepared detailed proposals—and General Sokolovsky the Russian deputy military governor, initiated discussions on them with Clay in the fall of 1946—designed to resolve the interlocking impasse on reparations, the import-export balance, and central administrations. Clay had the Russian proposals studied thoroughly by his staff, and he reported to Washington on October 11, 1946, that they were a reasonable basis for discussion.[12] Significantly, Marshall's remarks to Bevin during the Moscow CFM indicate that the Americans were actively considering the Russian proposals as late as April 1947. At Moscow, in the spring of 1947, "General Clay and his assistants on the Control Council" told a writer for *The New Republic* "that the Russians are tough horsetraders . . . but that we are negotiating with them daily on a basis of reasonable give and take and are not faring too badly. The French, with their demand for the Saar and the internationalization of the Ruhr, are far more intransigent."* But all of these and many more similar observations and facts seem to have been ignored and forgotten; they seem to have passed into the realm of non-history. The responsibility for that rests, in no small measure, with the Department of State.

THE STATE DEPARTMENT AND THE RUSSIANS

Louis J. Halle has written that even during the period of the Grand Alliance of World War II "there was no time when the danger from the Soviet Union was not a topic of anxious conversation among officers of the State Department; and by the winter of 1944–1945, as the day of victory approached, it became a predominant theme in Washington."[13] The process by which anxious conversations become transformed into a policy or a position is, perhaps, impossible to reconstruct by methods familiar to a historian. There are, however, certain events and relationships that are highly suggestive. I have noted in another context that the State Department's European experts, especially Riddleberger and Matthews, tried to shift the discussion to a catalog of Russian unilateral actions in Germany when Clay and Murphy demanded that pressure be brought upon France to cooperate in the ACC.[14] Both the tactic and the relationships the incident reveals are important.

The Army's strong and persistent pressure upon the State Department to bring France around in the ACC cut across the State Department's policy

---

* Arthur L. Mayer, "Winter of Discontent," *The New Republic*, 116 (March 10, 1947), 19. See also Anne Whyte, "Quadripartite Rule in Berlin: An Interim Record of the First Year of the Allied Control Authority," *International Affairs*, XXIII (Jan. 1947), 33, for the statement that "it has been the French who have consistently refused to agree to any step towards unity, even when a four power meteorological station for all of Germany was proposed. . . . The original difficulty lay in the attitude of the French, which, during the vital formative months of 1945, forced each zone to operate separately."

to make concessions to French prestige, to treat France on the basis of her potential power, and to restore France as a bulwark of democracy in Europe. To offset the threat to State Department policy and to guard against the persistent efforts of the Army to make Germany run and to disregard the vital needs of the liberated areas—as Matthews had expressed it to McCloy in June 1945—State Department functionaries seem to have fallen into the practice of defending the Department's own policies and priorities by expressing anxiety about Russian intentions. They were obviously encouraged and fortified in the practice by the De Gaulle–Bidault theory that any solution other than France's for the Saar, the Ruhr, the Rhineland, and Germany's western boundaries promised not only to threaten the stability of the French provisional government but also to make undue concessions to the Russians. Bidault and De Gaulle had warned Byrnes and Truman about Russian intentions in August 1945, and Ambassador Caffery reported time and time again that establishment of German central administrations would bring the Russians to the French frontier, probably topple the French provisional government, and cause political uncertainty at best or a leftist/ Communist victory at worst. State Department functionaries were, of course, also influenced by experience. Various factors entered the complex picture: Russian practices in Germany, in Eastern Europe, and elsewhere; the toughness of Molotov as a negotiator; the Russian encouragement of German Communists, such as Walter Ulbricht; and the difficulties of reaching a reparations agreement. The State Department's interpretations of these experiences were, however, countered regularly by Eisenhower and Clay, who cited examples of Russian cooperation and compromises and who seemed to think the Americans were a match for the Russians in the ACC and in Germany.

There is no evidence that the State Department's practice of defending France by expressing anxiety about Russia began as a result of intellectual conception or a rational plan. It seems to have developed quite naturally, in the context of the bureaucratic wrangling that I have already described. But when the practice did occur, it became a matter of record: a memorandum; a minute; a phrase, line, or sentence in a speech; or an imprint on the memory of the user. The records accumulated. In time, these accumulated records of tactical maneuvers came to be used as though they were historical records: as events followed events in Europe; as decisions followed decisions; as personnel and assignments in the State Department changed; as the Army, the British, and the Russians lost patience with the State Department's tender, loving care of France; as the American public became restive with the cost of the occupation; as politicians saw great political advantage in claiming that American policy in Germany was a failure (during the November 1946 Congressional elections, for example); and as members of Congress began to search for Communists in high places and to raise questions about the competence and the loyalty of State Department functionaries. Part of this complex and irrational development can be demonstrated, beginning with the point at which the State Department's earlier hit-and-miss practice received a patron with ideas.

George F. Kennan and the Impasse in Germany

George F. Kennan, the United States Chargé in the Soviet Union, began to apply the analysis of his famous long telegram of February 22, 1946, to the problems of the German occupation early in March 1946. The State Department (apparently Matthews, the head of the European desk) had asked him to comment on a cable of February 24, 1946, from Murphy. It may be recalled, for context, that Murphy had asked Matthews on January 29 whether he had "formulated an opinion by now regarding a way out of the impasse" in Germany, adding, "We have exhausted every argument we know here." Matthews eventually recommended to Byrnes that the United States agree to permanent French occupation of the Saar in return for French willingness "to treat this question as a part of the whole settlement of French policy toward Germany." Apparently sensing the obvious—neither France nor the Army would be pacified by that—Matthews also turned to Kennan. Matthews had been convinced earlier "of the soundness of George Kennan's excellent recent telegrams evaluating Soviet policy," and it was he who had asked Kennan to comment on Stalin's election speech of February 9 and thus inspired the long telegram of February 22, 1946. Matthews was absolutely enthralled by the latter. He sent Ambassador Caffery a copy on February 26, saying, "it is about as fine a piece of writing and as clear an analysis of a highly complicated and vital situation as has ever come out of the Foreign Service."[15] The next day the State Department asked Kennan for his comments on Murphy's message of February 24, 1946.

Murphy's message from Berlin was filled with warnings and spliced with the strongest recommendations he had yet made. "The time is overdue when a firmer and more aggressive stand should be taken" on central agencies and the implementation of the Potsdam Agreement. Ulbricht and the German Communists (supported by the Russians) were making political capital with their slogans: "The Ruhr is and must remain German; Germany cannot live without the Ruhr; we stand for a united Reich." The French remained intransigent, Murphy continued, and neither the Russians nor the Germans believed that France had acted without real or tacit British and American approval. Meanwhile, the Russians had "taken full advantage of French obstructionism to consolidate the Soviet position in eastern Germany." Russia was, in fact, laying the basis for close affiliation with the new Germany of the future. According to Murphy, that carried with it "grave implications" for the future. If the French could not be persuaded by discussion, he concluded, "the question is asked whether it might not be desirable temporarily to withhold cooperation in other fields from the French until a more favorable attitude might develop."[16]

As Matthews apparently expected, Kennan's comment on Murphy's message was the analysis of the long telegram adapted to the German situation. Kennan detected a two-phased Russian program for Germany, which would lead to creation of a "Soviet Socialist state," preferably flanked in the West by "a France extensively under Soviet influence." He speculated on the sources of Soviet conduct in Germany, and he said he "would by no means accept it as foregone conclusion that Russians have really been eager, up to this time, to see central German administrative agencies established." They had been "gingerly carrying water on both shoulders" and awaiting future events. Yet, "they doubtless feel that in the end they cannot lose." They had been happy with French intransigence in Berlin, and Kennan thought the French Communists' opposition to central agencies was proof of that. Central agencies, he warned, "are plainly [a] two-edged sword," and it was unduly optimistic to assume that their existence would "break down exclusive Soviet control in Soviet zone." The United States and Britain should show less enthusiasm for a united Germany and more for constructive programs in their zones. This would bring the Russians "tapping insistently at the back door." The establishment of the Oder-Neisse boundary line sealed the fate of Germany to two alternatives: nominal union, "vulnerable to Soviet political penetration and influence," or partition, with western Germany walled off "against eastern penetration" and integrated into an internationally organized Western Europe.[17]

But Kennan was not finished. On March 20, 1946—as if to warn against the undue optimism he had detected in Murphy's message from Berlin— he cabled to express his "concern and alarm" about an idea currently circulating in the United States that Russian suspicions "could be altered or assuaged by personal contacts, rational arguments or official assurances." Such a belief, Kennan asserted, "reflects a serious misunderstanding about Soviet realities and constitutes, in our opinion, the most insidious and dangerous single error which Americans can make in their thinking about this country." He interpreted: the official Soviet thesis is "that outside world is hostile and menacing." He warned: "Suspicion is basic in Soviet Government. It affects everything and everyone." Finally, he admonished: "To this climate, and not to wishful preconceptions, we must adjust our diplomacy."[18]

Soon after Kennan entered the debate on Russian motives and policies in Germany, Clay and Murphy made known the disparity between Kennan's analysis and the Russians' behavior in Berlin. They also expressed their anger at what they regarded as a deliberate attempt by the State Department to use Kennan's views to stir up anti-Russian sentiments. Murphy wrote to Matthews on April 3, 1946, to complain about how widely Kennan's long telegram was circulating within the bureaucracy and to report Clay's belief that it was distributed to Army commanders at the instigation of the Department of State. Matthews replied that he had "no time to argue the matter at length," but he cautioned Murphy that while his and Clay's account of good relations with the Soviets in Berlin was accurate, "you get an entirely distorted picture if you attempt to draw general conclusions from it." Echoing Kennan, Matthews lectured Murphy that it was

basic doctrine in the Kremlin that the Soviet and non-Soviet systems cannot exist in this world side by side. This basic belief amounts to a religion to the true Communist and its implications make it impossible to visualize real peace in the world unless or until there is a fundamental change in Soviet thinking. This being so, the Soviet leaders (and the generals [presumably those in Berlin with whom Clay and Murphy associated] have nothing to do with Soviet policy) want no peace, or stability or rehabilitation in Europe—or at least west of the Iron Curtain—for under such conditions their infiltration and communization methods do not prosper.[19]

Kennan's theories prevailed over the facts in Berlin. By May 1946 Kennan thought "we must declare our independence of the Potsdam agreement." He said the United States should announce that it was no longer bound by Potsdam and propose economic unification within Germany's old boundaries, excluding East Prussia. Such action, he predicted, would disarm the French "and put the matter squarely to the Russians."[20] The State Department had already decided to do the latter.

Testing the Russians

Clay's suspension of reparations deliveries from the American zone on May 3, 1946, provided a context for putting the matter "squarely to the Russians." Clay's action was serious indeed. He had said in April that reparations and common import-export policies depended upon prior resolution of the central administrations question, and he had referred the issue to government level. His reparations suspension was thus, in effect, forcing the State Department to do something about France's vetoes of central administrations. But, as I have shown earlier, Clay's expectations and the State Department's response were incongruous. Acheson and Hilldring sent Byrnes a plan "designed . . . *above all*, to put Soviet protestations of loyalty to Potsdam to [a] final test."[21]

Byrnes accepted the proposal for a test, but he constructed his own questions. As described earlier, he presented them to the Paris CFM on May 15, 1946, in the form of a proposal to appoint and instruct special deputies for Germany. When he returned from Paris, Byrnes referred to his special-deputies proposal and its reception in a radio report he made to the American people. He said the United States had proposed the establishment of central administrations, economic unity, and a balanced export-import program for Germany. "The French Government, which had previously opposed the establishment of central administrative agencies, indicated their willingness to accept our proposal when we suggested that the Saar be excluded from the jurisdiction of these agencies. The British agreed." Byrnes said the Soviets would "not agree to exclusion of the Saar without further study, and therefore no immediate progress was possible." He then described his invitation to the other occupation powers to join their zones with the American zone in economic unity and concluded: "We will either secure economic co-operation between the zones *or place the responsibility for the violation of the Potsdam agreement.*"[22]

Clay's and Murphy's responses to the Acheson-Hilldring test plan are not recorded in the available accounts. They met Byrnes at the CFM meetings in Paris and they may have discussed it orally with him. But there are records showing that both protested when they read Byrnes's radio address in the newspapers. Clay cabled the War Department that France had not agreed to the American position on central administrations. The French were, in fact, talking about a plan that would be a step backward. Murphy cabled Benjamin V. Cohen, the author of Byrnes's address, and said his own notes on the CFM meetings in Paris did not support the conclusions in Byrnes's speech. In effect, Clay and Murphy both said Byrnes was letting France off the hook and heaping blame on Molotov and the Russians. Cohen's reply to Murphy admitted indirectly that Clay and Murphy were correct. He said he was aware that "there may not be complete meeting of minds between Secretary and Bidault on central agencies," but that an effort should be made to "minimize if not obviate" their differences. Byrnes hoped "that we may find a *modus vivendi* with the French if we avoid clash on verbal differences upon which their political situation may cause them to put exaggerated importance."[23] Clay and Murphy had insisted, however, that the differences were fundamental, not verbal, and Clay had judged the French position to be a step backward.

While the State Department and Byrnes used the reparations suspension as a point of departure for testing the Russians, Clay and Murphy tried to set the record straight on the reasons for Clay's suspension of reparations from the American zone. In Washington and in the American press, Clay's action was being interpreted as a move against Russia. Clay tried to correct the misapprehension in a Berlin press conference on May 27, 1946. He said the suspension did not apply to Russia alone, but was directed at "everybody." He was simply refusing to dismantle further plants until "the economic unity on which reparations is based has been attained."[24] In the meantime, the State and War Departments had worked up a plan to ship reparations to the so-called IARA (Inter-Allied Reparations Agency) countries and to set aside for future deliveries—after German unification—to Russia and Poland the 25 percent that was due them under the Potsdam reparations agreement. The plan's stated purpose was to strengthen Clay's bargaining position vis-à-vis the Russians and to continue to ship reparations plants to other countries anxious to have them for postwar economic development. The cable that transmitted the plan to Berlin said: "Plan could be negotiated quickly in Washington on diplomatic level if tripartite character would embarrass you in Berlin."[25] Clay protested on June 5. He said any tripartite arrangement "would be particularly undesirable since stoppage of dismantling [was] not directed at any one nation but simply adopted as a measure to prevent removal of plants needed in case Potsdam provision for economic unity and central administrative agencies not actually implemented." Clay said he did not want to deny legitimate reparations to the IARA countries, to the Soviet Union, or to Poland, "but we

cannot agree to carry out [the] reparations plan and actually ship designated plants until we know whether the basis on which the reparations
plan was developed is to be carried out or not."[26]

Murphy corrected the State Department as pointedly as Clay did the War
Department. Anticipating criticism of the reparations suspension in the
IARA, the State Department had prepared a guidance paper on Clay's suspension and, on June 11, 1946, sent it to Russell H. Dorr, the American representative to the IARA in Brussels, with an information copy to Murphy
in Berlin. The guidance paper instructed Dorr to emphasize the failure to
agree on economic unity and common trade policies as the primary reason
for the reparations suspension. It also advised Dorr that "you may in your
discretion point out that failure to implement Potsdam first-charge principle
and continuation of reparation from current output in Soviet zone has produced heavy German import deficit and prevented treatment of Germany
as economic unit and that accordingly Soviet undertaking to treat Germany
as economic unit would permit prompt resumption of reparation in capital
equipment."[27] Murphy's correction said if Dorr mentioned Russian reparations from current output and the like, he should also mention the similar
reparations that France was taking from the French zone. He went on
to detail France's current-production and industrial-equipment removals,
France's opposition to the principles of Potsdam, to political parties, to
central agencies, and to trade unions, and he said France's position on the
Saar, the Ruhr, and the Rhineland "directly conflict with the principle of
Germany as an economic whole." Murphy concluded: "*If a fair representation of the matter is to be made by Dorr*," he should mention France's actions.[28]

Acheson replied to Murphy's correction on June 24, 1946, saying simply
that the State Department concurred in his observations.[29] But the Department's functionaries found it difficult to reconcile that concurrence with
what they knew to be the case, perhaps with what they believed to be necessary regardless of truth. The condition is revealed in a memorandum of
June 10, 1946, from Walt W. Rostow, the Assistant Chief, to Charles P.
Kindleberger, the Chief of the German-Austrian Economic Affairs Division
of the State Department. According to Rostow, who had just returned from
a consulting visit in Germany, American officials in Berlin were cautiously
optimistic about the Soviets. Their experience had shown them, he wrote
that "hard-bargaining straight-forward Americans who know their objectives, and who have reasonable objectives, can do business with the Rus-

sians." They insisted "that Soviet policy has up to the present consistently looked towards treating Germany as an economic unit," and recent events had not altered that general view. Then, clearly revealing the differences between Berlin and Washington, Rostow wrote: *"Whether correct or not it is the Berlin view that Clay's hold-up of reparations is designed rather more to get the French obstruction cleared up than to show up Soviet intentions."*[30]

Despite the doubts in the Washington bureaus, and despite the inclinations of the American press to blame the Russians for the problems in Berlin, the State Department remained firm in Acheson's concurrence with Murphy—at least for a time.[31] An official policy summary of August 5, 1946, attributed the reparations suspension to the impasse on economic unity and central agencies and did not mention Russia or France. In September, Russell H. Dorr cabled from Brussels that in forthcoming reparations discussions he assumed that he was "authorized to put onus on France and Russia for failure to live up to the economic unit provisions [of] Potsdam." But the State Department instructed him, instead, to reiterate the American position on the relationship of reparations, economic unity, and central agencies; to refer to Byrnes's Stuttgart speech; to emphasize the American desire to implement Potsdam; and to "avoid acrimonious participation in debate."[32] The minutes of a January 24, 1947, State Department staff conference on policy for the Moscow CFM show apparent agreement that resumption of reparations should be conditioned by Russian and French actions on economic unity. The policy papers prepared by the State Department for the Moscow CFM state that "General Clay halted reparation removals from the United States zone of occupation because of the French failure to agree to the creation of central administrative departments, provided for in the Berlin Protocol, and because of Soviet unwillingness to agree on common policies for the operation of German foreign trade."* Finally, Marshall's statement of March 17, 1947, at the Moscow CFM emphasized the protective nature of the reparations suspension. He said the United States could not permit further removals in the face of recurring German financial deficits and until the United States zone was assured a share in all of Germany's resources. He did not mention France or Russia.[33]

---

* *FRUS*, 1947, II, 199, 217. There is a subtlety, easily missed, in the quoted statement. The addition of the phrase "provided for in the Berlin Protocol" lets the French off the hook, technically, for failing to agree to central agencies, because they never approved the Berlin Protocol. State Department functionaries were not unaware of that; in fact, the Acheson-Hilldring test plan of May 9, 1946, said so flatly.

Scoring the test and scorching the Russians. During the course of the Moscow CFM, at the time when the vital decisions leading to the Marshall Plan for European economic recovery were made, the State Department withdrew its concurrences, threw caution to the winds, and leveled its guns on the Russians. For example, early in 1947 the State Department released a publication that contained a deliberate and calculated distortion of the historical record on the reparations suspension. The distorted record was Byrnes's radio report to the American people after his return from the Paris CFM in May 1946. He had said the following about the reparations suspension:

I asked that the Special Deputies on Germany be instructed to report on several pressing problems, including boundary and economic questions. We cannot, for example, continue to carry out the reparation program if Germany is not to be administered as an economic unit as agreed upon at Potsdam. Whatever boundaries are agreed upon for Germany, she must be able to subsist without external assistance. We cannot subsidize Germany to enable her to pay reparations to other nations.[34]

The State Department publication of 1947 paraphrased and quoted Byrnes's remarks of May 1946 as follows:

The United States, Mr. Byrnes said, could not continue to carry out the program of reparations removals from the American zone in Germany to the Soviet Union if Germany was not to be administered as an economic unit as agreed upon at Potsdam. Furthermore, declared Mr. Byrnes, "Whatever boundaries are agreed upon for Germany, she must be able to subsist without external assistance. We cannot subsidize Germany to enable her to pay reparations to other nations."[35]

The direct quotation leaves no doubt about the Byrnes statement being used, and the addition of the phrase *to the Soviet Union* in the paraphrased portion leaves little doubt about the deliberate distortion.

Upon his return from Moscow, Marshall himself took up the State Department's new emphasis and he was soon joined by others. In a radio report to the American people on the Moscow CFM, Marshall said, "the unwillingness of the Soviet authorities to cooperate in establishing a balanced economy for Germany as agreed upon at Potsdam has been the most serious check on the development of a self-supporting Germany." The Soviets, he said, had attacked the union of the British and American zones as a step in the division of Germany and as a violation of the Potsdam Agreement. In doing so, they ignored "the plain fact that their refusal to carry out that agreement was the sole cause of the merger." Kennan, the recently appointed head of the State Department's Policy Planning Staff and thus in a position to act on German affairs rather than comment on them from Moscow, said on May 6, 1947, that the Russians had refused to agree to restore the German economy and that "we cannot wait for Russian agreement to achieve that restoration." Edward S. Mason, one of Marshall's advisers at the Moscow CFM, wrote during the summer of 1947 that "at Moscow the Soviet Government in effect repudiated Potsdam." In September the State Department released a note it had sent to Russia, saying that the revised bizonal level of industry was needed to relieve the heavy financial burden of the occupation being borne by the United States and caused by "the failure of the Soviet Government to implement the Berlin Agreement." The State Department also prepared for the Herter Committee (the House Select Committee on Foreign Aid, 80th Congress) and the House Foreign Affairs Committee a statement that reportedly charged the Russians with being "the principal obstructions" in Berlin and with "blocking the treatment of Germany as an economic whole."[36]

As the nation and the Congress debated the Marshall Plan, the idea that Russia had blocked progress in Germany and in Europe apparently became fixed permanently. Marshall testified before the House Foreign Affairs Committee in November 1947, saying, "the war ended with the armies of the major allies meeting in the heart [of the European community of nations]. The policies of three of them have been directed to the restoration of that European community. It is now clear that only one power, the Soviet Union, does not for its own reasons share this aim."[37] Marshall simply transformed France—one of the three—from the negative, obstructionist power it had been in 1945–46 into a positive force in the restoration of the European community. Vandenberg, speaking on the Senate floor in December 1947 in opposition to a resolution to stop dismantling of factories in Germany, protested nevertheless that "it does not disturb me in the slightest that this would be a unilateral breach of the Potsdam agreement, because in my book the Potsdam agreement was breached long ago by Soviet Russia. . . . I think the Potsdam agreement became a scrap of paper a long time ago as a result of Soviet repudiation of many of its obligations."[38] Vandenberg had "kept book" during his participation in the CFM in London and Paris in 1945–46, and presumably during his frequent conferences with Marshall after the latter's Harvard speech. On January 5, 1948, Charles E. Bohlen, the Counselor of the State Department, told a Wisconsin audience that "the Soviet Union, at first by devious means and later openly," had blocked the revival of Europe, which the Western democracies sought. Later in January Marshall told an audience of businessmen in Pittsburgh that "the refusal of the Soviets to cooperate in establishing a unified economy for Germany invalidated the level of industry and reparation calculations made at Potsdam." A day earlier Secretary of the Army Kenneth C. Royall had testified in the Senate Foreign Relations Committee that "the Soviets have prevented economic and political unity with the western zones." State Department notes to the Soviet Union in February and March 1948—both published at the time—continued to stress Soviet responsibility for the failure to treat Germany as an economic unit. Willard L. Thorp, the Assistant Secretary of State for Economic Affairs, repeated the idea in a public forum in New York on March 6, 1948, and Charles E. Saltzman, the Assistant Secretary of State for Occupied Areas, wrote in July 1948 that Soviet obstructionism caused the failure of Potsdam.[39]

The catalog is longer. As for its impact, it is perhaps sufficient to note that not even Clay was immune to the trend of the times. On January 22, 1948, in testimony in the House Appropriations Committee, he said: "It became evident at the very early stages in the game that our objectives in Germany were considerably different from some of those of the other occupying powers. The result was that everything conducive to constructive government presented in the Allied Council was blocked by representatives of the Soviet Government, so that operations under the quadripartite agreement for Germany have been impossible."[40] One may detect in the first sentence a veiled reference to Clay's recollection of the many problems he had had with France, but he nevertheless singled out the Soviet Union as the trouble maker, as was the custom.

The Truman administration, the Congress, and the American public debated the Marshall Plan for European economic recovery with a great deal of anti-Soviet rhetoric, as the State Department intended they should. Historians have interpreted the origins of the plan similarly, and—in the fashion established by the public debate—they have neglected the economic problems of the German occupation that gave rise to the Marshall Plan.

THE GERMAN ECONOMIC JUNGLE

CHAPTER ELEVEN

Unilateral Reparations Removals

E ACH OCCUPATION POWER took reparations unilaterally from its own zone of occupation. Unilateral removals did not necessarily impinge upon the program to change Germany's production from heavy industry, chemicals, machine tools, and so on, to domestic and peaceful industries and to reduce the German level of industry and standard of living to the European average. Except for those taken as war trophies or war booty, unilateral reparations could have been accounted for as removals provided for in the level-of-industry and reparations plan of March 1946. In fact, however, the failure of the four powers to cooperate on uniform reporting and accounting practices and the failure to agree on administrative machinery to do the latter resulted in continuing uncertainties about the amount of reparations Germany was paying or would pay. This in turn made it impossible for the Allied Control Commission to establish a German economy able to sustain itself without outside assistance.

There appears to be no way to calculate or reasonably estimate the total amount removed unilaterally by the four powers as reparations. One can, however, illustrate the character and the style of those removals by each of the four.

THE ZONAL STYLES

The Russians, who justified their unilateral actions by strict interpretation of the Potsdam zonal reparations plan, changed their earlier plant removals program to a current-production reparations program in the spring of 1946, a change they justified by a broad interpretation of the Potsdam Agreement, which had remained silent on current-production reparations. The decision to change was apparently based on experience: dismantling and transporting entire plants from their locations in Germany for reassembly in the Soviet Union had proved to be difficult, unproductive, and basically uneconomic.[1] According to James P. Warburg, "The Russians ...

decided that they would rather have the golden eggs laid by the goose than the goose itself."[2] Whether the change was more a function of the Russian experience or of the long-range economic decisions made in Russia in conjunction with the new five-year plan of 1946, or simply a desperate response to the impasse in Berlin and the needs of Russia for postwar reconstruction is beyond my ken. Perhaps it was for all of these reasons.* In any case, in June 1946 the Russian military government combined some 200 enterprises in the Soviet zone into a series of Soviet corporations (*Aktiengesellschaften*, generally called Soviet AGs), in which the Russians retained control of 51 percent or more of the interest. Comprising some 25 to 30 percent of the productive capacity of the Soviet zone and employing workers estimated to have been between 300,000 and 400,000, the Soviet AGs produced goods and services for the Soviet Union's reparations account and apparently also for reexport from the Soviet Union by the Russian state-trading companies.[3]

The French, who had reservations about the Potsdam Agreement, which they had not helped to negotiate, systematically removed machines, equipment, and current-production reparations from the French zone. In June 1946, for example, OMGUS reported that France had removed unilaterally some 5,000 machine tools from the French zone. OMGUS made similar, detailed reports of French removals in July, August, September, and December 1946, and in January 1947.[4] What the French did on their own behalf, they eventually did for their friends. In doing the latter they followed a British precedent and example.

The British, who agreed neither with Clay's unilateral suspension of reparations shipments from the American zone nor with his refusal to agree to ACC allocations of reparations from the other zones during the impasse that resulted, finally worked out an emergency unilateral reparations program for the British zone.[5] In November 1946, having decided that Clay's continuing blockage was unduly harmful to the liberated countries, the British asked the IARA nations to submit lists of machines, machine tools, cranes, and other equipment that they wanted as reparations. The British offered prompt delivery directly to the IARA of such materials as were available from their zone, to an amount no greater than RM 75 million in

---

* See James P. Warburg, *Germany: Nation or No-Man's-Land* (Headline Series, No. 60; New York, Foreign Policy Association, 1946), p. 44, for the observation that "the Soviet Union had readjusted its original policy when it became evident in the winter of 1945–1946 that French obstructionism would continue. Instead of taking plant and equipment for reparations account, as per Potsdam, it switched to leaving the plants in Germany and taking out a large part of their current production."

value. The French soon followed the British example, but they reversed the procedure. France, in the first instance, reported to the IARA the equipment and machinery it was making available for reparations from the French zone. It asked the IARA to submit the lists to its member nations and allocate the machines and equipment to the receiving countries according to the standing procedures of the IARA.[6]

The Americans, who opposed unilateral removals on principle and objected repeatedly to such removals and the failure to account for them, nevertheless engaged in the practice they protested.[7] For example, in May 1946, the Army, the Navy, and the Bureau of Mines requested certain equipment from Germany that they had identified from the so-called FIAT lists that had been prepared by American teams of scientists who had roamed over Germany after 1945 in search of scientific know-how. When Clay discovered that the United States representative in the IARA could not guarantee IARA allocation to the United States, he recommended direct shipment back to the United States. He said a report of the shipment and its value could be made to the IARA for its use in calculating the final United States reparations account. After considerable hesitation and negotiation, the State and War Departments approved Clay's recommendation, but they also suggested that a larger unilateral reparations program might be implemented—similar to the ones later adopted by Britain and France in November 1946—to satisfy the reparations demands of the non-occupation powers represented in the IARA.[8] The unilateral program was never implemented, in part because Clay insisted that his reparations suspension was not a decision to deny reparations selectively, but a tactic to force government resolution of the impasse on central administrations and economic unity.

A similar removal of special equipment by the United States occurred in June 1946. The incident shows the pressure for such removals as well as the United States hesitancy to engage in them. According to a State Department memorandum, various agencies in Washington were pressing OMGUS to bypass the normal IARA reparations allocation procedure and to ship certain scientific and technical equipment directly to the United States. The memorandum said: "Permission to ship implicitly involves the judgment that the gain to the United States from receiving the equipment outweighs the cost in good relations with non-occupying countries, which are receiving no reparation currently. The basic question is whether the Department prefers to embarrass the War Department, Commerce Department and American Industry, or itself in its relations with other countries." The State Department eventually embarrassed itself, but with the understanding of all parties that this would be the last such shipment made to the United States outside the regular reparations allocation channels.[9] How and whether it was done after that are not revealed in the available records. The removal of scientific know-how and other things is recorded, however.

SCIENTIFIC KNOWLEDGE AS REPARATIONS

Each of the four occupation powers removed from Germany technical, industrial, and scientific information—including the human beings who possessed it or who could further its effective use. Such removals from Germany were never calculated for reparations, even though no less a policy-maker than Dean Acheson once referred to such exploitation as a unique type of reparations.[10] Neither were such removals ever evaluated commercially as exports of goods and services, even though Clay declared that such exploitation entered "squarely into the commercial field," once the need for scientific data to fight the war in Japan no longer existed.[11] The British, French, and Russian technical and scientific removal programs cannot be documented. That condition—the reader should be strongly cautioned—reflects the policies of those governments regarding access of scholars to government records, rather than the extent and nature of their removals from Germany. The American program can be documented. Clarence G. Lasby's book, *Project Paperclip*, is a careful and fascinating study of the American exploitation of German scientists.[12] Project Paperclip was, however, but one aspect of a larger program.

Field Intelligence Agency, Technical

The American decision to engage in systematic, budget-supported technical and scientific intelligence activities may be dated from October 14, 1944, when the JCS created the Technical Industrial Intelligence Commission (TIIC). The Commission obtained a budget of $2 million from the Foreign Economic Administration (FEA), and it was attached for operations to United States Forces, European Theater (USFET), where it functioned as the Field Intelligence Agency, Technical (FIAT). When the FEA was dissolved, the JCS transferred the TIIC's Washington offices to the Department of Commerce on October 21, 1945. The Commerce Department provided funds, secured personnel in the United States, processed film, compiled reports, published bibliographies and reports, and sold the latter through its Office of Technical Services. It also gave the TIIC a stronger business-and-industry orientation than it had had under the FEA. Operations in the field (FIAT) were always a military responsibility. The War Department processed the FIAT personnel for service in Europe and issued directives to USFET. USFET supervised and controlled the agency, furnished offices, billets, rations, transportation, and such German personnel as was needed.[13]

The size and scope of the operation are revealed in a Department of Commerce report to the War Department, in materials collected by a Senate committee, and in reports and correspondence of the American military government in Germany. In October 1946, after Clay had convinced the War Department that the FIAT operation would have to be cut back and eventually discontinued, the Commerce Department reported that it had a total of 200 civilians working in the program abroad. Another 600 technical investigators, who had been recruited from American science and industry, had already completed their surveys and returned to the United States. In addition, the Commerce Department had 600 technical and scientific consultants available on a continuing basis for evaluation of data and compilation of reports in the United States. The so-called Meader Committee of the Senate found, on October 31, 1946, that there were 290 people in the European theater, 190 paid personnel working in the Commerce Department as document screeners, microfilm operators, and so on, and an additional 100 investigators working under various contracts.[14]

The FIAT teams in Europe combed the German countryside for scientists and technicians; for scientific, industrial, and technical information; for documents, new formulas, new processes; for sample machines and equipment; and for a host of other things. The scope of their activity may be inferred from a notice in the *Science News Letter* for May 4, 1946, advising that any industrial and scientific group wishing to go to Germany to "investigate German industrial methods" might do so under the auspices of the United States government. The notice, which was based on a Commerce Department release, said the investigations would have to promise benefits to American industry as a whole. Competent people were being sought for chemicals, aeronautics, the automotive industry, machine tools, industrial equipment, fuels and lubricants, metals and minerals, communications equipment, scientific instruments, shipbuilding, and textiles.[15] In February 1947, John C. Green, the Director of the Department of Commerce's Office of Technical Services, declared in public that when the program would be closed out in June 1947, every important plant in the American zone "will have given up its industrial secrets." He reported that no fewer than 130 reels of film had been processed on the Leica camera works alone. He observed that 600 German scientists were working "in the field of pure sciences" on projects never before made public, but he insisted that even more could be done if American manufacturers would send their engineers to Germany. They would have to act quickly, however, as the United States government could not hold open the door much longer.[16] Clay was, in fact, trying to push the door shut, as I shall note later.

The projects on which German scientists worked in Germany may be sketched from the very limited available evidence contained in OMGUS reports and papers. In December 1946, for example, an exchange of correspondence between OMGUS and the Office of Military Government for Bavaria reveals that an optical firm in Munich was producing cameras and other equipment for the Air Force under ten separate projects. It reveals also that the Navy, the Army Signal Corps, and the Surgeon General's Office had placed orders with the firm. In May 1947 an OMGUS summary report for the War Department shows that 201 authorized German research establishments were engaged in 1,120 sponsored projects. Of these, 18 were in food and agriculture; 16 in biology and bacteriology; nine in public health; eight in medical physics; 20 in biochemistry; 18 in general, analytical, and physical chemistry; 16 in industrial chemistry; 13 in organic chemistry; 18 in physics and mathematics; 13 in electrical engineering; 23 in mechanical engineering; four in civil engineering; and two in textiles.[17]

FIAT Accounting and Termination

The many published guesses notwithstanding, the total value of the materials and scientific know-how removed from Germany appears to be beyond calculation. When Clay tried to get an accounting, he first met resistance, and then ran up against a stone wall in Washington. On October 4, 1946, Clay wrote the War Department asking for a policy regarding the trade processes and advanced scientific information being removed from Germany by the FIAT teams. He thought these things should be valued in monetary terms for possible assignment as reparations and to give German scientists a basis for filing claims against a future German government. Clay argued that the materials in question had considerable value for American industry and science, and he believed that FIAT operations had fallen "squarely into the commercial field" after the war with Japan ended.

He also observed that in taking the FIAT information "we are perhaps doing the same thing that Russia is doing in taking current production from Germany without accounting, and that France is doing in removing capital equipment from Germany without accounting."[18]

Clay's letter activated an issue that had been making the rounds in Washington since at least July 1946, when the Secretary General of the IARA in Brussels had formally asked Britain, France, and the United States for an accounting of unilateral removals from the western zones of Germany.[19] On October 16, 1946, the War Department advised Clay that it was impractical to fix a value on the FIAT materials, because there was no way to predict how the materials would be used commercially in the future. Furthermore, the War Department thought FIAT evaluations were primarily an international problem and that the State Department should make them. It also suggested that they might be made by the IARA in Brussels.[20] The conclusion is inescapable: The War Department wanted someone else to do it, if it was to be done at all. A week later Byrnes advised Russell H. Dorr in Brussels that the State Department could not make a report on unilateral removals for another two or three months. The IARA would have to wait until the State Department collected information and reports from Germany and from the various agencies that had actually received the materials. Byrnes also warned Dorr that there were problems, particularly in determining what was legitimate war booty and what should be reported as reparations.[21]

Clay took up the issue with the War Department again on January 22, 1947. He repeated the essence of his letter of October 4, 1946, which had produced no effective response in the meantime.[22] Clay was anxious to balance accounts and promote the bizonal self-sufficiency envisaged by the Bevin-Byrnes bizonal fusion agreement, which had gone into effect on January 1, 1947. His determination became clear on January 30, 1947, when he proposed to cut off further FIAT field investigations in Germany, effective on March 31, 1947.[23] Clay eventually got a stoppage, but not on March 31, 1947, and only after he fought off the Commerce Department's efforts in Washington and London to continue the program. The Commerce Department was apparently impressed by what a later writer called "an unparalleled opportunity to cash in on research and discovery paid for by our enemies."[24] Secretary of Commerce Harriman agreed to pay the costs of a continuing European operation from Commerce Department funds, and he assured the War Department that Congress would supply the money despite its economy drive.[25] Clay, pleading lack of space, facilities, and personnel, reported that he would close down the FIAT operation anyway unless ordered not to do so by the War Department.[26] How he was dissuaded is not clear, but the program phased out gradually during the remainder of 1947. Meanwhile, Clay's request for an accounting of the FIAT removals simmered in Washington while the reparations issue boiled in Moscow.

The IARA Assembly in Brussels passed a resolution early in October 1946, deploring the slow rate at which industrial capital equipment was being made available from Germany. Early in 1947 it resolved to address a memorandum to the CFM deputies who were meeting in London, and it requested a hearing for IARA representatives at the CFM in Moscow. The United States, wanting especially to avoid discussion of Clay's reparations suspension, abstained from voting on the IARA protest in October and agreed that a factual report might be made by the IARA to the CFM, but did not favor inviting IARA representatives to the Moscow CFM.[27] They were invited nevertheless, and an effort to give them a hearing produced serious recriminations, as well as statements by Marshall that had the effect of foreclosing whatever possibility there might have been for Clay to get his accounting.

At Moscow, Molotov and Bidault wanted to hear the IARA representatives. Marshall and Bevin did not, and they maneuvered to have the CFM deputies hear them in the first instance. Molotov threw verbal darts. He said his government did "not conceal the fact that it wants reparations from Germany, nor does it conceal the amount which it wants." From statements made by "representatives of the western powers," Molotov said, "one might think that the western powers do not want reparations." But, according to Molotov, they had received gold, German external assets, the German commercial fleet, and German patents and inventions estimated in press reports to be worth more than $10 billion. Furthermore, Molotov concluded, Britain, France, and the United States were taking reparation from current production in the form of coal and timber.[28]

Unlike Byrnes when Molotov demolished the draft-treaty proposal in Paris, Marshall seems to have been prepared for Molotov's thrust. He replied in detail to the charges, even though little progress had been made in Washington on Clay's request for a United States reparations accounting. With respect to German scientific information and patents, Marshall said the United States was publishing in pamphlets all of the information it had obtained and that it was making those pamphlets available "to the rest of the world" at a nominal fee. He said AMTORG, the Soviet purchasing agency in the United States, had been the largest single purchaser. Marshall then read a letter in which John C. Green, the Director of the Department of Commerce's Office of Technical Services, had asked him to make inquiries in Moscow about Russia's scientific and technical removals and about whether the United States might have access to the removed material on terms similar to those prevailing in the United States.[29]

To emphasize and record the minimal reparations taken by the United States in Germany, and to reemphasize his declaration that "we will not follow Mr. Molotov in a retreat from Potsdam to Yalta" on the reparations issue, Marshall released a statement to the press on the United States reparations receipts from Germany. It showed United States reparations receipts to have been less than $275 million in value, broken down as follows: receipts through IARA, valued at $66,666; U.S. direct removals "ordered to further our war effort prior to the Japanese surrender," valued at less than $10 million; ships, valued at $5 million; German external assets, valued between $150 and $250 million; current production, none; and gold, none.[30]

Marshall's publication of United States reparations receipts at the Moscow CFM was to have a deleterious influence on the way Americans treated the issue later, for Marshall had been less than candid. His assertion that the United States was making the scientific and technical knowledge available to the rest of the world skirted the fact that the JCS had established a screening process to sort out the materials it did not want released to American industry or to other nations (except Britain).[31] The $10 million in direct removals by the United States "ordered to further our war effort prior to the Japanese surrender" undoubtedly occurred, but Marshall's statement was innocent of any suggestion that such removals continued after V-J Day and that they had entered "squarely into the commercial field," as Clay put it. Marshall failed also to mention that the United States removed FIAT materials outside the normal reparations channels during 1946, after Clay had suspended reparations deliveries from the American zone.[32] Marshall remained silent on Molotov's charge that German coal and timber were being delivered as current reparations. Bidault had asserted on March 18, 1947, that France had been paying for all products it received from Germany, and that coal in particular had been paid for in dollars. Since Molotov had not challenged Bidault, it probably seemed to Marshall to be the better part of wisdom not to raise the issue once more. Finally, Marshall mentioned only a small portion of the scientific and technical materials the United States had removed under the FIAT program and he made no effort to value them, even though Clay had argued in January 1947 that, whereas the United States made the knowledge available to all others, its own industrial development was advanced to a point where the knowledge was most valuable to the United States.[33]

Marshall promised at Moscow to give an accounting to the CFM and the IARA of the American direct removals "ordered to further our war effort prior to the Japanese surrender." The issue bounced around the Washington bureaucracy after that. Finally, on August 8, 1947, SWNCC approved by "informal action" a policy for evaluating and reporting on materials and equipment removed from Germany. The policy listed ten categories of war matériel that the reporting agencies might *exclude* from their reparations-accounting reports. It provided, further, that any agency that had received war matériel not included in the exclusion lists might appeal to a special ad hoc committee of SWNCC for their exclusion. The SWNCC policy stated, finally, that agencies need not report properties removed to meet military needs during the combat period, properties removed by individuals without authority, and *intangible technical, industrial and scientific data of all types*.[34] What the reporting agencies were to understand intangible data to be was, perhaps mercifully, left to the imagination.

Meanwhile, the Army had been using Clay's requests of October 4, 1946, and January 22, 1947, to get from the State and Commerce Departments an evaluation of the scientific expertise that had been removed from Germany. On August 11, 1947, soon after Clay had pressed his point again during Army Secretary Royall's visit in Berlin, the Army used the SWNCC policy guidance of August 8, 1947, as leverage on the State Department. General Daniel Noce, the Director of the Army's Civil Affairs Division, wrote to Assistant Secretary of State Hilldring, referring to the current program of declaring a value on the reparations removals from Germany. He quoted portions of Clay's previous statements and recommendations, and asked for the State Department's views and for any advice it might offer.[35]

Charles E. Saltzman, a special assistant to the Secretary of State, replied on August 29, 1947, saying the State Department had concluded that the disadvantages of evaluating the FIAT removals for reparations accounting far outweighed the advantages that might accrue. Saltzman noted that Clay and the Army had argued that an American accounting would give Clay political leverage to demand that Russia and France evaluate and declare their current-production and other reparations removals. But the State Department believed it would be safer for the United States to maintain the position that it had received no special benefits from the FIAT removals, since they were being released into the public domain. It believed that to admit now that the United States could evaluate these removals would leave it open to charges from the Soviets that Americans had removed more than they had heretofore reported. Saltzman said Molotov had made such charges *ad hominem* in Moscow in the spring of 1947. What emerges rather strikingly is the fact that Marshall's less than candid responses to Molotov's charges at the Moscow CFM made it virtually impossible to declare the values, except at the risk of great embarrassment to Marshall—and perhaps at the risk of even greater embarrassment to the State Department functionaries who had advised him and prepared his statements in Moscow. Saltzman's statement continued: the State Department could not agree with Clay's argument that the United States derived greatest benefit from the FIAT materials because of its higher level of industrialization. One might argue, Saltzman wrote, that the less industrialized countries would receive more benefit than the United States. According to Saltzman, the Army's desire to charge the FIAT materials against the United States share of reparations from Germany raised two serious problems. First, the IARA countries would probably object to having their reparations accounts charged similarly. Second, the American agencies that had benefited from the FIAT removals would not agree to having their budgeted appropriations charged for the FIAT receipts. In short, they did not want to pay for them. As for Clay's argument that the German scientists needed a basis for filing claims in the future for their intellectual contributions, Saltzman said the State Department believed that a future German government could take care of that without a United States evaluation of the materials for reparations.[36]

On September 17, 1947, the War Department sent Clay a copy of Saltzman's letter of August 29, 1947, and it attached some of the correspondence and memoranda that it had accumulated on the issue since Clay's original request of October 4, 1946. Clay replied on October 2: "I have no comment relative to your letter of 17 September. We here and the Department of the Army have been honest in expressing our views; the State Department has taken the responsibility and, there, I am willing for it to rest."[37]

The State Department had assumed many other responsibilities regarding the German economy. In the interests of its policy to rehabilitate the liberated countries, it was in fact requiring the Army to subsidize huge sums of "hidden reparations" to Germany's neighbors.

CHAPTER TWELVE

Hidden Reparations: Coal

HIDDEN REPARATIONS were those items of value taken from Germany over and above the reparations provided for in the Potsdam Agreement and the ACC's level-of-industry and reparations plan of March 26, 1946. As such, they were a fundamental cause of the failure of the ACC to apply the economic principle that Germany would sustain itself without external assistance at about the level of the European average. Hidden reparations did not include the German navy and merchant marine, the gold reserves, the external assets, or the foreign balances seized and confiscated by the victorious powers. Neither did they include the properties returned from Germany to their legitimate owners as restitutions. They did not include the costs incurred as a result of requisitioned housing, office buildings, facilities, and other materials normally considered to be legitimate "occupation costs." Neither did they include the industrial plants, part plants, and equipment that were to be removed in accord with the ACC agreement on Germany's postwar level of industry and standard of living. Hidden reparations did include removals from Germany in the form of labor services; transport services; seaport services; technical and scientific knowledge, processes, and personnel; "restitutions" that were in fact reparations; and various unilateral removals that defy classification, except as loot.

GERMANY'S COAL RESOURCES AFTER 1945

The three major coal-mining regions of Central Europe lay outside the American jurisdiction in Germany. The Silesian coal beds were under the control of the Soviet Union and Poland, the Ruhr was in the British zone, and the Saar was under French control. As early as October 1945, Murphy observed that Eisenhower and Clay presented American views on a balanced German economy forcibly, but that the "power to implement American wishes" on coal production and export had "passed from direct American control." Possessing less than 2 percent of the German coal resources in their own zone, "the Americans were left locally without a single blue chip." The Russians had, in fact, assigned the Silesian coal fields to Poland before the Potsdam Conference, and both countries subsequently regarded those resources as Polish national assets.[1]

Saar coal production went the way Silesian coal production did, so far as the German economy was concerned. France never considered Saar coal to be a German asset after 1945. Bidault informed Byrnes in August 1945 that France wanted German coal as a major reparations item. If, as Byrnes suggested, coal was to be exported from Germany with the requirement that it be paid for in dollars to satisfy the "first-charge" principle, "France would actually obtain no reparation except what she might have been able to seize on the spot." France seized the Saar mines on the spot. In November 1945 the French sought American support for their demand that the Saar mines be regarded as French property. In February 1946 France wanted the ACC to exclude the resources of the Saar as it drew up the level-of-industry and reparations plan, and the French sought British, American, and Russian approval of France's annexation of the Saar. In April Bidault asked the CFM to approve France's proposal that the Saar mines be the property of France. On September 23, 1946, after Byrnes had pledged American support for France's Saar claims (through diplomatic channels, at the Paris CFM, and in his Stuttgart speech), Bidault advised Byrnes that what France wanted was not support for its claims to the Saar, but the Saar itself. Byrnes thereupon repeated his pledges, but cautioned Bidault against taking unilateral action.[2] When it became obvious that France would go ahead anyway, Acheson cabled Murphy early in December 1946, saying that he and Clay might "upon appropriate occasion" inform the French that unilateral action on the Saar was "most unwise and a regrettable precedent."[3] On December 9, 1946, Bidault advised the CFM in New York that France was, in effect, separating the Saar from Germany. Clay protested to Byrnes that France's unilateral action was "another example of French contempt and disregard of" the ACC and a defeat for four-power government. Byrnes admitted that the CFM had not agreed to Bidault's announcement on December 9, 1946, but he said the French interpreted the CFM's failure to protest as assent. In February 1947, after a dispute in Berlin regarding cultural exchanges between the Saar and the rest of Germany, the War Department advised Clay not to make an issue of the Saar, because of Byrnes's previous commitments and pledges and because Germany would be discussed at the Moscow CFM.[4]

The Ruhr, by all measures the heart of Germany's coal-mining and export industry before the war, produced only limited amounts of coal for the ultimate benefit of the German economy between 1945 and 1947. The drastic production cuts caused by wartime destruction and Germany's defeat notwithstanding, Truman's coal directive of July 1945 required German coal exports of 10 million tons in 1945 and an additional 15 million tons by the end of April 1946.[5] Despite British qualms, General Montgomery's protests and resistance, and Ambassador Pauley's frustrations, Truman's coal directive was issued regardless of the consequences it would have in Germany, and without a decision on whether such exports would be charged to commercial accounts or to reparations. In the end, the estimated total tonnage exported under the directive was 8.2 million tons, or slightly less than one-third of the 25-million-ton total.[6]

The French complained regularly about the failure of the ACC to export sufficient coal from Germany to France and to other countries. In October 1945 the French member of the ACC's Fuel Committee demanded a 50 percent increase in German coal exports. He brushed aside a Russian argument that exports be allocated only after the needs of all the zones of occupation had been met, and he reminded his colleagues that France was not bound by the Potsdam formula for German economic unity.* The British were, in fact, ignoring the export targets of the Truman coal directive and simply making sure that German coal consumption was no greater than that of the liberated countries.[7] Unable to get satisfaction in Berlin, the French complained in Washington, apparently having sensed the State Department's inclination to protect the liberated countries from the occupation armies in Germany. In February 1946, for example, the French government protested to the State Department that on January 10, 1946, the United States member of the ACC Economics Directorate had objected to increased German coal exports because German domestic coal requirements were not being met. Presumably recognizing in this an example of the Army's priority for German recovery, Byrnes asked Murphy for a full report of the January 10 meeting and then relayed Murphy's reply to the French ambassador personally. But before Byrnes had gotten back to Ambassador Bonnet,

---

* USPOLAD to SecState, Oct. 31, 1945, *FRUS*, 1945, III, 1537. The State Department's reaction to the French position (in *ibid.*, note 96) is interesting. State agreed in principle with the implications of the Russian position that goods should move freely between the zones, but in practice the State Department said it could not approve shipment of goods in short supply, such as coal, unless the Russians permitted free movement of goods out of their zone. See also Murphy to SecState, Dec. 11, 1945, *ibid.*, 858.

the French had protested again, on March 8, 1946. Then, on March 14—encouraged by Byrnes's assurances to Bonnet that he too wanted to maximize German coal exports—the French Embassy asked "that the United States representative on the Coordinating Committee [Clay] *be instructed* to consider the needs of the French economy when coal was discussed at the Coordinating Committee meeting scheduled for March 18."[8]

France's stake in German coal was extremely high, and the United States government was determined to do what it could to satisfy France. The two conditions may be illustrated from the records of the French-American financial negotiations which Léon Blum began informally in Washington on March 19, 1946. Blum outlined France's coal needs and expressed France's hopes to fill those needs from Germany. France could import coal from the United States, Blum said, "but it is expensive to pay for in dollars and ship in US vessels."[9] Jean Monnet, the Commissioner General of France's postwar Reequipment and Modernization Plan, and French technical experts filled in the details of France's needs and recovery plans in subsequent meetings: France planned to increase her industrial production by 1950 to about 150 percent of the 1938 level. Steel production would be at 12 million tons, roughly double the prewar levels; electric power at 200 percent of 1938; transport industries at 150 percent of 1938; the mechanical industry at 160 percent of 1938; and a "sizeable" machine-tool industry would be built. French coal production, on the other hand, would be less than 120 percent of the 1938 level.[10] The French had, in fact, outlined a long-range economic development program for France to absorb Germany's industrial base which the ACC's level-of-industry and reparations plan of March 26, 1946, had assumed would have to be transferred out of Germany. The French plan also dovetailed neatly with the State Department's policy to restore France as a major power, as the bulwark of democracy on the continent of Europe.

The French plan (which eventually became the "Monnet Plan") seemed irresistible in Washington. E. M. Bernstein, a former "Morgenthau planner" who had criticized the Army while he served in Germany, was convinced that "the European industrial needs that used to be met by Germany will have to be filled by someone, probably by France and the U.K. if Germany is not to meet them again." Clayton thought that "coal is such a critical item that it must be assumed that the French will get the coal they need." Later, in the continuing deliberations on the French loan request, Secretary of the Treasury Fred M. Vinson saw great financial wisdom in letting

France obtain her coal imports from the Ruhr, where, he said, coal cost $10 per ton less than in the United States. (Actually, under existing practice the delivered price to France was about $14 per ton less, that figure being the difference between $8 per ton, at which the British billed the French after July 1946, and $22 per ton, at which American coal was being landed at Le Havre.) Clayton agreed with Vinson and said most of the 20 million tons France would need during the period of the loan "would have to come from the Ruhr."[11]

Charles P. Kindleberger, who was in the State Department in 1946, wrote later that underpriced coal from Germany was hardly more than an academic problem in Washington at the time. "German imports were paid for largely by the United States, which was also helping to support a number of Germany's customers for coal. If the price had been raised, it might have earned more for the United States in Germany, but cost us more in other countries."[12] But the problem of underpriced German export coal was academic for neither the American Army nor the British. In July 1945 Truman had ordered the Army to assume responsibility for procurement and financing in Germany to serve the purposes of the United States government. In part to overcome the Army's original refusal to assume such responsibility, and in part based on principle, on Roosevelt's earlier orders, and on prior policy decisions, the State Department reiterated its policy to make imports a first charge on Germany's capacity to pay. As Clayton had explained it to McCloy, "Imports into Germany should be a first charge on all German exports from current production or stocks on hand," and any claims for reimbursement of interim outlays by the Army "should rank above reparation."[13] But the State Department's policy to restore the liberated countries first, particularly its policy to restore France, caused a gradual erosion of the commitments it had made to the Army and the British during discussions of the coal directive in the summer of 1945. Both the British and the American Army feared the economic and financial consequences of such erosion—for the disease and unrest it foreshadowed in Germany and for the increased costs of the occupation it promised under existing pricing and payments practices.

German Coal and the British

The British, heeding General Montgomery's warnings of dire consequences in Germany and mindful of the costs to the British government, had released Montgomery from the absolute quotas of Truman's coal directive in November 1945. In March 1946, apparently believing they could gain economic advantage by managing their own coal exports from the Ruhr, the British wanted to terminate a Clay-Robertson informal agreement of September 1945, according to which the two zones pooled their export receipts to pay for necessary imports. The Americans would not agree to such termination, however. In June 1946 the British considered— then shelved—a decision to establish "a complete moratorium on coal exports from the Ruhr."[14] The British may have refrained from pressing the issue at the time because they expected the American loan being negotiated for France to provide France with sufficient funds to pay for Ruhr coal. Significantly, after the loan to France had been approved, American, British, and French negotiators met informally in Paris between July 4 and 8, 1946, and reached an agreement that all coal exports from Germany (including those previously delivered under quantitative receipts) would be promptly billed and the bills would be presented for payment. The agreement also provided that no further coal shipments would be made to countries that refused to pay or delayed payments unreasonably. The coal that the British had been delivering at the German border against quantitative receipts since the summer of 1945 would now be billed to the receiving countries at no less than 80 percent of the coal's value—actually at slightly more than one-third of the market price for American coal in Europe, and at approximately half the price that Polish and British coal sold for in Europe in the immediate postwar period.[15] Britain's financial stress was hardly relieved by that, and Bevin's action at the CFM in July is evidence of Britain's continuing frustration.

After Molotov summarily rejected a British proposal for export-import decisions regarding all of Germany, Bevin threatened on July 11, 1946, that the British would go it alone in their zone. He said that the British were "obliged to organize the British Zone" and "to produce for export in order to reduce the burden on the British taxpayer."[16] Long since aware of the Army's desire to reduce costs to the American taxpayer, fully aware of the paucity of the resources in the American zone to accomplish the task, conscious of the Army's continuing desire to shift its financial responsibilities for the occupation to the State Department, and mindful of the larger European program envisioned by his own Department, Byrnes headed the British off. He responded to the British threat—in the "hope that we can avoid the situation outlined by Mr. Bevin"—by inviting the other occupation powers to join their zones with the American zone in economic unity. Britain's eventual decision to accept Byrnes's invitation—a decision Bevin did not make immediately, as Byrnes and others would have one believe— was apparently influenced by American assurances that the two zones could do better what the British threatened to do alone. The Americans could provide the dollars needed by Germany's customers to pay for the exports the British wanted to produce and sell. But the time for the Marshall Plan had not yet arrived, and the Army and the British were to be saddled with heavy financial and supply burdens in Germany for a time longer.

German Coal and the Army

During the CORC meeting of March 18, 1946—the meeting for which France had asked the State Department to instruct Clay "to consider the needs of the French economy" for coal—Clay denied sharply the French allegation that coal allocations "excessively favored domestic German needs at [the] expense of exports." Among other things, Clay said, the United States "contemplated expenditures of 200 million dollars" to bring food into Germany and that "no payments for exports" had been made in dollars. Two days later McNarney repeated Clay's arguments in the ACC and reminded his colleagues that the United States "had no intention either directly or indirectly of financing reparations and restitution from Germany."[17] But that is precisely what the United States was doing.

Murphy, in the message in which he referred to "French sabotage of the Potsdam decision," warned Washington on April 4, 1946, that the stalemate in Berlin on central administrations would, "in the absence of a substantial volume of exports paid for in dollars," inevitably result in the United States financing of reparations, "a proposition" that it had "vigorously opposed" at Potsdam.[18] Nevertheless, the War Department advised Clay on April 26, 1946, that the "continued discussion of the coal problem" between the French and the State Department in Washington "is making it evident to this office that some formal revision of coal allocation policy will be insisted upon by the State Department." As expected, Clayton said on May 6, 1946, that France would have to import about 20 million tons of coal from the Ruhr.[19]

In July and August 1946, while underpriced, unbilled, and unpaid coal and other "exports" continued to cross the German borders, Clay commented on three occasions on the significance of current American policy and practice in Germany. On July 12, 1946, the Paris CFM approved a French resolution to have the ACC appoint a committee of experts and instruct them to make recommendations to increase German coal production and to recommend proper apportionment of German coal "as between domestic consumption and exports."[20] Recognizing in the resolution the fruits of the Franco-American discussions in Washington, about which the War Department had warned him in April, Clay responded on July 16, 1946: To satisfy current demands for exports and domestic needs in Germany, German coal production would have to be brought back approximately to prewar levels as quickly as possible. To accomplish that, it would be necessary to increase German production in other industries, including steel, on which the coal industry depended. To do the latter, German coal exports would have to be reduced—at least temporarily—because there was little coal for export anywhere in the world, and because the occupation powers could not afford to sell German coal abroad cheaply and buy foreign coal dearly without multiplying their costs in Germany. Although he did not say so precisely, Clay's observations were, in reality, arguments for an upward revision of the level-of-industry plan of March 26, 1946, if current demands on the German economy were to be met and satisfied.[21] Upward revision of the level of industry naturally also meant downward revision of the reparations plan, since under the latter reparations were to be in the form of residues.

Three days later, though not addressing himself to the coal problem specifically, Clay bore down on the reparations issue directly and identified the fundamental problem created by hidden reparations. "The reparations payments to be exacted from Germany will leave it with a minimum economy. If this reparations program is to be carried further to give commercial advantages to other nations ... then the reparations program must be revised. We cannot in conscience exact reparations as now contemplated and further limit the German economy in fields not contemplated in the reparations program."[22]

In August 1946 Clay told State Department visitors in Berlin that the Army was being pushed and pulled between two conflicting policies. Basic American policy for Germany, such as JCS 1067 and the Potsdam Agreement, provided for the first-charge principle. But, Clay continued, American policy for the liberated countries assigned to them first priority for recovery and rehabilitation at the expense of Germany. The result was "that the deficit incurred by the US for civilian supply in Germany is ascribed in the mind of US public to feeding the enemy," whereas many of the Army's costs were for non-German purposes; for recovery and rehabilitation of the liberated countries.[23]

Clay's comments and observations suggest at least three possible approaches—or their combination—that would have satisfied the Army (and probably the British) at the time: (1) an upward revision of the German level of industry, which would have provided production sufficient to meet the demands of Germany's neighbors and the needs of the German domestic economy, (2) a reduction in reparations removals, which would have automatically left a greater production base in Germany, and (3) a realistic accounting, pricing, and payments program, which would have assigned costs, profits, and losses where they occurred—rather than exclusively to the German economy (and thus ultimately to the American and British military governments).

The Army and the British thought the Bevin-Byrnes bizonal fusion agreement of December 2, 1946, solved some of their problems. The agreement provided that the two zones would develop a three-year plan designed to achieve self-sufficiency in the British-American combined zones by 1949. Until self-sufficiency would be achieved, the governments agreed to defray the costs of necessary outlays in Germany from appropriated funds. Although the published agreement nowhere said so, the Army understood (and the British apparently did too) that German exports would henceforth be delivered on a cash basis and in strict conformity with the principle that imports were a first charge on Germany's proceeds from exports.[24] As a matter of fact, the British wanted to bill France for German exports *retroactive* to the date France had rejected the invitation to zonal fusion, but the final Bevin-Byrnes agreement rested on the assumption that for the time being the bizonal authorities would not attempt to use the proceeds from bizonal exports to recover previous outlays. The previous outlays were, in fact, covered by funds supplied to the bizone by the governments themselves to give the Joint Export-Import Agency its initial grant of working capital.[25] The agreement nevertheless projected economic self-sufficiency (essentially a balance of imports and exports) for the two zones by 1949, and the bizonal authorities used that projection as a policy basis for demanding that bizonal exports were to be paid for in dollars, on a cash basis, beginning in January 1947. The Army-British understanding was false—or the implied agreement was fragile. The bizonal cash-payment policy caused trouble from the beginning. The French protested immediately, and they did so on behalf of the other liberated countries as well.[26] Similar protests came from Czecho-slovakia and other countries. Faced with such protests, the State Department ordered the Army (and thus required the British) to abandon the cash-payment and first-charge principles in the interests of using the German economy to advance its program of rehabilitation in other countries.

Policy on German coal exports to Austria may be used to illustrate the State Department's position as well as the error of the Army's assumption that the bizonal fusion agreement provided a basis for establishing a self-sustaining economy in the two zones. As early as July 1946, the State Department advised the Army that it would have to abandon the policy that required Austria to pay for all imports and that it would have to forgo implementation of the policy that American advances to pay for Austrian imports would be carried as a first charge against the proceeds of Austria's exports. According to the State Department, Austria had received a United States credit of $10 million to purchase surplus property, and the Export-Import Bank was considering another Austrian loan request. The State Department believed "that repayment of loans and credits of this type should have priority over reimbursement for past imports furnished by the oc-cupying powers in the period of military supply responsibility."[27] In other words, the Army's claims on Austria were simply assigned a lower-than-first-charge priority. In November 1946, as it prepared for the financial dis-cussions leading to bizonal fusion, OMGUS reported to the War Depart-ment that Austria owed Germany (actually the British and American military governments) $21 million for coal exports and that "these unpaid bills in fact constitute a German subsidy of [the] Austrian economy."[28] In January 1947, when the cash-payment policy of the bizonal authorities threatened to wipe out the "German subsidy of [the] Austrian economy," when the full consequences of the Army's (and Britain's) interpretation of the bizonal fusion agreement began to emerge clearly, the War Depart-ment wired Clay not to implement the bizonal cash-payments policy with respect to Austria. Clay cabled on January 28, 1947, noting that his under-standing of the bizonal fusion negotiations in Washington (in which he had participated) was that credits to Austria and others would not be con-tinued, because such credits nullified the bizonal fusion agreement. Clay asked for verification of his understanding of the War Department's new instructions: OMGUS was to continue to sell coal to Austria on credit under the presumption that at some time in the future sufficient dollar funds would be made available to Austria to pay for the coal. The new instructions, Clay emphasized, would mean that American and British appropriations would be forthcoming soon to make it possible for Austria to purchase coal for cash. "When dollar and sterling funds are made available to Austria, it is assumed here that the Austrian government will be advised that coal payments represent a first charge."[29]

Some of the funds in question—or rather, the American share of those funds not written off in a bizonal-Austrian coal–electric power exchange-agreement of July 1947—were eventually made available to Austria from appropriations under U.S. Public Law 84, the so-called Interim-Aid Law of 1947.[30] The remaining funds were apparently made available from Marshall Plan funds. In any case, there is little basis for questioning the assumption that there is a direct and fundamental linkage between the American decisions on interim aid and the Marshall Plan and the determination to solve the problem of "hidden reparations" from Germany.

The decisions in Washington to assign lower priorities to the Army's right to recover current and prior financial outlays that it furnished to Austria until the interim-aid and Marshall Plan funds came to the rescue were paralleled by decisions regarding Germany. In the case of Germany, however, there were complicating factors: the loans and credits that were to have priority over the Army's recovery rights under the first-charge principle were not made to Germany (as they had been to Austria) but, in the first instance, to Britain as a joint occupying power and only in the second instance to France and others—the recipients of German coal (and other) exports. The recipients of American loans and credits—who were also the recipients and beneficiaries of Germany's exports—were not to be pressed by the Army in Germany to balance their accounts with Germany to the detriment of their ability to repay the loans and credits they received directly from the United States. In that context, the significance of a little-known fact becomes manifest: until October 1947 the monthly statistical reports published by OMGUS for the American zone and the bizone excluded valuations of German exports of "coal, timber, and invisibles."[31] After that they were listed and valued, apparently on the assumption that they could now be regarded as a credit to the German economy, which would be paid in the future when funds were made available under interim-aid legislation or the Marshall Plan. A policy decision to make such funds available, either directly to Germany or to the recipients of Germany's exports, had been hammered out by the Army and the State Department early in July 1947, in negotiations conducted frantically and hectically at several levels of authority and with little coordination between the levels.[32] Once the decision was reached, it was hastily "grafted" onto the new JCS policy directive on Germany which was sent to Clay on July 11, 1947, and released to the press on July 15, 1947. The graft is plain to see, but until the records upon which this study is based became available, the significance of its glaring inconsistency with other parts of the directive escaped my attention and apparently that of others as well. In one section the JCS directive 1779 states categorically that the United States government does not "agree to finance the payment of reparation by Germany to other United Nations by increasing its financial outlay in Germany or by postponing the achievement of a self-sustaining German economy." That had been policy since 1945, though it was—as a rule—not in accord with practices on coal and other things. The graft, which appears somewhat later in the text of the directive, said:

In cases where the restoration of normal international commercial relations between Germany and the rest of Europe would involve an increase of U.S. dollar expenditures for the government of Germany, or a delay in the attainment of a self-supporting German economy at an appropriate standard of living, funds for German expenditures shall be increased, or the German economy compensated through provision by the U.S. of sufficient relief monies to the country or countries so benefitted to enable them to pay Germany.[33]

That was the promise of the Marshall Plan.

In October 1947 OMGUS reported for the first time on the value of Germany's coal, timber, and invisible exports. The report estimated coal and timber exports alone to have been about 75 percent of Germany's exports in 1947. For October 1947 it reported coal, timber, and invisibles to have been 85 percent of the total exports of the combined British and American zones. The remaining 15 percent were exports of so-called contract items: textiles, toys, cameras, ceramics, musical instruments, and similar things. Few of the latter had been available for export under contract in 1945 and 1946.[34] Therefore, if figures were available for the earlier period, they would evidently show an even larger percentage of Germany's total exports to have been in the form of coal, timber, and invisibles. The significance of this is that *more than* 75 percent of Germany's exports between 1945 and October 1947 were not being paid for. They appeared to be commercial exports, but they were, in fact, "hidden reparations" that Germany was required to pay over and above the reparations provided for in the Potsdam Agreement and the level-of-industry plan.

Coal and timber exports were but two forms of "hidden reparations" that Germany was required to pay. Two other forms—transit and seaport services —may serve as evidence that "hidden reparations" were the rule, rather than the exception.

CHAPTER THIRTEEN

Hidden Reparations: Transit and Seaport Services

G ERMANY PROVIDED important water and land transit services for her neighbors before and after the war. Wartime destruction, the requisition of transit services and equipment by the occupation forces, and the allied removals of equipment, locomotives, freight cars, and rails after Germany's surrender greatly reduced Germany's ability to provide these services. The occupation powers found it to be virtually impossible to collect payment or accumulate foreign credits for even those reduced services, which were "current production" so far as the German economy was concerned. Though Austria, Italy, or the United Nations Relief and Rehabilitation Administration (UNRRA) might have served as case examples, I have chosen to illustrate the practices and the problems from the examples provided by Czechoslovakia, Belgium, and the Netherlands.

TRANSIT SERVICES FOR CZECHOSLOVAKIA

Despite the failure of the ACC to agree on a four-power export-import plan, the American occupation authorities tried to implement in their zone the ACC's policy that German exports must be paid for.[1] Czechoslovakia protested early against that policy. It tried to get the IARA in Brussels to charge the costs of German transit services for the benefit of Czechoslovakia to reparations.[2] The Czechs argued that they needed German transit services for goods shipped to and from France, for goods flowing through the ports of Rotterdam and Antwerp, and for goods flowing through the ports of Hamburg and Bremen. They insisted that the ACC's cash-payment policy would delay Czechoslovakia's recovery and rehabilitation, and on May 16, 1946, Czechoslovakia appealed to the State Department for a ruling that the charges for transit through the American zone would be set off against the amount Germany would pay to Czechoslovakia in reparations.[3]

Czechoslovakia's case required the State Department to choose between the policy of rehabilitating the liberated countries first and the policy that the proceeds from current German exports would be used in the first instance to pay for imports. Before making a decision, the State Department cabled Berlin and Prague to ask how much money was involved. It also cabled Russell H. Dorr in Brussels to ask what Czechoslovakia was doing about the matter in the IARA. Dorr reported that the Czechs had raised the issue in the IARA Assembly, but that the British and the Americans had been resisting effectively, "at least for the time being." Dorr noted, however, that Yugoslavia was also trying a similar tactic. Yugoslavia wanted the IARA to charge to the Yugoslav reparations account the costs of the teams Yugoslavia had in Germany to inspect reparations plants. The State Department's first decision was to remain firmly in favor of its first-charge policy, and it advised the Army in August 1946 that the United States position was that export proceeds from German current production of goods and services were to be used in the first instance to pay for imports.[4] In October 1946, after Byrnes had cancelled an approved Export-Import Bank loan for Czechoslovakia, the State Department cabled Dorr to confirm his instructions to oppose Czechoslovakia's efforts to convert the costs of transit services in Germany to reparations.[5] But in February 1947 the State Department began to have second thoughts. In fact, the consequences of actions taken by the British and American military governments impelled the State Department to reconsider its position.

Under the Bevin-Byrnes bizonal fusion agreement of December 2, 1946, British and American officials in Germany negotiated formal trade agreements with fourteen countries by October 1947.[6] The negotiations with Czechoslovakia broke down in February 1947. The bizonal officials insisted on a payments agreement making the German transit services payable in dollars on demand. The Czechs wanted to pay in sterling as well, and they reserved the right to present a claim to have the entire transit account (which obviously had not been paid) charged as reparations. The American and British negotiators for the bizone resisted the sterling-payment issue; they said they could not accept an agreement containing the Czech reservation on reparations, and they threatened to discontinue the services unless some form of payments agreement could be worked out. Clay reported the impasse to the War Department, assuring the Department that he did not intend to cut off the services arbitrarily. What he wanted, he said, was "government level" recognition of the dollar-payment principle.[7]

The Czechs, apparently believing that Clay had negotiated under instructions from Washington, appealed to the State Department. Perhaps they simply wanted to have him overruled, for they apparently told the State Department that Clay had threatened to suspend the transit services on February 15, 1947.[8] The State Department advised the Czech Embassy in Washington that Clay would not, in fact, suspend the Czech traffic through the American zone of Germany. At the same time, the War Department cabled Clay that the State Department believed it was in the interests of the United States to encourage Czech trade and economic relations with the West and that it feared political repercussions if Clay stopped Czech traffic through Germany. Although transit services could not be charged to reparations, the War Department said, OMGUS should nevertheless make every effort to reach an acceptable agreement with Czechoslovakia. It urged Clay to consider making bizonal purchases in Czechoslovakia; in effect, to consider a bilateral offset trade agreement regardless of the first-charge principle.[9]

Early in March 1947 OMGUS curtailed Czech transit services in Germany, claiming as the reason congested storage facilities in Bremen and other technical problems, but apparently not without hope of gaining Washington's recognition of dollar payments and the first-charge principle. In response the Czech military mission in Berlin threatened to suspend all Czech coal shipments to Germany, and a full-scale incident was in the making. OMGUS advised the War Department that—after various offsets and payments had been calculated—the Czechs owed the United States zone of Germany approximately $2 million as of March 1, 1947. Murphy advised the State Department that the Czechs were using every channel and every pressure to settle the transit services account in a way that would eventually require greater expenditures of United States funds in the American zone of Germany. If the Czechs were permitted to reduce their dollar payments to Germany, Murphy warned, the result would be an indirect subsidy of the Czechoslovakian economy at the expense of the American taxpayer. If the State and War Departments wanted to do that as a matter of policy, Murphy said, they should also be prepared to provide budgeted funds to implement the policy. The belief that the charges could be squeezed out of the bankrupt German economy was an illusion.[10]

Acheson's reply to Murphy described some of the factors and pressures that pushed the State Department ever closer to the solution that later became known as the Marshall Plan. Acheson thought the Czechs might turn the technical problem into a political and diplomatic issue if no agreement could be reached, and he implied that they would seek Russian support. According to Acheson, Czechoslovakia had a serious foreign-exchange problem and it was especially short on dollar resources. The State Department agreed in principle that the transit issue should not be settled to provide a subsidy to the Czechs through the German economy. On the other hand, there were political reasons for reaching a settlement satisfactory to Czechoslovakia, one being that the Czechs should continue to trade with the West through the American and British zones of Germany rather than shift their main trade channels to East Germany and Poland. In short, the State Department wanted to bring the Czechoslovakia-bizone trade talks to a successful conclusion, and it outlined the terms for an agreement that was negotiated in Prague late in July 1947.[11] The agreement provided for offset accounts for trade, goods, and services, and for periodic clearances by payments in dollars or sterling at the choice of the creditor. According to OMGUS, "the system of 'offset payments' facilitates payments for trade, as a minimum demand is placed upon the foreign countries for hard currency as payments for the net balance."[12] Meanwhile, the decision had been made in Washington that commercial relations between Germany and the rest of Europe that increased American expenditures or delayed a self-supporting German economy at a suitable standard of living would be subsidized by funds appropriated to the Army for use in Germany or by "relief monies" to the countries that needed to buy German goods and services.[13] The benefit Czechoslovakia was to draw from that policy decision was determined, in the end, by its failure to participate in the Marshall Plan.

THE NORTH SEA PORTS AND THE GERMAN ECONOMY

For financial and other reasons, the military authorities in Germany preferred to ship military and civilian supplies for their German operation through the ports of Bremen-Bremerhaven (American zone) and Hamburg (British zone). In May 1946 the Netherlands and Belgian governments, supported by France, asked the State Department to consider diverting the traffic to the ports of Antwerp and Rotterdam. At the request of the State Department, the War Department cabled USFET, the Army headquarters in Europe, asking for comment and a recommendation. USFET replied that the traffic's diversion would increase administrative problems and reduce the military's ability to safeguard the goods while in transit. Furthermore, it would cause trained personnel shortages unless the Bremerhaven-Bremen operation were shut down in the American zone. Finally, USFET noted, diversion would increase the cost of the occupation to the

American economy by approximately the amount the German economy was required to absorb in Belgian and Dutch port fees, transfer fees, and the like. In short, USFET preferred not to make the shift.[14]

USFET's objections notwithstanding, the State Department pressed the case for Belgium and the Netherlands. The Army advised Clay on July 2, 1946, that the State Department understood that diversion of traffic to Antwerp and Rotterdam would increase dollar costs and administrative problems, but it believed that "important considerations of foreign policy" made it "necessary to explore all practicable means to use Rotterdam and Antwerp for imports and exports from Germany."[15] Despite Clay's protests that American policy did not require him to provide commercial advantages to other countries at the expense of a minimum German economy, negotiations with the Dutch and the Belgians were the upshot.[16] During the negotiations both the Dutch and the Belgians made clear their desire for a revival of the German economy—a desire Murphy had reported to Matthews as early as May 1946, when he expressed surprise at the "reasonableness" of the Dutch and apparent satisfaction that they were concerned about "French extremism regarding the German problem." The negotiations were hung up, however, on the unwillingness of the Americans to divert traffic if additional dollar costs would result for the Army. Clay cabled on October 10, 1946, that he would continue to negotiate, provided that "all dollar costs for both imports and exports involved in the use of Rotterdam and Antwerp above present costs via Bremen" would be assumed by the Netherlands and Belgium.[17]

No agreement could be reached on Clay's terms, and the War Department supported Clay until May 1947. On May 1, 1947, SWNCC—perhaps reflecting the broader economic studies it had undertaken at Acheson's request in March—decided against the Army and in favor of the State Department's position. The War Department informed Clay on May 19, 1947, that "because of overriding political considerations" it would now agree to route portions of the supplies for Germany through Rotterdam and Antwerp.[18] Clay warned that any agreement acceptable to Belgium and the Netherlands would increase United States costs. He estimated that the Dutch and the Belgians would realize a net annual credit balance of about $5 million and that the German economy would lose an equivalent amount in revenues that it could otherwise apply to the payment of food and other exports. Given Germany's financial situation, the $5 million loss would inevitably fall back upon the British and American military governments—unless, of course, the latter were ready to reduce German food and other imports to inhumane and dangerous levels. Clay said he needed to know whether allied financial advances and credits could be carried as a charge against the German economy for future payment. If they could, Clay also needed to know whether the Dutch and the Belgian claims would have equality with the American and British claims against the German economy for essential imports. In other words, Clay wanted a verification of the first-charge principle, which he thought the State Department was prepared to abandon in this case. Clay agreed to negotiate whatever concessions Washington wanted him to make, but he would do so only under specific instructions, since it was a matter of United States–Belgian–Dutch relations rather than an internal German question.[19]

Washington's instructions to Clay are significant for their content and for their reflection of the discussions and decisions occurring in Washington regarding the German level of industry, bizonal rehabilitation, and the Marshall Plan. The Dutch and the Belgians had publicly stated their support for a revived German economy. Marshall had thrown the European recovery question to the Europeans for resolution. Short of a miracle, which no one expected, France would be difficult regarding German economic recovery. The Belgians and the Dutch might, therefore, help to swing European opinion to the side of the Americans. They might even help to bring France around. In any case, the War Department advised Clay—redundantly—that negotiations should begin as soon as possible, that further delay would have unfavorable results, and that delay should be avoided. Furthermore, if the Netherlands and Belgium would accept deferred settlement of their net credits, Washington would agree to give their claims against Germany equal priority with those of the United States and Britain for essential imports.

Clay balked, nevertheless—probably not because of the issue, but in principle. As I shall discuss more fully later, Clay had recently been dissuaded—by Eisenhower and others—from resigning in outrage at the State Department's orders to withhold publication of the bizonal level-of-industry plan and at Marshall's concessions to France, which Clay had read about in the Paris press. He rejected a draft agreement that would have given the Belgians and the Dutch a credit of $1 per ton for all goods shipped through Antwerp and Rotterdam to Germany, or about $1.7 million per year. Invoking a policy statement contained in JCS directive 1779 and relying on an interpretation he had received from the War Department

Clay argued that he was not obligated to enter into any agreements in Berlin that would increase costs in appropriated funds. Clay's instructions from the War Department stated clearly that decisions on such agreements were to be bucked back to Washington, where decisions would be made by the Committee of Three (the Secretaries of Navy, State, and War).[20]

Several "teams" went into action after that. Under Secretary of State Clayton, Ambassador Caffery, and Ambassador Lewis W. Douglas—meeting in Paris to further the Marshall planning—took up the issue in August. Caffery warned that the sixteen nations making up the Committee of European Economic Cooperation (CEEC), which drafted the Marshall Plan, were watching the seaports negotiations carefully for an indication of how far the United States was prepared to go to make the European recovery plan a success.[21] In September 1947 the War Department cabled Clay that Washington wanted negotiations with the Belgians and the Dutch to resume and instructed him to proceed with the least delay practical. The Low Countries were to be offered whatever conditions were necessary to achieve an agreement, and American negotiators were to refrain from driving such a hard bargain that the benefits of the agreement would be reduced by Belgian and Dutch dissatisfaction. OMGUS would be authorized to spend Government Aid and Relief for Occupied Areas (GARIO) funds sufficient to cover its outlays for the benefit of the Dutch and Belgians. Clay, now at loggerheads with the State Department after it took the level-of-industry plan negotiations out of his hands, resisted further. He quoted again his directive and instructions from the War Department and—in effect—said the decision to increase costs in Germany would have to be made in Washington, not in Berlin.[22]

The President's Committee on Foreign Aid (the Harriman Committee) entered the negotiations, and Robert Lovett conferred for the State Department with the Netherlands and Belgian ambassadors in Washington.[23] The problem was eventually resolved, I know not when or how. A memorandum of December 9, 1948, from Clay's Economics Adviser to the War Department referred to a gentlemen's agreement and noted that OMGUS had been scheduling a substantial volume of traffic through Antwerp and Rotterdam.[24]

The value of Germany's "hidden reparations" in coal, timber, and invisibles for 1945, 1946, and most of 1947 was never shown in the official statements purporting to be analyses of the German economy under the occupation and of Germany's capacity to pay its own way. Neither did such exports appear as offsets in the calculations designed to show Germany's export-import deficits. This permits the conclusion that the *actual* costs of the German occupation to the British and American taxpayers were much smaller than those to be found in the heavily inflated figures that circulated publicly and in the Congress at the time. Stated differently, the funds appropriated by the British and American governments from their public treasuries for use by their occupation forces in Germany carried a heavy override of costs not ultimately intended to benefit Germans, Germany, or the German economy. They were intended to benefit the liberated countries.

From 1945 onward, Germany's exports of coal, timber, and invisibles (85 percent of the total exports in October 1947, for example) were, in a sense, reparations from current production that were being underwritten by the British and American governments through the occupation forces in Germany. They were, however, never classified as reparations and they have not been regarded as such by historians. In part, that was due to the fact that Americans had said so often that they objected in principle to reparations from current production. In part, it was because Americans wanted to avoid opening the door to demands from the Soviet Union and other claimants for reparations from current production, even while they supplied them without nomenclature to the liberated countries in the interests of realizing the State Department's vision of what a future Europe should be like. In part, it was because Americans feared that a concession on the principle of current-production reparations would "legitimize" the Soviet corporations in East Germany (the Soviet AGs) and establish trading practices and patterns between Germany and Russia that could not be reversed after reparations had been paid. Furthermore, after Roosevelt, Truman, Byrnes, and a chorus of others had told each other so frequently and emphatically that the United States would never again advance dollars to Germany to help her pay reparations, apparently nobody wanted to admit that the United States was in fact repeating the performance of the 1920's, though not where it involved the Soviet Union and Eastern Europe. Maybe they actually believed what they repeated to themselves and each other. Whatever the truth, Germany's nonreparations exports were now considered to be commercial exports in a strict sense. As Clayton had expressed it in July 1945, "The question of whether these exports shall be charged to the receiving countries on reparations or commercial account will remain in suspense and supplies necessary for production as well as exports will move forward without reference to solution of this problem."[25] German nonreparations exports were simply removed from Germany under the superior orders of the military authorities and charged to the German economy. Under those conditions, the German economy could not function without subsidy, except at a cost in hunger, cold, and human deprivation that the Americans and the British assumed to be excessive—even for a defeated enemy. The charges to the German economy were thus ultimately shifted to the occupation powers that were unwilling to test the limits of human suffering in Germany.

The inherent beauty of the Marshall Plan, to which we may now turn, is that it solved these and other problems. It did so by giving American aid in lieu of the reparations that Germany's neighbors had expected to take directly from Germany. But the spokesmen for the Marshall Plan never discussed these things publicly. They preferred the more popular sport of "laying it on" the Russians and the Communists, as I have shown in a previous chapter.

MARSHALL'S PLAN

CHAPTER FOURTEEN

Marshall's Moscow Decisions on Germany

IN HIS LATER discussions of the Marshall Plan, George Marshall usually traced the plan's origins to certain actions he and British Foreign Secretary Bevin had taken in April 1947, during the Moscow Council of Foreign Ministers. In Moscow, he said on one occasion, "the United States put into effect certain measures susceptible of immediate application" in Germany, "where we have major responsibility as an occupying power."[1] What he never mentioned, apparently, is that he had been pressed by Bevin and the British and that he had been influenced by political developments in the United States. The latter may be considered first.

THE ARMY AND THE HERBERT HOOVER MISSION, 1947

Early in 1946 the Army had abandoned its *formal* efforts to shift responsibility for the civil functions of the occupation to the State Department. Byrnes, it will be recalled, had been adamantly opposed to a State Department takeover, and Truman had made a decision in favor of the State Department. Throughout 1946, as I have shown, the Army tried a variety of approaches to motivate the State Department to break the impasse in Berlin, to bring France around on central agencies and economic unity, to clarify policy and facilitate its implementation, and to alter its extreme emphasis on the rehabilitation of the liberated countries at the expense of the German economy and in disregard of the first-charge principle as well as the agreement at Potsdam to establish a German economy capable of sustaining itself without outside assistance. Meanwhile, the Army continued *informally* to try to get the State Department to plan for assumption of the political functions of military government in Germany. The State Department remained immovable, and when Byrnes returned from his long peace-treaty negotiations in Paris in the fall of 1946, he publicly dismissed the Army's concerns with a flippancy that seems to have been based on ignorance of or disdain for the Army's seriousness. In a press conference on October 31, 1946, Byrnes responded to a reporter's question about possible plans for a State Department takeover in Germany:

It [the takeover proposal] has frequently been made to me by Secretary of War Patterson. I think he mentioned it yesterday. I seldom see him that he does not mention it. There is always the same answer, that I think the State Department is a policy department. I think we have problems of our own and I see no evidence of the ability of the Department to reorganize as an operating department. Therefore, I have never given serious consideration to it. When the Secretary of War has some new headache and comes to me and wants me to take it over, I tell him I have enough of my own. The State Department is not going to do that, certainly if I have anything to do with it for some time to come.[2]

The State Department's responses to the Army's pleas, recommendations, and approaches since 1945 frustrated Secretary of War Patterson. He was aware that Byrnes remained adamantly opposed to a State Department takeover in Germany and was concerned about the Army's image as an administrator of a "failure" in Germany. Clay, Murphy, certain members of Congress, and some journalists reminded him often of the human suffering in Germany, and he was immediately mindful of the political climate in the United States during the Congressional election campaigns of 1946. Accordingly, he turned to Herbert Hoover for help. On election day, 1946, Patterson telegraphed Hoover in New York that "we have some problems on food that I should like very much to discuss with you. If you will let me know when you are coming [to Washington] I want to pay you a visit."[3] The two men met in Washington on Sunday, November 16, 1946, and Hoover agreed tentatively to go to Germany on a special mission for the Army.[4] Patterson assigned his special assistant, Tracy S. Voorhees—a friend of Arthur H. Vandenberg, the incoming chairman of the Senate Foreign Relations Committee—to negotiate the terms of Hoover's prospective mission. Early in December Voorhees talked in New York with Clay and General Hugh Hester, the Director of OMGUS's Food and Agriculture Division, and on December 21, 1946, he met with Hoover to discuss details. The details are significant.

Hoover told Voorhees that he would do what he could to support the Army's efforts to feed the people in the occupied territories. He thought "his principal service of value would be aid in holding the Republican Congress in line so that it will support [the Army's] program." He warned that some members of the Republican Party were determined to have a showdown with the administration on the German occupation. Citing particulars,

Hoover said the Republican members of the Senate committee that was looking into American policies in Germany had been frustrated by the administration's resistance to the committee's investigations. They were incensed by the decision of the Democratic Party members to release a report prematurely, a report that Hoover said gave little attention to things other than the love life of the occupation soldier. According to Voorhees, Hoover was certain that "as soon as Congress organizes and these men come into a majority on the Committee, they will immediately make an investigation on the spot in Germany." Such an investigation, Hoover predicted, would "result in an antagonistic report as to all policies," and it would be critical of the War Department, but even more critical of the State Department. Hoover thought he might be able to influence the Senate's investigation and final report by going to Germany as a special representative of the President, not simply as an expert on food problems but with a mandate to look into a broad range of policies, issues, and problems. Some of the issues that interested Hoover were Germany's confiscated liquid assets, reparations, the size of the American military presence in Europe, France's "sit-down strike" in Berlin, Britain's inclination to introduce socialism in the British zone, and the adoption of a realistic economic policy until such time (he thought about two years) as a peace treaty could be drawn up and agreed on. In general, he wanted to explore methods for relieving the burden of the occupation upon American taxpayers.[5]

Patterson's response to Hoover's request for a broad mandate from Truman shows precisely that he knew what was at issue. Assistant Secretary of War Petersen, who knew from firsthand experience how sensitive Byrnes and the State Department had been to the Meader Committee probes, advised Patterson early that Hoover should not be invited to go to Germany to look into matters other than food. On December 24, 1946, after learning of Voorhees's and Patterson's discussions with Hoover, Petersen reaffirmed his original advice, arguing that Hoover was concerned mainly with policy questions that were within the province of the State Department. He warned that Byrnes would object to Hoover's getting into that field, particularly since the CFM deputies for Germany would be meeting in London early in 1947 and the CFM would take up the German question in Moscow in March.[6] Patterson went ahead nevertheless.

Fully aware of Hoover's intentions—and apparently in agreement with them—Patterson wrote Truman on January 16, 1947, about the Army's feeding program and "the central problem" of obtaining "funds through the proposed deficiency appropriation and the 1948 budget to discharge our Government's responsibilities under the bizonal agreement, and to make effective the new and constructive economic plans for which the merger agreement was made." Patterson recommended an authoritative survey of food requirements in the bizonal area of Germany and Austria as a helpful approach, possibly as "an absolute necessity to secure the requisite funds." He said the survey would have to be "by a person whose conclusions would command the confidence of everyone, including the leadership of the new Congress," and he recommended Hoover as an ideal man for the mission. Patterson assured Truman that Secretary of Agriculture Anderson, Secretary of Commerce Harriman, and Under Secretary of State Clayton—all members of the Cabinet Committee on World Food Programs—agreed with his recommendation.[7]

Two days later, on January 18, 1947, Truman invited Hoover to make a survey in Europe and to report to him, particularly on food and funds for food purchases in the areas occupied by American forces in Europe as well as in the British zone of Germany. But Hoover negotiated with Truman for a broader mandate, observing that for his mission to succeed he would have to explore "what further immediate steps are possible to increase their exports and thus their ability to become self-supporting; what possibilities there are of payment otherwise; and when charity can be expected to end. Without some such inclusive report, the Congress and the taxpayer are left without hope."[8]

The State Department, which was preoccupied with preparations for the Moscow CFM and apparently handicapped by the effect of Byrnes's recent resignation and Marshall's unfamiliarity with his new assignment, does not appear to have participated directly in the negotiations between Hoover and Truman. Perhaps to cover himself if the State Department protested later, Patterson sent Truman a low-key warning on January 20, 1947, that the State Department would soon be opening negotiations on the German peace treaty and that Hoover's desire to broaden the scope of the survey would lead to a report that "may introduce confusion on economic matters in Germany."[9] In the end Truman rewrote his invitation on January 20—nevertheless dating it January 18—this time asking Hoover "to undertake this economic mission as to food and its collateral problems, and report to me upon it," and expressing the hope "that methods can be devised which will relieve some of the burdens on the American taxpayer."[10] The War Department subsequently advised McNarney and Clay that Truman's concession "opened the door" somewhat, but that it hoped Hoover's report would become the basis for a nonpartisan program that would gain support and appropriations from the new Congress despite the economy drive its leaders had pledged themselves to.[11]

The details of Hoover's mission need not be repeated here.[12] When he returned to the United States, he made three reports, the third of which was entitled "The Necessary Steps for Promotion of German Exports, so as to Relieve American Taxpayers of the Burdens of Relief and for Economic Recovery of Europe." It contained an analysis of the German economy, a list of American assumptions, a list of economic illusions, and a set of recommendations for a new economic policy toward Germany. Hoover believed that (1) German industry would ultimately have to be freed of its restrictions, except for such control as was needed to prevent a return to militarism, (2) the removal and destruction of factories and plants (except war plants) would have to be stopped, (3) the Soviet AGs would have to be dissolved, and (4) the Ruhr and Rhineland, "the heart of her industrial economy," would have to remain a part of Germany. Until such time as a peace treaty could be made, Hoover recommended that the economy of the combined American and British zones be made self-sustaining. The latter was simply a plea for implementing the Bevin-Byrnes bizonal fusion agreement of December 2, 1946, which—as I have noted previously—the French and Czechs objected to and the State Department had been expressing second thoughts on. According to Hoover, the British and Americans should stop using relief monies for "paying Russian and French reparations." They should bring an end to economic uncertainty caused by dismantling, currency inflation, denazification, and decartelization. They should stop transferring plants for reparations under the level-of-industry concept and use Germany's capital equipment for production, without which "the productivity of Europe cannot be restored." In summary, Hoover concluded, although building a lasting peace should be the primary objective, the British-American combined zones should proceed immediately to "build a self-sustaining economic community."[13]

THE HOOVER REPORTS IN WASHINGTON

The inclination of some State Department functionaries to blast Hoover gave way initially to a recommendation from John D. Hickerson, the deputy director of the European desk, to say nothing publicly, and finally to a decision by Acheson that the State Department's position would be to make no official comments on matters that were subjects of the Secretary of State's discussions at the Moscow CFM.[14] The State Department nevertheless remained alert to Hoover's activities and to the impact of his report in the cabinet, the Congress, and the press.[15] The State Department's major concerns were shared and stated fully by Edwin W. Pauley. Though he was no longer Truman's representative on the Allied Reparations Commission, Pauley wrote Truman that he felt "a duty to respond to Hoover's report nevertheless." He expressed "the deepest kind of apprehension over [Hoover's] proposal for the revival of German heavy industry," and he detailed the dangers of Hoover's other proposals. According to Pauley, Hoover would have the United States abandon both the Potsdam Agreement and the level-of-industry and reparations plan, which were designed to move Europe's major industrial concentrations "to countries that do not have the German record of aggression." Hoover's recommendations required a reversal of policy that would have recovery rather than security the principal goal in Germany.[16] A White House analysis of Hoover's report and Pauley's response concluded that "there must be other approaches to these problems than the revival of a German colossus along the lines suggested by Mr. Hoover." But by that time the dialectic produced by Hoover's report and the Army's initiative was well under way.[17]

After his return from Europe, Hoover maintained close liaison with the Army, even as he and his staff prepared the final reports of the mission. On March 5, 1947—on the same day that Acheson initiated the SWNCC studies that supposedly contributed so much to the Marshall Plan—the War Department reported by teleconference to Clay, Murphy, and General Draper (the head of OMGUS's economics division) in Berlin that on March 4, 1947, Patterson had made a broad policy decision that the War Department would accept and carry out Hoover's recommendations as a whole. Patterson's decision was based on the conviction that Hoover could secure Congressional approval for the Army's 1947 deficiency appropriation and for its 1948 budget request, and that the Army could not "merely select portions of the Hoover Program and reject others, and still obtain the necessary Congressional support."[18]

The political significance of Patterson's decision and of Hoover's cooperation with the Army emerged quickly and clearly. In a memorandum prepared on March 8, 1947, Voorhees summarized current developments for his Army superiors and colleagues. Hoover had already made clear to Congressional leaders that he opposed the State Department's $350 million post-UNRRA aid request for rehabilitation of certain liberated areas and that he supported the Army's deficiency appropriations requests in full. Furthermore, Hoover had "proposed to the State Department that the most effective agency to carry out this food and relief program in liberated areas would be the War Department." According to Voorhees, when the State Department "would have none of this," Hoover suggested that he might propose to the Congress that it be done "not through the State Department, which he thinks is not qualified to do it effectively," but through an official appointed by the President to be responsible "for food and relief in areas other than those for which the War Department is responsible."[19]

Less than two weeks later, Voorhees noted that Patterson had told the House Appropriations Committee that he had approved Hoover's entire report as the basis for the War Department's economic programs and as a foundation for its appropriations requests. According to Voorhees, the Committee had asked Hoover to appear before it, "and I believe it will largely follow his recommendations," depending on "how far we have gone in carrying out the advice Mr. Hoover has given us."[20] Meanwhile, Hoover had also convinced key cabinet members of the wisdom of his recommendations.

On March 20, 1947, Acheson reported to Marshall in Moscow that he had attended a meeting on March 13 in Secretary of Agriculture Anderson's office with Harriman, Patterson, Forrestal, Budget Director James E. Webb, and Hoover. Hoover outlined his proposals and recommendations on Germany, emphasizing his belief that "we should develop German heavy industry," because Germany's exports from light industries would either be insufficient to pay for her needed imports or they would be so extensive as to produce disaster in international trade. In short, German light-industries production and exports would help to flood world markets for such goods and thus have disastrous effects on those less highly developed nations of the world whose very existence depended on light-industries production and exports. Hoover believed German heavy industrial production, particularly of steel and machinery, was vital not only for Germany itself, but for the rest of Europe. According to Acheson, "it was recognized that [the] program suggested by Hoover would produce some complications arising out of competing demands of France for Ruhr coal," but the "Cabinet officers present seemed to concur in the views expressed."[21]

Marshall's regard for the political impact of Hoover's report is evident in the oral instructions he gave George Kennan on the purposes and functions of the Policy Planning Staff. Remembering Marshall's instructions, Kennan told Harry B. Price in February 1953 that when Marshall talked with him on April 29, 1947, "He was deeply perturbed. He said he wanted to take the initiative. 'I don't want to wait,' he said, 'for Congress to beat me over the head.' "[22] Joseph M. Jones, obviously relying on Kennan's memory, described the brief meeting as follows:

It was so clear that the world was falling down around our ears, the Secretary said, that Congress would soon be demanding action, suggesting all kinds of bright and unworkable ideas in an effort to force the Department's hand. This would put the government on the defensive, and that was inadmissible. The Secretary said he therefore wanted to take the offensive himself. Within ten days or two weeks he wanted from Kennan a paper containing an analysis of the problem of European reconstruction and recommendations for action.

At the end of their brief talk, Kennan asked the Secretary if there were any other instructions he wished to give him. Marshall's reply was: "Avoid trivia."[23]

Kennan's mandate was not as open-ended as he later told Price and Jones it was. Marshall had made concessions to Bevin in Moscow—concessions that provided leverage for the kind of program the Army, Hoover, and the Congress favored.

BEVIN, THE BRITISH, AND MARSHALL AT MOSCOW

The British had been unhappy with Truman's coal directive of 1945, and they tried several times to get out from under the financial burdens it imposed upon them. They had objected to administrative extension of the coal directive's purposes after April 1946, and they had considered declaring a moratorium on German coal exports in the spring of 1946, only to have the Americans dissuade them. In July 1946, in Paris, Bevin had threatened "to organize the British Zone" and "to produce for export in order to reduce the burdens on the British taxpayer," only to agree later to accept Byrnes's alternative—the fusion of the British zone with the American zone for economic unity. Meanwhile, the British had fought against the excessive restrictions of the level-of-industry and reparations plan of March 1946, only to bend under the strongest American pressure, provided that certain assumptions were made explicit in the plan, and provided that the plan be reviewed annually, beginning in January 1947.[24] Remaining consistent, Bevin had suggested that a revised German level of industry be an agenda item in the Anglo-American negotiations on bizonal organization and finances. But Hilldring told his British counterpart on November 22, 1946, that the level of industry was a matter for recommendation from Berlin, and that "while the British had a view that the level of industry of steel should be 11 million tons rather than 7.5 as at present, similar views could not be obtained on the American side in Washington."[25] The American position was that revision was not needed. Clay reportedly said in Washington that with current production in the two zones at less than 60 percent of capacity, a 40 percent increase was possible under existing agreements and plans.[26]

The British, pressed by the financial bind that had prompted them to agree to bizonal union and that would soon lead to their decision to withdraw from Greece, remained dissatisfied with the continuing costs of the German occupation under the Bevin-Byrnes agreement of December 2, 1946. They also disagreed with the American analysis of the economic viability of the new three-year plan for Bizonia—a view shared in public by American working-level administrators in Berlin. In any case, after a British military government spokesman in Berlin reportedly said that German steel production would have to be increased from 5.8 to 11 million tons annually, the British government admitted it had plans to do so. In a press conference in London on January 20, 1947, John B. Hynd, the British Minister for Occupied Territories, announced that the British government had prepared a level-of-industry plan to replace the one of March 1946, and that it had taken steps to prevent dismantling of plants and equipment that would be needed in the British zone for the proposed new plan.[27] Bevin pushed the British plan at Moscow.

The British plan for revision of the level of industry failed to receive four-power approval at the Moscow CFM, in part because France would not discuss an increase in the agreed level without a prior decision on France's demands for coal and security, and in part because the British, Americans, and Russians could not agree on a common definition of the relationship between the level of industry, exports and imports, and reparations (including reparations from current production).[28] In fact, the Big Three rehearsed the issues and the differences that had arisen at the Potsdam Conference. But Bevin and Marshall were prepared to try various alternatives to reach agreement. Even after Marshall declared publicly that the United States would not follow Molotov "in a retreat from Potsdam to Yalta,"[29] he talked to Bevin privately about Russia's desperate need for current-production reparations, and he admitted that the United States delegation was studying the matter. Marshall wanted "to see if there might be some procedure such as the operation in Germany of reparation plants for the benefit of the Soviets, they providing the raw materials, etc., which would permit a form of reparations from current production without delaying the creation of a self-supporting German economy."[30] Perhaps reflecting his knowledge of Hoover's activities in Washington—about which Acheson had reported two days earlier[31]—Marshall observed that such a plan would probably cause trouble with Congress on reparations.[32] Molotov's firm position "that German industry must be set at a level to insure her internal needs, payment of imports, and reparations" did not foreclose a compromise based on the studies Marshall said the United States delegation had underway.[33] But there was no compromise possible with France, whose report to the Moscow CFM had been described by Murphy as "confused and deceptive in its Byzantine complexity." The French remained firm in their demands for the Saar, for coal from Germany, and for Ruhr and Rhineland separation or control (a slight modification). Bidault went to Moscow with instructions "to raise the question of coal before considering the other political and economic problems concerning Germany," and on March 18 and 20, 1947, he outlined what those instructions meant. He said he could not agree to any decisions on economic unity, the level of industry, and reparations unless there was a prior agreement that France's coal requirements would be met. France wanted an international agency to control the allocation and use of German coal. It objected categorically to raising the March 1946 level of German steel production. It wanted a "special regime for the Ruhr" and it wanted the Saar integrated "at once into the economic and monetary system of France." Until the latter had been done, German economic unity was unacceptable. Furthermore, Bidault said, "France would not approve the creation of central German administrative agencies until the German frontiers were fixed."[34]

Bevin had anticipated the impasse that occurred in Moscow. He told Marshall on March 22, 1947, that Bidault had threatened even before the CFM met "that unless a suitable adjustment in coal was made for France, the French could not go through with this conference regarding other matters." Bevin said he had warned Bidault that this was "not acceptable procedure" and advised him "not to bring it up in the Conference." As noted previously, Bidault did so nevertheless, and Bevin lashed back, deploring the methods being used to oppose a peace settlement "which affects all the world."[35] Faced with the impasse, with the prospect of "a long period of months . . . before anything was done," and with a situation in Germany that was "urgent for correction," Bevin finally proposed joint British-American action.[36] The British were determined to reduce the cost of their occupation in Germany, and they were not prepared to accept American alternatives or delays as they had done throughout 1946.

THE BRITISH BIZONAL INITIATIVE

During a luncheon meeting in Moscow on April 8, 1947, Marshall and Bevin discussed conference procedures and the prospect that the foreign ministers would not complete their CFM agenda. They agreed to limit their own remarks in the CFM to such comments as were "absolutely necessary" and to insist that the CFM pass over items of disagreement and proceed to the next item on the agenda. Thereupon, "on his own initiative," Bevin explained what the British thought to be necessary if "we had to fall back for the time being on a bi-zonal procedure." Among other things, Bevin said the bizone should establish a new level of industry, using 10 million tons of steel production annually as a basis. According to Bevin, the new bizonal level-of-industry plan should be followed rapidly by decisions on what plants could be released and dismantled for reparations shipments to the IARA nations and to the Soviet Union and Poland. Three days later Marshall asked Acheson to be sure that Truman "had an opportunity to read the memoranda" of his conversations with Bevin, particularly the one of April 8, 1947,[37] since the British were pushing Bevin's initiative.

On April 11, 1947, William Draper (the OMGUS director of economics) cabled Clay, who was back in Berlin, that Bevin "plans to see you soon concerning a proposal on the level-of-industry." Clay and Sir Brian Robertson (the British military governor) had, in fact, already discussed the British proposals during their negotiations on how best to implement the Bevin-Byrnes fusion agreement of December 2, 1946.

Among other things, the British group wanted to concentrate the bizonal agencies in one city and to establish an advisory council composed of German political-party and trade-union representatives. They also wanted an upward revision of the bizonal level of industry and resumption of reparations deliveries. Draper advised Clay that Bevin's tactic in Moscow would be to propose a four-power agreement on a revised level of industry based on German steel production of 10 million tons annually (with 11.5 million tons capacity left in place). The British expected France to disagree because of the steel figure, and they expected Molotov to ask whether the new plan would provide for current-production reparations "in accordance with the Soviet demand. The answer being 'no,' it is expected that Soviet Delegation will not agree." Should events develop as expected, Draper continued, Bevin planned to state that he felt "free to take whatever action is appropriate regarding the level-of-industry." He would then seek a British-American agreement to revise the bizonal level of industry based on a 10-million-ton steel-production figure, to resume reparations deliveries as soon as plant-and-equipment removal lists could be compiled in accordance with the new level-of-industry plan, to make advance-type reparations deliveries in the meantime, and to allocate and ship plants and equipment to the East as well as to the West, in accord with the Potsdam formula.[38]

Clay objected to some elements of the British plan. Reflecting the difficulties he had had with the State Department on cash payments for coal, transit services, and seaport services, among other things, Clay insisted that "the basic difficulties in making the bizonal economic agencies effective are more fundamental than appear on the surface." Reflecting his knowledge of Hoover's apprehensions about Britain's plans for socialization in Germany and of the Army's acceptance of Hoover's reports, Clay noted that the British proposal to concentrate the bizonal agencies in one city would introduce excessive centralization. He thought the British plans for an advisory committee of political-party representatives and trade-unionists who were not elected by the German people would establish "a precedent for communist control." Though he had agreed with Robertson to study the level of industry and reparations, Clay thought the 10-million-ton steel-production figure had simply been "pulled out of the hat." Furthermore, he had reservations about resuming reparations deliveries and "would not want to agree to allocate any more plants to the Soviets prior to economic unification." In any case, he urged "that no bilateral agreements be made in Moscow until they have been studied here [in Berlin] to determine their full implications."[39] His advice was not to prevail.

Bevin wrote to Marshall on April 14, 1947, that he had had disturbing telegrams from Berlin regarding economic fusion of the zones. "There has even been an indication given that it might be better to cancel these arrangements and work our own Zones separately." In view of the seriousness of the matter, Bevin asked Marshall whether Clay might be brought back to Moscow for discussions with Robertson, Marshall, and Bevin.[40] But Marshall and Bevin finally reached an understanding between themselves in Moscow and then agreed informally to stop in Berlin on their return from

Moscow to discuss the understanding with the military governors (actually with Clay, since Robertson remained in Moscow during the negotiations there).[41]

Indicative of their determination not to be put off this time, the British opened the discussion with the Americans in Moscow by presenting a detailed memorandum of agreement, which included items on the location and powers of the bizonal agencies, the functions of the agencies' chairmen, the need for economic planning, freedom of trade, financial reform, a revised level-of-industry plan, and a new reparations list. The British proposed that the United States and Britain announce their intention to raise the level of industry for the bizone immediately after the CFM, that the new plan be made public by July 1, 1947, and that a revised list of plants and equipment for reparations removals be released by August 15, 1947. They suggested that, after allowances were made for a reserve to compensate for possible French annexation of the Saar and to cover possible excessive removals from the Russian zone, reparations plants should be offered to the ACC for allocation between Russia and the IARA. Once allocated, they would "be delivered both to the Western and to the Eastern Powers."[42]

After much discussion Marshall and Bevin agreed on a four-point memorandum on April 18, 1947. First, Clay and Robertson would study revision of the level-of-industry plan "for two or three weeks" and agree on a steel production figure, which Marshall hoped would come close to 10 million tons annually, and which Bevin said would be acceptable if "bracketed between ten and twelve which were the Russian brackets." Second, the plants and equipment to be made available for reparations under the revised level of industry would be allocated by the ACC and delivered to the IARA and the Soviet Union. Third, the bizonal economic agencies would be reorganized to make them more efficient, but not as a provisional government. Fourth, the bizonal agencies would be concentrated geographically as soon as accommodations could be arranged.[43]

Except for two "vetoes" by Marshall, and except for a major misunderstanding about what they had agreed on, the original British plan was the basis of the four-point memorandum of agreement. Marshall wanted to delay public announcement of the decision to revise the level-of-industry and reparations plan "for six weeks or so in order to avoid the implication that we had been insincere in our efforts in Moscow to agree on economic unity." Furthermore, he wanted to delay the news that the bizonal agencies would be concentrated in one city until accommodations could be arranged and "to avoid unfavorable reaction."* The misunderstanding was on the resumption of reparations deliveries. Marshall appears to have been either terribly confused or torn between Bevin's persuasiveness and the advice he got from his own staff. He cabled Acheson on April 19, 1947, that reparations deliveries to the IARA would have to be resumed, both for the benefit of the recipients and so the Germans would know where they stood. He noted, however, that he did "not believe it desirable politically to resume reparations deliveries except on basis of Potsdam division with four power allocation in ACC and deliveries to Soviet Union."[44] But that is precisely what the British wanted to do.

Marshall's confusion may have been caused by his State Department advisers. They had apparently convinced him that Clay's reparations suspension was originally caused by Russia's violation of the Potsdam decision, and he therefore concluded that resumption of deliveries to Russia should be delayed until the Russians accepted those decisions. His radio report to the American people after the Moscow CFM summarizes the advice he had been receiving:

One of the most serious difficulties encountered in the effort to secure economic unity has been the fact that the Soviet-occupied zone has operated practically without regard to the other zones and has made few if any reports of what has been occurring in that zone. . . . This unwillingness of the Soviet authorities to cooperate in establishing a balanced economy for Germany as agreed at Potsdam has been the most serious check on the development of a self-supporting Germany and a Germany capable of providing coal and other necessities for the neighboring states who have always been dependent on Germany for these items.[45]

Clay and Murphy had challenged the accuracy of such conclusions in 1946, but in 1947 they failed to do so. Perhaps they had come to resent Molotov's critical attacks on the bizone and the reparations suspension. Perhaps they were tired. Perhaps they felt defeated by the force of the State Department's and John Foster Dulles's influence on Marshall. Clay was certainly disillusioned. He wrote to a friend in April 1947, saying that after Byrnes resigned he had "not had the same heart" for his work. "This was particularly

* SecState to ActgSecState, April 19, 1947, *FRUS*, 1947, II, 357–58. It might be noted that Marshall later considered these decisions vital to the origins of the Marshall Plan. He told Harry Price, in 1952, that consideration was given to forming the plan at the end of the Moscow CFM, but that he had vetoed it because he did not want it to appear that the Western allies had come to Moscow with a plan to go ahead without the Russians. Harry B. Price, Notes on an Interview with George C. Marshall, Oct. 30, 1952, Truman Library.

true at Moscow, and after being there for two weeks I asked and received permission to return to my duties here in Germany." Less than a month later Clay wrote to Byrnes, expressing his fear that what Byrnes had said at Stuttgart "now has little significance in guiding our policy in Germany." He hoped "that in our political warfare with the U.S.S.R. we do not forget that here in Germany we have 70,000,000 human beings to remember."[46] But Marshall's and Bevin's Moscow decisions on Germany, the "measures susceptible of immediate application," had been made, and they caused a major crisis in the Washington bureaucracy.

CHAPTER FIFTEEN

The Moscow Decisions and the American Bureaucracy

ON HIS RETURN trip from the Moscow CFM, Marshall stopped in Berlin late in April 1947 to discuss his and Bevin's agreement with Clay and Murphy. According to Clay, Marshall instructed him "to proceed vigorously with the strengthening of the bizonal organization ... and to expedite the upward revision of the level of industry to ensure the self-sufficiency of the area."[1] Clay immediately sketched the difficulties he would have in carrying out Marshall's instructions and, on May 2, 1947, he detailed them in a letter for Marshall. His conclusion: Germany was bankrupt.

GERMANY'S BANKRUPTCY

Drawing upon his experience in Germany, Clay concluded that the bizone could not be made self-sustaining unless the German debt was calculated and fixed and unless Germany was "permitted to enter into trade relationships with other countries unhampered by the curse of her past political mistakes." Clay noted that the allies had removed as reparations all of Germany's gold reserves, foreign balances, and other external assets. American and British disease-and-unrest appropriations had provided food "to maintain an above starvation diet," but such appropriations were not available for recovery and rehabilitation. "Germany can not present a sound credit risk to prospective lenders," Clay wrote, and the only credits OMGUS had been able to negotiate for Germany had been "restricted to self-liquidating inventory advances, such as the $7.5 million advance for this purpose being made available by our R.F.C." Using such credits and capital built up "by initial exports literally squeezed from a bankrupt economy by the use of [the] meager stocks of remaining raw materials," the bizone had accumulated approximately $100 million, "a small capital fund with which to rebuild the economy of approximately one-half of Germany with a population of 40 millions." The bizonal authorities were fighting a losing battle, despite their strict policy of using Germany's capital funds only when their "expenditure will definitely stimulate an equal or greater amount of income from German exports," and despite their "niggardly" policy of demanding "that every export of goods or services from Germany be fully and promptly accounted for; ... our Allies, who have suffered at the hands of Germany, are extremely reluctant to deal with Germany in any way that brings a net profit to Germany." For example, Clay wrote, Belgium and the Netherlands were asking that Germany use Rotterdam and Antwerp as ports of entry and exit, "and that Germany pay foreign exchange for this use, despite the fact that Bremen and Hamburg have adequate port facilities available without foreign exchange costs." Czechoslovakia had been insisting that she not be required to pay for the use of German railroads and port facilities, and OMGUS was being pressured to provide free use or to set special rates and to charge them off as reparations. UNRRA accumulated a bill of over $1 million for freight and transit services through Germany to Czechoslovakia, and it wanted these charges to be "offset against UNRRA's much lesser charges for aid in the administration of the DP [Displaced Persons] program in the U.S. Zone." France, while demanding an increase in German coal exports, had retained German prisoners of war and was now recruiting them for voluntary work in France. Under existing French plans, such volunteers would be required to send their earnings to their dependents in Germany, a transaction that France proposed to pay for with "old German Reichsmarks left in France by the retreating German army." France, Clay continued, "would have the fruits of the labor, but Germany would pay the major part of the labor cost." Clay conceded that "it is difficult not to be sympathetic" with the demands of Germany's neighbors, but he argued that the United States would have to realize "that any transaction which brings a loss ostensibly to the US/UK Zones of Germany does, in fact, bring that loss to the US/UK Governments instead." Under the reparations agreements made at Potsdam and at the Paris reparations conference, Germany "is not able to finance a continuing hidden reparations program in the form of concessions in international trade forced upon her by the Allied nations through the Occupying Powers." The issue was not, Clay warned, "sympathy for Germany and the German people," but a need to reduce the financial burden of the occupation for Britain and the United States. "We have to recognize that it is not Germany who is paying the penalty today, but rather the taxpayers of the United States and Great Britain and that we can unburden ourselves of this expense only by returning Germany to a satisfactory trading position or by abandoning her to chaos."[2]

THE STATE DEPARTMENT AND THE FEAR FOR LIBERATED EUROPE

Four days after his conference with Clay in Berlin, and immediately upon his return to Washington, Marshall summoned Kennan and instructed him to cut short his assignment in the War College, to organize the Policy Planning Staff without delay, to prepare a study of the problem of European reconstruction, to make recommendations for action, and to "avoid trivia." The Congress, he said, would soon be demanding action and suggesting "all kinds of bright and unworkable ideas in an effort to force the Department's hand."[3] A day earlier, Marshall had reported to the cabinet on the Moscow Conference and told his colleagues of his and Bevin's decision to raise the German level of industry and to reorganize the bizonal administration by locating its "executive headquarters" in one central city. He apparently relied on Clay's analysis to outline some of the implications of the decisions for the remainder of Europe, because Forrestal recorded in his diary that "we must be very careful to preserve our good relationships with the 'fringe' countries in Europe—Belgium, France, Denmark, Norway, Sweden, Holland, etc., because otherwise Communism can infiltrate into all of them."[4] Seen in their historical context, Marshall's instructions to Kennan and the State Department Policy Planning Staff (PPS) were for staff studies and recommendations on how to implement the decisions he had already made in Moscow; on how to do so without upsetting the European economic and political system, without upsetting France, and without using the Hoover recommendations which were receiving so much attention in the Pentagon and in the Congress.

As it had been since 1945, coal was at the heart of the problem Marshall wanted resolved. At issue was whether to use the limited supply of Ruhr coal for German industrial rehabilitation to achieve self-sufficiency and to reduce the cost of the occupation to the Americans and the British, or whether to export Germany's coal to France and other countries in order to further the rehabilitation of liberated Europe and to transfer Europe's steel machine-tool, chemical, and other industries "to countries that do not have the German record of aggression," as Edwin W. Pauley had put it in April 1947.[5]

France had never relaxed its pressure for more coal from Germany. Once

France had formally adopted the Monnet Plan for postwar industrial development, and when the implications of the merger of the British and American zones became manifest, the French increased their pressure. During the Moscow Conference they seemed more determined than ever to get a firm, permanent commitment from the CFM on German coal exports. Late in February and early in March 1947, the French insisted in London and Washington that decisions be made in Berlin to satisfy France's coal needs, and they warned that France's delegation to the Moscow CFM was being instructed not to discuss the German economy, particularly not the level of industry, unless the question of German coal deliveries to France had been settled previously. Bevin warned Bidault about using such tactics at Moscow, but the State Department seemed inclined to "give full consideration" to France's needs. It did so despite Clay's objection to a State Department policy paper that he said was "devoted to emphasizing the export of coal rather than the utilization of coal to make the German economy self-sustaining and thus reduce or eliminate the present costs of the occupation."⁶ Marshall himself seemed to have an open mind on the question. He listened to France's demands on March 6, 1947, when he met in Paris with President Vincent Auriol and Acting Foreign Minister Pierre-Henri Teitgen. He said he understood the "critical character of the present situation," and advised Auriol and Teitgen that he intended "to meet with General Clay in Berlin, to inform myself concerning the coal problem in Germany and France."*

In Moscow Bevin and Marshall made concessions to France by agreeing

---

* Minutes of Marshall-Auriol Conversation, March 6, 1947, *FRUS*, 1947, II, esp. 193. Marshall's intention to inform himself in Berlin gave rise to an interesting and apparently desperate maneuver, which I admit I do not understand completely. Apparently in the hope of supporting the State Department's priority for coal exports from Germany to France, and apparently with the hope of counteracting what Clay would obviously tell Marshall in Berlin, Caffery cabled Marshall in Berlin on March 7 (*FRUS*, 1947, II, 189, note 54), reporting that "a French Foreign Office official had made the following comment in connection with the French coal problem and the Moscow Conference: 'If the United States could find a way to meet French views on German coal exports, he was certain that the French would find it possible to go along with United States' views on other German problems.' " Actually, the minutes in which the statement appears have the official (Teitgen) saying: "If we receive precise guarantees on coal, the political problems themselves would perhaps appear to us more simple." The more precise wording was added to the minutes in parentheses as a direct quotation, apparently when the minutes were approved by Teitgen and Auriol. The American Embassy claimed to have received the minutes from the French on March 8. But it had already sent the direct quotation to Marshall in Berlin on March 7. The question remaining open is whether Caffery had coached the French, or whether they did it on their own. If they did it on their own, however, there is a further question: how did Caffery get the direct quotation to send to Marshall before the "corrected" French minutes had been received? See *FRUS*, 1947, II, 191 and 190, note 58.

to the so-called Moscow sliding scale for German coal exports from the Western zones. But the agreement was precarious and incomplete. It was precarious because Britain demanded a new level of steel production in Germany, which would necessarily require greater amounts of German coal for domestic use. It was incomplete because Bidault wanted guarantees and commitments that would have converted Saar coal production into French "domestic" coal production for purposes of import allocations by the European Coal Organization. Even though Marshall approved the exchange of correspondence on the Moscow sliding scale, the United States had in fact reserved its position on the question of whether Saar coal would be French and whether, therefore, all French coal imports from Germany under the sliding scale would come from the Ruhr-Aachen coal fields of the British zone.[7] That the coal question and its ramifications hung heavy on Marshall's mind, that it was in fact the issue that caused him to give such urgent instructions to Kennan on April 29, 1947, is revealed in his report of the previous evening to the American people.

Marshall's Moscow CFM Report

Marshall's radio report of April 28, 1947, to the American people was, in many ways, a straightforward account of the failure of the CFM to agree on central agencies, a provisional German government, the nature of democracy, coal allocations, the level of the German economy, and the American draft treaty on German disarmament. But the speech was spliced with references and allusions to the decisions he and Bevin had made in Moscow and to his concern about their implications. In discussing coal, which he singled out for his first topic, Marshall observed that "the damaged mines, mine machinery, railroad communications and like facilities" would have to be rehabilitated before the allied nations could receive more coal from Germany. Rehabilitating the German mines would require coal for steel-making; "therefore, *and this is the point to be kept in mind*, while the necessary rehabilitation is in progress, *less coal* would be available in the immediate future for the neighboring Allied states." Perhaps remembering his conversations on the issue with Auriol and Teitgen in Paris, certainly remembering Bidault's demands and maneuvers in Moscow, Marshall noted that "the delay necessary to permit rehabilitation of the mines so vitally affects France that the settlement of this matter has become for her a critical issue." But, he intimated, there was no turning back. "The impoverished and suffering people of Europe ["the majority of whom," he said in the same speech, "are bitterly disposed towards the Germany that brought about this disastrous situation"] . . . are crying for help, for coal, for food, and for most of the necessities of life . . . [But] the people of Britain and the United States . . . cannot continue to pour out hundreds of millions of dollars for Germany. . . . The rehabilitation of Germany to the point where she is self-supporting demands immediate decision." According to Marshall, Russia's opposition to progress on a German settlement at the Moscow CFM—which Marshall took care to detail in his address—belied Stalin's words about possible compromises in the future, and it certainly foreshadowed endless delays. "We cannot ignore the factor of time involved here," Marshall concluded. "The recovery of Europe has been far slower than had been expected. Disintegrating forces are becoming evident. The patient is sinking while the doctors deliberate. So I believe that action cannot await compromise through exhaustion. New issues arise daily. Whatever action is possible to meet these pressing problems must be taken without delay."[8]

Kennan and the PPS Report of May 23, 1947

Kennan, who often discovered truths in his earlier positions that the Good Lord's other creatures had overlooked, wrote in his memoirs that the emphasis he placed "on the prompt and vigorous rehabilitation of the German economy . . . differed most sharply from the views then being held in other quarters of Washington." To illustrate what his views were, he summarized and commented at length on a speech he made at the War College on May 6, 1947, and he emphasized the following: "In my opinion it is imperatively urgent today that the improvement of the economic conditions and the revival of productive capacity in the west of Germany be made the primary object of our policy in that area and be given top priority in all our occupation policies; and that this principle be adopted as a general line of procedure of this government, binding on all of its departments and agencies."[9] But Marshall's actions, Britain's initiatives, Hoover's report and its acceptance by the Army and Congressional leaders, and Clay's analysis from Berlin make it clear that Kennan was unjustified in concluding that he was leading the vanguard for German recovery. In any case, the PPS report of May 23, 1947, speaks for itself. Even though it recommended a certain amount of German rehabilitation and recovery (particularly in the coal-mining and closely related industries), the PPS report remained remarkably consistent with the State Department's general policy to restore and rehabilitate France and the liberated countries first and to require the occupation authorities in Germany to adhere to that policy.

The PPS recommended a two-phased approach. Its report of May 23 said that "the production of coal in the Rhine Valley *and its movement to the places of consumption in Europe*" had been suggested as "the most suitable object" for immediate action.[10] Kennan had explained the short-run plan to Acheson four days earlier. It should be a "Coal for Europe" program to boost production. It should "be accomplished by maximum publicity and dramatization," and "be given as far as possible the character of an action not so much by the U.S. Government *to the French Government and other Governments of that area* but by the U.S. *public* to the peoples of those areas." Specifically, the United States should take measures to increase production, to procure coal-mining machinery, to make food available to coal-producing areas, to make special American government grants to help Britain overcome production difficulties in the Ruhr, and to ensure "maximum cooperation of our occupational authorities in Germany in providing labor, materials, etc. for the coal-producing areas."[11]

The PPS's recommendation for the long run was little more than a series of ideas, thoughts, and suggestions for dealing with the problems Clay had outlined for Marshall orally on April 25, 1947, and in writing on May 2, for making possible the German recovery envisaged by the Moscow decisions without raising the specter of the "old Germany" for Germany's neighbors. According to the PPS report, the enormously complex and difficult problem of European recovery should be resolved by the Europeans themselves: "This is the business of the Europeans." Letting the Europeans do it apparently promised a double advantage: it would ensure recovery of the liberated countries first and it would transfer out of the Washington bureaucracy some of the wrangling about funds, priorities, and objectives that had gone on there since the summer of 1945. But the PPS said the United States would not need to "stand aside or remain aloof from the elaboration of the overall European program. As a member of the United Nations and particularly of the Economic Commission for Europe, and as a power occupying certain European territories, it is entitled and obliged to participate in working out the program. Our position as an occupying power also makes it incumbent upon us to cooperate whole-heartedly in the execution of any program that may be evolved." In short, the vision of the PPS was that the State Department would participate with the Europeans in the development of a program and that the War Department would be obliged "to cooperate whole heartedly" in the execution of the program. The PPS recommended that the overall approach should "be informally and secretly discussed with British leaders at an early date and their assurances of support solicited."[12]

Discussions with the British were vital, in part because the British could help to prevent the Army from proceeding on the basis of the Hoover reports, in part because the British would have to moderate their determination to use Germany's coal resources to implement the Moscow decisions to increase the bizonal level of steel production to somewhere between 10 and 12 million tons annually, in part because the Rhine Valley coal mines were in the British zone, and in part because the Army and the Congress wanted to force the British to drop their plans for socialization of the German coal mines.

THE ARMY AND THE FEAR OF SOCIALISM

While Kennan organized the PPS in Washington, Clay and Sir Brian Robertson carried out their instructions to reorganize the bizonal administration in Germany. Clay objected to "excessive" bizonal centralization and to a bizonal advisory council made up of German political party representatives and trade unionists, and he appealed to the War Department for instructions and support.[13] Murphy relayed Clay's appeal directly to the State Department and said Clay needed "top level study and decision" on whether the United States was prepared to accept "rigid central economic controls and planning,...socialization of German enterprises...and...a far greater expenditure of U.S. appropriated funds than we shall be able even if willing to contribute."[14]

Clay told the War Department that he had done all he could to carry out Marshall's instructions to reach an agreement with Robertson. He said Robertson was under such strict instructions from his government that the Americans would have to make major concessions to the British plan in order to reach an agreement. The British wanted "a detailed regimentation of the German economy" and "Socialistic controls which would pave the way to the complete socialization of the bizonal area." They had supported the German Social Democratic Party in the maneuver that unseated Rudolf Mueller (a Christian Democrat from the American zone) and elected Victor Agartz (a Social Democrat from the British zone) as Chairman of the Bizonal Economic Administration. According to Clay, Agartz had "announced frequently that his principal mission is socialization." Aware of the mood of the Eightieth Congress, of Hoover's criticism of Britain's experiments with socialism, and of the Army's acceptance of the Hoover reports as the basis for its appropriations requests, Clay said that "acceptance of the British terms" was inconsistent with American political objectives in Germany. He was even more sure that Britain's terms "would not be acceptable to the American business men and bankers on whom we must depend in the final analysis for the success, not only of our export program, but for subsequent financing to enlarge the export program."[15]

Although Robertson appeared to have moderated his position somewhat after he talked with Bevin in Berlin on April 28, 1947, Clay continued to report that Britain wanted to use bizonal reorganization to further the German Social Democratic Party's program of nationalization. Should the British and the Social Democrats succeed, Clay warned, sufficient opposition might develop in the United States "to endanger our appropriations." He said Robertson seemed more ready to compromise after his talks with Bevin, and he thought he could work out an acceptable agreement in Berlin. But he needed "assurance from our Government that its desire to make economic fusion work does not make it willing to accept a highly centralized economic control, which will be utilized in the hands of the SPD with the support of British Military Government, to extend socialist influence."[16]

The State Department had responded to Clay's and Murphy's early warnings and drafted a permissive policy-guidance on socialization. The War Department, with an assist from Forrestal, aborted it.[17] It sent the State Department's policy draft to Clay on May 1, 1947, advising him that it was "not yet finalized," that the Army preferred to entrust the details of bizonal reorganization to Clay, and that it "hoped that within a reasonable time, you will be given firm instructions in accordance with" the Army's position.[18] The "reasonable time" turned out to be a week.

By May 7, 1947, SWNCC had drafted and the Committee of Three (the Secretaries of State, War, and the Navy) had approved detailed instructions for Clay's further negotiations with Robertson. The instructions said Washington shared Clay's fears of a highly centralized, controlled economy and of socialism, which would reinforce centralization. Clay could reduce the danger by using care in structuring the new bizonal organization, in defining and limiting the powers of the bizonal council, and in retaining the power of the military governors to give or withhold approval, particularly over Economic Council legislation. The instructions said there should be central determination of production, of export-import levels, and of fuel and materials allocations to industries, but that central powers should be defined so as to preclude socialization at the bizonal level and to require the *Länder* to administer central decisions as much as possible. Clay's veto power over Economic Council legislation, his instructions said, would give him control over excessive centralization and over all critical decisions. Should the military governors disagree, the issues were to be referred to the governments for decision. The inference was clear that Washington would back Clay in the event of difficulty with the British.[19] In short, socialization in Germany would be prevented for the time being, not by formal policy instructions, but by shrewd administrative reorganization and alert and careful administrative supervision and control.[20] Interestingly, Forrestal wanted more control and Patterson was worried: at the time Clay's instructions were approved by the Committee of Three, Forrestal demanded that "the government should make it clear that we do not propose to endorse socialization in Germany under any circumstances and this should be communicated [to the British] at the highest level." Patterson, who knew from Clay's reports that the German Social Democratic Party had plans of its own for nationalization, observed that Clay would still find it difficult to resist if the Germans themselves voted to nationalize industry.[21] Later, when Patterson's fears proved to have been justified; when the German Social Democrats' plans seemed to threaten the immediate, dramatic coal production program recommended by the PPS, the American government put pressure on the British and got them to curb the Social Democrats in the British zone. To that we shall return.

THE PPS'S "COAL FOR EUROPE" PROGRAM

Fascinated by the European (and the Russian) response to Marshall's invitation to implement the long-term recommendation of the PPS and apparently taken in by the official line on the constellation of events in June 1947, historians have neglected completely the PPS's "Coal for Europe" recommendation, which called for an American initiative and which Kennan described as "almost essential to the success of the general scheme."[22] Immediately after completing its first report on May 23, 1947, the PPS fulfilled its promise "to come up with more detailed suggestions" on the "production of coal in the Rhine Valley and its movement to the places of consumption in Europe." It completed a second paper, PPS/2, on June 2, 1947. Acheson sent it to Ambassador Lewis W. Douglas in London, and the War Department sent it to Clay. The message to Clay said the State Department would invite Britain to join in promoting an energetic coal production program in Europe. It referred to the psychological importance of immediate action and noted that "Germany is one and perhaps [the] most important element in [the] program." It assured Clay that the proposed action was not a critique of the existing Clay-Robertson plan for coal production, but an attempt to go beyond, perhaps by giving government support and by viewing the Ruhr-Aachen area in a broader context.[23] In short, German coal production was to become a key feature of a European recovery program.

The bizone, in fact, had had a high-priority coal production program under way since early 1947. It was the first major program to be implemented under the Bevin-Byrnes bizonal fusion agreement of December 2, 1946, and it was launched with considerable fanfare by the military governors themselves late in January 1947. Clay and Robertson, accompanied by their economic advisers, met in Minden, Essen, and Düsseldorf from January 23 to 25, 1947, with the bizonal administrators for economics, the German minister-presidents, their ministers for economics and labor, and certain trade-union and political-party leaders. The purpose of the meetings was to announce and outline a program to increase coal production to 300,-000 tons per day by the end of 1947 and to 400,000 tons daily in 1948.[24] Robertson announced a new miner's ration of 4,000 calories per day (more than two and a half times the normal consumer's ration), a 20 percent wage increase, a special retirement program, extra alcohol and tobacco rations for miners, and a general program for giving the Ruhr area priorities for textiles, consumer goods, and construction materials for homes and apartments. Clay outlined programs to recruit miners in the American zone, to send lumber and textiles from the American zone to the Ruhr, and to import $600 million in food to Germany in 1947. He also stated that no coal would be delivered as reparations, but that it would be exported and sold.[25]

Basic to the bizonal coal program was an understanding between Clay and Robertson that the British would abolish the control agencies they had established over the coal mines in 1945 and turn over control and management of the coal industry to German authorities by April 1, 1947. But Clay soured quickly on that agreement after the Social Democratic membership of the Bizonal Economic Administration unseated Rudolf Mueller (CDU) as chairman and elected Victor Agartz (SPD) on January 16, 1947. It may, in fact, be indicative of something that it was Agartz—not the military governors—who announced at Minden that the Germans would assume control on April 1, 1947. Clay later claimed to have intelligence reports showing that the British had backed Kurt Schumacher, Agartz, and the SPD in the manuever to unseat Mueller.[26] In any case, the turnover did not occur on April 1, 1947. It was held in abeyance while the British, the Americans, and the Germans wrangled over how much power would be delegated to Germans in the reorganized bizonal agencies and over the right of the Germans to set up a political control board over the agencies. That struggle over organizational, structural, and administrative questions assumed crisis proportions in February 1947, only to be shelved in a sort of *"Burgfrieden"* (palace peace) to await the results of the Moscow Conference. It was finally settled at the organizational, administrative level on May 29, 1947, after Clay had received from SWNCC the rather detailed and complicated instructions of May 7, 1947, which have been summarized above.[27]

The Social Democrats and the British were not defeated, however, and there is reason to believe that the British compromised with Clay on administrative and organizational details in the expectation that they would get their way in the end after all. During the election campaigns for the first state legislatures (*Landtage*) in the British zone—the elections ran concurrently with the later stages of the British and American negotiations on bizonal reorganization—the SPD discussed various schemes for socialization or "nationalization" at the state (*Land*) level. Once the elections were completed, some form of socialization seemed inevitable in every one of the British zone *Länder*. In the crucial *Land* of North Rhine–Westphalia (the Ruhr area), where the CDU had emerged with a plurality, the incoming minister-president, Karl Arnold (CDU), called for a new ordering of the economic life of the *Land* as a major item of business. "The capitalist economic system," he said, "has run itself into the ground under its own laws."[28] He went on to talk about a communal economy (*Gemeinwirtschaft*) in coal, steel, iron, and chemicals; an economy managed by business professionals with the participation of the state, the cities, the unions, and the cooperatives.

Echoing the State Department's permissive draft-policy of May 1, 1947, Murphy had assured Sir Sholto Douglas, the British Commander in Germany, and Lord Francis A. Pakenham, the Minister for German Affairs in the Foreign Office, that the United States "had no anxiety regarding [the] question of socialization of industry" so long as the German people decided the issue for themselves.[29] But the Army, Forrestal, Herbert Hoover, the Eightieth Congress, and some State Department functionaries (including Clayton and Douglas) combined forces after the *Landtag* elections in the British zone and compelled the State Department to abandon its moderate, neutralist views on socialism. The State Department eventually did so rather than risk defeat for its more important immediate objective of providing coal for Europe. As a result, the State Department also talked about production rather than experimentation. Significantly, however, the production advocated by the State Department was to be in coal and related industries, not in machine tools, steel, chemicals, and the like. The State Department's restricted view of German production increases was, of course, in accord with the PPS's recommendation, and it remained consistent with the policy to shift Europe's industrial bases from Germany to Germany's neighbors. The vigor and passion with which the State Department held to its policies of long standing are revealed in its dispute with the Army over the bizonal level of industry and in its determination to require Clay to conform his policies to the general European recovery program that would be developed by the Europeans (with "friendly aid" from Washington) in accordance with the PPS's long-term recommendation and Marshall's invitation of June 5, 1947. To these issues I shall return after describing the State Department's turnabout on socialization.

CHAPTER SIXTEEN

No Time for Experiments

THE CONTEXT of the State Department's shift from its moderate, permissive policy on socialism in Germany to its decision to press Britain to abandon socialist experiments in Germany and to require the German Social Democrats to suspend their plans reveals a great deal about the purposes of the Marshall Plan. Although the Army and the State Department finally took the same side on socialization (as they were to do on the bizonal level of industry), they did not do so for similar reasons. The Army wanted socialization suspended in principle and because it saw socialization as a hindrance to the implementation of the Moscow decisions to make the bizone self-sufficient and less costly. The State Department agreed to suspend socialization in the interests of the Coal for Europe program, as the best practical method for furthering its policy of using German coal to rehabilitate liberated Europe.

Marshall's and Bevin's Moscow decisions on Germany had threatened to undo the victory the State Department had won over the Army (and the British) on the question of coal and related policies in the summer of 1945. The victory had been threatened before: by the British effort to place a moratorium on coal exports in the spring of 1946; by Bevin's announcement of July 11, 1946, that the British would organize their zone to produce for export and self-sufficiency; and by the bizonal administration's determination to use the Bevin-Byrnes fusion agreement of December 2, 1946, to put the two zones on a cash-payment basis in the interests of the economic self-sufficiency promised by that agreement. Responding to various pressures and forces already described, Marshall came close to abandoning the State Department's policy at Moscow. He and Bevin had opted for a bizonal policy that was remarkably similar to the one Clayton had described in 1945 as a "narrow view," and that Matthews had warned McCloy would encourage "the natural human tendency of all our high-powered people in

Germany to use the German economy to make that country run and to disregard completely in practice the vital needs of the liberated areas."[1]

Marshall realized at the time that the Moscow decisions were a major adjustment in policy, for he wanted their announcement delayed for about six weeks. When he heard from Clay and his State Department advisers what the full implications of his and Bevin's decisions were, he instructed Kennan and the PPS to develop a crash program of studies and recommendations. On June 20, 1947, he came close to admitting the "mistake" he had made in Moscow, when he instructed Clayton on what to say to the British about socialization during the latter's consultations in London on the implementation of the Harvard speech. Marshall told Clayton he had not been sufficiently informed in Moscow to take the firm stand he was about to take. In Moscow he had had only the advice and information from the occupation authorities in Germany. But since his return from Moscow he had "had information and advice from other sources" and he was now convinced "that the British have made an absolute failure in the Ruhr."[2] Four days after talking with Clayton—possibly moved by conscience and probably to let Clay down easy—Marshall responded to Clay's "Germany is bankrupt" letter of May 2, 1947, saying that since he had seen Clay he had "listened to a great many presentations of the complications regarding dollar assets or transactions in connection with your zone and also the bi-zonal complications particularly as relate to the Ruhr."[3] He told Clay that he was taking action to bring the British around on socialization, but he said nothing about how that action was related to the State Department's plans to replace the Moscow German decisions with a *European* economic program.

PRESSING THE BRITISH

Assistant Secretary of War Petersen, who had been on the scene in Germany during the crucial negotiations on bizonal reorganization, returned to Washington in a lather early in June 1947. He wrote to Secretary of War Patterson on June 12, 1947, that the War Department needed a Presidential decision on socialization and on raising the German food ration from 1,550 to 1,800 calories per day. He reported that he had talked with Lord Pakenham in Berlin about increasing bizonal coal production to the 300,000 ton daily production target set by Clay and Robertson in January,* but he thought Lord Pakenham was more interested in nationaliz-

---

* Production had reached a high of 238,000 tons daily in March and had fallen to 215,000 tons in June.

tion of the coal mines than in production. Petersen complained to Patterson that the United States had taken no real stand on the issue, and he predicted that German industry would be socialized by "default" unless the United States did something immediately. Petersen said he had tried unsuccessfully for about six months to get a policy from the State Department. All he got, he said, was a negative statement that said "anything goes (presumably even communism) so long as it is the result of the freely expressed will of the German people." Petersen thought the United States should emphasize production as its first objective and it should insist that economic and social reform not be allowed to interfere with that. If the State Department would not make strong representations against the British program, the War Department should ask the President to do so. Petersen thought Patterson might first bring the matter to the Committee of Three, where he could count on Forrestal for support.[4]

Following Petersen's advice, Secretary of War Patterson asked Marshall for a discussion of socialization in the Committee of Three, and the urgency of his request was made manifest by the news from Berlin.[5] On June 17, 1947, Murphy relayed Clay's comments on the State Department's Coal for Europe program and added a warning of his own on socialization. Clay disagreed with all of the PPS's specific recommendations for increasing coal production and focused instead on the socialization issue as the real problem. He objected to the PPS's suggestion for a capital loan secured by Germany's coal exports. Such a loan would be unpopular, he said, and it would actually retard recovery because it proposed to tie Germany's export receipts to a specific objective. Clay also thought the PPS's proposal to supply additional machinery and equipment was unnecessary: the Germans needed no extra machines until production increased and they could make their own machines when they needed them. "In other words," Clay concluded, "capital is not the immediate problem in coal production." The major problems were the generally low level of the Ruhr economy, the managers' and miners' lack of a sense of responsibility for Germany's economic life and future, and the continuing uncertainty regarding the future ownership of the mines. Clay reported he had proposed to Robertson that the management of the mines be turned over to German trustees subject to the Bipartite Board (the military governors) until such time as the Germans could decide what the future of the mines would be. Adding his own comments to the "eyes-only" telegram for Marshall, Murphy reported that the Army believed it had received no effective guidance on socialization from the State Department, that Ambassador Douglas (who was also in Berlin) thought the British would push their socialization program very hard, and that he himself thought Clay's trusteeship idea might be "an admirable compromise."[6]

The Committee of Three met on June 19, 1947, and decided that Marshall should make "strong representations ... to the British Government to the effect that it must cease or defer any experiments in socialization of the German coal mines." Forrestal wanted to stop socialization cold, because it was "an opening wedge for communism," and he wanted Marshall to approach the British "at the highest level." Patterson thought the OMGUS trusteeship plan was sufficient to get an increase in production under way and to delay things until the Germans could decide the question of ownership for themselves. Marshall wondered whether the trusteeship plan would remove the uncertainties that Clay had identified as a problem, but he also seemed concerned about "reaction in this country if we should be found supporting a nationalization of industry program in Germany."[7] The final decision was to press the British.

Clayton, who was scheduled to go to London to discuss Marshall's Harvard invitation with the British, was assigned to make representations to the British on socialization. Marshall instructed him to "make it quite clear to Mr. Bevin" that the United States considered the British management of the Ruhr coal mines to be "pathetic." Clayton was to tell Bevin that Ruhr coal production was essential to European recovery and that the United States could not "participate in any big new commitments to help Europe back on its feet unless we know that the problem of producing coal in the Ruhr will be licked and quickly." The United States, Marshall said, "could not sit by while the British" experimented "with socialization of coal mines; time does not permit of experimentation." Clayton passed the word to Bevin and the British cabinet on June 24 and 25, 1947.[8] Meanwhile, the pot was boiling over in Berlin and the State Department took additional steps—before Clayton had had time to report on his representations in London.

Clay and Murphy reported urgently on the socialization issue to their respective departments in Washington on June 24, 1947. Clay's message said that General Draper had presented the American five-year trusteeship proposal to his British counterpart and that Robertson had then referred the proposal to London for instructions. Murphy had learned that the British government was disturbed by the trusteeship proposal, because Britain favored socialization of the mines on a *Land* (state) basis, with ownership vested in *Land* North Rhine–Westphalia. According to Clay, the British seemed to think that he would accept socialization if it occurred on a *Land* basis, but Clay protested that he had never agreed to that. Clay said he had never favored socialization by *Land* North Rhine–Westphalia, since that would give one *Land* the dominant position in the German economy and in a future German government. He had told the British repeatedly that the United States might accept socialization if it were undertaken as the result of the freely expressed desire of the German people. Now Clay predicted that he would have great difficulty in maintaining his position unless the United States government was prepared to define what constituted a free expression of German opinion. He wanted to know, for example, whether the present unstable conditions were serious enough to preclude the kind of intelligent and protracted discussion necessary for a free expression of opinion. The United States could take a strong position now, he said, or it could defer the decision until reasonably stable conditions were achieved. On the other hand, if it wanted to accept socialization without making an effort to maintain a reasonable degree of free enterprise, he should be instructed accordingly so he could cease his unnecessary opposition in the bizonal administration. In any case, Clay concluded, he needed an immediate and urgent decision as to whether the United States wanted to accept or reject socialization or to defer the issue for a definite period of time so the bizonal agencies could function smoothly.[9] Murphy summarized Clay's message for the State Department and asked "for the benefit" of the Department's thinking on the subject. He said British officials in Berlin had told him that their discussions with German officials had gone so far that the movement in North Rhine–Westphalia could not be stopped.[10]

The British-American Coal Conference

Apparently panic-stricken by Clay's and Murphy's news from Berlin—in any case before Clayton had time to report on the results of his representations in London—the State Department decided to invite the British to a coal conference in Washington.[11] When he heard about that, Clay cabled to Washington, saying that Robertson had in the meantime agreed in principle to the trusteeship plan and that he had reason to believe that Robertson's concession reflected the official position Britain would eventually take. He therefore thought the entire matter could be settled in Berlin without further discussions and conferences with the British in Washington. But it was too late. Petersen advised Clay that the prevailing opinion in Washington was that increased coal production was the key to European recovery, that the socialization issue had to be settled, and that the coal conference should proceed as planned.[12] Clay, whose experience had taught him to be wary of State Department participation in decisions affecting German coal production and consumption, complained to the War Department that negotiations regarding German internal affairs were being conducted at so many places and on so many levels that no single person or agency could comprehend them all. Petersen agreed with Clay, but explained that the War Department was not protesting at the moment because the State Department had become actively interested in solving some of Clay's problems, particularly on socialization and increased coal production.[13]

Clay's apprehensions about the coal conference were matched by Bevin's, whose fears were in turn sharpened by suspicions about the State Department's intentions.[14] Bevin agreed to coal talks in Washington and said he might attend himself, "because of the extreme importance of German coal for production." But Marshall cabled Ambassador Douglas to dissuade Bevin from coming. Marshall said Bevin's presence in Washington so soon after the failure of the Paris three-power talks on the Marshall Plan would cause "considerable confusion in the public mind both here and abroad." He thought that if Bevin attended nothing would change the impression that Bevin was in Washington to get instructions for the scheduled Paris conference of the sixteen nations on the Marshall Plan, and he said "the Soviet propaganda machine would have a field day." Bevin understood that all right, but he was puzzled by the State Department's limited coal-conference agenda.[15] He wanted to talk about broad economic questions and said the real problems to be resolved were not the technical aspects of coal production—which the occupation authorities themselves could deal with—but whether the German economy would be permitted a balanced production sufficient to relieve the taxpayers in Britain and the United States. The coal conference, he said, should be devoted to finances, to export-import arrangements, to food rations (1,800 calories per day), and to general economic policies such as currency reform and the exchange rate of the German mark.*

The State Department would not agree to Bevin's proposed expansion of the coal-conference agenda. Neither would it agree to delete the item on "elimination of uncertainty in the ownership status of the mines," which Bevin objected to. Although the American five-year trusteeship proposal was

---

* Bevin feared the adverse political reaction a five-year delay in socialization would produce in the House of Commons and in the German SPD. He also argued for consultations with the French, Belgians, Dutch, and Luxembourgers, who had a vital interest in the production of the Ruhr mines. See Douglas to SecState, July 12, 1947, *FRUS*, 1947, II, 936–38.

clearly the United States position, Marshall instructed Douglas to advise Bevin that the continued American desire to discuss the uncertainty in the ownership status of the mines was not with "intentions here to prejudge solution." As for the broader questions that Bevin wanted to discuss, the United States preferred to delay such discussions until the "Paris deliberations [on the Marshall Plan] take on clearer form." Marshall admitted that food was a problem, but he said the United States preferred to focus on coal to avoid "diffusion of discussion."[16]

If the State Department would discuss nothing but coal, Bevin said he could not justify sending a delegation to Washington: "Decisions on coal alone could, in Bevin's view, just as well be reached in Berlin." But the State Department wanted the talks in Washington and it reminded the British that they had accepted the invitation, that General Draper had already arrived in Washington from Berlin for the discussions, that the press had been informed of the British acceptance and of the reasons for Draper's presence in Washington, and it warned that "if talks are not held, it would seem that considerable misunderstanding would result and unfortunate implications drawn." Marshall also advised Bevin that he knew the broader questions that interested the British would have to be discussed sometime in the future.[17]

The British cabinet finally agreed to send a small delegation to Washington for the coal conference, but only on the condition that Bevin received an amplification of the agenda. The Americans finally admitted that nationalization would be discussed under the item to be devoted to uncertainty of mine ownership. They observed that financial matters would undoubtedly be discussed, but warned that the United States "could make no commitments" that affected Congressional appropriations.[18] A day later Draper reported to Clay that Bevin was ready to put nationalization on ice, but that the cabinet was resisting. As for the coal conference, Draper said the original agenda would remain and the technical aspects would be emphasized, because France was concerned about the level of German industry and the rate of German recovery.[19] In fact, France's concerns were the basis for the State Department's position, its maneuvers, and its pushing and pulling with the British and Clay on the coal issue. Before dealing with that, however, a brief word is in order about the coal conference, which *did* eventually take place.

When the eighteen-member British delegation arrived in Washington for the coal conference's opening session on August 12, 1947, they were met by forty-seven American participants from the State, War, Commerce, Interior, Agriculture, and Treasury Departments. A Congressional delegation had been persuaded not to attend the opening session, because "it was felt" that the presence of members of Congress would "place the British delegation in an embarrassing, unbalanced and difficult position."[20] During the course of the conversations, which lasted until September 10, 1947, the Americans kept pushing for adoption of the five-year trusteeship plan, which had in fact been agreed on between Clay and Robertson in Berlin on July 16, 1947. The British delegation, which was headed by Sir William Strang (Murphy's counterpart in Berlin), received the American proposals, but informed the Americans that they were "not authorized to conclude any agreement." Furthermore, the British made clear on August 23, 1947, that they wanted a revision of the bizonal financial agreement of December 2, 1946, as an absolute condition of any agreement they might make on a coal export program that would increase the costs to the occupation authorities in Germany.[21] In other words, if the Americans were going to require the occupation authorities in Germany to produce coal for the recovery of Europe in general, the British would insist that the costs be borne as part of the European recovery plans and not as costs to the German economy (and therefore as costs to the British Treasury). The Americans, who had already agreed internally in July 1947 that they were prepared to do what the British wanted, were nevertheless not yet ready to make firm commitments in the absence of Congressional consideration and in the absence of a final European recovery plan, which had run into snags in Paris. They finally agreed to financial discussions with the British at an "early date," hoping to salvage what they could of the coal conference, which they had publicly described as being very important. But Clay cabled that early financial discussions with the British in Washington were out of the question if he and Murphy were expected to participate. September was Congressional tour month in Germany, he said, and he was expecting delegations in Berlin almost every day of the month. The Congressmen generally wanted to see top people, he said, and if he and Murphy were in Washington when they arrived, the delegations might be severely critical of OMGUS for having given inadequate attention to the Congress.[22]

Bevin finally agreed to delay the financial talks and he approved the trusteeship plan in principle. But he outlined a chronological sequence of events, decisions, and consultations that would have to take place before he could give final approval. The State Department's patience ran out. It wanted its coal-management plan and it would not "agree to further delay." It informed Ambassador Douglas that "if there is to be a blow-up concerning the composition of the US/UK Control Group, we prefer to have it now rather than postpone it for the subsequent financial discussions." Douglas was to tell Bevin that the United States planned to end the coal conference "tomorrow either with or without an agreement," and that "under any circumstances" it would "announce agreement in principle on the Management Plan and specific agreement on the US/UK Control Group being put into effect immediately at the close of the Conference tomorrow." Faced with the inevitable, Bevin protested the Americans' distrust of his intentions and "the generally cavalier and abrupt manner" with which they were proposing to deal with the Benelux countries.[23] The German coal-management plan was formally approved by the military governors in Berlin on November 11, 1947, and it was announced on November 14, 1947.[24]

The State Department finally forced the British to put socialization of the coal mines on ice—as Draper, Acheson, and others expressed it.[25] But what began as a pragmatic effort to ensure the success of the PPS's Coal for Europe program ended in the adoption of a general policy statement on socialization that proved to be agreeable to Clay, Forrestal, and the leadership of the Eightieth Congress. On June 19, 1947, when the Committee of Three decided to make representations to the British to "defer any experiments in socialization of the German coal mines," it also asked for development of an agreed United States policy statement "regarding public ownership of enterprises in Germany."[26] In drafting the statement, the State Department apparently tried to keep clear the distinction between the tactic it had adopted for getting more coal mined (the pressure on the British to defer experimentation) and its general position on public ownership. It proposed the following as a general policy statement: "Since the question is one for decision by the German people, you will refrain from interfering in the question of public ownership of enterprises in Germany to ensure that any choice for or against public ownership is made freely through the normal processes of democratic government."

The Army objected, but finally agreed on the condition that the State Department version be altered to read: "While it is your duty to emphasize to the German authorities the principles and advantages of free enterprise, you will otherwise refrain from interfering . . ." The record shows that the State Department found the Army's compromise to be unacceptable, but it appears nevertheless as a paragraph in the JCS directive 1779, which was issued on July 15, 1947.[27]

Clay recorded his satisfaction with the directive in October 1947, after

Kenneth Royall and Forrestal had asked whether he needed additional directives on nationalization. Clay said he needed nothing further, for he had taken the position that "there must be economic and political stability in Germany before the German people can be expected to freely express their views." The British were tacitly accepting his interpretation, Clay said, and "time is on our side. If we can thus defer the issue while free enterprise continues to operate and economic improvement results, it may never even become an issue before the German people." Perhaps fearful that the State Department and the British might revive the question again, Clay promised that "if I see weakness develop in Germany or in connection with CFM meetings in London, I shall report immediately and ask for whatever help then appears appropriate."[28]

A Comment on Clay's Views

Clay seems to have thought that he was protecting the Germans from the British, from the State Department, and possibly from their own desperation and folly. During the coal conference, when the controversy with the British was at its height, Clay had cabled the War Department that the United States had always insisted that the German people had the ultimate right to decide the question of socialization, and he recalled that he had said as much in approving the American-zone *Land* constitutions. OMGUS had not interfered with the *Länder*, the counties, and the cities when they established public ownership of utilities and other enterprises. The Hessian coal mines had been socialized and they were state property, with the former management functioning as custodians responsible to the Hessian Minister of Economics.[29] But Clay argued that Ruhr coal was a property of *national* significance, for without it Germany could not establish a viable economy. "It is unthinkable," he said, that North Rhine–Westphalia should take over the assets of the Ruhr "unless desired by the German people." The German people were, however, in no position to express their desires until Germany's boundaries had been drawn, until someone decided what electorate would be given a free choice. Clay believed that, if the decision were left to the bizonal Economic Council, it would not approve socialization of the coal mines by *Land* North Rhine–Westphalia, and it would probably also reject socialization in principle. "It is a great mistake to assume that extreme Socialists represent present majority viewpoint now in Germany.... In spite of these factors," Clay concluded, "an election at the present time or in the immediate future would be a great mistake as it would develop bitter political controversy which would be exploited in every possible way by the Communist Party and would certainly interfere seriously with the rate of economic recovery."[30]

Clay summarized his views publicly in Germany. Speaking to the *Länderrat* of the American zone on September 9, 1947, he observed that much had been said about American opposition to socialism and noted that much of what had been said was inaccurate. "I would not be frank with you if I did not say to you that America believes in free enterprise. We believe neither in monopolies nor in cartels in restraint of trade. We are convinced that we have attained a high standard of living for our people through a system of free enterprise. Nevertheless, as strongly as my country believes in free enterprise, it believes even more strongly in democracy." The United States would not impose an economic structure in Germany against the will of the German people. But the German will would have to be expressed by the entire German people. If a *Land* wanted to socialize, that was its concern. But if a *Land* wanted to socialize an industry important to all of Germany, the rest of Germany would have to have a voice in that decision.[31]

A Comment on the State Department's Acquiescence

The State Department's position on socialization was much more complex than Clay's or the Army's. Its draft policy-statements consistently proposed to leave the choice to the Germans. Its internal memoranda reveal judgments that the political trend in Europe was toward the left, and at least one of them recommended support and encouragement for the German Social Democrats.[32] But the record shows that the State Department put pressure on the British to suspend the plans for socialization of the coal mines and that it concurred in the directive that Clay and the Army used to prevent socialization during the occupation period.

The State Department's inconsistency and vacillation on socialization must be seen against the background of its Coal for Europe program, its policy to restore the economies of the liberated European countries first, and its policy to rebuild France as the bulwark of democracy on the continent of Europe. In its decision to pressure the British to suspend and delay socialization, the State Department was influenced by its knowledge that Kurt Schumacher's socialism was strongly "nationalistic" in emphasis, and by its knowledge that Schumacher and the German Social Democrats would insist that the socialized German coal mines produce in the first instance for German needs, rather than for liberated Europe. The German

Social Democrats would not have agreed peaceably to continued production for "hidden reparations," and they would have resisted exports of coal that the German economy could use more advantageously to produce export goods and services and to provide employment. In short, the State Department was not prepared to permit Social Democrats to interfere with its mission in Europe, any more than it was prepared to permit the American Army to do so. Its actions in response to Clay's and Robertson's decision to raise the export price of German coal are germane to that conclusion.

The price of coal. In accord with the bizonal fusion agreement of December 2, 1946, and in response to the Bevin-Marshall decisions in Moscow, Clay and Robertson decided early in July 1947 to raise the export price of Ruhr coal from about $10 to about $15 per ton.[33] When the State Department got the news, it prepared an instruction for Clay to defer the decision until the issue could be discussed at the Washington coal conference. It sent the instruction to the War Department for concurrence and transmittal to Berlin, and it advised Murphy directly. For some reason the cable for Clay "languished" in the War Department for eight days, while Clay got the news from Murphy.[34] Clay protested immediately that production costs and competitive European coal prices fully justified the price rise. Whereas low coal prices might be desirable for United States foreign policy, Clay continued, they would make continued American and British subsidies of German coal exports necessary. In fact, Clay argued, Germany would never achieve self-sufficiency if the bizonal authorities could not set prices to obtain justified revenues.[35]

Clay's arguments in favor of the coal price rise arrived at the Pentagon during the furor over the State Department's instructions to delay publication of the revised level-of-industry plan for the bizone, an incident to which we shall return. For reasons that are not clear, the Army's Civil Affairs Division then sent the price-rise instruction it had received from the State Department eight days earlier (the one Clay had gotten from Murphy and to which he had already responded), and it did so without clearing the message with either Assistant Secretary Petersen or Secretary Patterson.[36] Patterson stormed at Marshall two days later, accusing the State Department of avoiding the agreed channel of communication with Clay and protesting the interference from Washington in the export price of coal and other decisions (the level-of-industry plan, in context), which Patterson thought were properly made in Berlin. Patterson then resigned, as Petersen had done four days earlier—both ostensibly in anticipation of the unification of the armed forces.[37] Patterson subsequently apologized to Marshall for having mistakenly accused the State Department of avoiding channels, but he repeated his argument that decisions such as the price of export coal should be left to Clay.[38]

The authority to set the price of German export coal was finally left to the military governors. The State Department relented to severe Army pressure late in July and to British demands during the early stages of the coal conference.[39] By that time the passion and desperation of the early controversy had subsided, in part because a policy decision had been made in Washington to increase appropriated funds to Germany to cover the losses arising from the export sale of underpriced coal or to give France and other countries "sufficient relief monies" to pay Germany for the coal.[40]

The State Department's position in the coal-price controversy and its reversal of policy on socialization are examples of the State Department's determination to let nothing happen in Germany that promised to threaten its priority for liberated Europe, especially France. Significantly, when the military governors announced the price rise, France protested on September 4, September 10, and September 17, 1947, adding to the last protest a complaint that the British were regarding "as interest-bearing loans the subventions paid from zonal budget to mines covering differences between cost of production and sales prices of coal." In effect, France was protesting Britain's decision to stop "hidden reparations" in coal. The State Department passed France's protests to the War Department, asking that it solicit suggestions from OMGUS for the State Department's reply. Clay noted that the new price of $15 per ton was still below the prevailing coal prices in Europe and that even with the higher price the United States and Britain would have to continue to subsidize the German economy for some time. Perhaps realizing how futile a factual analysis was, Clay concluded that the logical extension of France's arguments would lead to a policy of giving Germany's exports away free so as not to consume the foreign exchange resources of other European countries.[41]

The problem of reconciling the Army's plans for reasonable German economic recovery, the Bevin-Marshall decisions in Moscow, and the State Department's priority for France and the liberated countries is revealed most dramatically and sharply in the battle that raged over the revision of the bizonal level of industry.

CHAPTER SEVENTEEN

The Bizonal Level-of-Industry Plan

C LAY AND ROBERTSON, who had agreed between themselves to study revision of the bizonal level of industry even before Bevin and Marshall
instructed them to do so in Moscow, established working groups in Berlin
to develop a plan within six weeks after the Moscow CFM meeting.[1] The
groups in Berlin worked without specific instructions, perhaps because so
much energy was being expended in Washington on bizonal reorganization, socialization, "excessive" centralization, coal, the PPS's crash program
of studies, and the SWNCC study. A memorandum prepared by James W.
Riddleberger on May 28, 1947, for Marshall's use in a press conference noted
that instructions for Clay on revision of the level of industry were being
considered by SWNCC, but that nothing had been approved as yet.[2] Assistant Secretary of War Petersen, who was in Berlin, cabled the War Department on June 2 that Clay had gone ahead on the basis of Marshall's oral
instructions of April 25, 1947, to negotiate a level-of-industry plan with the
British. He reported that the negotiations had gone well, that they were
nearing completion, and that formal instructions from Washington at
that point would only delay matters. The few points remaining to be agreed
upon, especially the level of steel production, would be submitted to Washington for approval as soon as the negotiations in Berlin were completed.[3]

LEVEL-OF-INDUSTRY INSTRUCTIONS FOR CLAY

If Petersen hoped his explanations and assurances would keep the State
Department from interfering, he was disappointed indeed. The record
shows that while SWNCC was considering instructions for Clay, the State
Department learned from its own sources that the British-American working groups in Berlin were going considerably beyond the instructions being
considered in SWNCC. Clay and Robertson were, of course, taking quite
literally their oral instructions to make the bizone self-sufficient, and they

were projecting production levels and export targets that would have increased Germany's requirements for Ruhr coal and decreased the number of plants available for reparations. After learning what Clay and Robertson were planning, the State Department drafted instructions for Clay on its own initiative—rather than through SWNCC—only to have the Army, Forrestal, Harriman, and the cabinet intervene.

When Petersen saw the State Department's draft level-of-industry instructions, he objected to those portions calling for resumption of reparations deliveries to the Soviet Union. Even though the State Department's position was fully in accord with the written memorandum of the Bevin-Marshall understanding of April 18, 1947,[4] Petersen took his objections to Patterson, who took them up with Marshall, who took the dispute to a cabinet meeting on June 27, 1947. The cabinet discussion appears to have gone in several directions, probably because the cabinet members had been misled about the reasons for Clay's original reparations suspension, certainly because they feared the unfavorable impact a reversal of Clay's reparations suspension would have on public opinion and the Congress, and specifically because Patterson, Forrestal, Harriman, and Anderson did not want to ship any more reparations supplies to Russia. The cabinet finally decided to hold the reparations issue in abeyance, pending the results of scheduled discussions in Paris between Bevin, Bidault, and Molotov on Marshall's Harvard invitation.[5]

Petersen admitted to Clay later that his and Patterson's intense concentration on blocking the State Department's attempt to issue instructions for the resumption of reparations deliveries to the Soviet Union had caused the War Department to let a more fundamental policy decision on the level of industry slip through as an apparent compromise. The instructions that finally went to Clay on July 2, 1947, contained two paragraphs directing him to plan a level of industry that would make the bizone economically self-sufficient and a third paragraph instructing him to make sure that the new level-of-industry plan would provide for substantial reparations deliveries to the countries devastated by Germany. The question of resuming actual deliveries would be the subject of future instructions, the cable said, but the United States was committed to deliver complete and usable capital equipment as reparations from Germany, and it would do so even at the expense of Germany's future living standard.[6]

Clay responded to the instructions four days later by asking for clarification of the basic contradiction they contained. Making the bizone self-sufficient and providing an adequate schedule of reparations for the IARA countries, Clay said, could not "be accomplished at the same time." The revised level of industry would leave little complete and usable German capital equipment of the type that the IARA nations wanted. It would leave steel plants, miscellaneous plants, and separate machines of various kinds, Clay noted, but the IARA nations were not interested in residues. They wanted the same plants and equipment that were needed in Germany to increase Germany's exports and to produce for the immediate needs of European recovery and rehabilitation. Calculations in Berlin had been based on the needs of German industry to establish a self-supporting German economy with a low but reasonable standard of living and the ability to contribute to European recovery. If OMGUS was now to proceed from another basis, Washington would have to instruct it on whether German self-sufficiency or reparations were to be the governing factor. If reparations were to govern, Clay said he needed advice on the minimum needs of the IARA nations. Those needs would, in effect, automatically fix the level of industry to be left in bizonal Germany. "We are fully prepared to carry out any instructions relative to meeting IARA needs," Clay concluded, "but we cannot negotiate under indefinite instructions which approve a revised level of industry only in the understanding that it also produces substantial reparation deliveries of complete and usable German capital equipment to carry out previous US commitments to IARA countries."[7]

On July 8, 1947, Petersen explained to Clay how the contradictory instructions had come to be issued, and he commented on the discussions and disagreements in Washington regarding Germany's participation in the European recovery program. According to Petersen, the State Department's view was that OMGUS should always weigh the costs to the German economy against the advantages that would accrue to the United States from aid given to another country. The State Department thought OMGUS should emphasize German production of export goods needed by the liberated countries, even though doing so would be an indirect subsidization of the liberated areas at the expense of Germany or of American dollar appropriations for Germany. The Army, in turn, argued against using Germany as a base from which to subsidize the liberated areas, either by draining off German production or by requiring additional United States appropriations there in the form of funds to prevent disease and unrest. Petersen reported that Marshall seemed willing to consider a reasonable compromise of the differences. As I shall show, the compromise became the heart of the Marshall Plan: Germany would be made economically self-supporting to satisfy the Army, but not at the cost of abandoning the State Department's policy to rehabilitate the liberated countries.[8]

The immediate upshot of the disagreements and negotiations in Washington was that Clay never got the clarification of policy he asked for on July 6, 1947. He did, however, get a statement of principles and policy on the relationship of Germany to European recovery. The statement had been hammered out in its final form by SWNCC and the Committee of Three on July 2 and 3, 1947, and it was transmitted to Clay by the Army on July 10, 1947.[9] The statement was, in fact, the first clear indication that the Washington bureaucracy was moving in the direction of Marshall's compromise.

POLICY ON GERMANY AND EUROPEAN RECOVERY

It will be recalled that Acheson created a State Department policy study committee on July 31, 1946, and instructed it "to consider and report on long-range United States Policy for Germany." The committee, which was chaired by James W. Riddleberger, the head of the Central European desk, made its studies and then reported on September 13, 1946. But no formal policy statement resulted, even though the report produced a great deal of pushing and pulling during the fall of 1946. In October the committee apparently decided that its work was finished and that it could not "be reconvened to make any corrections." Its report was nevertheless used as a basis for the studies and papers that were prepared for the CFM meetings in New York in December 1946 and in Moscow in March–April 1947.[10] In January 1947 the project to issue a German policy and information statement was deferred until after the Moscow CFM. It was resumed—apparently early in May—and a draft of a revised and updated version of JCS directive 1067 was sent to Berlin late in May.[11]

The economic and financial sections of the revised directive were completed on May 19, 1947, *four days before* the PPS issued its first recommendations on the European recovery program. The timing is particularly significant, because the changes that were made in the draft directive between May 19 and July 10, 1947, show precisely the policy decisions made in Washington with respect to Germany as a result of the PPS report of May 23 and Marshall's Harvard invitation of June 5, 1947. The economic-disarmament and reparations paragraphs of the May 19 draft of what became JCS directive 1779 contained the following key section:

Your Government does not agree to reparation from Germany greater than that provided by the Potsdam Agreement. Nor does your Government agree to finance the payment of reparation by Germany to other United Nations by increasing its financial outlay in Germany or by postponing the achievement of a self-sustaining German economy. Your Government reaffirms the principle that the proceeds of authorized exports shall be used in the first place for the payment of authorized imports.

The finance paragraph stated, among other things, that

(4) you will use the resources of the German economy to the maximum extent possible in order to reduce expenditures from appropriated funds of your government. You are authorized, as provided in the Potsdam Agreement, to use the proceeds of exports to pay for imports which you deem essential, subject to strict accounting and auditing procedures; (5) you will continue to aid economic recovery by collection of full payment for exports of German goods and services; and (6) you will continue to prevent non-essential imports.[12]

The July 10, 1947, policy statement on the relationship of Germany to European recovery revised the foregoing economic and finance paragraphs of the May 19 draft policy completely. It also reversed the priorities implied in the Bevin-Marshall decisions on Germany taken at Moscow on April 18, 1947. First, the July 10 policy stated that no initiative was to be taken in the matter by the United States zone of Germany, but that "the occupied area must be represented when European recovery plans are being prepared." Second, the new policy affirmed that if the restoration of European trade required an increase in American expenditures in Germany, or if it set German self-sufficiency back, appropriated funds for Germany would be increased or the German economy would be compensated by American grants of relief monies to the country or countries that benefited from Germany's trade losses so that the country or countries in question would be able to pay Germany. Third, the new policy directed the American commander in Europe to consult with European countries and international organizations and to ensure that Germany produced and exported goods needed by the European countries for their economic recovery and rehabilitation.[13] In short, German and European recovery would have to occur simultaneously.

Although Marshall, Patterson, and Forrestal agreed to the July 10, 1947, statement of principles as a reasonable compromise, the lower levels of the State Department feared that the Army would not conform willingly.[14] The Office of European Affairs, from which criticism of the Army's policies and Clay's practices had originated often in the past, was in fact convinced that

Clay had to be brought in line. According to a memorandum of July 11, 1947, which reflected internal discussion on the question of Germany's role in the contemplated European recovery program,

Instructions must be prepared which will force Clay to give the necessary cooperation and to view our operations and policies in Germany in the light of our over-all interests in Europe. I do not believe that a mere instruction to him "to cooperate" is good enough. Something must come from the Secretary of War, and preferably from the President, telling Clay that the success of the European recovery plan is of vital importance to this country and that our representatives in Germany must do everything possible to contribute to its success. He should also be told of the political pitfalls ahead and warned not to make statements or take action which might upset the applecart.[15]

THE BIZONAL LEVEL-OF-INDUSTRY PLAN

As if to prove the validity of the State Department's fears, but actually because the negotiations begun in Berlin in April 1947 had moved to a natural conclusion, Clay reported on July 12, 1947, that he and Robertson had reached agreement on a level-of-industry plan to make the bizone self-supporting. The plan proposed to leave enough facilities in Germany to produce 10.7 million tons of steel annually in the two zones, or 11.5 million tons for all of Germany. It allowed for overall production at about the 1936 level, whereas the March 1946 ACC plan had allowed about 70 to 75 percent of the 1936 level. Heavy machinery production would be at 80 percent of the 1936 level, precision optics at a level sufficient for domestic consumption and the 1936 level of exports, photo equipment at a level sufficient to export 150 percent of "prewar" amounts, and so on. According to Murphy, the new plan's major departure from the ACC's 1946 plan was in its increase in the production levels of metals, chemicals, and machinery (to about 90 or 95 percent of the 1936 levels). Those were the very industries from which the largest shares of reparations were to have been drawn. But Murphy argued that the 1946 plan had already set "maximum and in some cases unrealistic levels for non-reparations industries," and there was thus no room for expansion in them.[16]

Clay explained on July 12, 1947, that he and Robertson had agreed to send a preview copy of the plan to the IARA and then to publish it by joint US/UK release in Berlin on July 16, 1947. As soon as possible after that, he and Robertson would publish a list of the plants that would be available for reparations under the new plan. The list would, in effect, show the plants that were to be removed from the reparations lists based on the March 1946 level-of-industry plan. Commenting on the question on which he had sought clarification six days earlier without success, Clay observed that the new level of industry would leave a number of plants for reparations, but not in quantities sufficient to satisfy the IARA nations. Referring to the issue on which he had been promised further instructions after the cabinet had decided what they would be, Clay reported his intentions not to resume reparations deliveries until he had a policy instruction. For what it was worth, he recommended a policy of no further deliveries (to anyone, it should be noted) until the question of German economic unity was settled. He thought an alternative might be to deliver plants and equipment over and above the amounts that would be needed for the new level of industry to the IARA nations only, pending Soviet fulfillment of the Potsdam provisions.[17]

Panic in Paris

State Department functionaries, apparently vigilant against acts that threatened the Department's European policy, predicted how France would respond to the revised level-of-industry plan. H. Freeman Matthews, the head of the European desk, relying upon an earlier memorandum prepared by Counselor Charles E. Bohlen, warned on July 11, 1947, that conversations in Berlin were about to result in an agreement to increase German industry and to decrease German coal exports. "If France cannot derive some compensating advantage in the reorganization of [the] German economy," Matthews said, "it will become a serious political problem for the present government and in this respect add to the difficulties facing it."[18]

The French were, indeed, worried about American and British plans for Germany, and Clayton—who was in Europe for discussions on the Marshall Plan—discovered that they wanted to talk about little else. Prime Minister Paul Ramadier, with whom Clayton wanted to discuss Europe's general economic and political problems, brought up the German question on his own. He talked about coal, the Ruhr, reparations, and a German "federal solution," insisting that satisfactory decisions on these issues were "conditions" for the success of the Marshall Plan.[19] Bidault laid it on the line later in the day.

Apparently anticipating what Clayton planned to discuss with him, Bidault made brief remarks about the urgency of the Paris talks on the Marshall Plan and then zeroed in on the German problem: The French government had not changed its views on reparations and the Ruhr. If France were pressured to change its policies in the interests of German recovery, the French Communists would have a field day. On the Ruhr, Bidault said, "no decision should be taken which might prejudice the final status." Clearly revealing knowledge of the Coal for Europe program and the American plan to turn the mines over to German trustees, Bidault warned that "a change in the Ruhr institutions, a change decided upon separately, would be dangerous and would put the French Government in a difficult position."

Clayton talked about the new coal program, the world shortage of steel, and the State Department's "diagnosis of Europe's economic situation and possible methods of dealing with the problem," but Bidault's fears and anger increased as his knowledge increased. He was especially upset by Clayton's reference to the Ruhr and coal exports. He said his critics were charging that "to assemble a conference at Paris to examine the Marshall proposals amounts to the same thing as abandonment of reparations and modification of the French position as regards the Ruhr." France could not accept a decision on the Ruhr that "would upset the definitive settlement of the German question." With respect to increased steel production, Bidault "saw no reason to raise the ceiling fixed in March 1946." In the first place, German production had not yet reached the ceilings set in 1946, and, in the second place, "France was capable, if it receives sufficient coke from the Ruhr, of increasing its steel production very substantially and of meeting, with the help of Belgium and Luxembourg, *all the requirements of western Europe, including German needs*." Anticipating the Clay-Robertson plan which was completed in Berlin a day later, Bidault warned against a "decision raising substantially the German industrial level." Lashing back at Clayton's observations that dismantling was uneconomic and that the question of Germany's level of industry would have to be settled rapidly, Bidault protested "energetically" that "there must be no repetition of the error of Potsdam, where German questions were settled without France." No French government, he said, could consent to a European economic program that included "abandoning reparations" and "raising the level of German industry." Dismantling should, in fact, "be pursued at an accelerated rate," and France should "receive a much more substantial share of reparations in equipment and in capital goods."

Apparently realizing in the end that Clayton's remarks and observations were based on policy decisions already made in Washington, Bidault suggested a procedure that would permit implementation of those decisions without immediately threatening his and the French government's political future. According to Ambassador Caffery's report of the Bidault-Clayton conversation, Bidault argued emphatically "against any public statement which could lead the French people and Europe to believe that reparations had been abandoned" or that Germany's economic potential would be increased. "If such a declaration were made, the Conference [on the Marshall Plan] which is to meet Saturday would be doomed to failure and 'there would be no Europe.' Nevertheless if you are determined to do some of this, as much as we dislike it, do it without any public announcements." Taking their cues from Bidault, Clayton and Caffery recommended to Washington that "extreme care ... be taken to avoid any public statement at this juncture" on reparations, the level of industry, and related matters. Such a statement could jeopardize the Paris conference on the Marshall Plan "or strengthen the Communists in their effort to discredit its efforts and those of the French Government."[20]

Publication Delayed in Washington

Contemporary press reports and the conclusions of my previous book notwithstanding, the decision to delay publishing the level-of-industry plan for the bizone was made in the State Department *before* the British suggested it and *before* the French knew what the details of the plan were. When the State Department learned that Clay and Robertson would publish the plan in Berlin on July 16, 1947, it responded on the basis of Clayton's and Caffery's warning and recommendation of July 11 from Paris and prepared a draft cable directing Clay to hold up things, to take "no final action to conclude agreement," and not to publicize anything until he had received an answer to his cable of July 6, 1947—the one in which he had asked for clarification of his contradictory instructions of July 2, 1947.[21] The State Department delivered the draft cable to the Pentagon for transmission to Clay late in the day on July 14, 1947. The British *aide-memoire*—based on a telegram from Bevin in Paris, warning that "any immediate publication ... would be a tragic mistake"—was delivered to Under Secretary Lovett at the State Department the next day, on July 15, 1947.[22] After Bevin's views came in, the draft cable of July 14 was revised to incorporate Bevin's views, to state that publication of the plan in Berlin would disrupt the Paris conference on the Marshall Plan, and to instruct Clay to give no further publicity to the agreement and to do his best to ensure against leaks in information.[23]

Having seen the draft cable of July 14 and knowing the inclinations and priorities in the State Department, Assistant Secretary of War Petersen warned Assistant Secretary of State Hilldring about using the delay to accommodate France. Advising the French before publication was one thing, he said, but to consult with them was something else. The French had always refused to agree on matters dealing with the German economy and German unity, whether quadripartite or tripartite. They would oppose the new level of industry on the familiar ground that an increase in German steel production would mean less German coal for export. "It will be a great sign of weakness, and lack of leadership," Petersen continued, "to consult with the French or other nations on this matter." If the State Department gave in to pressures and permitted the desire for reparations to determine the German industry level, there would be little production in Germany for European recovery.[24]

Despite Petersen's warning, the Americans eventually caved in. Interestingly, the British did not. Bidault had approached Bevin on July 15, asking for details on what the bizonal authorities were doing in Berlin on the German level of industry. Bevin advised the Americans that he would have to give Bidault the story, and the British did so the next day. Making clear that they were not consulting the French, the British informed French foreign office officials that the military governors had reached "a firm agreement subject only to minor amendment." The British delegation, which was headed by Sir Edmund Hall-Patch, explained the plan and answered questions from the French. Among other things, Hall-Patch argued that the two powers had to do something to "prevent the continuation of the present intolerable drain on the US and UK taxpayers," and he reminded the French that the two powers "had not pressed on with these questions as much as self-interest would have dictated since we had hoped for economic unity *or at least French cooperation.* We were now acting out of sheer necessity."[25] After additional pushing and pulling, the British cabinet finally decided, on July 24, 1947, to delay the plan until September (presumably until the Paris conference on the Marshall Plan had completed its work) and "to consider any representations that the French Government may care to make to them" (but not to the Paris conference on the Marshall Plan) on the level of German industry and the coal-management plan.[26] In short, the British would listen to France's representations, but they would not *consult* the French. The Americans took another route, and they eventually brought the British along.

The French-American Connection

Harriman, traveling in Europe as Secretary of Commerce and as Chairman of the President's Committee on Foreign Aid, conferred with Bidault on July 16, 1947, about an hour after British officials had begun to explain the bizonal level-of-industry plan to French officials. Hervé Alphand, the Director of Economic Services in the French foreign office, had come out of that meeting and briefed Bidault hurriedly before he received Harriman and Ambassador Caffery. According to Caffery, "we found Bidault in a hysterical condition."[27] Bidault was alarmed about the measures being taken to centralize Germany, to reestablish the Germans in the mines, and to raise the steel production level. Even if he wanted to, Bidault said, he could not overcome the simultaneous opposition of De Gaulle, the Communists, and some of his friends to the proposed developments in Germany. He warned that the Communists would use the level-of-industry plan to support their charges that Germany would be rebuilt first, and that his government would fall if he tried to explain to the French parliament—in which there were 180 Communists and 120 Socialists—the Truman Doctrine, the Bidault-Bevin-Molotov meeting in Paris on the Marshall Plan, "the outright breaking with the Soviets," and the bizonal plans for the Ruhr and German production.[28]

On the following day, perhaps assuming that Harriman's visit was evidence that the Americans were reaching the point of no return on Germany and European recovery, Bidault combined official threats to the two governments with a personal, handwritten plea to Marshall (and perhaps to Bevin too). In identical notes to the United States and Britain, Bidault claimed that the French government had been greatly surprised by the details of the bizonal plans for Germany. He asserted that the bizonal military governors had exceeded their administrative authority and had made major political decisions affecting the future. France could not agree that the British acting alone, or in concert with the Americans, were "qualified to act in so far as the control of mines in the Ruhr and the industrial level of Germany are concerned." Such decisions were within the province of the CFM and the future peace conference, and nothing the Americans or the British did could be regarded "legally or de facto" as binding. Should the two powers now "confirm the proposals" Clay and Robertson had made regarding the Ruhr and the level of industry, "the French Government will be forced to protest solemnly and publicly, and to make all reservations as to the various consequences which will inevitably follow."

Writing to Marshall personally, Bidault emphasized the political ramifications of the German decisions. France had "burned its bridges" early in July at the Bevin-Bidault-Molotov meeting in Paris. Having opted for the British/American position, France was now confronted with "an absolutely unexpected situation" requiring an additional vital decision. "I went straight ahead in all tranquility," Bidault summarized. "I committed my country. I regret nothing that I have done. But I fear, if the plans of which I was given a glimpse materialize at this time, not only will all my efforts have been in vain, but they will be turned against the cause I served.... I, personally, would be unable to continue my task."[29]

Confronted with the threat of a French public protest on the bizonal level of industry and apparently moved by Bidault's pleas, the State Department moved toward concessions. Caffery reported again on Bidault's panic, noted his threat to resign, and observed that there was no predicting what the outcome would be.[30] Clayton thought that "any firm decision raising [the] German level of industry should be postponed for further consideration and consultation."[31] After talking with Maurice Schumann and "other prominent and decidedly friendly Cabinet Ministers," Caffery reported that "the majority of responsible French leaders" supported the policy of using German industrial capacity for German and European reconstruction, "but beg, repeat beg, that no further measures for German rehabilitation be announced until European plan under Marshall proposal be prepared, *when German program can be made to dovetail with it*."[32] The basic strategy of the PPS had been to dovetail the Moscow decisions on German economic recovery with a larger European program. Now that France seemed ready to go along with that plan, the only problem remaining was to coordinate and time the various decisions so as to bring France and the Army along together. Bringing the Army around proved to be difficult.

The Army continued to press for an early release of the level-of-industry plan without consulting the French. Patterson resigned as Secretary of War, apparently disgusted with the course events were taking, but only after he and Marshall had agreed that the plan would stand even though its announcement would be postponed for a few weeks to avoid a possible blow-up of the Paris conference on the Marshall Plan.[33] But the strategy of delay without consultations was doomed to failure, because of French adamance and the State Department's priorities. As Harriman, the British, and others had done earlier in Paris, Under Secretary of State Lovett tried to reason with Ambassador Bonnet in Washington about the need for a measure of German recovery. Lovett talked about the heavy costs of the occupation to the United States and Britain, and he warned that the Congress was getting tired of carrying the German financial burden with appropriations. Bonnet replied by predicting a crisis for the French government and implying that it would have to withdraw from the Paris talks on the Marshall Plan.[34] Kennan—remaining precisely consistent with the PPS's original strategy—concluded that Bidault's difficulties should be resolved by consultations. The consultations could be informal and no agreement was needed: just an understanding or a general consensus on what had to be done to raise production in Germany. He therefore recommended tripartite talks with the French on Germany in the interests of putting the issue squarely to the French: "a rise in German production or no European recovery financed by the U.S." Meanwhile, "I am afraid we must insist that instructions be sent to General Clay to the effect that the agreement arrived at between him and General Robertson should be held in abeyance pending final approval by the two governments in the light of the development of the general situation in Europe."[35]

Marshall and Bevin, independently of each other, decided to hold up things and to concert their respective responses to Bidault's threats and pleas, and they advised each other of their decisions in messages that crossed. Marshall suggested they inform Bidault that they would "suspend further announcement on the agreed plan...until the French Government has reasonable opportunity to present its views for full consideration."[36] Bevin cabled that he was planning to consult the cabinet in the light of Bidault's messages and expressed the hope that Britain and the United States could develop a common position. Meanwhile, he was instructing Robertson to suspend action on the level-of-industry and the coal-management plans, to make no announcements, and to give out no publicity "either official or unofficial" in Berlin or to the IARA.[37] Bevin hoped Marshall could send similar instructions to Clay, which for some reason Marshall did not do. Perhaps he was too busy with his other problems, perhaps he thought sending additional instructions would stir up more trouble than not sending them, and perhaps he assumed (mistakenly, as it turned out) that the Army's cable of July 15, 1947, asking Clay to hold things up, was sufficient.

Marshall's and Bevin's gestures did not satisfy France. The French wanted to participate in the decisions on Germany, and they would not be put off by promises of a "reasonable opportunity" to present their views on an agreed plan. Jean Monnet told Clayton as much in Geneva, and Marshall and Matthews got the word in Washington from Ambassador Bonnet.[38] Bonnet told Marshall that France objected to restoration of European steel production "on the same pattern as before the war," because France wanted French steel production to replace German steel production. That was one of the primary objectives of the Monnet Plan. According to Bonnet, Bidault was "prepared to take a plane for Washington" to discuss these things as well as France's readiness "to join her zone to the British-American zones" if the CFM failed to reach four-power agreement in London in November. Marshall then gave Bonnet a copy of a message he had already dispatched to Paris for Bidault. It said that the level-of-industry plan would be suspended until discussions could be held between the Americans, the British, and the French.[39] In short, the State Department was no longer talking about an "agreed plan," but was interpreting the pledge to give France a "reasonable opportunity to present its views for full consideration" to mean *discussions*. Bonnet said the message would please Bidault, but it had the effect of a declaration of war on the American Army.

CHAPTER EIGHTEEN

Battling on the Potomac

M ARSHALL AGREED to discussions with the French on the Ruhr and the bizonal level of industry without having received Bevin's agreement to do so and despite Petersen's heated protest that consultation would be a grave mistake as well as a sign of weakness and lack of leadership.[1] His message of July 21, 1947, to Bidault promised to suspend announcement of the level-of-industry plan "until the French Government has had a reasonable opportunity to discuss these questions with the United States and United Kingdom Governments," and until "full consideration" could be given to France's views. Marshall said he had been in touch with Bevin, that the British government was "considering the whole question," and that he hoped to be able to arrange soon the manner in which the issues could be considered.*

The British were not prepared to go as far as Marshall had gone, and they proposed to tell the French as much. They wanted Clay and Robertson to use the new level-of-industry plan when submitting data to the CEEC for its studies on the Marshall Plan in Paris, and they suggested that the implementation of the plan be delayed only until the beginning of September. In the meantime the two governments should "be prepared to consider any representations that the French Government may care to make to them on the subject of the level of industry plan." Since France had not agreed to zonal fusion, Britain would not concede to France "an equal right with themselves to determine the level of industry in the bi-zonal area." Neither would Britain look with favor upon a decision of France to make representations to the Paris conference on the Marshall Plan.[2]

The Americans tried to get the British to modify their position and to refrain from lecturing the French about their rights. Matthews, who was

---

* SecState to Bidault, July 21, 1947, *FRUS*, 1947, II, 1003–4. Interestingly, no information copy of the cable was sent to Berlin for Murphy, though to have done so would have been normal procedure. Neither was Clay advised.

deeply involved in the State Department's difficult negotiations with the Army on French consultations, told British representatives in Washington that Marshall's message of July 21, 1947, would probably satisfy Bidault for a few days and suggested that no further messages be sent to him for the time being. If Bevin thought otherwise, the Americans hoped he would try to delay things somewhat and merely tell Bidault that there would be discussions, but without commenting on the form they would take.[3] Apparently aware of the battle raging between the two departments in Washington, Bevin agreed on July 25, 1947, that no consultations with the French would occur until the Americans and British had worked out the form they would take.[4] In the end, the Army forced the State Department to accept the British plan to receive representations from the French rather than to discuss the issues with them. Although that position was soon to be reversed, the battle that produced it is noteworthy.

THE LINE OF BATTLE

The State Department had apparently overcome the Army's initial objection to Marshall's July 21, 1947, message to Bidault by promising to negotiate with the Army on Germany's participation in European recovery and on the form the discussions with France would take. In any case, Assistant Secretary of State Hilldring prepared a position paper on the two issues for Marshall's use in a meeting he planned to have with the newly appointed Secretary of the Army, Kenneth C. Royall. Hilldring suggested that Marshall make clear to Royall that the State Department "possesses an awareness of . . . the problems faced by our military authorities in Germany." Marshall might tell Royall that the State Department had gotten assurances from the French that they would fuse their zone with the bizone, possibly in November; that it had gotten Bevin's agreement to put socialization "in cold storage"; and that it was "prepared to defend [the Clay-Robertson level-of-industry plan] with the utmost vigor against suggestions for modification," even though it could not guarantee against "conceivably meritorious" changes in the interests of security and European recovery.[5] But before Marshall got around to telling Royall these things in Washington, the pot boiled over in Berlin.

Bidault had leaked the news of Marshall's commitment to discuss the bizonal level of industry, apparently soon after he received the message himself on July 22, 1947. Clay and Murphy got the news for the first time by reading it in the Paris newspapers, and on July 24, 1947, Clay fumed to

Petersen in a teleconference. He was furious because Marshall had agreed to consult France and because no one had advised him officially. When Petersen informed him that Royall and the Army had learned of Marshall's decision with "shocked surprise," Clay thought both he and the Army had had enough. He said the United States had recently announced a new policy for Germany (JCS 1779), but that it would obviously not implement it. "I think we are facing disaster in Germany and I don't like to head a failure which I can do nothing about. Under present conditions, it seems to me War Department should disdain further economic responsibility and insist now on a civilian takeover by State." Clay asked twice during the conference for an invitation to attend the coal conference in Washington, making clear his intention not to return to his assignment in Berlin.[6]

Eisenhower advised Clay to stick it out rather than resign, among other things asking Clay to "please remember that now abide Faith, Hope and Charity, these three, and the greater than any is a sense of humor." Though Clay took the advice, he did not drop the issue. He complained to Daniel Noce, the Director of the War Department's Civil Affairs Division, that he had negotiated the level-of-industry plan with Robertson under a broad authorization from Marshall to do so, only to have it jerked out of his hands without even a notification as to why. He reminded Noce that he had protested the same kind of end run by the British on the coal-management and socialization issues and recalled that on those occasions the Army and the State Department had backed him and pressured the British to let the decisions be made in Berlin.[7]

Meanwhile, Marshall and Royall reached a tentative—though incomplete —understanding that the two departments would defend the Clay-Robertson plan "unless amendment may be found necessary in case of [a] genuine threat to the success of the European economic plan (Marshall Plan) or in the face of a threatened collapse of democracy in France." They agreed that decisions on bizonal matters rested exclusively with the American and British governments and that "in view of the recognized urgency of the situation in Germany" the level-of-industry agreement should be announced as soon as possible, hopefully no later than September 1, 1947. Last, they agreed to continue their discussions regarding implementation of the level-of-industry plan and "various questions relating to the Ruhr coal matter" and to advise Clay and Murphy as soon as they reached "an understanding on those or related matters."[8]

Upon receiving the details of the Marshall-Royall understanding, Clay cabled Royall that he could accept the idea that the agreed level of industry might have to be amended in the interests of the Marshall Plan, but he argued that "only security and not economic reasons" could justify a lower level. He warned that France would demand reductions for reasons of competition; and he commented on the difficulty of evaluating the threat that British-American policies in Germany posed for French democracy: "France has consistently argued that democratic government in France would fall if French communists could appeal to [the] French people that French government had yielded to a planned restoration of Germany either economically or politically.... Nevertheless, some time this risk must be taken as [the] French government will continue to insist that this will result and no one can prove otherwise except by actual test."[9]

On the same day, July 28, 1947, Marshall and Royall reworked their tentative understanding of July 26, and recorded their agreement in written form, not unlike the form of a treaty between two sovereign nations:

1. No other country will have any vote, veto or power of decision as to the bi-zonal level of industry, and no liaison representative or other representative of any other government will participate in any bi-zonal or other U.S.–U.K. conferences as to the bi-zonal level of industry.

2. If any government presents to the U.S. Government its views as to the level of industry plan, the State Department may transmit these views to the bi-zonal authorities for their consideration. Such views will be appraised by the bi-zonal authorities and given such weight as is thought proper, and their recommendation on the fundamental questions of the level of industry forwarded to the U.S. and U.K. Governments for approval.

3. ... public announcement of the new bi-zonal level of industry agreement will be made at the earliest possible date and is expected, in any case, to be not later than September 1, 1947....

4. If an invitation from the Paris Conference for American representation is accepted the delegation would be expected to include representatives of the War Department and the Theater Commander....

5. The U.S.–U.K. coal conference will take place in Washington as scheduled and no other government will be invited to participate. No other country will have any vote, veto or power of decision as to the ownership, management or other matter affecting the coal industry in the bi-zonal area....

6. If any government presents to the State Department its views as to coal in the bi-zonal area, the State Department may transmit these views to the members of the coal conference, if then in session, and to the bi-zonal authorities for their consideration. Such views will be appraised by the bi-zonal authorities and given such weight as is thought proper....

7. It is agreed that the export price of coal is a matter for final determination and announcement by the bi-zonal authorities subject to any immediate increase in price being confirmed by the coal conference.[10]

The conclusion is inescapable: Patterson's resignation, Petersen's resignation, Clay's threats to resign, the Army's determined support of Clay's views, its threat to demand an immediate State Department takeover in Germany, and the sympathy of Congressional leaders for Hoover's recommendations, as well as the State Department's knowledge that the British cabinet had already taken a position on Germany similar to Clay's and the Army's, helped Royall to achieve a remarkable victory in his negotiations with Marshall.

Royall went to Berlin immediately after his "treaty" with Marshall. According to Petersen, he went to obtain Clay's views on the German situation and to develop a basis for "his further negotiations" with the State Department on the level of industry and coal.[11] While he was in Berlin, Royall held a press conference, during which he reportedly said he felt free to boost German industrial production without consulting the French and that he knew "of no agreement by the War Department to consult with France before promulgation of the plan to raise the level of industry in Western Germany."[12]

One may doubt that Royall planned it that way, but Bidault now read in the newspapers about a decision taken in Washington—as Clay and Murphy had done a week earlier. Bidault's response was no less dramatic. Ambassador Bonnet called Under Secretary of State Lovett at his home on Saturday evening, August 2, 1947, telling him that he had had three telephone calls and a long cable from Paris during the day—all on Royall's remarks in Berlin. The French government regarded Royall's statements as proof that the United States was insincere in its agreement to consider French views regarding the level of industry and the Ruhr. Meeting Bonnet again on Sunday, Lovett tried to calm him by suggesting that Royall might have been misquoted. But Bonnet had various press clippings and news stories and would not be put off. More important, Bonnet had seen the draft of a message the State Department and the British planned to deliver to Bidault the following morning, and he was convinced it proved "that the Army would go ahead and 'do what they had always intended to do.' "[13] The message, when read in the light of Royall's remarks in Berlin, suggested to Bonnet that the Americans and the British would listen to the French and then go ahead with the level-of-industry plan no matter what the French had said.

Bonnet and the French were, in fact, interpreting things correctly. After the Marshall-Royall "treaty" of July 28, 1947, the British and American governments had adopted a common position on July 30, 1947, and agreed to inform Bidault in separate but identical messages as soon as possible.[14] The State Department transmitted its text to Caffery on August 2, 1947, and he prepared it for delivery to Bidault on August 4. The message—which was the one Bonnet had seen in Washington before his talks with Lovett on August 3, 1947—referred to Marshall's agreement to suspend announcement of the level-of-industry plan until France "had had a reasonable opportunity to present its views for full consideration." It stated that the United States was "now prepared to give careful consideration to any representations which the French Government may care to make" on the level of industry and asked for "an early expression of French views." Noting that the issue might complicate the work of the CEEC's Paris deliberations on the Marshall Plan if it was discussed there, the message asked the French to "communicate their views directly to the British and United States Governments, rather than at the Conference." It also stated American readiness to receive and consider French views "with respect to the management and control of the coal industry in Germany."[15] In short, France could make representations, but there would be no formal *discussions* or *consultations*.

SAVING THE FRENCH

Having listened for a weekend to French reactions to Royall's press conference remarks in Berlin, to complaints that France had been sold out in the interests of German recovery, to threats that France would withdraw from the Marshall Plan talks in Paris, and to warnings that political deluge was imminent in France, Lovett in Washington and Clayton, Caffery, Douglas, and Murphy—who were in Paris to be near the CEEC talks—conferred by teleconference on August 4, 1947. Clayton wanted to delay delivery of the latest note to Bidault, and his colleagues in Paris agreed. He thought "it would be better to have informal talks with the French on these two questions rather than request them for a formal expression of their views because political considerations would probably compel them to express in writing more extreme views than if substantial agreement could first be reached informally. Once having expressed such extreme views, it would be very difficult to change." But it was too late. The British had already delivered the identical note to Bidault. Caffery interrupted the teleconference to report that the French had " 'blown up' over the British note." Lovett thereupon urged Caffery "to calm Bidault" by assuring him "that any French views would receive full consideration."[16]

Lovett's and Caffery's assurances to Bidault were soon transformed into fixed policy. Marshall eventually got the cabinet's endorsement for a recommendation to consult with the French; he got Bevin's agreement to discussions with the French, albeit "on an informal and noncommittal basis"; and he advised the French of his decision, for which Bidault expressed his "gratitude" for a "most constructive step."[17] But the decision to consult France required the State Department to break the Marshall-Royall formal agreement of July 28, 1947, and to somehow make peace with the Army over the conflicting bureaucratic objectives in Germany and Europe. Some State Department functionaries believed the only way to proceed was to demand greater discipline from the Army and particularly from Clay. Others thought the State Department should finally agree to relieve the Army of its political-economic responsibilities in Europe and thus free the State Department to follow its own objectives in Europe.

The Urge to Discipline the Army

During his teleconference with Clayton and others in Paris on August 4, 1947, Lovett said the French wanted "to sit down with UK and US and talk matters over," but that the War Department would not agree. He said the matter was "likely to go to highest level" for decision.[18] Lovett had, in fact, prepared a memorandum for Marshall on August 3, in which he denounced Royall's press-conference remarks as evidence of the unworkable and dangerous nature of any understanding with the War Department on American foreign policy. He argued that the Clay-Robertson plan and the Marshall-Royall understanding of July 28 were limiting the Secretary of State's freedom of action in the conduct of American foreign relations, and he complained that "we are unable ... to live up to our assurances to the French and are exposing the United States in its relations with France to a justified charge of duplicity and dishonest dealing." He concluded that "we are now forced to ask for a reconsideration of our understanding with the War Department," because it was impossible to conduct American foreign relations "on the basis of any such understanding."[19]

Marshall received Bonnet on August 5, 1947, and heard that France "must insist on a frank discussion" rather than a written presentation. Bonnet said the French interpreted Marshall's July 21 message as a commitment to hold discussions, and they linked such talks with France's continued participation "in the work of the Paris Conference." If the United States was now prepared "to abandon the idea of tripartite conversations," Bonnet said, "M. Bidault is ready to proceed immediately to Washington to explain

France's position directly to the Secretary of State and to set forth the consequences of any refusal to discuss these problems with the French Government." The French realized that the United States Congress would not accept a European recovery program that did not include Germany, Bonnet continued, but France would not accept a program "built around an agreement with respect to German industry in which it had not participated."[20]

Marshall refrained from immediate comment on either the French memorandum of August 5, 1947, or Bonnet's oral elaborations on it. But he was subjected to strong pressure from within the State Department for a decision favorable to France. Clayton, who had already recommended discussions *before* the latest uproar, recommended "strongly" that the United States "come to some arrangement with Bidault." After talking with Bidault and Monnet, he reported that the French had dropped their demands for separation of the Ruhr and the Rhineland and that they were now talking about a more "reasonable" solution. They wanted assurances of "access by Europe to the products of the Ruhr," and they had suggested creation of an "international board which would allocate the Ruhr production of coal, iron, and steel and perhaps chemicals between Germany and other countries."[21] Meanwhile, State Department functionaries studied the Clay-Robertson plan. They admitted that they had neither adequate information nor precise data on the plan, but they concluded nevertheless that the plan had "no claim to scientific accuracy" and suggested that it be revised to make it more "palatable and convincing." The final push apparently came from Caffery, who reported on August 8, 1947, that "all work of technical committees of conference on European Economic Cooperation responsible for steel, coal and coke has come to a stop because the French are reluctant to participate in preparation of reports based on answers to questionnaires submitted by bizonal authorities on these commodities. It will be recalled that these answers were based on assumption 10 million tons steel output 1951." The French, Caffery continued, had told the British privately that they would participate again "as soon as satisfactory arrangements have been made for level of industry discussions."[22]

Marshall took the issues to the cabinet meeting on August 8, 1947. I have found no records of what was decided there, but Marshall left the meeting apparently determined that the Marshall Plan would have to be made to work. He advised Lovett afterwards that Royall had "accepted my views regarding a tripartite meeting with the French in London on the Clay and Robertson level of industry agreement." According to Marshall, Clay—who had threatened again to resign—would be Royall's problem. Royall "was going to give him orders and drop further discussions."[23]

But Clay, who had written to Byrnes in May expressing concern for the 70 million human beings in Germany and complaining that "we cannot place Germany in a vacuum while we solve world problems as if it did not exist," was in no mood to accept orders without further discussion.[24] Murphy cabled that the decision to hold tripartite talks on the level of industry and the control of Ruhr coal mines was unacceptable to Clay. Clay had told Murphy that he would not go to London for the talks and that he planned to cable the Army Chief of Staff asking for immediate retirement. "He further said that all of this would make some form of public statement by him inevitable." Murphy said he had tried to reason with Clay, but that he seemed "determined to proceed with [his] request for retirement."[25] Douglas also tried to unruffle Clay and get him to change his mind, but the arguments that finally persuaded him to do so came from Royall. Royall told him that "the export coal price, the freight charges and other specific matters" would be "solved promptly." He also promised to try "to induce State to take over Military Government," and he assured Clay that "if State does not take over promptly, I will seek approval of a broad directive to that end," presumably from Truman.[26]

The Urge to Replace the Army

Even before Royall threatened to go to Truman for a decision, the State Department had, in fact, been moving independently toward a State Department takeover in Germany. Unlike Byrnes and Acheson, who had repeatedly made clear the State Department's terror at the prospect of assuming administrative responsibility for military government, Marshall initiated discussions with the Army on the issue. Marshall, who knew the Army well, decided early that the Marshall Plan could not be implemented with the Army in command in Germany. It is probably not a coincidence that he wrote to Patterson on May 23, 1947—on the day that Kennan completed the PPS's initial report—and raised the issue of transfer of responsibility. It was certainly the first time in two years that the State Department took the initiative on that issue. Marshall suggested to Patterson that the two departments coordinate plans for the eventual assumption by the State Department of administrative responsibility for the occupied areas. He named Hilldring the State Department's planning officer and asked Patterson to appoint someone with whom Hilldring might deal in the Pentagon.[27] Hilldring's office began immediately to draw up plans, proposals, recommendations, organization charts, and other materials typical of a staff study. But there is no evidence that Hilldring's studies led to action until late in August 1947, after Royall had promised Clay to "induce State to take over Military Government" and after he had talked with Marshall about making the transfer by the "stroke-of-a-pen."[28]

Meanwhile, attitudes in the lower levels of the State Department had shifted from the urge to discipline Clay and the Army to the urge to replace them. The shift is traceable. As late as May 1947, Matthews recorded his shock and disappointment at OMGUS's unwillingness to buy Iceland fish for $2 million, and he protested that "OMGUS continues to be indifferent to any policy or proposal which does not seem to bring immediate benefit to the German economy." He concluded that "the question of Iceland fish purchases seems to be taking its place along with coal exports, Czech transit traffic, and Hungarian restitution, as matters in which OMGUS will only cooperate under extreme pressure." In June 1947, State Department functionaries "believed that under the plan for recovery of Europe we will be required to view Germany as being another European country, rather than an American enclave and that General Clay will be required to deal with German problems in the ECE on this basis." By July, a member of Matthews's staff thought it was time to "force Clay to give the necessary cooperation and to view our operations and policies in Germany in light of our over-all interests in Europe." He argued that a "mere instruction to [Clay] 'to cooperate' " was not enough. Something had to come from the Secretary of War or "preferably from the President," warning Clay not to make statements or take actions that "might upset the applecart."[29] But finally, by August 1947, James A. Stillwell, a special assistant to Clayton, recommended that the State Department "immediately take over the direction of the civil affairs of Germany" and borrow from the Army the "present military staffs, both in the field and in Washington," the latter to be accomplished by relieving Clay as military governor and replacing him with a High Commissioner "directly responsible to the State Department." Stillwell's argument was that Clay was "still operating on disease and unrest and economic self-sufficiency ideas," whereas the "main objective of our occupation policy henceforth is to direct the German economy so it will be able to play its rightful share in the Marshall Plan for the Recovery of Europe." What that meant was "that the coal and other industrial production of the Ruhr are absolutely essential to any economic recovery plan which may come out of the Paris Conference" and that neither the Army nor the Germans should have the right to determine how this production would be allocated and used.[30]

True to his promise to Clay, Royall discussed the State Department's take-over with Marshall late in August 1947. He followed the informal discussions with a formal proposal on September 3, 1947. With respect to Germany —where he wanted the turnover to occur first—Royall suggested the appointment of a High Commissioner by October 10, 1947, and the transfer of functions, personnel, budget balances, and responsibilities by November 1, 1947.[31] As it had always done when it faced the prospect of administering the policies it would have preferred to "force" Clay and the Army to administer, the State Department recoiled. Having already agreed to the transfer in principle, however, this time it objected to details and specifics, and it argued that it could not meet the rigid target dates suggested by Royall. The discussions continued, nevertheless, and a meeting of top-level State Department and Army officials with Clay on October 18, 1947, reveals an apparent move to work out a compromise arrangement whereby Clay would be made High Commissioner. The available documents do not show that Clay was approached directly to be High Commissioner, but they do suggest that he knew or suspected what was under way. He reviewed cases (Czech transit services, restitution, and inland waterways) to illustrate that the State Department had consistently interfered with the implementation of his directives. He said the State Department had instructed him on details in violation of his general directives. It had also sent instructions without permitting OMGUS an opportunity to make recommendations or state its position. He concluded that "if a high commissioner were appointed for Germany no self-respecting man would continue to operate with the degree of interference he had experienced and he, himself, would not be willing to continue under these conditions for another year."[32]

Two days after the meeting with Clay, the State Department released a statement that it had "no present intention to take over responsibility for the administration of occupied areas from the Army" and that consideration of the takeover had "been indefinitely postponed."[33] But Clay and the Army forced the issue. Clay asked Royall and Eisenhower for greater authority as military governor, and he apparently made clear his intention to retire rather than continue under the prevailing conditions.[34] Royall approached Marshall personally on October 31, 1947, and then drafted a memorandum of "understanding" which he asked Marshall to approve on November 5, 1947. The memorandum said:

The directives issued by the United States Government to overseas commanders in their capacity as Military Governors constitute statements of the objectives of military government and prescribe basic policies which our Government wishes given effect. It is intended that Military Governors broadly construe their authority and be empowered to take action consistent with relevant international agreements, general foreign policies of the Government, and governmental directives, appropriate or desirable to attain military government objectives or to meet military exigencies.[35]

Hilldring analyzed Royall's memorandum for Marshall and warned that it would be a mistake to give Clay additional authority. He reviewed the history of Clay's efforts to get broader instructions since the day in April 1945 when he read the first drafts of JCS 1067. According to Hilldring, Clay—with War Department support—had always treated the administration of Germany as though Germany represented the only United States interest in Europe and he had done a magnificent job. "But it is not unfair to him to say that he has been far less objective and wise in blending his administration of Germany with the equally worthy purposes of the United States in Austria, France, Italy, Belgium and the Netherlands." What was needed, according to Hilldring, was not an assignment of greater authority to the War Department or the military governor, but a decision to turn "the administration of military government over to the State Department."[36]

The records do not show exactly how and when it was done, but Marshall and Royall apparently agreed informally to plan the State Department takeover by July 1, 1948, and to withhold any announcement of the decision until after the London CFM. Marshall said as much to the Senate Foreign Relations Committee on January 8, 1948, and an Army memorandum of January 19, 1948, reveals some of the details. But after the London CFM, the State Department still wanted to avoid a formal public announcement of the decision and the target date, so as to permit a change in the event of a world crisis. Royall finally went ahead anyway on January 27, 1948. As if to prove that the State Department was correct, on March 23, 1948—three days after the Russians had walked out of the ACC in Berlin—Truman announced that after a review of the situation he had decided not to make any changes in the administrative arrangements in Germany. Clay would remain as military governor and Commander in Chief of United States forces in Europe.[37]

Truman's announcement said that the decision to keep the Army in control would not change American policy to develop German self-government and administrative responsibility. The Army, Clay in particular, used that pledge to encourage, promote, and literally force the rapid creation of a West German government which could assume the responsibilities the Army did not want anymore—and which it had exercised unwillingly since the early summer of 1945. What I know of that development has been published previously, but I might note here that the firm and decisive support for German self-government and eventually for the Basic Law came, in the first instance, from Clay and the American Army, who saw these things as means to be relieved of some of their political and economic responsibilities in Germany.[38]

CHAPTER NINETEEN

Germany and the Marshall Plan

THE COMPLICATED negotiations with Britain, France, and the Army on the bizonal level of industry and the Ruhr coal-management plan finally convinced the State Department that it would eventually have to assume administrative responsibility for the policies it wanted implemented from the American base in Germany. Faced with the financial responsibilities that accompanied administrative responsibilities in Germany, the State Department moved toward a position it had prevented the Army from taking for more than two years: it became more critical of France's aims and objectives regarding Germany and the future of Europe, and it finally concluded that France's territorial and economic demands were, in fact, incompatible with any program that would have Germany achieve a viable economy in the future.

Though much has been written about the continuing influence of a Morgenthau-plan mentality on American policy in Germany, the issues were much more complex than that.[1] Riddleberger had, in fact, outlined the American dilemma in Europe as early as November 24, 1945, when he discussed the pitfalls of a policy that would try to destroy Germany's industrial war potential on the one hand and prevent the creation of a "soup kitchen" economy on the other.[2] Essentially, the problem was and remained one of achieving balance, moderation, and a "golden mean," which—as I have shown—the French would not discuss, much less consider; which the State Department would not further unless France was satisfied; and which the Army would not pursue, in part because it wanted to promote sufficient economic recovery to make a case for relief from the civil-political responsibilities of the occupation and in part because it was out of sympathy with the State Department's broader politico-economic mission in Europe.*

---

* Interestingly, the Russians made specific proposals that would have had the effect of achieving a balance between reparations, exports and imports, and German consumption, and they did so repeatedly—at Potsdam, during the Clay-Sokolovsky discussions in Berlin late in 1946, and at the Moscow CFM in 1947. See *FRUS*, 1945, Potsdam II, 810, for the Soviet pro-

Late in April 1947, when Marshall learned from Clay and from his own advisers what the political and economic consequences of his and Bevin's Moscow decisions on Germany were likely to be, he instructed Kennan and the PPS to initiate studies that would, in effect, look toward a balanced solution of Europe's economic problems, rather than toward the unilateral rehabilitation of the bizone which the Army, the British, Herbert Hoover, and the Eightieth Congress seemed to prefer. As noted previously, the PPS divided the problem, recommending a limited German recovery program (the Coal for Europe plan) and a long-term European program to be developed by the Europeans themselves, albeit with American "friendly aid in the drafting."[3] Both recommendations were essential elements of the Marshall Plan, the first one to pacify the Army and the second one to pacify the Europeans and the State Department.

The Marshall Plan emerged issue by issue during 1947, but in conformity with the PPS's two major recommendations and with remarkable clarity and consistency. A limited amount of general German economic recovery would have to occur as an essential component of the Coal for Europe program, and perhaps to satisfy the Army, the British, the Congress, and the American public. But Germany's recovery would have to be controlled in such a way as to satisfy the political interests of Bidault and to ensure the prior recovery of Germany's neighbors and provide for their security.[4] In the interests of better control, neither the American Army, nor the British, nor the German Socialists would be permitted a free hand in the Ruhr and the Rhineland. Furthermore, the announcement of German recovery programs, such as those provided for by the Bevin-Marshall decisions in Moscow and detailed in the Clay-Robertson level-of-industry plan, would have to be coordinated with the long-term program for European recovery; their implementation would have to be delayed until the Europeans agreed upon

---

posal of July 23, 1945, which said: "In working out the economic balance of Germany the necessary means must be provided for payment for imports approved by the Control Council. In case the means are insufficient to pay simultaneously on reparations account and for approved imports, all kinds of deliveries (internal consumption, exports, reparations) have to be proportionally reduced." See *FRUS*, 1945, Potsdam II, 276–81, for a discussion of the Russian proposal, and Clay to War Dept., for Echols, Oct. 11, 1946, RG 165, file WDSCA 387.6, Sec. IV, Box 351, NA, for the Russian proposal in the fall of 1946, a proposal that Clay considered to be "a reasonable basis for discussion." Clay's judgment that the Soviet proposal violated neither the Potsdam Agreement nor the level-of-industry plan may be found in Clay to War Dept., for Noce, Jan. 22, 1947, RG 165, file WDSCA 387.6, Sec. VIII, Box 354, NA. See SecState to the President and ActgSecState, March 19, 1947, *FRUS*, 1947, II, 264, for the statement that at Moscow Molotov "insisted that German industry must be set at a level to insure her internal needs, payment of imports, and reparations."

a common recovery plan, and—if necessary—those aspects of the German recovery program that were ready for implementation before the common plan could be developed would have to be kept under wraps until it was politically opportune to reveal them to Germany's neighbors or to make them public.

As Kennan's committee had recommended, the German-recovery phase of the PPS report (the Coal for Europe program) went forward immediately, even while the long-term program was still very much in its embryo and developmental states, and long before the Americans had a clear conception of the general European plan. That condition produced the events and situations already described: the British-American coal talks, the wrangling over the coal-management plan and socialization, the dispute about the export price of coal, and the conflict between Berlin and Washington on the bizonal level-of-industry plan. The condition also confronted the State Department with the task of reconciling its limited German recovery program—which was moving ahead more rapidly than the general European recovery program—with its own priorities and with France's demands for security, territory, coal, a decimated German economy, and a decentralized German political structure. The latter remains to be described.

Early in June 1947 the State Department urged OMGUS to proceed rapidly with the British to develop a coal-production program in Germany. Later in June the Committee of Three asked Clay and Murphy to report on what was needed to permit the German economy to contribute actively to European recovery and to bizonal self-sufficiency.[5] On July 2, 1947, the State Department instructed Clay to make sure that the level of industry being planned for the bizone would provide for a self-supporting German economy, but also to make sure that substantial reparations deliveries from Germany would occur, even though doing the latter might be at the expense of Germany's future standard of living.[6] One day later the Committee of Three combined these and other instructions and adopted a policy statement on Germany and the Marshall Plan:

1. The United States would make known publicly its willingness to have its zone of Germany collaborate in the European recovery program, but no initiative was to come from Berlin even though "the occupied area must be represented when European recovery plans are being prepared."

2. If the restoration of European international commercial relations required an increase in American expenditures in Germany, or if such restora-

tion would set back German self-sufficiency, American expenditures in Germany would be increased, or the German economy would be compensated by provision of American relief monies to the country or countries benefiting from Germany's trade so as to enable them to pay Germany.

3. The American commander in Europe would consult with European countries and international organizations regarding German production and trade and ensure that emphasis was given to the export of German goods needed by the European countries for their economic recovery and rehabilitation.

4. Transactions of a substantial nature, or those which resulted in trade exchanges between Germany and other European countries—but not in conformity with the three preceding principles—were to be referred to Washington for decision.[7]

According to Petersen, who sent the policy statement to Clay on July 10, 1947, paragraph 2 was a frank admission that United States policies and programs in the interests of general European recovery might delay a self-sustaining German economy and require an increase in funds for Germany or for other countries so they could pay Germany for her exports.[8] That paragraph was, in fact, a hasty and uncoordinated reversal of previous policy, and when it was grafted onto the draft of JCS directive 1779 on July 11, 1947, it stood there in flat contradiction of another section of the same directive, which stated that the United States would "not agree to finance the payment of reparation by Germany to other United Nations by increasing its financial outlay in Germany or by postponing the achievement of a self-sustaining German economy."[9]

The flow, the content, and the contradictions of the policy instructions and directives that went from Washington to Berlin in June and July 1947 testify to the State Department's attempt to reconcile the irreconcilable: German recovery to self-sufficiency and France's demands for coal, security, and economic advantage. Matthews, who had worried similarly to McCloy in 1945, warned Lovett on July 11, 1947, that "conversations looking toward the level of increase in German industry are about to result in an agreement between the British and ourselves with benefit to the economy of Germany," that German coal exports would be reduced, and that unless France received compensating benefits the French government would face serious political problems.[10] On the same day, Clayton and Caffery heard from Ramadier and Bidault that France had not changed its German policies and demands, and that if France could not be accommodated there would be no Marshall

Plan. They advised Marshall immediately to use "extreme care ... in dealing with this matter."[11]

Neither extreme care, nor caution, nor attempts at rational argument or persuasion were enough to allay France's fears, and Bidault's warnings of impending doom for France, the Marshall Plan, and Europe increased with multiplier effect as he received more and more information about the British-American plans for the bizone. Bevin, who was in Paris, warned that publication of the level-of-industry plan "would be a tragic mistake." The Army ordered Clay to hold up everything for the time being. Harriman, who "found Bidault in a hysterical condition," tried to convince him of the absolute necessity for a new level of industry in the bizone and claimed "that the point had been reached where measures had to be taken." But Bidault had already told him he was "very alarmed about developments in Germany," and he warned that "he would be compelled to protest" if the Americans went ahead with their plans.[12]

Marshall finally capitulated and advised Bidault on July 21, 1947, that no further action on German recovery plans would be taken until "the French Government has had a reasonable opportunity to discuss these questions with the United States and United Kingdom Governments."[13] Marshall had been influenced by a personal plea from Bidault, by official demands from the French government, by suggestions from Bevin, and by advice from Kennan to hold tripartite talks and use the occasion to "place squarely before the French the choice between a rise in German production or no European recovery financed by the U.S."[14] Marshall's sensitivity to the political tightrope on which he was walking is revealed most clearly in a memorandum he wrote to Secretary of Agriculture Anderson on July 22, 1947. Anderson had been in Europe from July 1 to 14, 1947. Upon his return he wrote a report for Truman and asked the State Department for advice on its possible publication. In reply, Marshall assured Anderson that he had been "tremendously impressed" with Anderson's report to the cabinet, but that recent French reactions to the level-of-industry plan for Germany had "produced a very delicate situation, particularly with regard to the development of the meetings of the sixteen nations in Paris." Under the circumstances, Marshall said, the publication of Anderson's report would be unwise "for the reason that it stresses the economic reconstruction of Germany virtually to the exclusion of any mention of our interest in the reconstruction of the liberated areas—which is the basis of the Paris conference." In other words, Marshall liked the report but feared that its publication

would "add fuel to the flames now raging by reason of the agreement negotiated between General Clay and General Robertson."[15]

As noted previously, Marshall agreed to discussions on Germany with the
French for political reasons, and he did so before the Americans and British
had agreed on what they would discuss. What the two powers finally discussed with France is conveniently summarized in the State Department's
instructions of August 12, 1947, to Ambassador Douglas, who was the
American delegate and the chairman of the London tripartite discussions.
The French were to be given every opportunity to make a full statement,
but Douglas was to "make it clear that in the absence of a fusion of the
French zone with the US and UK zones, the US and UK are responsible
for and will take final decision on all matters regarding the bizonal areas."
Douglas was to defend the Clay-Robertson plan vigorously against modification, but "if in your judgment there is a genuine threat to the success of
the European economic plan or if democracy in France will be threatened
unless changes are made," the issue was to be referred to Washington for
further instructions. Douglas was to discuss neither the resumption of
reparations nor the rate of reactivation of Germany industry. If the French
raised the Ruhr management issue, Douglas was to tell them that "acceptance" was not involved, but that the matter could be discussed in the CFM
scheduled for November. If France raised the question of the French zone's
union with bizonia, Douglas was to make clear that the United States
desired such union, but that it would not hold up the new level-of-industry
plan pending a French proposal and its discussion. If France wanted to discuss the Saar, Douglas was to say that he had no instructions and that the
matter was being dealt with through diplomatic channels.[16]

As Clay had predicted in July, the French made clear in London that
their major objection to the bizonal level-of-industry plan was that it threatened the Monnet Plan's projected steel production figure of 12 million tons
per year. At issue were France's plans to replace German steel production
with French steel production, ostensibly to ensure permanently France's
economic and political security. The French said they could not accept the
plan in the absence of a prior agreement that made certain Germany would
have to export "sufficient coal and coke to insure that German steel production will not absorb so much German coal as to hamper the steel production of other countries, particularly French Monnet plan."[17] Before the

London talks were over, the United States instructed Douglas to advise the French of American willingness to discuss the matter and to "give sympathetic consideration" to the proposal for a Ruhr authority which would assure "that access to production of the Ruhr shall not in the future...be subject to the will of Germany." According to Douglas, the British were prepared to cause trouble on the issue, and he therefore decided to take a chance and try to get France to approve the final communiqué without using the policy statement.[18] He hardly needed to do so, since he, Clayton, and Caffery had already told Bidault on August 19, 1947, that they had instructions to postpone further informal discussion with the French on the question of an international board for the Ruhr, but that they "were authorized to say...that at some more appropriate time we would be glad to give sympathetic consideration to the French position on the Ruhr."[19] Although Bidault was disappointed, "even" chagrined, and threatened once again that "no French Government, neither the present one nor any succeeding one, could ever agree to a revised level of industry for Germany, without some assurances as to French security and access by Europe to the products of the Ruhr," he finally became reconciled—particularly after the three Americans said they would recommend that discussions be held on the issues immediately after the London tripartite talks.[20]

The political considerations that were so important to the decision to hold the tripartite talks on Germany also dictated the content and the emphasis of the final communiqué. The communiqué covered up disagreements, played down the many issues that had not been resolved, and failed to make clear that France continued to object to the level-of-industry plan and its implications.[21] The talks and the communiqué nevertheless gave both sides what they wanted: Bidault got the political leverage he said consultations would give him to forestall political crisis and to remain in control in France. The British and Americans could now publish the Clay-Robertson bizonal level-of-industry plan and use it officially as the basis for Germany's contribution to the Marshall Plan for European economic recovery.

The issues that were not agreed upon during the London tripartite talks were the subjects of continuing discussions and negotiations in Berlin, Paris, London, and Washington throughout 1947 and on into 1948. For example, the military governments in Berlin negotiated agreements on the Saar, coal, coke, and the Moscow sliding scale for German coal exports.[22] In Paris, Clayton, Caffery, and Douglas—seconded by Kennan and Charles H. Bonesteel (a colonel on the War Department General Staff, on assignment with the State Department)—initiated informal talks with the French on the international board for the Ruhr, thus laying the basis for the final agreement on a Ruhr coal and steel authority, which came out of the London six-power talks of 1948.[23]

Interesting and significant though the continuing negotiations are, they are beyond the scope of this study. Once the Americans had reasonable assurances that the French would not (could not, since they had been consulted) *openly* and *publicly* protest the Ruhr coal-management plan, the price of export coal, and the Clay-Robertson level-of-industry plan, they concentrated on giving "friendly aid" to the CEEC in Paris on the form, structure, technicalities, and nature of the European recovery program. In the end, they made sure that the German decisions that Marshall and Bevin had made in Moscow would be implemented.

Germany and the CEEC

A convincing body of evidence now available makes clear that the Americans conceived and developed the Marshall Plan as a method for resolving the United States economic dilemma of the German occupation. There are, for example, Marshall's and Dulles's reports on the Moscow CFM;[24] the PPS's report of May 23, 1947, with its emphasis on German coal for Europe; and the SWNCC message of June 19, 1947, to Clay, which said that "any program of European reconstruction must necessarily take Germany into account." There is a record of Clayton's remarks to Bevin and the British cabinet members that "a radical change is needed in approaching the German coal problem as *sine qua non* to any consideration of the over-all European problem." Finally, there is the Committee of Three's policy decision of July 2, 1947, which said that "the occupied area must be represented when European recovery plans are being prepared."[25]

Kennan's recommendation that the Europeans themselves develop the long-term program of European recovery, together with the political decision to have them do so despite Clayton's vigorous protests that "*the United States must run this show*," and the continuing public posture taken by Marshall and others that the United States would limit its role to "friendly aid," all made it difficult for the Americans to get the kind of German program they wanted and needed. Interestingly, Molotov seems to have sensed that there was more to the Marshall invitation than met the eye, for he asked Bevin and Bidault in Paris whether they had additional information from the Americans.[26] Though I have no way to demonstrate the conclusion, Molotov's performance at Paris late in June and early in July 1947 makes sense if one assumes that the Soviets detected either duplicity or a political-economic trap in the Marshall Plan. Why else would Molotov ask, as the first order of business, whether Bevin and Bidault had "inside" information from the United States or whether they had made any "deals" among themselves? Why would he ask the two unanswerable questions he proposed they send to Washington: How much money was the United States prepared to spend on European recovery, and would the Congress vote to approve the credits? Perhaps Molotov knew from Russia's own experience with economic planning that the grand plan implied by Marshall's invitation was impossible to achieve—either because the capitalistic economic systems would refuse to stand still for that, or because the various nations would not accept the encroachments on their national sovereignty implied in the program, or because of the sheer *technical* impossibility of constructing the economic input-output tables that would be required for the task. Since its economic objectives were either unbelievable or impossible to achieve, Molotov's assumption that the Marshall Plan was essentially a political program, not unlike the imperialism that Marxist-Leninists were inclined to see, has a certain logic.

Molotov's departure from Paris on July 3, 1947, undoubtedly helped to narrow the range of political disagreement after that, but it did not pave the way for the kind of German-based European recovery program the Americans had in mind. On July 20, 1947, Caffery reported on the first week of the CEEC's Marshall Plan talks in Paris, concluding that the "French, of course, have not abandoned outwardly their ... 'pastoral' approach to [the] German problem and contend that security lies in 'pulling heavy industrial teeth' of Germany."[27] On August 6, 1947, after a three-day round of discussions on the progress of the CEEC and on the latest PPS paper (of July 23, 1947), Clayton, Caffery, Douglas, Murphy, and Paul H. Nitze (the Deputy Director of the Office of International Trade Policy, State Department) recommended formally that it was time to give "friendly aid" to the Paris conference. The recommendation produced considerable discussion in Washington and Paris on how to give "friendly aid" without facing charges of dictation and on how to develop a "united front" in Washington to ensure against contradictory "friendly aid" from the War Department and the State Department.[28] On August 14, 1947, the State Department sent guidelines to Paris for Clayton's and Caffery's use in "informal talks with appropriate committee chairmen and others."

These guidelines were vague and cautious on details, but firm on principles that would require effective German participation in European recovery. The guidelines said the participating countries were paying too little attention to Marshall's call for self-help and mutual aid. "An itemized bill summing up prospective deficits against a background of present policies and arrangements will definitely not be sufficient." The Americans expected the production programs of participating countries to be based not only on their own needs, but also on fulfilling the needs of the other participating countries. Apparently to ensure that Germany would be included as a full participating country, the guidelines concluded by stating that "further aid can be given [regarding the] role of western Germany."[29] The importance of the latter emerged in future exchanges.

Clayton and Caffery reported on August 20, 1947, on their "friendly aid" in Paris, noting—as one example of a fundamental problem—that the combined steel-production figures submitted by the bizone and France would require more coke than would be available anywhere.[30] Douglas believed that the "French must be persuaded to abandon [their] present position that original Monnet plan must be accepted practically unchanged no matter what the cost to US or to general recovery," and he thought the United States would have to be represented in Paris to defend the bizonal production plans against the competing demands of the Monnet Plan. Though the United States need not take the lead, Douglas said, "neither should we hang back."[31]

Meanwhile, in Washington, further discussion within the State Department produced the consensus "that sufficient friendly aid is not being given." Two days later, Lovett cabled Marshall (who was attending an inter-American conference on peace and security at Petropolis, Brazil) that the CEEC was scheduled to produce a report within a week, and that the news was all bad. The CEEC was going to come out with sixteen shopping lists that would require an unreasonably large grant of American aid and that would in the end fail to establish European self-sufficiency by 1951. Lovett said the conference had gone ahead despite Clayton's and Caffery's instructions of August 14. The United States had "pointed out [the] necessity for primary emphasis on efficient utilization of existing capacity rather than on capital development," but "adequate results have not ensued." According to Lovett, "the time has now arrived for us to give some indications that the present plan is not acceptable and to do so promptly." He recommended that Clayton and Caffery be instructed to press for a European plan based upon self-help and mutual aid rather than on long-term capital improvements in the individual nations. They should "emphasize the breaking of specific bottle-necks well known to them and to us."[32]

Lovett talked about shopping lists, costs, and principles, but he also al-luded to the fundamental issues at stake. The "specific bottlenecks well known to them and to us" referred to the Ruhr and the Rhineland, to the PPS's Coal for Europe program, and to the limited rehabilitation of trans-portation and of steel and machinery production that was needed in Ger-many to implement the coal-recovery program. Lovett's insistence on self-help and mutual aid rather than on long-term capital improvements re-ferred to the conflicting demands for coal, coke, steel, manpower, and other factors of production between the Monnet Plan and the Clay-Robertson bizonal level-of-industry plan. Finally, his note that the Americans wanted "primary emphasis on efficient utilization of existing capacity rather than on capital development" meant that the Americans had opted for the Clay-Robertson plan for Germany rather than the Monnet Plan for France; for European recovery that would include substantial German recovery rather than for European recovery that would, in the first instance, benefit France. It was well known that the greatest source in Europe of idle or under-utilized capital equipment—on which the Americans wanted to put "pri-mary emphasis"—was in Germany. The Harriman Committee, for example, referred to that knowledge when it observed that "over-all production in some European countries has shown remarkable recovery, [but] it is still true that Europe's total production, *especially when Germany is taken into account,* is well below prewar levels, with the critical item of coal a prime example."[33] Marshall himself referred to it in a speech he made to the Chicago Council on Foreign Relations on November 18, 1947: "The truth is that far from being accorded a preference over any Allied country, Ger-man recovery has lagged so far behind that of the other countries of Europe as to retard the whole effort for European recovery. At the present time in-dustrial production in Western Germany is less than one-half that of pre-war."[34]

Armed with a State Department policy statement of August 26, 1947, and assisted by Charles H. Bonesteel and Kennan (who supplied additional, oral instructions "relating to general political situation"), the Americans in Paris, with Marshall's approval, told the CEEC what they wanted. The fundamental objectives of the program were "to move entire area" toward a "working economy independent of abnormal outside support." To do that "participants must ... foster European recovery as a whole, and ...

make national contributions to this common goal." In order to maximize self-help and mutual aid, the "program must ... concentrate initially on elimination of bottlenecks and [on] other opportunities for greatest immediate recovery at lowest cost in scarce resources," and—as if to nail down the German contribution firmly—the "program must be directed primarily toward short-run recovery rather than long-run development; full use of existing or readily repairable capacity and restoration of normal domestic and intra-European intercourse therefore have priority ..." Clayton and his colleagues in Paris translated their instructions into seven "conditions," which they presented to the leadership of the CEEC on August 30, 1947. The "condition" providing specifically for Germany's recovery stated that "long-run development projects should not be allowed to interfere with the reactivation of the most efficient existing productive facilities. The latter must have first priority."[35]

AMERICAN STRATEGY AND THE CEEC

The State Department's strategy was to dovetail German rehabilitation with the general European recovery program and to present to the United States Congress a single foreign-aid package. To do that, it sought acceptance in Paris of a set of broad, general principles that would permit implementation of the level-of-industry plan for the bizone and allow a rate of reactivation of German industry that would also be acceptable to the Army, the British, the Congress, and ultimately the American public. The strategy, to be followed on three fronts, was outlined in detail by Charles Bonesteel in a memorandum of August 27, 1947, to Robert Lovett.

In Paris, "the United States will state to the participating countries that it is our intent to meet their views with regard to bizonal matters in so far as is possible, consistent with our responsibilities as the military governors. This intention to be based clearly on the assumption that the Paris conferees give assurances of an equal intent with regard to their national programs, and further demonstrate this intent by their actions at Paris. The demonstration of their intent requires, in effect, that discussions of the German zones are part of a broader discussion of all national programs."

In London, Douglas would consult with the British to get them to agree to the proposed discussions in Paris.

In Washington, the difficult assignment of satisfying the Army would go to Lovett, Bohlen, and Saltzman, who would meet with Royall, Eisenhower, Draper, Lauris Norstad (the Director, Plans and Operations Division), "and no others," if that could be arranged. According to Bonesteel, the State Department approach to the Army should be "educational, with a slight dictatorial flavor." Lovett and Bohlen could "present the broad global picture, bringing out the two-world assumption" and emphasizing the need to counterbalance the "Soviet world" and to treat "Europe west of the Iron Curtain on a regional basis." With respect to budget and finances, the State Department might assure the Army that it was committed to obtaining "considerably greater sums for Germany as part of the regional program." Last, the Army should be told of "the requirement that the German economic matters be discussed at Paris," emphasizing the "security aspect of drawing more closely to us the nations of Western Europe now wavering between communism and us."[36]

Implementing the Strategy

The Army. The State Department's grand strategy proved difficult to implement, even though the Army and the Harriman Committee (the President's Committee on Foreign Aid) fell into line readily. The Army accepted the strategy and agreed to discussions in the CEEC regarding integration of the bizone into the European recovery program. Clay accepted the decision taken in Washington, but he apparently did so on the assumption that he was leaving, for he later made clear that "no self-respecting man would continue to operate with the degree of interference he had experienced" and that he "would not be willing to continue under these conditions for another year."[37]

The Harriman Committee. Convincing the Harriman Committee was easy. Harriman had endorsed Herbert Hoover's report on Germany in March 1947, and he had been promoting Hoover's recommendations since then. After Truman created the Committee in June 1947, Harriman arranged for it to hear reports from Marshall, Kennan (on the political background of the Marshall Plan), Eisenhower (on economic stability and national security), and others.[38] The records of an August 15 meeting of the subcommittee for economic and financial analysis—whose membership included Calvin B. Hoover, former Chairman of the German Standard-of-Living Board in Berlin—reveal a strong bias in favor of stimulating coal production in the Ruhr and Rhineland, increasing the bizonal level of industry, and (in the interests of speedy European recovery) reactivating plants that were in excess of those needed by the German economy under the level-of-industry plan.[39] On September 10 and 11, 1947, the full Harriman Committee heard speeches and reports by several government functionaries, including Kennan, Bonesteel, and Lovett. Lovett reviewed the developments in Paris, summarized the State Department's August 14 guidelines, "which will not be compromised," and described the Clayton-Kennan-Bonesteel attempt to get the technical experts in Paris to modify the requirements for American aid. He concluded that the current CEEC documents and reports could not be translated into a workable program, and he observed that "the Department of State desires that the work to date not be considered as constituting a program."[40]

The message the Harriman Committee got on September 10 and 11, 1947, is described in a letter of September 12, from Owen D. Young, the chairman of the subcommittee on economic and financial analysis, to Harriman. It said, in part:

I share fully the apprehension of the State Department that if we fail to meet the present food and fuel emergency which faces the German people and if we fail to help them develop promptly a long range program of rehabilitation, which will enable them to support themselves, there is grave danger that western Germany will become communistic and will be taken over by Russia. If Russia could supplement her present vast resources of raw materials and manpower with the creative, productive and organizing capacity of the German people, she would become shortly the most powerful nation in the world. The result very likely would be that all of Western Europe would be forced to accept a communistic program. The United States would then be faced with a menace which would make the Hitler threat in perspective look like child's play.[41]

It is needless to push the point further, for the published report of the Harriman Committee is filled with statements and allusions attesting to the Committee's acceptance of the State Department's strategy and policy. There is, for example, the statement that "the amount of aid allotted to Germany may have to be higher than was set at Paris." Further: "In the opinion of the Committee...it is the policies pursued in Germany by our own Government which are of all-importance to the success of any aid program." In addition: "It cannot be too strongly emphasized that the producing and purchasing power of Germany, and, through Germany, the producing and purchasing power of all Central Europe, is indispensable to the recovery of Western Europe." Finally, there is the entire section entitled "Report on the Special Position of the Bizone."[42]

The British. The British initially rejected Washington's proposal to have the CEEC discuss the integration of the bizone into the European recovery program, and the Americans eventually had to seek Britain's support by roundabout means. Perhaps the British agreed with Murphy, who warned on September 8, 1947, that if Germany were discussed in the CEEC the European countries would try to obtain indirect financing from the United States through Germany.[43] Upon hearing of the British rejection, Marshall cabled Douglas to impress upon Bevin the seriousness with which he regarded the British opposition. Marshall noted that "the force of US pressure" to get a cooperative, regional approach at the expense of national programs such as the Monnet Plan "is seriously weakened if the one European area in which the US has direct responsibility abstains." He argued that Germany had not been adequately included in the CEEC reports, and he noted as evidence that the bizone's CEEC questionnaire had reported that mining-machinery production would reach about $1,000 million in 1951, but that the CEEC experts had planned for *only* $13 million in mining-machinery exports from Germany between 1948 and 1951. Further, he noted, the CEEC reports contemplated *no* net steel exports from Germany after 1947.[44]

Douglas was unable to turn Bevin and the British around. Harried by problems in Paris, confronted with the CEEC delegates' resistance to excessive American "friendly aid," and warned by Bevin that direct United States interference would delay the CEEC reports, Douglas asked the State Department to go more slowly. On September 12, 1947, he reported that he had not brought up the bizonal-inclusion question with the British because of the other difficulties he and Clayton were having in Paris. He and Clayton suggested that it might be "more appropriate to ask for the inclusion of the bizonal areas when the conference is reconvened after the submission of the 'provisional' or 'first report.' "[45] Five days later Douglas repeated his advice, saying that the United States could press for inclusion of the bizonal areas after the first CEEC report had been received by the United States government "and when, should it be necessary, the conference is reconvened for the purpose of modifying the first report or preparing a second."[46] In the end, Britain accepted the State Department's strategy and policy on Germany during the broader negotiations in the CEEC and in Washington.

The CEEC. Irony of ironies—in view of what had happened since 1945— as the Marshall Plan talks progressed in 1947, the State Department began to press actively for German recovery over the objections of the liberated countries. It apparently did so roughly in correspondence to its accumulating knowledge of the costs of a European recovery program unless something more was done in Germany than to implement Kennan's Coal for

Europe program. Late in August 1947, after Clayton and others had reviewed the draft CEEC reports being prepared in Paris, Clayton advised Sir Oliver Franks, the President of the CEEC in Bevin's absence, that the $28.2 billion Marshall Plan aid figure that was emerging "was out of the question." He reported to Washington that he was "convinced there is no other way to deal with this situation than to impose certain necessary conditions."[47] The State Department responded with a flurry of activity, much of which mocked the concept of "friendly aid."

On August 26, 1947, the State Department sent Clayton and Caffery a policy statement listing certain fundamental objectives and conditions, which have been summarized previously. It also outlined a procedure for informal and formal American review of the CEEC reports with respect to "both general policy matters and technical questions." It said Germany was to be "covered fully into program" with the revised bizonal level-of-industry plan as the basis. The latter might be changed in the interests of general European recovery as "recommended by conference on same basis that conference makes similar recommendations for changes in Monnet or other national plans."[48] On August 30, 1947, Clayton and Caffery presented the American "conditions" to the Executive Committee of the CEEC. They told the Committee that the preliminary materials and reports they had examined were "disappointing," that the $29.2 billion preliminary aid figure was "much too large." They insisted that the CEEC had to develop a common, regional approach rather than simply add up the uncoordinated national requests. Significantly, the Americans illustrated their arguments from the example of coal and steel, remarking that the CEEC report on steel assumed that all existing steel plants in the sixteen nations would operate at full capacity from 1948 on, even though there was insufficient coal and transportation for this purpose. Confronted with the "conditions," and advised of Clayton's opinion that the existing conclusions of the CEEC "might, if formally advanced, prejudice the success of the entire Marshall program," the Executive Committee gave up "any idea of completing the report by September 1."[49]

A MISSIONARY'S REPORT

Kennan and Bonesteel—who had been present when the "conditions" were discussed with the CEEC Executive Committee in Paris—reported independently to Lovett. They endorsed the official Clayton-Caffery-Douglas "suggestion that the time has come to present our views to [the] governments directly,"[50] and Kennan filed a personal, fascinating analysis of the reasons for the failure of the Paris Conference to develop a satisfactory European recovery program.

Kennan concluded that the United States "must not look to the people in Paris to accomplish the impossible. . . . No bold or original approach to Europe's problems will be forthcoming. . . . Worst of all: the report will not fulfill all of the essential requirements listed by Mr. Clayton . . . on August 30." None of the CEEC delegates was a strong political figure at home, Kennan said, and none could afford to "take extensive liberties with the anxious reservations of the home governments." Furthermore, since the Russians were not present, "the gathering has reverted, with a certain sense of emotional release, to the pattern of old-world courtesy and cordiality in which many of the participants were reared and for which they have instinctively longed throughout the rigors of a post-war diplomacy dominated by the Russian presence." That condition had "practically ruled out any critical examination of the other fellow's figures—particularly as most of the delegates must have lively doubts as to the entire validity of some of their own, and cannot be eager to enter a name calling contest between pot and kettle." At bottom, however, the CEEC delegates' difficulties were compounded by three basic problems and conditions, none of which "can be corrected within the brief period of grace which still remains." Britain's sociopolitical sickness was one of the basic problems. Another was the failure to integrate Germany into the European program. The third was the general political weakness of the participating governments.

According to Kennan, Marshall's Harvard speech had put the European nations to a test, which they had failed. The United States could let things ride, "receive a report which will not really be satisfactory, review it and reject it in due course, making no further effort to aid." Another alternative —"the one we should adopt"—would be for the United States to "make efforts to have the report presented in such a way as to avoid any impression of finality; let it come to us on the understanding that it will be used only as a basis of further discussion; try to whittle it down as much as possible by negotiation; then give it final consideration in the Executive Branch of our Government and decide unilaterally what we finally wish to present to Congress. This would mean that we would listen to all that the Europeans had to say, but in the end we would not *ask* them, we would just *tell* them what they would get." That, according to Kennan, was "what some of the more far-sighted of the Europeans hope we will do."[51]

Three days after Kennan's report, and on Caffery's renewed request for "vigorous and direct representations" to the governments concerned, Lovett sent a circular telegram to the American representatives accredited to the CEEC nations. He instructed them to see the respective foreign ministers or prime ministers as soon as possible and to say that the CEEC plan had "numerous deficiencies" that would make it "unacceptable" to the State Department, "undoubtedly evoke strong criticism" in the United States, and "endanger" the entire program. The amount of aid to be requested was too high, Lovett continued, and the "whole program shows little more than lip service to principles of European self help and mutual help." The telegram summarized the American "conditions," generally went on in the same uncompromising way, and closed with the information that the State Department was trying to get the British to agree to an American proposal to discuss the bizonal plans in the CEEC and integrate Germany into the recovery program.[52]

A footnote in *Foreign Relations* states that "replies from the American missions indicated that these views received sympathetic consideration by the various foreign ministers." But if the British response is indicative, and if Bevin's conclusions are accurate, the footnote is a pure fabrication. Bevin, Sir Edmund Hall-Patch, and Roger M. Makins told Douglas that the seven "essentials" were not new to them, that it was impossible to postpone the scheduled date for the CEEC's report in order to meet the American demands, that the participating countries had already cooperated as much as was possible, and that "any effort to press further would ... so impair national sovereignty that many countries would rebel." In reporting these things to Washington, Douglas noted that "in view of the foregoing, it would have been futile to press for a decision" on CEEC discussion of the bizone and its integration into the general plan.[53]

The American effort to have the CEEC report delayed and revised failed also. The Executive Committee told Clayton and his colleagues on September 10, 1947, that "to meet entirely the US conception of a program would require a change in the terms of reference and this would mean a new conference." There was, in fact, "no possibility of the present Conference agreeing on an integrated plan." The most the Executive Committee would agree to do was to label the CEEC's report as "provisional," with the understanding that they would go to Washington—along with selected technical experts—to review the program there.[54]

While Marshall tried to arouse British sympathy for the American approach and expressed a veiled threat to take unilateral action regarding the bizone, Clayton and his colleagues tried again to move the Executive Committee in Paris. They finally reached an understanding to delay the CEEC's report for about a week and to let American technical experts work *directly* with the CEEC technical committees in Paris to improve the report. Meanwhile, the Americans and the Executive Committee would continue to discuss what further actions would be taken after the provisional report was issued. At this point Bevin asked Douglas to advise Marshall of his earnest "hope that the United States Government, having made its views known, will now allow the Conference to work upon them and complete its report in an atmosphere of calm and without any feeling of external pressure." It is also the point at which Clayton and Douglas decided not to push the question of German discussions in the CEEC and to advise Washington that "it would be more appropriate to ask for the inclusion of the bizonal areas when the conference is reconvened after the submission of the 'provisional' or 'first report' and press for inclusion during the remaining 8 days of the present phase of the work of the conference."[55]

The final result of all these things was the adoption of a procedure remarkably similar to the one Kennan had outlined on September 4, 1947. The CEEC issued a "first report" on September 22, 1947, and sent it to Washington as the European plan called for in the Harvard speech. In Washington the Advisory Steering Committee on European Economic Recovery reviewed the report. The committee had been established late in August when the decision to offer more "friendly aid" was made. It met for the first time on September 9, 1947, under tight secrecy and security rules. At one time it seems to have had about a third of the personnel of the State, Commerce, and Treasury Departments working for it.[56] The Advisory Steering Committee coordinated the CEEC reports with the Harriman Committee and other groups, and it finally met with the CEEC Executive Committee and selected technical experts in Washington in October and November to work out the outlines of the proposal that would be presented by the administration to the Congress.[57]

According to Ernst H. Van Der Beugel, a Dutch foreign affairs expert who participated in the Washington meetings, the discussions in Washington were largely technical but highly informative to the Europeans for what they revealed about the way the American system worked. The Americans, he said, used the Europeans as "part of a team charged with the difficult task of making the Paris Report as attractive as possible for the presentation to Congress." In the process, Van Der Beugel continued, "there was an inclination on the part of the Administration to change accents, to color presentations, to minimize some problems and overemphasize others, to hide existing shortcomings and to applaud practically non-existing achievements, in its efforts to win Congressional approval.... The aim was Congressional approval for a program created solely for the benefit of the Europeans. It was no wonder ... that [the Europeans] had some difficulty, not only in adjusting ... to this situation, but suddenly becoming part of this process."[58]

What the administration did—in fact needed to do—is perhaps illustrated best by quoting portions of an exchange between Vandenberg and Marshall during the Senate Foreign Relations Committee hearings on the European recovery program. According to Vandenberg, the first question he wanted to ask Marshall was also the one he considered to be most basic— too important to be left to Royall, who would appear before the Committee later for the Army.

Vandenberg: What I want to ask you is for your comment as to whether there is any dependable hope for this program without a restabilization and integration of western Germany into the program.

Marshall: The inclusion, or integration, of western Germany into the program is essential. Coal alone provides one of the great essentials to the recovery program, and Germany is a major source of coal. I merely say that it is essential that western Germany be considered an integral part of the program.

Vandenberg: That does not quite go far enough.... I would think that it was just as essential that we had a rather definite and hopeful program for the stabilization of western Germany without too long a delay as it is to have a program for any of the rest of these countries, and to whatever extent you are able to make the statement I should like your comment as to the progress that is being made in that direction, and what the prospects are.

Marshall talked then in rather vague and general terms about coal, about conversations with the French, about administrative reorganization in Germany, and other things.

Vandenberg: To get down to the bare bones of the thing, would it be fair to say that within the limitations of whatever four-power agreements are binding upon us, we are no longer proposing to await decisions of the Council of Foreign Ministers in respect to the mutual integration of the three other zones ... and that we are now proceeding ... without waiting for programs from the Council of Foreign Ministers, always intending ... to leave our programs open to any who wish to subscribe?

Marshall: That is correct, Senator. We are going ahead exactly on that basis.[59]

CHAPTER TWENTY

Of Myths and Realities

THE BACKGROUND and origins of the Marshall Plan for European economic recovery described in this study suggest that neither the official
and orthodox interpretations of its inception and purposes nor the ones
offered by the revisionists are complete and credible.

CONTAINMENT

It would be ridiculous indeed to deny that the doctrine of containment
and the hope for a Communist rollback were features of the discussion and
debate on the European recovery program.[1] Kennan's chairmanship of the
PPS would have been an anomaly if it had been otherwise. But Kennan
and the PPS actually recommended on May 23, 1947, that "immediate
measures be taken to straighten out public opinion on some implications of
the President's message on Greece and Turkey." The PPS did not see "communist activities as the root of the difficulties of western Europe," and it
wanted "to clarify what the press has unfortunately come to identify as the
'Truman Doctrine,' and to remove in particular two damaging impressions
which are current in large sections of American public opinion." The two
impressions were, first, "that the United States approach to world problems
is a defensive reaction to communist pressure and that the effort to restore
sound economic conditions in other countries is only a by-product of this
reaction and not something we would be interested in doing if there were
no communist menace," and second, "that the Truman Doctrine is a blank
check to give economic and military aid to any area in the world where
the communists show signs of being successful."[2]

But, as it turned out, there was no containing the doctrine of containment, to which Kennan himself contributed with his article in *Foreign
Affairs*.[3] The State Department could not carry out the PPS's recommendation, because to do so effectively would have required a forthright discus-

sion of German recovery, which was so essential to the Marshall Plan. As I have shown, a forthright discussion of the German problem aroused Bidault and threatened the political stability of France. Closer to home in the State Department, a forthright discussion of Germany would have called into question the "official" explanations for the difficulties in Germany since 1945. It would have called into question Byrnes's explanations of his failures in the CFM and of the origins of the bizone. It would have called into question the State Department's interpretation of Clay's reparations suspension, and it would inevitably have opened the subject of "hidden reparations." It would have called into question Marshall's explanations of the failure of the Moscow CFM, and it would have challenged the credibility of other pronouncements, releases, and statements—all of which were public knowledge. In a sense, Kennan, Acheson, Matthews, Cohen, Bohlen, and others in the State Department lived to reap the fruits of their own suspicions and of the various tests they had devised and used to frustrate the Russians and keep Clay and the Army off France's back in 1945 and 1946.

An effort to contain the doctrine of containment in 1947 and 1948 would also have flown in the face of a broad spectrum of opinion in the newly elected Eightieth Congress, where the State Department's wartime and immediate postwar stewardship was already under attack for "appeasement" of Russia. Scaring hell out of the Congress and the American people and emphasizing the Communist menace to promote the Greece-Turkey aid bill had paid off, as Joseph Jones pointed out so clearly.[4] In any case, the State Department took a pragmatic approach, rather than follow the PPS's recommendation to correct the anti-Communist emphasis of the Truman Doctrine. It chose to ride the Marshall Plan home safely on the high tide of anti-Communist rhetoric and opinion (which it had helped to further), rather than to risk the plan's defeat and the consequent rehabilitation of Germany by the Army and the Congress on the advice and recommendations of Herbert Hoover—or according to some other "bright and unworkable ideas," as Marshall put it.[5] Naturally, the flow of events themselves contributed to the State Department's option. How would it have been able to abandon the anti-Communist line and reconcile that with Molotov's behavior in Paris in June and July 1947; with the Soviet Union's pressure on Poland and Czechoslovakia not to participate in the Marshall Plan; with the creation of the Cominform in October 1947; and with the coup in Czechoslovakia in 1948?

OPEN-DOOR DIPLOMACY

It would be futile to deny that the concepts that have been described as characteristic of the diplomacy of the open door influenced and guided American policymakers in the inception, discussion, debate, and passage of the European recovery program. But to conclude, as William A. Williams did for example, that "the problem was to coerce the Russians, help western Europe, and thereby establish the reality of an open door system throughout the world" is to ignore the evidence and resort to a secular devil-theory of historical causation designed, perhaps, to bolster those already converted and to spread the gospel among the gullible and the naive.[6] Politicians, along with other mortals, never stand naked of the robes of the past as they make their way toward decisions; they do not go from day to day and issue to issue with an ideological blank slate. In other words, unless one expects miraculous conversions or a revolution, one can hardly expect the policymakers of 1947 to have forgotten or rejected Cordell Hull, Woodrow Wilson, and a host of others as they moved toward resolution of one of the major postwar problems with which they were faced: making peace with Germany and reconstructing war-torn Europe.

In any case, if published analyses and public rhetoric are reliable, there is little doubt that the American policymaking establishment was imbued with, permeated by, and committed to the private-enterprise economic system. American leaders wanted to create and preserve the forms of political and social organization and the patterns of international trade (multilateralism) most conducive to the free-enterprise economic system. They wanted an interlocking, worldwide system of production and consumption, and they apparently believed that that was the most efficient, effective, and just foundation for peace, prosperity, and a rising standard of living for all.[7] The "conditions" laid down by the Americans in Paris late in August 1947 included demands that the participating countries undertake internal financial and monetary reforms, stabilization of currencies, the establishment of proper rates of exchange, as well as "steps to facilitate the greatest practicable interchange of goods and services among themselves, adopting definite measures directed toward the progressive reduction and eventual elimination of barriers to trade within the area, in accordance with the principles of the ITO Charter."[8] The American determination to achieve these and other objectives in Europe helps to explain the progressive shift from the *invitation* of June 1947 to the *dictation* of October 1947: the progressive shift from letting the Europeans draft their own recovery program, to "friendly aid in the drafting," to Clayton's personal missionary work in the capitals of Europe in June and July, to the more stringent (but informal) advice and requirements of mid-August, to the presentation of "conditions" and "essentials" to the CEEC in Paris late in August and to the governments themselves early in September, and finally to the outright intervention in the development of the CEEC's program in September, October, and November. But, as I have shown in the analysis, the progressive shift from the *invitation* of June to the *dictation* of October was also heavily influenced and conditioned by the immediate objective of ensuring Germany's rehabilitation, which was to be dovetailed with the larger European program. In fact, it can be argued that the attempt to resolve the German dilemma was the occasion for calling forth the principles of the open door, rather than the reverse. Significantly, Kennan—who had insisted in May (over the fierce protests of Clayton) that the Europeans themselves draft the plan—was the one who marshaled the major arguments in September for United States dictation of the final program of European recovery. In the end, he said, the United States should not ask the Europeans, but should just tell them what they would get. Kennan's reversal suggests that there was no clear "open door" plan when Marshall spoke in June, and it supports the idea that bureaucratic tinkering to solve the economic dilemma in Germany give rise to the Marshall Plan.

FORESTALLING AN AMERICAN DEPRESSION

As with the other elements of the prevailing interpretations, it would be inaccurate to deny that American policymakers were influenced by fears of a domestic recession as they originated, discussed, debated, and passed the European recovery program.[9] Observers of the political scene in 1947 discussed the recession issue openly and often. Freda Kirchwey, writing in *The Nation* in June 1947, remarked that "the Marshall plan, put simply, is an attempt to reestablish the capacity of the world, starting with our best customers, to buy American goods. Our own economy will slump, our prosperity will disappear overnight, if the huge output of American factories, whose capacity to produce ... increased 50 percent during the war, cannot find overflow markets outside the United States." John H. Williams, writing in *Foreign Affairs* later in 1947, referred to the widespread discussion of that view. He noted that Bevin had said similar things and that the

Soviets had made it an important element of their criticism of the Marshall Plan. Lewis H. Brown, the chairman of Johns Manville Corporation and a visiting expert in Germany in 1947, told the Academy of Political Science in New York that "a restored Europe will buy far more American goods than is now possible and will help to prevent a depression and unemployment in the United States."[10] Meanwhile, administration and Congressional spokesmen used the theme for what they thought it was worth. Harriman testified in the House Foreign Affairs Committee hearings in November 1947, saying that interim aid would reduce the United States export surplus and "would check the downward trend [of the economy] that has been in evidence since last spring."[11] The Harriman Committee's report to the President said the continuation of American trade with Europe was one of the reasons the Marshall Plan was needed, and it predicted that serious problems would occur if Europe's projected $7 billion deficit with the American continent came to pass in 1948.[12] Truman's own report to the Congress stated that, "Considered in terms of our own economy, European recovery is essential."[13] And, as a last, extreme example, chosen from many others that might have been listed, Senator Henry Cabot Lodge seemed pleased to observe in March 1948 that "the bill covers the French Empire, the Dutch Empire, and the British Empire, which possess vast quantities of materials which would be useful to us."[14]

Despite the widespread popular use of the theme that the Marshall Plan was a scheme to prevent a postwar depression in the United States—Molotov, Bidault, and Bevin seem to have thought it was such a scheme, as did some 47 percent of the Frenchmen polled in September 1947—there is evidence of dissension within the Harriman Committee itself.[15] Calvin B. Hoover, whose analysis of the German economy in 1945 had not enhanced his influence in the State Department, wrote to Marshall on July 28, 1947, suggesting that he consider making a speech in response to a *New York Times* story that reported Bidault to have said the United States needed to lend as much as France needed to borrow. Hoover observed that Bevin had been saying some of the same things and that both Bevin and Bidault were repeating the Soviet position, albeit not with the same vehemence. Hoover noted that it was tempting to justify the Marshall Plan as good business and that "indeed some supporters of the policy are already advancing arguments of this type." Not only would such arguments do harm to the United States abroad, he asserted, but they were "bound to boomerang when the matter comes up for consideration by Congress." His reasoning was that any competent economist could show that export surpluses would disappear if there was an increase of consumer purchasing power and higher wages. According to Hoover, the real argument for the Marshall Plan was to be found in the hard evidence that the Europeans needed aid for postwar reconstruction and the achievement of political and economic stability, both of which were so essential to American national interests as to justify the heavy costs involved. "What I am concerned about," he concluded, "is the possibility that we will find ourselves defending a thoroughly sound policy with arguments so unsound that we will find ourselves vulnerable both at home and abroad."[16]

Marshall and the State Department—more concerned with selling the program than with describing its essence—were apparently as unwilling to risk alienating potential and committed supporters of the plan on the recession issue as they were unwilling to risk losing supporters on the containment issue, for I have found no evidence that they ever made an effort to deal with the question on its merits. They simply marshaled and gathered the votes that were needed, regardless of their source or the intellectual foundations on which they rested. Hoover, unwilling to trade principles for votes to the end, continued to argue that the plan was fundamentally sound and that the anti-recession arguments being used to promote it were fundamentally wrong. He told the Senate Foreign Relations Committee on January 23, 1948:

We do not need to give foreign countries money to buy our surplus goods. There need never be any net surplus of goods which cannot be easily disposed of to our own citizens, either by lowering taxes or by raising real wages or by other means of increasing purchasing power whenever such action is appropriate. *Just now, of course, it is obvious that we have no general net surplus of goods and services at all.* We could easily consume much more in the form of goods and services than we are currently able to produce. There can be no question, therefore, but that the goods which we furnish Europe must come out of our own potential standard of living and not out of some mythical surplus. This answers both the argument about ERP providing a market for our surplus goods and the ERP as a means for preventing a depression in the United States. *These are both spurious arguments*, and incidentally they have been used with some effect by the Russians as propaganda against us.[17]

Calvin Hoover's words and other similar analyses went unheeded in 1948, and they have apparently been ignored and neglected by historians as well. The standard accounts of the postwar period rely heavily on such conditions as containment, open-door diplomacy, multilateralism, and the need to forestall a postwar American depression for their explanations of the Marshall Plan. But one might ask, on reflection, what all of these conditions tell us *specifically* about the *origins* of the Marshall Plan. More precisely, one might ask whether these conditions are indeed useful in explaining why the Marshall Plan originated in the spring of 1947, rather than in 1946, or 1948, or 1949, or at any other time in the twentieth century. Historians of the Marshall Plan have fallen into a familiar trap. They have used their extensive knowledge of the issues raised and discussed in the public debate on the Marshall Plan in order to explain and describe what *must have been* the reasons for the origins of the Marshall Plan. In short, the origins of the Marshall Plan have been explained by extrapolation, rather than by interpretation of documents, sources, and contemporary evidence. As I have shown repeatedly in the foregoing analysis, government officials were not averse to misleading the public. State Department and other officials often simply told the Congress, the press, the American people, or whomever, *what they wanted to tell them* at a given time, and they often did so without regard for what was true and accurate. The advocates and the spokesmen for the Marshall Plan did the same thing during the public discussion of the Marshall Plan in 1947 and 1948. That accounts, in large measure, for the multiple reasons that have been advanced for the Marshall Plan, reasons that I listed at the beginning of this study.

Significantly, both opponents and friends of the Marshall Plan found the methods used by the administration to sell the program to be less than commendable, if not downright objectionable. For example, Senator Robert A. Taft of Ohio complained in November 1947 that "we have seen in the past 3 months the development of a carefully planned propaganda for the Marshall plan, stimulated by the State Department by widespread publicity and secret meetings of influential people in Washington and Hot Springs."[18] Walter Lippmann wrote in January 1948 that "there is a notion, held by some in Washington, that the only way to win the support of Congress for the Marshall Plan is to frighten it."[19] The previously cited remarks by Van Der Beugel are doubly appropriate here. As "part of a team charged with the difficult task of making the Paris Report as attractive as possible for the presentation to Congress," he observed the "inclination on the part of the Administration to change accents, to color presentations, to minimize some problems and overemphasize others, to hide existing shortcomings and to applaud practically non-existing achievements."[20] A less diplomatic critic remarked in February 1948 that "the administration has not been truthful and fair with the American people."[21]

MARSHALL'S PLAN

Current interpretations of the Marshall Plan are all predicated, in some respect or other, on the assumption that there existed a rational plan or policy for European recovery in June 1947. But Marshall later denied that he had a plan at the time, and my study has demonstrated that his statements were accurate. When he spoke at Harvard on June 5, 1947, Marshall had no plan for European recovery, for containment, for creating a multilateral trade world, for promoting the open door in Europe, for forestalling a postwar American depression. He had a practical problem that he thought would have to be resolved, for its own sake and before someone with "all kinds of bright and unworkable ideas" tried to do it. With that in mind, the origins of the Marshall Plan may be reviewed.

Faced with the post-Potsdam impasse in Germany caused by France's actions, and appalled at the high cost of the occupation in appropriated dollars, the Army and Clay maneuvered for two years to try to bring France around. But the State Department refused either to apply sanctions against France or to admit publicly that France was indeed the major problem in Germany. Instead, State Department functionaries expressed suspicions about Russian intentions and long-range objectives, and they did so despite the Army's protests, despite the Army's evidence that the Russians were cooperating in Berlin to fulfill the terms of the Potsdam Agreement. Eventually, the State Department devised tests of Russian intentions, and finally its officials asserted openly that Russia had violated the Potsdam Agreement and other things. Meanwhile, the Russians went their own way in their zone. The British, who agreed with the Army on the need to reduce occupation costs in Germany, threatened several times to adopt unilateral policies in their zone. In July 1946 Bevin outlined a British plan to promote a self-sufficient economy in the British zone, which included the Ruhr. Searching for an alternative to Britain's plan for unilateral action in the Ruhr, Byrnes invited all the occupation powers to join their zones with the American zone in economic unity. Britain eventually accepted Byrnes's invitation, but France and Russia did not. Britain and the American Army expected zonal union to result in substantial reductions in the financial burdens of the occupation, and the two military governments developed a three-year plan to make the bizone economically self-supporting by 1949. But the State Department, which made policy for the United States in Germany, would not agree to economic policies in bizonal Germany that impinged on its plans for rehabilitating liberated Europe first. Neither would the State Department accept bizonal policies and practices that threatened France's political stability or left France's expectations for German coal exports unfulfilled.

Early in 1947 the Army and the British got an ally. The Republican leaders of the newly elected Eightieth Congress were determined to cut costs and to wrest power from the Executive Branch, from the Democratic administration. Some of them were prepared to conduct an investigation into the causes of the "failure" in Germany; some were prepared to review the State Department's wartime and postwar stewardship of American foreign policy; many of them were spoiling for a political showdown with the party of the New Deal. The combination of Congress's inclination to intervene in the German occupation, the Army's restlessness, the CFM's failure to make progress on a German settlement in Moscow, a British decision to increase German production, and Marshall's steady hand in the State Department finally broke the post-Potsdam impasse and inspired the Marshall Plan.

At the Moscow CFM in April 1947, Marshall agreed privately with Bevin to reorganize the British and American zones, to raise the German level of industry, and to make the two zones economically self-sustaining by 1949. Marshall was relatively new to his job at the time. He was burdened with the normal demands of bringing order to the shambles of policy left by Byrnes, who reportedly had carried the State Department around the world in his briefcase. Marshall's well-developed sense of procedure, order, and harmony was heavily taxed by the Greece-Turkey aid bill, the Austrian treaty, the Truman Doctrine, and the CFM in Moscow. He was pushed and pulled by advice from the State Department, the War Department, Dulles, and OMGUS; by France's demands for coal and other concessions; by Britain's initiatives to reduce Britain's dollar costs in Germany; and by Herbert Hoover's "independent" actions regarding German policy. But he was also mindful of the political currents in the United States that had brought forth the Eightieth Congress, pledged to economy in government; to reducing the power of the Executive Branch; to fighting communism at home and abroad; to turning around the diplomacy that had produced Yalta, Potsdam, the changes in Eastern Europe, and the "failure" in Germany. Instinctively sensing that the Moscow decisions on Germany would cause trouble, Marshall prevailed upon Bevin to agree to a six-week delay in announcing them. Upon further reflection, and after consultations with Dulles, Clay, and his State Department advisers, he concluded that the Moscow decisions on Germany were politically dangerous and economically unwise. Although they might solve the German problem, they would do so at economic and political costs that his own department would not accept, and that would be virtually impossible to justify to potential critics who would charge the United States with rehabilitating its recently defeated enemy ahead of its friends and allies. The Moscow decisions on Germany threatened to cause political disaster in France. They would certainly bring heavy criticism from France, from Russia, from German hard-liners in the United States (such as Henry Morgenthau and the Society for the Prevention of World War III), from the liberal press in the United States (such as *PM* and the *New Republic*), and from leftists and Communists everywhere. Marshall decided that his commitment to Bevin would have to be modified, and that the Army's, Hoover's, and the Congress's plans for German recovery would have to be headed off.

True to his training and experience—and perhaps to his instincts as well—Marshall called for the equivalent of military staff studies on his problems. Immediately upon his return from the Moscow CFM he instructed Kennan to activate the Policy Planning Staff in the State Department and to prepare the studies that eventually became the basis for the Marshall Plan. Kennan and the PPS tried to resolve Marshall's post-Moscow dilemma by recommending a short-term program (Coal for Europe) that would do in Germany much of what he and Bevin had already decided in Moscow to do, and a long-term program of European economic recovery to be developed by the Europeans themselves. The short-term program would be merged with the long-term program and thus diffuse domestic criticism of Germany's recovery and help to ensure against the economic and political disaster that a "Germany first" program threatened to call forth, particularly in France, but not exclusively there. The PPS proposal of May 23, 1947, was in fact a plan to implement and gain acceptance for the German decisions that Marshall and Bevin had already made; decisions that raised the specter of a restored Germany equipped with the manpower, the resources, and the technical facilities that Germans had used with such profound effect in the past.

As Marshall said over and over, and as I have demonstrated, there was no "Marshall Plan" in June 1947. When Clayton went to Europe for consultations late in June, he had specific instructions about a German-based Coal for Europe program and about socialization, but he had only very general and vague conceptions of what was to become the European recovery program. What he did in the capitals of Europe with respect to the latter eventually caused much concern in the State Department. The minutes of a round of discussions in the State Department in August 1947 show a "consensus that Mr. Clayton, while generally aware of departmental thinking with regard to the 'Plan,' holds fundamental divergent views on some aspects." The minutes also make clear that "a comprehensive departmental position has not been officially approved," and they show that "the time has come to firm up the overall departmental position."[22] The upshot was a formal policy statement, which was sent to Clayton and Caffery on August 26, 1947, nearly three months after the Harvard speech. But the "plan" was still incomplete, for Kennan and Bonesteel were dispatched to Paris personally to deliver oral instructions and policies regarding the "general political situation."[23] In short, what existed in the summer and fall of 1947 were the Bevin-Marshall decisions taken at the Moscow CFM, decisions that raised a spectrum of actual and potential domestic and foreign problems that would have to be resolved, defused, and—if necessary—kept from the arena of public discussion and debate, at least for a time.

Perhaps typical of the system that gave rise to it, the Marshall Plan was actually a series of pragmatic bureaucratic decisions, maneuvers, compromises, and actions. Typically also, contemporaries, commentators, and historians have construed the entire series as a plan for purposes of communication and rationalization (and maybe for other reasons). The questions that bureaucrats struggled with included the following: How could they sell a European recovery program to the American public and to an American Congress publicly committed to economy and reduced government spending? How could they explain a new foreign aid program to members of Congress who had already criticized wartime lend-lease and postwar United Nations (UNRRA) aid? How could they reconcile the fundamental differences between the Army and the State Department regarding the purposes, objectives, and length of the American presence in Europe? How could they reconcile the demands of France for German coal to implement the Monnet Plan and the demands of the American and British military governments for coal to provide a self-sufficient German economy? How could they increase coal production in the Ruhr and prevent the British and the German Social Democrats from alienating the American Congress and others by nationalizing the German coal industry? How could they reconcile the conflicting demands of the victorious powers for German reparations and of the military governments for a German industrial base with which to achieve self-sufficiency for the bizone? How could they reconcile the conflicting demands of Germany's neighbors for cheap German imports and of the military governments for sufficient German export proceeds with which to pay for needed food and raw materials imports, and for previous outlays for such imports?

The series of pragmatic bureaucratic decisions and compromises that became the Marshall Plan included the decisions to do something about German recovery. Neither the Army, nor the British, nor the Congress would settle for less. It included the maneuvers to prevent socialization or nationalization in the Ruhr, and perhaps in all of Germany. Neither the Army, nor Forrestal, nor the Congress would settle for less. It included the actions and maneuvers to restore France and maintain Bidault in power—at least to prevent a leftist United Front in France, and definitely to forestall Communist ascendancy there. Neither the French government nor the State Department would settle for less. It included actions to rehabilitate the liberated nations and Germany's neighbors other than France, some of whom (especially Belgium, Luxembourg, and the Netherlands) were sympathetic to the economic rehabilitation of Germany while mindful of the need for continued security. It included a decision to reduce Germany's economic potential for war by resuming dismantling and reparations, a decision that was in turn countered by actions to rehabilitate Germany's coal, steel, transport, and other industries in the interests of short-term, speedy, and less costly European recovery, and of creating or promoting the eventual formation of a Western European economic and perhaps political union. The series included maneuvers to satisfy France's demands for coal, coke, security, and territory, but there were also actions that forestalled complete satisfaction of France's demands. It included compromises to satisfy Congressional demands for economy and an end to foreign aid, but there were also requests for billions of dollars of foreign assistance that somehow had to be made acceptable to the Congress. To satisfy the Congress and the public, the Truman administration talked about the advantages of multilateral trade and the free flow of goods which foreign aid would stimulate. It talked about the immediate effects of bad crops in Europe; about the hardships caused by the blizzards and the hard winter of 1946–47. It talked about the Marshall Plan as a one-shot deal,[24] as an experiment in pump-priming, as a means to forestall a postwar recession, as a humanitarian act, as an economic effort that would reduce the need for military preparedness, as a measure for ensuring access to strategic resources, and as a hard-headed venture in the promotion of peace and security.[25] But the State Department also resorted to a practice it had used with effect before: it described and analyzed "the broad global picture" by emphasizing "the two-world assumption," the need to counterbalance the "Soviet World," and the desirability of "treating Europe west of the Iron Curtain on a regional basis."[26]

Interestingly, Bidault's and Molotov's actions in 1947 show that both France and Russia understood the primary motivation for the Marshall Plan to have been the American economic dilemma in Germany. Typically, the French would not even discuss Germany at first. When Bidault learned from Clayton and Harriman about the plans the Americans had for increasing coal production in the Ruhr and raising the level of industry of the bizone, he threatened to sabotage the Paris Marshall Plan talks and warned that if he did so there would be no Europe. As I have shown, Bidault and the French eventually bowed to the inevitable, but only after they realized that the State Department was as determined in 1947 to solve the German problem as the Army had been in 1945 and 1946. Unlike the Army, however, the State Department gave Bidault an opportunity to compromise and retreat without loss of face and power. As a result, the French modified their demands for separation of the Ruhr and Rhineland from Germany, and they agreed to negotiate on reparations, restitutions, and other economic questions arising from French annexation of the Saar. In turn, the State Department advised France that the United States supported in principle some form of international board that would control and allocate the basic production of the Ruhr. Molotov—also typically—protested the Marshall Plan procedures, probably for substantive reasons. He objected to making decisions on Germany outside the organized Council of Foreign Ministers. The State Department never gave *him* an opportunity to retreat gracefully or politically, and he apparently tried to find out what the Americans had promised Bidault and Bevin as a *quid pro quo* for their support of the Marshall Plan. He asked Bidault and Bevin directly whether they had inside information on the plan, he warned them of the serious consequences of any independent actions they might take in concert with the

Americans, and then he left the Paris talks on the Marshall Plan early in July 1947. He interpreted Marshall's initiative in terms of the Marxist-Leninist dialectic, and, after he left Paris, he apparently contributed to the decisions in Moscow to establish the Cominform, to implement the so-called "Molotov Plan," and to organize and mobilize the vanguard that would lead mankind into the future.

SOURCES AND NOTES

A Note on Sources

THE PUBLISHED materials used directly to prepare this study are identified in the notes. The unpublished materials may be identified and described as follows.

The War/Army Department and OMGUS papers were the major collection used. The OMGUS papers, which I used extensively in a previous book, served as a foundation and starting point, but the papers of Lucius D. Clay, the files of the War Department's Civil Affairs Division, and the official papers of Assistant Secretary of War Howard C. Petersen, Under Secretary of War William H. Draper, and Secretary of War Robert P. Patterson were essential for this one. I also used the extensive War Department decimal files, the Army's records of the so-called Committee of Three (the Secretaries of State, War, and the Navy), the declassified files of the Joint Chiefs of Staff, and the American records of the British-American Combined Civil Affairs Committee. When I began the study, I needed security clearance to use the materials in the custody of the Army. The classified records I wanted to use directly were declassified by the custodians on request, or else I took classified notes, which were then screened for declassification. In no case did this present a problem, except that it was a rather cumbersome and time-consuming procedure, and except that the State Department apparently insisted that *it* review documents and notes that were of a political-diplomatic nature. Initially, the State Department reviewed and declassified only a very limited number of documents and notes. Finally, invoking its rule that no access would be granted to State Department records for the years for which the appropriate *Foreign Relations* volumes had not been published, it refused to receive notes from the Army for review, screening, or declassification. Once the appropriate *Foreign Relations* volumes had appeared (first for 1945, then for 1946, and then for 1947—in successive years), the Army—presumably with State Department agreement—cleared the documents it would have sent to the State Department for review under the earlier procedures. Perhaps it sent them to the State Department. I do not know. In the end, all the materials I wanted were made available for my use, though in some cases I had to wait for as long as three years. The War/Army Department papers are in the Modern Military Records Branch of the National Archives in Washington, D.C. The OMGUS papers are physically located in the Federal Records Center, Suitland, Maryland, but they are under the jurisdiction of the Modern Military Records Branch of the National Archives. *The Papers of General Lucius D. Clay, Germany, 1945–1949*, edited by Jean Edward Smith, were published by the Institute of German Studies at Indiana University in 1974. My citations are to the archival locations of the papers, where I found them.

The records of the Joint Chiefs of Staff and the Combined Civil Affairs Committee were made available only after they had been screened and de-classified under the Freedom of Information Act. Researchers not familiar with the way the Act has been implemented may be warned that the limitations to access are still severe under the Freedom of Information Act, unless the researcher knows precisely what he wants to see and is able to provide some detail about the specific document or documents he wants to see. In the implementation of the Act, declassification teams have reviewed records and record groups according to general declassification guidelines adopted by the various agencies that have jurisdiction. The teams have in fact screened the records, declassifying some of them (probably most), and sim-ply removing from the files those that are not to be declassified. The re-searcher has no sure way of identifying or knowing what has been screened out during the declassification review. He can, of course, see the "out-cards" sticking in the files that are open to him. But the out-cards contain only brief notations, typically the file number and date of the removed document, the date on which it was removed, and the initials of the person who re-moved it. Presumably the records thus removed will eventually be declassi-fied and returned to the original files, but that will depend on time, person-nel, circumstances, finances, and budgets. So far as I can determine, there is no one engaged in the work of returning files at this time. In any case, some record groups have been screened rather thoroughly. The JCS papers are a case in point, for if the JCS records that are now open without restric-tions are indicative of what the agency actually did between 1945 and 1948 regarding the occupation of Germany, the Joint Chiefs of Staff had a lot of time for tennis.

State Department files and records were a second major collection used. Many of the State Department's papers have been published and may therefore be conveniently consulted in the *Foreign Relations of the United States*. In addition to the published records, I used the decimal files of the State Department through 1947. They too have been screened. I also had access to the papers and memoranda of H. Freeman Matthews, the papers and memoranda of John D. Hickerson, the files and papers of the Office of European Affairs of the State Department, and the papers and files collected by Edwin W. Pauley when he was Truman's personal ambassador on the Moscow Reparations Commission. The Pauley materials are still in the custody of the Department of State, and they must be used there. The remaining records and papers are in the Diplomatic Records Branch of the National Archives. Unfortunately, the files and papers of Robert Murphy and the Office of the United States Political Adviser in Berlin (USPOLAD) are not available at this time. They are in the custody of the National Archives, but they were shipped there as a separate "lot" which has a cut-off date in the 1950's. They will, therefore, not become available for researchers until the *Foreign Relations* volumes for the appropriate cut-off year have been published, even though the files contain USPOLAD materials beginning in 1945.

The Truman Library holdings were the third major collection used in the study. The record groups consulted were the William L. Clayton papers, the Ellen Clayton Garwood papers, the Joseph M. Jones papers, the Clark M. Clifford files and papers, the Charles G. Ross files, the John R. Steelman files, the J. Howard McGrath papers, the Thomas C. Blaisdell papers, the John W. Snyder papers, the Frank McNaughton papers, the Samuel I. Rosenman papers, the George M. Elsey papers, the records and files of the President's Committee on Foreign Aid (the Harriman Committee), the records of the Committee for the Marshall Plan, and the official files of the President. The Truman Library papers are in Independence, Missouri.

Congressional Committee files and papers—for the 79th and 80th Congresses—were also helpful. They are, however, not as full and revealing as one might expect. One gets the impression that they were severely screened before they were transferred to the National Archives. The specific materials consulted were those of the House Committee on Postwar Economic Policy and Planning, the House Committee on Military Affairs, the House Committee on Foreign Affairs, the Select Committee on Foreign Aid (the Herter Committee), the Senate Special Committee Investigating the National Defense Program (variously known as the Truman Committee, the Kilgore Committee, and the Meader Committee), and the Senate Committee on Foreign Relations. The Congressional files and papers are in the National Archives.

The notes and transcripts of Harry B. Price's interviews with various officials and with participants in the Marshall Plan are a helpful source. Price did the interviews when he wrote his book *The Marshall Plan and Its Meaning*. The notes and transcripts are in the Truman Library.

There is a second collection of notes and transcripts of interviews on the Marshall Plan and its implementation, available in the Truman Library. Philip C. Brooks, the former director of the Truman Library, conducted the interviews in the United States and Europe. They are a fine international oral-history record.

The James F. Byrnes papers are in the Robert Muldrow Cooper Library at Clemson University, Clemson, South Carolina. It is a sizable collection. Using it is facilitated by a detailed and carefully compiled index, and by the kindness and helpfulness of the staff. The papers themselves are more difficult, in part because there are materials in the collection that were apparently added as Byrnes and his official biographers worked through the materials to write his memoirs. There are, for example, marginal notations on certain letters, memoranda, and other materials that were apparently entered by Byrnes at the time to help his assistants.

The Lewis W. Douglas papers are in the University of Arizona Library, at Tucson. Douglas's participation in the negotiations on the Marshall Plan in the summer of 1947 make them a vital source. The papers are, however, not nearly as complete and revealing as one might wish.

The OMGUS papers, and the German records, documents, and papers of the occupation period—without which this study could not have been written (indeed, without which this study would never have occurred to me)—are identified and described fully in the Note on Sources of my previous book, *The American Occupation of Germany: Politics and the Military, 1945–1949* (Stanford, Calif., 1968). Though I went back to the OMGUS papers and the German records for additional details and to research specific topics more fully, the only new German occupation materials used specifically for this study are a collection of papers of the German Ministry for the Marshall Plan. They are in the archives of the Federal Republic of Germany, in Koblenz. The papers are, naturally, full and complete on the implementation of the program in Germany, but they are relatively unrevealing for the period of the Marshall Plan's origins. The bizonal papers, also in Koblenz, are more helpful for that aspect of the Marshall Plan.

Notes

Chapter Two

1. *Congressional Record*, House, 80th Cong., 2d Sess., Jan. 26, 1948, p. 576. Jenkins was a member of the Select Committee on Foreign Aid and had been to Europe in the summer of 1947 as a member of the subcommittee on Italy, Greece, and Trieste.

2. Moore to Wilcox, July 28, 1947, *Foreign Relations of the United States* (hereafter cited as *FRUS*), 1947, III, 239–41.

3. *FRUS*, 1947, III, 237–39.

4. SecState to AmEmbassy, Paris, June 12, 1947, *FRUS*, 1947, III, 249–51.

5. Memorandum Prepared for the Use of the Under Secretary of State for Economic Affairs (Clayton), June 1947, *FRUS*, 1947, III, 247–49.

6. Memorandum of Conversation, June 25 [26?], 1947, *FRUS*, 1947, III, 283–84; June 26, 1947, *ibid.*, 288–93.

7. Lovett to Clayton, July 10, 1947, *FRUS*, 1947, III, 324–26.

8. Kennan to Thorp, June 24, 1947, *FRUS*, 1947, III, 267–68; Memorandum Prepared by PPS, July 21?, 1947, *ibid.*, 335–37.

9. Max Beloff, *The United States and the Unity of Europe* (London, 1963); Joseph M. Jones, *The Fifteen Weeks (February 21–June 5, 1947)* (New York, 1955); Harry B. Price, *The Marshall Plan and Its Meaning* (Ithaca, N.Y., 1955); William C. Mallalieu, "The Origins of the Marshall Plan: A Study in Policy Formation and National Leadership," *Political Science Quarterly*, LXXIII (Dec. 1958), 481–504; Ellen Clayton Garwood, *Will Clayton: A Short Biography* (Austin, Tex., 1958). See also Ross J. Pritchard, "Will Clayton: A Study of Business-Statesmanship in the Formulation of United States Economic Foreign Policy" (Ph.D. dissertation, The Fletcher School of Law and Diplomacy, 1956); and Robert H. Ferrell, *George C. Marshall*, in Ferrell, ed., *The American Secretaries of State and Their Diplomacy*, vol. XV (New York, 1966).

10. Moscow CFM, Report by Secretary Marshall, printed in U.S. Dept. of State, Office of Public Affairs, *Germany, 1947–1949: The Story in Documents*, Pub. 3556, European and British Commonwealth Series 9 (Washington, 1950), p. 63.

11. Pritchard, "Will Clayton," p. 282.

12. Pritchard, pp. 285–95; Garwood, pp. 13–14; 118–21; Ferrell, pp. 280–81; Dean Acheson, *Present at the Creation: My Years in the State Department* (New

York, 1969), pp. 230–31; George F. Kennan, *Memoirs, 1925–1950* (Boston, 1967), p. 329.

13. Acheson to Patterson, March 5, 1947, *FRUS*, 1947, III, 197–98; Memorandum by the State Dept. Member, SWNCC (Hilldring), March 17, 1947, *ibid.*, 198–99.

14. Jones, pp. 200–206.

15. Report of the Special "Ad Hoc" Committee of the State-War-Navy Coordinating Committee, April 21, 1947, *FRUS*, 1947, III, 204–19, and 219, note 6.

16. Jones, p. 241.

17. Kennan, p. 335.

18. Kennan to Acheson, May 23, 1947, *FRUS*, 1947, III, 223.

19. Kennan to Acheson, May 16, 1947, *FRUS*, 1947, III, 220–23.

20. Kennan, p. 352.

21. Kennan to Thorp, June 24, 1947, *FRUS*, 1947, III, 267–68.

22. PPS, "Certain Aspects of the European Recovery Problem from the United States Standpoint," Preliminary Report, July 23, 1947, in Clifford Papers, ERP Reports folder, Truman Library.

23. Kennan to Acheson, with enclosed PPS Report, May 23, 1947, *FRUS*, 1947, III, 223–29.

24. Garwood, p. 10; Pritchard, pp. 273–77.

25. Clayton, Memorandum, March 5, 1947, in Clayton Papers (Confidential Marshall Plan Memos, General File), Truman Library.

26. Summary of Discussion on Problems of Relief, Rehabilitation and Reconstruction of Europe, *FRUS*, 1947, III, 236; Minutes of Meeting on Marshall "Plan," Aug. 22, 1947, *ibid.*, 370.

27. Notes of Harry B. Price interview with George C. Marshall, Oct. 30, 1952, Truman Library. See also Price, p. 21; Herbert Feis, *From Trust to Terror: The Onset of the Cold War, 1945–1950* (New York, 1970), p. 239; *New York Times*, June 6, 1949, p. 1; Robert Murphy, *Diplomat Among Warriors* (Garden City, N.Y., 1964), pp. 306–8; and John Foster Dulles, *War or Peace* (New York, 1950), p. 105.

28. Speech by Marshall to Governors Conference, Salt Lake City, July 14, 1947, copy in Jackson Papers (European Recovery Program), Truman Library.

29. Marshall, "The Stake of the Businessman in the European Recovery Program," Jan. 15, 1948, copy of speech in Holland Papers (Marshall Plan), Truman Library.

Chapter Three

1. Paul Y. Hammond, "Directives for the Occupation of Germany: The Washington Controversy," in Harold Stein, ed., *American Civil-Military Decisions: A Book of Case Studies* (University, Ala., 1963), p. 426.

2. The report was the work of the American-British Combined Production and Resources Board (London Branch), and was signed by C. J. Potter, Lord

Hyndley, Thomas C. Blaisdell, and J. Eaton Griffith. See *FRUS*, 1945, Potsdam I, 614–21.

3. Clay to McCloy, April 26, 1945, Record Group (hereafter RG) 165, file ASW 370.8, Germany—Control Group, National Archives (hereafter NA); Henry L. Stimson and McGeorge Bundy, *On Active Service in Peace and War* (New York, 1947), p. 583; Clay to McCloy, June 16, 1945, RG 165, file ASW 370.8, Germany—Communications for Clay, NA; Stimson to Truman, July 16, 1945, *FRUS*, 1945, Potsdam I, 754–57.

4. Matthews to McCloy, June 15, 1945, RG 59, H. Freeman Matthews files, Box 1, folder M, NA.

5. Clayton to McCloy, June 18, 1945, *FRUS*, 1945, Potsdam I, 470.

6. McCloy to Clayton, June 21, 1945, *FRUS*, 1945, Potsdam I, 470–71.

7. Clayton to McCloy, June 30, 1945, *FRUS*, 1945, Potsdam I, 477–78; June 18, 1945, *ibid.*, 468–70.

8. SecState to President, July 5, 1945, *FRUS*, 1945, Potsdam I, 491–93.

9. Collado to Clayton, July 18, 1945, *FRUS*, 1945, Potsdam II, 779–80; McCloy to Clayton, July 20, 1945, *ibid.*, 800–801; the President to SecWar, July 29, 1945, *ibid.*, 821–23.

10. Eventually Article II, Section B, paragraph 15 (a), (b), (c), and (d) of the Potsdam Protocol, printed in U.S. Dept. of State, Office of Public Affairs, *Germany, 1947–1949: The Story in Documents*, Pub. 3556, European and British Commonwealth Series 9 (Washington, 1950), p. 50.

11. The President to SecWar, July 29, 1945, *FRUS*, 1945, Potsdam II, 821–23.

12. Lucius D. Clay, *Decision in Germany* (Garden City, N.Y., 1950), p. 54.

13. Murphy to SecState, Aug. 20, 1945, *FRUS*, 1945, III, 957–58; *ibid.*, 960; John Gimbel, *The American Occupation of Germany: Politics and the Military, 1945–1949* (Stanford, Calif., 1968), esp. pp. 36–44, 47–51; Clay, p. 88.

14. Eisenhower to Marshall, Oct. 13, 1945, RG 165, file WDSCA CAD 321, Sec. I, Box 202, NA.

15. Hilldring to SecWar, Subj: Transfer of Responsibility for Military Government from Military to Civilian Control, Oct. 21, 1945, RG 165, file WDSCA CAD 321, Box 202, NA; Minutes of Meeting of SecState, War, Navy, Washington, Oct. 23, 1945, *FRUS*, 1945, III, 989.

16. Eisenhower to Truman, Oct. 26, 1945, in State Dept. *Bulletin*, XIII (Nov. 4, 1945), 711.

17. SecWar to SecState, Nov. 2, 1945, *FRUS*, 1945, III, 996–97.

18. Donald Russell to SecState, Subj: Administrative Responsibility for German Control, Dec. 29, 1945, Byrnes Papers, folder 611(1), Clemson University Library.

19. Minutes of Meeting of SecState, War, Navy, Washington, Oct. 23, 1945, *FRUS*, 1945, III, 989.

20. Russell to Murphy, Oct. 15, 1945, Byrnes Papers, folder 611(1), Clemson University Library.

21. Patterson to Eisenhower and Hilldring, Dec. 21, 1945, RG 165, file WDSCA CAD 321, Sec. I, Box 202, NA; Russell to SecState, Subj: Administrative Responsibility for German Control, Jan. 2, 1946, RG 59, file 740.00119 Control (Germany), Box 3729, NA.

22. SecWar to ActgSecState, Dec. 22, 1945, *FRUS*, 1945, III, 1019–21.

23. SecWar to SecState, Dec. 29, 1945, RG 165, file OSW 091 Germany, NA; Eisenhower to Patterson (copy), n.d., filed Jan. 2, 1946, RG 59, file 740.00119 Control (Germany), Box C-131, NA.

24. Russell to SecState, Jan. 2, 1946, RG 59, file 740.00119 Control (Germany), Box 3729, NA.

25. Matthews to McCloy, June 15, 1945, RG 59, H. Freeman Matthews files, Box 1, folder M, NA.

26. Clayton to McCloy, June 18, 1945, *FRUS*, 1945, Potsdam I, 468–70; Sec-State to the President, July 5, 1945, *ibid.*, 491–93; the President to SecWar, July 29, 1945, *FRUS*, 1945, Potsdam II, 821–23.

27. Ickes to Truman, June 14, 1945, RG 165, file OSW 463.3, NA; Ickes to Truman, June 18, 1945, file OF 198 (1945–Apr. 1950), Truman Library.

28. Pauley to SecState, July 7, 1945, *FRUS*, 1945, Potsdam I, 630; Clayton to Pauley, July 3, 1945, *ibid.*, 623; Clayton to Blaisdell, July 4, 1945, *ibid.*, 627.

29. ActgSecState to AmEmbassy, London, June 24, 1945, *FRUS*, 1945, Potsdam I, 612–14. See *FRUS*, 1945, Potsdam II, 1028–30, for final version.

30. Chargé of SovUnion (Novikov) to SecState, May 17, 1945, *FRUS*, 1945, II, 1449–51.

31. BrEmbassy to SecState, July 3, 1945, *FRUS*, 1945, Potsdam I, 624–25; Sec-State to BrEmbassy, July 11, 1945, *ibid.*, 636–38; Eden to SecState, July 23, 1945, *FRUS*, 1945, Potsdam II, 1026–27.

32. Doc. 1046, *FRUS*, 1945, Potsdam II, 1028–30; Truman to Stalin, July 27, 1945, *ibid.*; Stalin to Truman, July 29, 1945, *ibid.*, 1031; Bob Koenig to Carl Mabley, July 30, 1945, RG 165, file WDSCA 463.3, Box 221, NA; Byrnes to addressees, Aug. 11, 1945, *ibid.*

33. Clay to McCloy, Sept. 6, 1945, RG 165, file WDSCA 463.3, Sec. I, Box 221, NA.

34. F. S. V. Donnison, *Civil Affairs and Military Government: North-West Europe, 1944–1946* (London, 1961), pp. 414–15.

35. Hilldring to Meader, Oct. 28, 1946, RG 46, SEN 79A–F30, National Defense Committee, OP-58, Box 1011, NA; Byrnes to Truman, Oct. 30, 1946, RG 59, file 740.00119 Control (Germany), Box 3741, NA.

36. George Meader, Memorandum of Conversation with James Byrnes in Paris, Oct. 13, 1946, RG 46, SEN 79A–F30, National Defense Committee, OP-58, Box 1010, NA.

37. Meader, Interview with Colonel D. L. Robinson, Control Officer, OMGUS, Oct. 16, 1946, RG 46, SEN 79A–F30, National Defense Committee, OP-58, Box 991, NA.

38. Hilldring to Meader, Oct. 28, 1946, RG 46, SEN 79A–F30, National Defense Committee, OP-58, Box 1011, NA.

39. Memorandum, Sparks to Meader, Oct. 25, 1946, RG 46, SEN 79A–F30, National Defense Committee, OP-58, Box 994, NA.

Chapter Four

1. Memorandum, Hickerson to SWNCC, Nov. 29, 1945, *FRUS*, 1945, III, 1432–35, esp. 1434.

2. Memorandum, Hickerson to SWNCC, Nov. 29, 1945, *FRUS*, 1945, III, 1434.

3. SecState to the President, Jan. 4, 1945, *FRUS*, 1945, Yalta, 293–94; SecState to the President, Jan. 5, 1945, *ibid.*, 295. See *FRUS*, 1945, III, 161–62, 163–64, 177–78, 181, 183–85, for further documentation of the issue.

4. Briefing Book Paper, France, *FRUS*, 1945, Yalta, 300–304.

5. Briefing Book Paper, June 23, 1945, *FRUS*, 1945, Potsdam I, 251–53.

6. Memorandum, Sparks to Meader, Oct. 25, 1946, RG 46, SEN 79A–F30, National Defense Committee, OP-58, Box 994, NA.

7. Memorandum of Bidault-Byrnes Conversation, Aug. 24, 1945, *FRUS*, 1945, IV, 722–24; Matthews's Memorandum of Byrnes-Bidault Conversation, Sept. 24, 1946, *FRUS*, 1946, V, 607–10; Harris's Memorandum of Bérard-Wallner-Harris Conversation, Sept. 24, 1946, *ibid.*, 693–94.

8. Murphy to SecState, April 4, 1946, *FRUS*, 1946, V, 536–37.

9. Memorandum of Truman–De Gaulle Conversation, Aug. 22, 1945, *FRUS*, 1945, IV, 709–10.

10. Memorandum of Bidault-Byrnes Conversation, Aug. 23, 1945, *FRUS*, 1945, IV, 711–21; Aug. 24, 1945, *ibid.*, 722–24. See also *FRUS*, 1945, Potsdam II, Doc. 1414, 1557–64; and RG 59, Box 3851, NA.

11. *FRUS*, 1945, II, 177–79. The document, CFM(45)17, is dated Sept. 13, 1945, but the record of the conference shows that Bidault circulated it on Sept. 14. See also *FRUS*, 1945, III, 869–71, and *Europa-Archiv*, 9.J.(July 20, 1954), 6747.

12. Murphy to SecState, Sept. 23, 1945, *FRUS*, 1945, III, 871–73. See also Murphy to SecState, *FRUS*, 1945, III, 831, for a cable reporting a French reservation of Aug. 10, justified by France's absence at Potsdam and lack of instructions.

13. Caffery to SecState, Sept. 27, 1945, *FRUS*, 1945, III, 878; Murphy to SecState, Sept. 29, 1945, *FRUS*, 1945, III, 879; Oct. 1, 1945, 843–44; Oct. 13, 1945, 882–83; Oct. 18, 1945, 883–84; War Dept. to OMGUS, Oct. 20, 1945, RG 218, file CCAC 014 Germany, Sec. 9, Box 125, NA; Murphy to SecState, Oct. 20, 1945, *FRUS*, 1945, III, 884–85. (Emphasis added.)

14. Lucius D. Clay, *Decision in Germany* (Garden City, N.Y., 1950), p. 72; Robert Murphy, *Diplomat Among Warriors* (Garden City, N.Y., 1964), p. 285.

15. Hilldring, Memorandum, Nov. 10, 1945; Hilldring to AsstSecWar, Subj:

Subjects Discussed with General Clay in Washington (Nov. 1–5, 1945), Nov. 7, 1945; Hilldring, "Resumé of Meeting at State Department, Nov. 3, 1945," RG 165, file WDSCA 014 Germany, Sec. III, Box 175, NA; Dept. of State, Memorandum of Conversation, Nov. 3, 1945, OMGUS Papers, file AG 091.2, Box 5-1/1, NA. *FRUS*, 1945, III, 892–93, note 55, says there are no records of these talks in State Department files. That is incredible, given the profusion of records in the Army files, the fact that William Clayton, Willard L. Thorp, H. Freeman Matthews, James W. Riddleberger, and others participated for the State Department, and the fact that a State Department memorandum of at least one of the conversations is in the OMGUS papers.

16. Extracts of Minutes of Meeting of SecWar, SecState, and SecNavy, Nov. 6, 1945, *FRUS*, 1945, III, 892–93.

17. SecWar to SecState, Nov. 21, 1945, *FRUS*, 1945, III, 908–9; Dec. 10, 1945, *ibid.*, 917; SecWar to ActgSecState, Dec. 28, 1945, *ibid.*, 922–23.

18. SecWar to SecState, Feb. 25, 1946, RG 165, file WDSCA 014 Germany, Sec. IV, NA.

19. Hilldring, "Resumé of Meeting at State Department, Nov. 3, 1945," RG 165, file WDSCA 014 Germany, Sec. III, Box 175, NA. See also John Gimbel, *The American Occupation of Germany* (Stanford, Calif., 1968), pp. 26–30.

20. Extracts of Minutes of Meeting of SecWar, SecState, and SecNavy, Nov. 6, 1945, *FRUS*, 1945, III, 892–93; Memorandum to the President, Subj: Byron Price's Report on Germany, Nov. 24, 1945, RG 59, file 740.00119 Control (Germany), Box 3727, NA; Murphy to SecState, Oct. 20, 1945, *FRUS*, 1945, III, 884–85; Memorandum, Hickerson to SWNCC, Nov. 29, 1945, *ibid.*, 1432–35.

21. Matthews to McCloy, June 15, 1945, RG 59, H. Freeman Matthews files, Box 1, folder M, NA; Matthews to Acheson, Jan. 22, 1946, *ibid.*, Box 2, folder Memoranda 1946, NA.

22. ActgSecState to SecWar, Dec. 12, 1945, *FRUS*, 1945, III, 919–20.

23. ActgSecState to SecWar, Jan. 12, 1946, *FRUS*, 1945, III, 923–25.

24. Memorandum of Byrnes–De Murville Conversation, Nov. 20, 1945, *FRUS*, 1945, III, 907–8; Dept. of State, Memorandum of Press and Radio News Conference, Dec. 5, 1945, Byrnes Papers, folder 555, Clemson University Library; SecState to Caffery, Dec. 6, 1945, *FRUS*, 1945, III, 916, and note 8, referring to Caffery to SecState, Dec. 8, 1945.

25. SecState to Caffery, Feb. 1, 1946, *FRUS*, 1946, V, 496–98.

26. Caffery to SecState, March 2, 1946, *FRUS*, 1946, V, 512–15.

27. Caffery to SecState, March 1, 1946, *FRUS*, 1946, V, 509–11; Byrnes to Caffery, March 2, 1946, RG 59, file 740.00119 Control (Germany), Box C-134, NA. See *FRUS*, 1946, V, 511, note 50, for a quotation of a portion of Byrnes's cable to Caffery.

28. SecState to French Ambassador, March 22, 1946, *FRUS*, 1946, V, 528–29.

29. Acheson, Memorandum for the President, March 26, 1946, RG 59, file 740.00119 Control (Germany), Box C-135, NA.

30. Murphy to SecState, April 4, 1946, *FRUS*, 1946, V, 536–37.

31. OMGUS to SecState and SecAgr, April 11, 1946, *FRUS*, 1946, V, 540, and note 86. See also OMGUS to War Dept., April 11, 1946, RG 319, file ARMY CAD Messages, CM-IN's 1946, Box 19, NA; Matthews to Petersen, April 17, 1946, RG 59, file 740.00119 Control (Germany), Box C-137, NA.

32. SecState to SecWar, April 10, 1946, *FRUS*, 1946, V, 539–40, and note 86, for a reference to Acheson to Patterson, April 24, 1946.

33. Caffery to SecState, March 2, 1946, *FRUS*, 1946, V, 512–15, esp. 515.

34. Byrnes's Report on Paris CFM, June 15 to July 12, 1946, July 15, 1946, State Dept. *Bulletin*, 15 (July 28, 1946), 167–72.

35. Clay to AGWAR, Subj: U.S. and French Position on Central German Administrative Agencies, July 18, 1946, OMGUS Papers, Box 166-1/3, NA.

36. Murphy to SecState, July 18, 1946, *FRUS*, 1946, V, 577–78.

37. U.S. Delegation Record, CFM, July 10, 1946, *FRUS*, 1946, V, 861, 875.

38. SecState, from Cohen, to Murphy, July 19, 1946, *FRUS*, 1946, V, 579–80.

39. George Meader, Memorandum of Conversation with Byrnes, Oct. 13, 1946, RG 46, SEN 79A–F30, National Defense Committee, OP-58, Box 1010, NA; Sparks to Meader, Oct. 25, 1946, *ibid.*, Box 994; Hilldring to Meader, Oct. 28, 1946, *ibid.*, Box 1011.

40. John Foster Dulles, *War or Peace* (New York, 1950), esp. ch. 9.

41. Minutes of Marshall-Auriol Conversation, March 6, 1947, *FRUS*, 1947, III, 190–95.

Chapter Five

1. See Les K. Adler and Thomas G. Paterson, "Red Fascism: The Merger of Nazi Germany and Soviet Russia in the American Image of Totalitarianism, 1930's–1950's," *American Historical Review*, LXXV (April 1970), 1046–64, for a discussion in detail.

2. Briefing Book Paper, Reparation and Restitution Policy Toward Germany, Jan. 16, 1945, *FRUS*, 1945, Yalta, 194–96. See also John L. Gaddis, *The United States and the Origins of the Cold War, 1941–1947* (New York, 1972), p. 127.

3. *FRUS*, 1945, Potsdam I, 436–38, note 7, contains the March 23, 1945, policy memorandum. See also Informal Notes, Meeting in the Office of the Secretary of State, March 15, 1945, to Discuss the President's Directives for Carrying Out of the Crimea Decisions . . . , RG 59, Box 3721, NA.

4. Instructions for the United States Representative on the Allied Commission on Reparations (Pauley), May 18, 1945, *FRUS*, 1945, III, 1222–27. See Isador Lubin, "Reparations Problems," *Proceedings of the Academy of Political Science*, XXI (Jan. 1946), 522–32, for a discussion, and Bruce Kuklick, "The Division of Germany and American Policy on Reparations," *The Western Political Quarterly*, XXIII (June 1970), 276–93, for the assertion that Pauley formulated the first-charge position "on a practical as well as an intellectual level" (p. 280), and for the argument that "When the Americans proclaimed to the U.S.S.R. the

sanctity of the first charge principle, they were saying they would finance German multilateralism but not aid Soviet Allies" (p. 282).

5. See Bruce Kuklick, *American Policy and the Division of Germany: The Clash with Russia over Reparations* (Ithaca, N.Y., 1972).

6. Pauley to SecState, June 19, 1945, *FRUS*, 1945, Potsdam I, 510–11.

7. SecState to Pauley, July 2, 1945, *FRUS*, 1945, Potsdam I, 521; Pauley to SecState, July 6, 1945, *ibid.*, 527–28.

8. ActgSecState to SecState, July 7, 1945, *FRUS*, 1945, Potsdam I, 530.

9. Pauley to SecState, July 14, 1945, *FRUS*, 1945, Potsdam I, 537. Principle 8 is quoted in Pauley to SecState, July 6, 1945, *ibid.*, 528.

10. Memorandum by the Political Adviser in Germany (Murphy), July 20, 1945, *FRUS*, 1945, Potsdam II, 141–42.

11. Dept. of State Minutes, 6th Meeting of Foreign Ministers, July 23, 1945, *FRUS*, 1945, Potsdam II, 279.

12. Edwin Pauley, Report on German Reparations to the President of the United States, Feb. to Sept. 1945, *FRUS*, 1945, Potsdam II, 943.

13. Pauley to Maisky, July 27, 1945, *FRUS*, 1945, Potsdam II, 896.

14. Clayton to McCloy, June 18, 1945, *FRUS*, 1945, Potsdam I, 468–70; June 30, 1945, *ibid.*, 477–78.

15. Collado to Thorp and Reinstein, July 23, 1945, *FRUS*, 1945, Potsdam II, 812.

16. Informal Meeting of Foreign Ministers, July 23, 1945, *FRUS*, 1945, Potsdam II, 296.

17. Dept. of State Minutes, 6th Meeting of Foreign Ministers, July 23, 1945, *FRUS*, 1945, Potsdam II, 279–80; Bohlen Minutes of Byrnes-Molotov Meeting, July 23, 1945, *ibid.*, 274–75; Informal Meeting of Foreign Ministers, July 23, 1945, *ibid.*, 296–97; Bohlen Minutes, Truman-Molotov Meeting, July 29, 1945, *ibid.*, 471–76.

18. Dept. of State Minutes, 10th Meeting of Foreign Ministers, July 30, 1945, *FRUS*, 1945, Potsdam II, 483ff, 921; Dept. of State Minutes, 11th Plenary Meeting, CFM, July 31, 1945, *ibid.*, 511–17; Potsdam Protocol, III, 4a and b, printed in U.S. Dept. of State, *Germany, 1947–1949*, Pub. 3556 (Washington, 1950), p. 51.

19. Dept. of State Minutes, 11th Plenary Meeting, July 31, 1945, *FRUS*, 1945, Potsdam II, 514; Pauley to Clay, Aug. 11, 1945, *FRUS*, 1945, III, 1251–53; R. G. Sproul and Luther Gulick to J. R. Parten, Subj: Meeting with Colonel Jefferson, Aug. 11, 1945, dated Aug. 12, 1945, RG 59, Lot M-17, Box 26, Pauley Reparations Mission, 1945–46 files, State Dept.; Pauley to SecState, Sept. 14, 1945, *FRUS*, 1945, III, 1290–93; Pauley to Clay, Aug. 4, 1945, *ibid.*, 1240–43; Pauley, Transcript of Press and Radio Conference, Aug. 30, 1945, Official Reporter Files, 28, Truman Library; Llewellyn Woodward, *British Foreign Policy in the Second World War* (London, 1962), p. 566.

20. From a memorandum by Thorp for the Committee, SC Minutes, Secre-

tary's Staff Committee Minutes, July 28, 1945, State Dept. files, Lot 122, No. 6, as cited in Kuklick, p. 162.

21. Clayton and Collado to Thorp, Aug. 16, 1945, *FRUS*, 1945, Potsdam II, 829–30, 938–40.

22. Memorandum of Conversation between Harriman (with Pauley, Lubin, and others) and Molotov (with Pavlov), Subj: Reparations Commission, Aug. 10, 1945, RG 59, Pauley Reparations Mission 1945–46 files, Lot M-17, Box 27, State Dept.; OMGUS, Monthly Report of the Military Governor, No. 1, Aug. 1945, p. 1; Record of Decisions, CFM, London, Sept. 25, 1945, *FRUS*, 1945, II, 370–71.

23. Pauley to Truman, June 11, 1945, RG 218, file CCS 007 (3/13/45), Sec. 1, NA.

24. Pauley to SecState, Aug. 20, 1945, *FRUS*, 1945, III, 1262–63; Caffery to SecState, Aug. 17, 1945, *FRUS*, 1945, IV, 705–7; Sept. 11, 1945, *FRUS*, 1945, III, 1286–87.

25. *FRUS*, 1945, Potsdam II, 934–35. Pauley to Clayton, Aug. 4, 1945, RG 59, file 740.00119 Control (Germany), Box 3851, NA; SecState to Winant for Clayton, Aug. 8, 1945, *FRUS*, 1945, III, 1245; Pauley to Eisenhower, Aug. 19, 1945, *ibid.*, 1260–61; Murphy to SecState, Sept. 4, 1945, *ibid.*, 1282–83; ActgSecState to Winant, Sept. 17, 1945, *ibid.*, 1293–94.

26. USGroupCC, Memorandum, Subj: Restitution Policy and Procedure, Sept. 24, 1945, RG 59, file 740.00119 Control (Germany), Box 3724, NA; Record of Decisions, CFM, London, Sept. 25, 1945, *FRUS*, 1945, II, 371.

27. Winant to ActgSecState, Oct. 4, 1945, *FRUS*, 1945, III, 1324–29.

28. Winant to ActgSecState, Oct. 4, 1945, *FRUS*, 1945, III, 1326.

29. SecState to Caffery, Oct. 18, 1945, *FRUS*, 1945, III, 1349–50; Caffery to SecState, Oct. 23, 1945, RG 59, Box C-242, NA.

30. The Potsdam Protocol called for reparations in "usable and complete industrial capital equipment." Potsdam Protocol, III, 4a and b, printed in U.S. Dept. of State, *Germany, 1947–1949*, p. 51.

31. Hilldring, "Resumé of Meeting at State Department, Nov. 3, 1945," RG 165, file WDSCA 014 Germany, Sec. III, Box 175, NA.

32. USPOLAD to SecState, Nov. 7, 1945, RG 59, file 740.00119 Control (Germany), Box C-129, NA; Nov. 13, 1945, *ibid.*; Murphy to SecState, Nov. 17, 1945, *FRUS*, 1945, III, 1390–92.

33. Murphy to SecState, Dec. 4, 1945, RG 59, file 740.00119 Control (Germany), Box C-130, NA; French Embassy, Aide-Mémoire, Dec. 17, 1945, RG 59, Box 3729, *ibid.*

34. Murphy reported, at the time, that Koeltz said Clay's compromise was unacceptable to the French government. See Murphy to SecState, Dec. 4, 1945, RG 59, file 740.00119 Control (Germany), Box C-130, NA.

35. Clay to AGWAR for Hilldring, CC-21041, Dec. 29, 1945, RG 316, Clay Papers, Box 3, NA.

36. JCS to Clark and McNarney, Nov. 29, 1945, *FRUS*, 1945, III, 1427–29.

37. Murphy to ActgSecState, Jan. 19, 1946, *FRUS*, 1946, V, 488–89 and note 18.

38. Memorandum, French Embassy to Dept. of State, Feb. 4, 1946, RG 59, file 740.00119 EW, Box 3857, NA.

39. Memorandum, Hilldring to Byrnes, July 19, 1946, RG 59, file 740.00119 Control (Germany), Box 3737, NA.

40. See JCS to McNarney, Clay, and Clark, June 15, 1946, RG 218, file CCS 007 (3/13/45), Sec. 4, NA, for the statement that U.S. economic aid to countries such as Italy and Austria could be "reduced through restitution of economic resources without corresponding increase of economic burden in Germany."

41. OMGUS to War Dept., June 23, 1947, RG 165, file WDSCA 387.6, Sec. XIII, Box 356, NA.

Chapter Six

1. Potsdam Protocol, III, 6, in U.S. Dept. of State, *Germany, 1947–1949*, Pub. 3556 (Washington, 1950), p. 51.

2. B. U. Ratchford and William D. Ross, *Berlin Reparations Assignment: Round One of the German Peace Settlement* (Chapel Hill, N.C., 1947), esp. pp. 26 and 78 for references to lack of equipment.

3. John H. Backer, *Priming the German Economy: American Occupational Policies, 1945–1948* (Durham, N.C., 1971), pp. 74–76; John Gimbel, *The American Occupation of Germany* (Stanford, Calif., 1968), pp. 20–21.

4. Ratchford and Ross, p. 79.

5. *Ibid.*, p. 80.

6. Draft of a Preliminary Report to the German Standard-of-Living Board, by the Working Staff of the Board on "A Minimum German Standard of Living in Relation to Industrial Disarmament and Reparations," Sept. 10, 1945, OMGUS Papers, Box 149-2/3, NA.

7. Clay to McCloy, June 29, 1945, OMGUS Papers, Box 410/3, NA; US-GroupCC to War Dept., Sept. 26, 1945, War Dept. Papers, file WDSCA 014 Germany, 15 Sept.–15 Oct. 1945, Sec. II, NA; Clay to McCloy, Oct. 3, 1945, War Dept. Papers, file ASW 370.8, Germany—Control Council, NA.

8. Hilldring, Memorandum for SecWar, Subj: Comments on Preliminary Report by the Working Staff of the German Standard-of-Living Board, Oct. 9, 1945, War Dept. Papers, file ASW 370.8, Germany—Control Council, NA; *Time*, 46 (Oct. 22, 1945), 27–28.

9. Clayton to Murphy, Oct. 12, 1945, *FRUS*, 1945, III, 1341–43.

10. Hilldring, "Resumé of Meeting at State Department, Nov. 3, 1945," RG 165, file WDSCA 014 Germany, Sec. III, Box 175, NA.

11. SecWar to SecState, Nov. 21, 1945, *FRUS*, 1945, III, 908–9.

12. ActgSecState to SecWar, Dec. 12, 1945, *FRUS*, 1945, III, 919–20.

13. SecWar to ActgSecState, Dec. 28, 1945, *FRUS*, 1945, III, 922–23. The

memorandum of November 30 was a draft of "The Reparation Settlement and the Peacetime Economy of Germany," eventually released to the press on Dec. 12, 1945, and published in the State Dept. *Bulletin*, XIII (Dec. 16, 1945), 960–63.

14. ActgSecState to SecWar, Jan. 12, 1946, *FRUS*, 1945, III, 923–25.

15. For discussion of the Price Report see John Gimbel, *The American Occupation of Germany* (Stanford, Calif., 1968), pp. 21–23; for the State Dept. studies see Thorp to Langer, Sept. 6, 1945, RG 59, Box 3852, NA; for the SWNCC studies see SWNCC 210, "The Determination of the Amount and Character of Reparation Removals from Germany in Relation to the German 'Peacetime' Economy," Oct. 31, 1945, RG 59, file 740.00119 EW, Box C-242, NA. Hilldring's assertion of Feb. 13, 1946, that his office had "not only propounded the questions, but also prepared Mr. Byrnes' statement," though probably correct in its specific detail, does not give credit to the wide background of studies and pressures that led to the December 12 statement. Hilldring to Petersen, Subj: Statement of U.S. Political Policies in Germany, Feb. 13, 1946, RG 165, file WDSCA 014 Germany, Sec. V, Box 176, NA.

16. James W. Riddleberger, "United States Policy on the Treatment of Germany," State Dept. *Bulletin*, XIII (Nov. 25, 1945), 841–49. Two recent studies revealing little or no appreciation of the State Department's dilemma are Lloyd C. Gardner, "America and the German 'Problem,' 1945–1949," in Barton J. Bernstein, ed., *Politics and Policies of the Truman Administration* (Chicago, 1970), pp. 113–48, and Wolfgang Schlauch, "American Policy Towards Germany, 1945," *Journal of Contemporary History*, V, No. 7 (1970), 113–28.

17. U.S. Dept. of State, *United States Economic Policy Toward Postwar Germany*, Pub. 2630, European Series 15 (Washington, 1946), pp. 101–4.

18. State Dept. *Bulletin*, XIII (Dec. 16, 1945), 960–63.

19. Byrnes to Walter F. George [and others], Dec. 11, 1945, RG 59, file 740.00119 EW, Box 3855, NA; Hans J. Morgenthau, *Germany Is Our Problem* (New York, 1945).

20. *The Nation* (editorial), 161 (Dec. 22, 1945), 675–76.

21. Hilldring to AsstSecWar, Subj: Transmittal of Summary of "Level of Industry Report" for Germany, Feb. 12, 1946, RG 165, file WDSCA 319.1, Box 191, NA.

22. Hajo Holborn, *American Military Government: Its Organization and Policies* (Washington, 1947), app. xviii, pp. 226–30; R. G. Hawtrey, "The Economic State of Europe," in Peter Calvocoressi, *Survey of International Affairs, 1947–1948* (London, 1952), p. 65; OMGUS, Monthly Report of the Military Governor, No. 9, April 20, 1946, Reparations and Restitutions (Cumulative Review), 4; OMGUS, *A Year of Potsdam: The German Economy Since the Surrender* (Berlin, n.d.), pp. 31–32.

23. OMGUS, Activities of the Directorate of Economics, ACA, 1945–48, Special Report of the Office of the Economic Adviser, Aug. 1949, p. 222, in JCS Records, file CCS 323.81 Germany (2/22/44), Sec. 3, NA; Holborn, p. 65. The

German census of 1946 showed an actual population of 65,911,190, an increase of 10.2 percent between 1939 and 1946. Experts differed on the analysis of the effects of disease, hunger, emigration, refugee movements, birthrates, death rates, the eventual settlement of the displaced persons, etc. The OMGUS German Standard-of-Living Board had estimated the German postwar population at 70,000,000; another committee of experts thought it might reach 74,000,000. See OMGUS, The Population of Germany, Special Report of the Military Governor, U.S. Zone, March 15, 1947, OMGUS Papers, Box 147-2/11, NA; and Ferdinand A. Hermens, "The Economics of Potsdam," *The Review of Politics*, VIII (July 1946), 402.

24. Murphy to SecState, Jan. 11, 1946, *FRUS*, 1946, V, 482–84; Jan. 13, 1946, *ibid.*, 484–86; Jan. 18, 1946, *ibid.*, 486–88.

25. Memorandum of Conversation with Lord Halifax, Jan. 28, 1946, *FRUS*, 1946, V, 493–94; Murphy to SecState, Jan. 31, 1946, *ibid.*, 494–96; March 22, 1946, *ibid.*, 529–31.

26. Murphy to SecState, Feb. 5, 1946, RG 59, file 740.00119 Control (Germany), Box C-132, NA.

27. SecWar to SecState, Feb. 13, 1946, *FRUS*, 1946, V, 501–3.

28. Matthews to SecState, Feb. 28, 1946, *FRUS*, 1946, V, 507–8.

29. Murphy to SecState, March 8, 1946, *FRUS*, 1946, V, 524.

30. Murphy to SecState, March 22, 1946, *FRUS*, 1946, V, 529–31.

31. Murphy to SecState, March 27, 1946, *FRUS*, 1946, V, 533–34.

32. Murphy to SecState, March 22, 1946, *FRUS*, 1946, V, 529–31; March 27, 1946, *ibid.*, 533–34.

Chapter Seven

1. Clayton and Collado to Thorp, Aug. 16, 1945, *FRUS*, 1945, Potsdam II, 938–40, 829–30.

2. Clayton to Harriman for Draper, Sept. 6, 1945, *FRUS*, 1945, III, 1283–85.

3. Kennan to SecState, Sept. 18, 1945, *FRUS*, 1945, III, 1294–96.

4. French Notes of Aug. 7, 1945, *FRUS*, 1945, Potsdam II, 1543–47, 1551–55; Murphy to SecState, Aug. 10, 1945, *FRUS*, 1945, III, 831.

5. Memorandum of Bidault-Byrnes Conversation, Aug. 23, 1945, *FRUS*, 1945, IV, 711–21. See also *FRUS*, 1945, Potsdam II, Doc. 1414, p. 1563.

6. CFM(45)17, Sept. 13, 1945, *FRUS*, 1945, III, 869–71.

7. OMGUS, Monthly Report of the Military Governor, No. 2, Sept. 20, 1945, p. 1; Thilo Vogelsang, "Die Bemühungen um eine deutsche Zentralverwaltung 1945/46," *Vierteljahrshefte für Zeitgeschichte,* 18.J.Heft 4 (Oktober 1970), 513–14.

8. Murphy to SecState, Sept. 23, 1945, *FRUS*, 1945, III, 871–73; Sept. 28, 1945, *ibid.*, 878–79; CONL/P(45)42, Sept. 28, 1945, *ibid.*, 841–42 and note 5.

9. Caffery to SecState, Sept. 27, 1945, *FRUS*, 1945, III, 878; Murphy to SecState, Oct. 2, 1945, *ibid.*, 843–44.

10. Murphy to SecState, Oct. 13, 1945, *FRUS*, 1945, III, 882–83; Oct. 18, 1945, *ibid.*, 883–84; War Dept. to OMGUS, Oct. 20, 1945, RG 218, file CCAC 014 Germany, Sec. 9, Box 125, NA.

11. Murphy to SecState, Oct. 20, 1945, *FRUS*, 1945, III, 884–85.

12. *Ibid.*, 846–48, 887–88.

13. OMGUS, Monthly Report of the Military Governor, No. 3, Oct. 20, 1945, p. 1. The December report said central agencies "would provide a focal point" for economic coordination, but the French had prevented their establishment. The January 1946 report repeated the theme. See *ibid.*, No. 5, Dec. 20, 1945, p. 7; *ibid.*, No. 6, Jan. 20, 1946, p. 1.

14. Memorandum of Byrnes–De Murville Conversation, Nov. 20, 1945, *FRUS*, 1945, III, 907–8.

15. Murphy to SecState, Nov. 24, 1945, *FRUS*, 1945, III, 911.

16. *FRUS*, 1945, III, 921, note 88; Murphy to SecState, Dec. 7, 1945, *ibid.*, 1553.

17. SecState to Caffery, Dec. 6, 1945, *FRUS*, 1945, III, 916, and note 81; Caffery to SecState, Dec. 18, 1945, *ibid.*, 921–22.

18. Murphy to SecState, Jan. 23, 1946, RG 59, file 740.00119 Control (Germany), Box 3730, NA.

19. Murphy to Matthews, Jan. 29, 1946, RG 59, file 740.00119 Control (Germany), Box C-132, NA; OMGUS, Monthly Report of the Military Governor. No. 7, Feb. 20, 1946, p. 1.

20. SecState to Caffery, Feb. 1, 1946, *FRUS*, 1946, V, 496–98; Memorandum of Byrnes-Bonnet Conversation, Feb. 6, 1946, RG 59, file 740.00119 Control (Germany), Box C-132, NA.

21. Thorp to SecState, Feb. 9, 1946, RG 59, file 740.00119 Control (Germany), Box 3731, NA.

22. Caffery to SecState, March 1, 1946, *FRUS*, 1946, V, 509–11.

23. Caffery to SecState, March 2, 1946, *FRUS*, 1946, V, 512–15.

24. Byrnes to Caffery, March 2, 1946, RG 59, file 740.00119 Control (Germany), Box C-134, NA. Quoted in part in *FRUS*, 1946, V, 511, note 50.

25. Murphy to SecState, Oct. 11, 1945, *FRUS*, 1945, III, 1531–33; OMGUS to War Dept., Oct. 25, 1945, RG 218, file CCAC 091.31 Germany, Box 126, NA; JCS to McNarney, Nov. 24, 1945, *FRUS*, 1945, III, 1547–49; Murphy to SecState, Dec. 7, 1945, *ibid.*, 1553; Feb. 19, 1946, *FRUS*, 1946, V, 503–4; March 1, 1946, *ibid.*, 511–12.

26. SecState to Diplomatic Representatives, Nov. 8, 1945, *FRUS*, 1945, III, 1539–40.

27. SecState to Murphy, Nov. 29, 1945, *FRUS*, 1945, III, 1550–52; Murphy to SecState, Dec. 7, 1945, *ibid.*, 1553; ActgSecState to Murphy, Dec. 28, 1945, *ibid.*, 1556–57; Murphy to SecState, Sept. 23, 1945, *ibid.*, 1529–30.

28. Murphy to SecState, March 20, 1946, *FRUS*, 1946, V, 768–69; ACC, Minutes of 23d Meeting, March 20, 1946, CONL/M(46)8, RG 59, file 740.00119 Control (Germany), Box C-136, NA. Clay estimated in November 1946—during

the negotiations on the bizonal fusion agreement—that unpaid exports from the two zones through March 31, 1946, were valued at approximately $58 million, calculated at the ratio of RM 10 to the dollar and from coal prices approximately one-half their competitive market value. See "Pooling of Past Proceeds of Exports from the British and U.S. Zones. Synopsis of the Problem," GEP/SEC/41, Nov. 18, 1946, attached to Memorandum of Conversation, Subj: Financial Aspects of Bizonal Unity in Germany, Nov. 19, 1946, RG 59, file 740.00119 Control (Germany), Box C-146, NA.

29. ACA, Coordinating Committee, Creation of an Interim Allied Export/Import Bureau, CORC/P(46)119, March 27, 1946, RG 59, file 740.00119 Control (Germany), Box C-136, NA; ACA, Coordinating Committee, Minutes, CORC/M(46)19, April 2, 1946, *ibid.*; Murphy to SecState, April 4, 1946, *FRUS*, 1946, V, 536–37; OMGUS to War Dept., CC 2626, April 5, 1946, RG 218, JCS 1946–48 Papers, file CCS 091.31 Germany (11/16/45), NA.

30. Murphy to SecState, April 4, 1946, *FRUS*, 1946, V, 536–37.

31. Lucius D. Clay, *Decision in Germany* (Garden City, N.Y., 1950), p. 121.

32. Statement by K. I. Koval at ACA, April 5, 1946, OMGUS Papers, Box 4-1/1, NA, as printed in John H. Backer, *Priming the German Economy* (Durham, N.C., 1971), p. 109.

33. Quoted from Backer, p. 109. Cf. Murphy's version in Murphy to SecState, April 10, 1946, *FRUS*, 1946, V, 538.

34. OMGUS from Clay to AGWAR for Echols, CC 2693, April 8, 1946, RG 316, Clay Papers, Box 3, NA.

35. Murphy to SecState, April 18, 1946, RG 59, file 740.00119 Control (Germany), Box C-137, NA.

36. Murphy to SecState, May 2, 1946, *FRUS*, 1946, V, 546 (emphasis added).

37. Dept. of State Minutes, 10th Meeting of Foreign Ministers, July 30, 1945, *FRUS*, 1945, Potsdam II, 491.

38. Clay, pp. 121–22.

39. Murphy to SecState, May 2, 1946, *FRUS*, 1946, V, 547.

Chapter Eight

1. Murphy to SecState, Feb. 24, 1946, *FRUS*, 1946, V, 506.

2. Lucius D. Clay, *Decision in Germany* (Garden City, N.Y., 1950), p. 39.

3. Byrnes to Caffery, March 2, 1946, RG 59, file 740.00119 Control (Germany), Box C-134, NA, quoted in part in *FRUS*, 1946, V, 511, note 50; Acheson to Truman, March 26, 1946, RG 59, file 740.00119 Control (Germany), Box C-135, NA.

4. OMGUS to AGWAR, May 3, 1946, CC 4277, OMGUS Papers, Box 427-2/3, NA, as printed in John H. Backer, *Priming the German Economy* (Durham, N.C., 1971), pp. 110–11.

5. See W. W. Rostow to C. P. Kindleberger, Subj: Coal and Other Matters, June 10, 1946, with Cover Memorandum from Kindleberger to Riddleberger, June 11, 1946, RG 59, file 740.00119 Control (Germany), Box 3735, NA.

6. Acheson and Hilldring to SecState, May 9, 1946, *FRUS*, 1946, V, 549, 550–55.

7. The proposal is printed as two memoranda, "Proposal for the Preparation of the Peace Settlement for Germany" and "The German Problem," dated May 15, 1946, in *FRUS*, 1946, II, 400–402. The quotations and paraphrases that follow are from the two memoranda.

8. Acheson and Hilldring to SecState, May 9, 1946, *FRUS*, 1946, V, 551.

9. For George Kennan's warning from Moscow, see Kennan to SecState, March 6, 1946, *FRUS*, 1946, V, 517: "I would by no means accept it as foregone conclusion that Russians have really been eager, up to this time, to see central German administrative agencies established." For examples of the theme's recurrence in the literature, see James F. Byrnes, *Speaking Frankly* (New York, 1947), p. 169; Clay, p. 40; Jens Hacker, *Sowjetunion und DDR zum Potsdamer Abkommen* (Köln, 1969), p. 126; Tilman Pünder, *Das Bizonale Interregnum: Die Geschichte des Vereinigten Wirtschaftsgebiets, 1946–1949* (Waiblingen, 1966), pp. 54–55; Philip Windsor, "The Occupation of Germany," *History Today*, XIII (Feb. 1963), 79; Eli Whitney Debevoise, "The Occupation of Germany: United States' Objectives and Participation," *Journal of International Affairs*, XIII, No. 2 (1954), 173; Andreas Dorpalen, "The Split Occupation of Germany," *The Virginia Quarterly Review*, XXII (Autumn, 1946), 581–82; Ferenc A. Vali, *The Quest for a United Germany* (Baltimore, 1967), p. 16; and Herbert Feis, *From Trust to Terror* (New York, 1970), pp. 58–59, who wrote that "France's refusal to permit central economic agencies to operate, France's restrictions on trade between its zone and others, and France's requisitions of German products gave the Russians a reason, which they did not need, for defending their refusal to allow exports from the East zone to the West."

10. Acheson and Hilldring to SecState, May 9, 1946, *FRUS*, 1946, V, 550–55. The "shifting Russian tactics" were identified as those occurring during the discussions on the import-export plan in the ACC, when Clay finally reached his decision to announce the dismantling suspension.

11. U.S. Delegation Record, CFM, May 15, 1946, *FRUS*, 1946, II, 398–99.

12. *Ibid.*, May 16, 1946, *FRUS*, 1946, II, 426–27.

13. Later, on July 12, Molotov said further study was needed before he could take a position. *Ibid.*, July 12, 1946, *FRUS*, 1946, II, 935.

14. *Ibid.*, May 16, 1946, *FRUS*, 1946, II, 427.

15. *Ibid.*, 428–29. Bidault's remarks are in *FRUS*, 1945, II, 179, 407–10; III, 871. In 1946 the French were, in fact, sending "observers" rather than delegates to the committees and directorates of the ACC. See *FRUS*, 1946, V, 587–88, for a report on that situation.

16. U.S. Delegation Record, CFM, May 16, 1946, *FRUS*, 1946, II, 430, 433.

17. *Ibid.*, 435.

18. *Ibid.*, July 10, 1946, *FRUS*, 1946, II, 873, 875.

19. *Ibid.*, 861.

20. *Ibid.*, 875–76.

21. *Ibid.*, July 11, 1946, *FRUS*, 1946, II, 900; *ibid.*, July 10, 1946, *FRUS*, 1946, II, 876–77.

22. Byrnes, *Speaking Frankly*, pp. 195–96; Byrnes, "The Big Four Paris Conference: Report to Nation," *Vital Speeches*, XII (Aug. 1, 1946), 610–13; George Curry, "James F. Byrnes," in Robert Ferrell, ed., *The American Secretaries of State and Their Diplomacy*, 14 (New York, 1965), 235; Feis, pp. 134–35. Curry wrote that Byrnes had listened to Molotov's German policy speech on July 10, and that he and his advisers huddled with Senators Vandenberg and Connally that night, and together they decided to issue the invitation as a last resort. He said Byrnes made his "carefully phrased offer" the next morning. Feis follows Byrnes and Curry.

23. U.S. Delegation Record, CFM, July 11, 1946, *FRUS*, 1946, II, 881–82.

24. *Ibid.*, 890.

25. *Ibid.*, 896, 899.

26. F. S. V. Donnison, *Civil Affairs and Military Government: North-West Europe* (London, 1961), p. 415.

27. Minutes of . . . National Advisory Council on International Monetary and Financial Problems, April 25, 1946, *FRUS*, 1946, V, 433. The statement is attributed to Clayton. For a reference to the State Department's long-range plans for the European economy, see Russell H. Dorr to Kindleberger, June 13, 1946, RG 59, file 740.00119 EW, Box 3865, NA: "I have borne in mind some of our discussions in Washington before I came over here [to Brussels as U.S. representative to the IARA] in regard to the Department's hope that reparations could be made an instrument of decentralizing European industry, building up economic strength in countries other than Germany and generally securing a better European balance."

28. Byrnes, "The Big Four Paris Conference," pp. 610–13; Byrnes, *Speaking Frankly*, pp. 195–96; Feis, pp. 134–35; Curry, p. 235.

29. Murphy to SecState, July 20, 1946, *FRUS*, 1946, V, 580–81.

30. Murphy to SecState, July 30, 1946, *FRUS*, 1946, V, 585–86; Aug. 3, 1946, *ibid.*, 587–88.

31. Murphy to SecState, Aug. 3, 1946, *FRUS*, 1946, V, 587–88; Aug. 11, 1946, *ibid.*, 590–92.

32. Murphy to SecState, Aug. 17, 1946, *FRUS*, 1946, V, 592–93; Aug. 29, 1946, *ibid.*, 595–96.

33. John Gimbel, *The American Occupation of Germany* (Stanford, Calif., 1968), pp. 80–85.

34. U.S. Delegation Record, CFM, July 12, 1946, *FRUS*, 1946, II, 909.

35. U.S. Military Attaché, London, to War Dept., July 28, 1946, RG 319, file CAD Messages, CM-IN's 1946, Box 19, NA.

36. War Dept. to OMGUS for McNarney and Clay, July 18, 1946, RG 165, file WDSCA 014 Germany, Sec. X, NA. (Excerpts in *FRUS*, 1946, V, 578–79.)

37. Clay, pp. 73–78; OMGUS to AGWAR, May 26, 1946, OMGUS Papers, Box 177-3/3, NA.

38. AGWAR to OMGUS for Clay, June 14, 1946, OMGUS Papers, file AG 091.31, Box 211-3/5, NA.

39. P. P. Claxton to Hilldring, Subj: Agenda and Preparatory Studies for Special Conference on Germany, July 1, 1946, RG 59, file 740.00119 Control (Germany), Box C-141, NA.

40. Cramer, Claxton, and O'Sullivan to Hilldring, Subj: Development of a Program and Announcement of U.S. Policy, July 16, 1946, RG 59, file 740.00119 Control (Germany), Box C-141, NA.

Chapter Nine

1. Staff Committee Paper, June 22, 1945, *FRUS*, 1945, Potsdam I, 191.

2. Briefing Book Paper, June 27, 1945, *FRUS*, 1945, Potsdam I, 450–52; Sec-State to the President, June 30, 1945, *ibid.*, 204.

3. Memorandum of Bidault-Byrnes Conversation, Aug. 24, 1945, *FRUS*, 1945, IV, 722–24.

4. Bohlen's Memorandum of Byrnes-Molotov Conversation, Sept. 20, 1945, *FRUS*, 1945, II, 267–68.

5. James F. Byrnes, "Our Peace Offensive Has Only Begun," *Vital Speeches*, XII (June 1, 1946), 487; Byrnes, *Speaking Frankly* (New York, 1947), p. 172.

6. Byrnes to AmEmbassy, London and Moscow, Feb. 12, 1946, RG 59, file 740.00119 Control (Germany), Box C-133, NA; Byrnes to Caffery, Feb. 22, 1946, *ibid.*

7. Murphy to Matthews, Jan. 29, 1946, RG 59, file 740.00119 Control (Germany), Box C-132, NA; Report of Press Conference on Civil Administration in Germany, Jan. 29, 1946, State Dept. *Bulletin*, 14 (Feb. 10, 1946), 197; OMGUS, Monthly Report of the Military Governor, No. 7, Feb. 20, 1946, p. 1; SecState to Caffery, Feb. 1, 1946, *FRUS*, 1946, V, 496–98; Memorandum of Byrnes-Bonnet Conversation, Feb. 6, 1946, RG 59, file 740.00119 Control (Germany), Box C-132, NA; Thorp to SecState, Feb. 9, 1946, RG 59, Box 3731, *ibid.*

8. Caffery to SecState, March 14, 1946, RG 59, file 740.00119 EW, Box C-246, NA. See also *FRUS*, 1946, II, 57, note 78.

9. SecState to AmEmbassy, Moscow, April 16, 1946, *FRUS*, 1946, II, 62–63, and note 83.

10. Caffery to SecState, April 16, 1946, *FRUS*, 1946, II, 56–58. More than a year later André Gérard wrote in "Can France Again Be a Great Power?" *Foreign Affairs*, XXVI (Oct. 1947), 32, that "to quote as an alternative to international control [of the Ruhr] the four-power treaty of guarantee offered by Mr. Byrnes last year is to shirk the real issue." See also "Two Worlds at Moscow," *The New Statesman and Nation*, XXXIII (April 26, 1947), 290, for a critical commentary on the treaty, as well as for the observation that Bidault said it was a "jolly good idea," but that when one got the French alone they compared it with the Briand-Kellogg Pact and other platonic declarations.

11. Molotov to SecState, April 20, 1946, *FRUS*, 1946, II, 83.

12. U.S. Delegation Record, CFM, April 29, 1946, *FRUS*, 1946, II, 167–68.

13. Bohlen's Memorandum of Molotov-Byrnes Conversation, April 28, 1946, *FRUS*, 1946, II, 146–57; U.S. Delegation Record, CFM, April 29, 1946, *ibid.*, 166–73; U.S. Delegation Record, CFM, July 9, 1946, *ibid.*, 842–47.

14. Minutes of a Marshall-Bidault Conversation, March 13, 1947, *FRUS*, 1947, II, 246–49.

15. Memorandum by the French Delegation, CFM (46) 1, April 25, 1946, *FRUS*, 1946, II, 109–12.

16. Clayton to SecState, April 22, 1946, *FRUS*, 1946, V, 541–42; Report on French-American Conversations, Washington, Nov. 13–20, 1945, *FRUS*, 1945, III, 899; Caffery to SecState, April 16, 1946, *FRUS*, 1946, II, 56–58; U.S. Delegation Record, CFM, May 15, 1946, *ibid.*, 394–96.

17. Arthur H. Vandenberg, "Peace with Justice the Supreme Necessity," *Vital Speeches*, XII (Aug. 1, 1946), 618. See also Memorandum of Conversation, Subj: Relation to United Nations of 25-Year Draft Treaty for German Disarmament, May 16, 1946, RG 59, file 740.00119 EW, Box 3864, NA; Harold Callender, in *New York Times*, April 20, 1946, in DNC Clippings, Box 144, Truman Library; "Who Failed at Paris?" (editorial), *The New Republic*, 114 (May 27, 1946), 747–48; and "Disillusion at Paris," *The Christian Century*, 63 (May 15, 1946), 615–17, for the views of journalists that Byrnes's proposal was received with little enthusiasm. Freda Kirchwey, "No Peace in Paris," *The Nation*, 162 (May 11, 1946), 557, said "the proposal was received coldly, almost indifferently, by every French newspaper."

18. Matthews's Memorandum of Byrnes-Bidault Conversation, Sept. 24, 1946, *FRUS*, 1946, V, 607–10. Bidault was advising Byrnes that France would annex the Saar unilaterally.

19. Harris's Memorandum of Bérard-Wallner-Harris Conversation, Sept. 24, 1946, *FRUS*, 1946, V, 693–94.

20. Office Memorandum, David Harris to Riddleberger and Matthews, March 26, 1946, RG 59, file 740.00119 Control (Germany), Box 3732, NA; Matthews to Acheson, April 3, 1946, *ibid.*

21. Drafts and Notes in RG 59, file 740.00119 Control (Germany), Box C-137, NA.

22. Lucius D. Clay, *Decision in Germany* (Garden City, N.Y., 1950), pp. 73–78; OMGUS to AGWAR, May 26, 1946, OMGUS Papers, Box 177-3/3, NA.

23. AGWAR to OMGUS for Clay, June 14, 1946, OMGUS Papers, file AG 091.31, Box 211-3/5, NA; OMGUS from Clay to USFET, June 15, 1946, CC 7029, RG 316, Clay Papers, Box 3, NA; OMGUS from Clay to AGWAR for Echols, June 17, 1946, *ibid.*

24. OMGUS from Clay to Echols, July 19, 1946, War Dept. Papers, file WDSCA 014 Germany, Sec. XI, June 11, 1946– , NA. See John Gimbel, *The American Occupation of Germany* (Stanford, Calif., 1968), pp. 61–68, 74–76, for a lengthy summary of Clay's statement and for a discussion of Clay's hope that it might help to promote a plan to encourage the Council of Minister-Presidents of the American zone to expand and develop into an ad hoc provisional govern-

ment of all four zones, in the absence of the central German economic administrations that had been provided for in the Potsdam Agreement and which France had blocked. See also John Gimbel, "On the Implementation of the Potsdam Agreement: An Essay on U.S. Postwar German Policy," *Political Science Quarterly*, LXXXVII (June 1972), 242–69.

25. Petersen to Clay, Aug. 5, 1946, War Dept. Papers, file ASW 091 Germany, NA. Patterson's praise of the statement is in Patterson to Clay, Aug. 6, 1946, OMGUS Papers, Box 177-3/3, NA.

26. Acheson to Riddleberger, Galbraith, Leverich, and Mason, July 31, 1946, RG 59, file 740.00119 Control (Germany), Box 3737, NA; Acheson to Murphy, Aug. 7, 1946, RG 59, Box C-142, *ibid.*

27. OMGUS to AGWAR, August 7, 1946, CC 1378, OMGUS Papers, Box 177-3/3, NA; AGWAR to OMGUS for Clay, Aug. 12, 1946, *ibid.*

28. Clay to Patterson, Aug. 16, 1946, OMGUS Papers, Box 177-3/3, NA; OMGUS from Clay to AGWAR, Aug. 13, 1946, OMGUS Papers, file AG 092.3, Box 5-2/1, NA; Clay to Byrnes, Aug. 19, 1946, Byrnes Papers, folder 469, Clemson University Library; Major Gerard B. Crook to War Dept., Subj: Report on Visit to U.S. Forces, European Theater, Sept. 23, 1946, RG 165, file WDSCA 319.1, Sec. V, Box 312, NA.

29. Hilldring(?) to Cohen, Aug. 24, 1946 (copy), RG 59, file 740.00119 Control (Germany), Box C-143, NA.

30. Robert Murphy, *Diplomat Among Warriors* (Garden City, N.Y., 1964), pp. 302–3.

31. Particularly Anne O'Hare McCormick of the *New York Times*, who read a draft of the speech, commented on it, and then accompanied Byrnes to Stuttgart for its delivery. Anne OH McCormick to Byrnes, n.d., RG 59, file 740.00119 Control (Germany), Box C-144, NA.

32. Byrnes to Truman, Sept. 2, 1946, RG 59, file 740.00119 Control (Germany), Box C-144, NA.

33. For an example of the French argument, see Murphy to SecState, Feb. 24, 1946, *FRUS*, 1946, V, 505–7: "Members of the French delegation here [in Berlin] have admitted privately that French policy is based not simply on fear of future German aggression but equally, if not more, on fear that the United States will lose interest, eventually withdraw from Germany, and some fine morning they will wake up and find themselves face to face with the Russians on the Rhine."

34. See my "On the Implementation of the Potsdam Agreement," esp. pp. 246–48.

35. U.S. Dept. of State, *Germany, 1947–1949*, Pub. 3556 (Washington, 1950), pp. 3–13.

36. Frank Spencer, "The United States and Germany in the Aftermath of War," *International Affairs*, 44 (Jan. 1968), 60.

37. "Pax Americana," *The New Statesman and Nation*, XXXII (Sept. 14, 1946), 181.

38. Memorandum of Bérard-Kindleberger Conversation, Sept. 9, 1946, *FRUS*, 1946, V, 603–4.

39. Harris's Memorandum of a Bérard-Wallner-Harris Conversation, Sept. 24, 1946, *FRUS*, 1946, V, 693–94.

40. Matthews's Memorandum of a Bidault-Byrnes Conversation, Sept. 24, 1946, *FRUS*, 1946, V, 607–10.

41. Murphy to Harris, Oct. 5, 1946, RG 59, file 740.00119 Control (Germany), Box C-145, NA.

Chapter Ten

1. OMGUS, Monthly Report of the Military Governor, No. 2, Sept. 20, 1945, p. 1.

2. Murphy to SecState, Sept. 11, 1945, *FRUS*, 1945, III, 868–69.

3. Murphy to SecState, Sept. 5, 1945, *FRUS*, 1945, III, 1048. The Americans and the British had similar programs.

4. Hilldring, "Resumé of Meeting at State Department, Nov. 3, 1945," RG 165, file WDSCA 014 Germany, Sec. III, Box 175, NA.

5. John J. McCloy, "American Occupation Policies in Germany," *Proceedings of the Academy of Political Science*, XXI (Jan. 1946), 550.

6. U.S. Congress, Senate, 79th Cong., 1st Sess., Committee on Military Affairs, *Elimination of German Resources for War, Hearings . . .* part 8, Dec. 11 and 12, 1945, p. 1058.

7. Lucius D. Clay, *Decision in Germany* (Garden City, N.Y., 1950), pp. 73–78.

8. James P. Warburg, *Germany, Key to Peace* (Cambridge, Mass., 1953), p. 31; Warburg, *The United States in the Postwar World: What We Have Done, What We Have Left Undone, and What We Can and Must Do* (New York, 1966), p. 17.

9. George Meader, Interview with Colonel D. L. Robinson, Oct. 16, 1946, p. 50, RG 46, SEN 79A–F30, OP-58, Box 991, NA.

10. David L. Glickman, *The Big 4 in Germany: The Treatment of Germany as an Economic Unit*, National Planning Association Pamphlets 54–55 (Washington, 1947), p. 48.

11. OMGUS, Public Relations Release, Clay Press Conference, Nov. 4, 1946, OMGUS Papers, Box 1-1/4, NA.

12. Clay to War Dept., Oct. 11, 1946, RG 165, file WDSCA 387.6, Sec. IV, Box 351, NA.

13. Louis J. Halle, *The Cold War as History* (New York, 1967), p. 38.

14. Hilldring, "Resumé of Meeting at State Department, Nov. 3, 1945," RG 165, file WDSCA 014 Germany, Sec. III, Box 175, NA.

15. Murphy to Matthews, Jan. 29, 1946, RG 59, file 740.00119 Control (Germany), Box C-132, NA; Matthews to SecState, Feb. 28, 1946, *FRUS*, 1946, V, 508; Matthews to Acheson and Mr. Secretary, Feb. 11, 1946, RG 59, H. Freeman Matthews files, folder Memoranda 1946, Box 2, NA; Matthews to Caffery, Feb. 26, 1946, *ibid.*, Box 1, folder C, NA.

16. Murphy to SecState, Feb. 24, 1946, *FRUS*, 1946, V, 505–7.

17. Kennan to SecState, March 6, 1946, *FRUS*, 1946, V, 516–20.

18. Kennan to SecState, March 20, 1946, *FRUS*, 1946, VI, 721–23.

19. Matthews to Murphy, April 18, 1946, RG 59, Records of the Office of European Affairs, folder: Mr. Murphy letters, 1947, Box 13, NA.

20. Kennan to Carmel Office, May 10, 1946, *FRUS*, 1946, V, 555–56.

21. Acheson and Hilldring to SecState, May 9, 1946, *FRUS*, 1946, V, 549 (emphasis added).

22. James F. Byrnes, "The Big Four Paris Conference: Report to Nation," *Vital Speeches*, XII (Aug. 1, 1946), 613 (emphasis added).

23. OMGUS from Clay to AGWAR, July 18, 1946, Subj: U.S. and French Position re Central German Administrative Agencies, OMGUS Papers, Box 166-1/3, NA; Murphy to SecState, July 18, 1946, *FRUS*, 1946, V, 577–78; SecState from Cohen to Murphy, July 19, 1946, *ibid.*, 579–80.

24. OMGUS, Public Relations Office, Transcript of Clay Press Conference, May 27, 1946, OMGUS Papers, Box 1-1/4, NA.

25. War Dept. cable, repeated in Byrnes to AmEmbassy, Brussels, for Dorr, May 29, 1946, RG 59, file 740.00119 EW, Box C-248, NA.

26. OMGUS from Clay to War Dept., June 5, 1946, RG 165, file WDSCA 387.6, Sec. II, Box 351, NA.

27. Byrnes to AmEmbassy, Brussels, for Dorr, June 11, 1946, RG 59, file 740.00119 EW, Box C-248, NA.

28. Murphy to SecState, June 18, 1946, RG 59, file 740.00119 EW, Box C-248, NA (emphasis added).

29. Acheson to Murphy, June 24, 1946, RG 59, file 740.00119 EW, Box C-248, **NA.**

30. W. W. Rostow to C. P. Kindleberger, Subj: Coal and Other Matters, June 10, 1946, with Cover Memorandum from Kindleberger to Riddleberger, June 11, 1946, RG 59, file 740.00119 Control (Germany), Box 3735, NA.

31. See, for examples, *Time*, 47 (May 6, 1946), 35; *The Christian Century*, 63 (Sept. 25, 1946), 1142; and esp. Edd Johnson, "Cold War: The 'German Problem' Is Easy," *The New Republic*, 117 (Sept. 15, 1947), 17, for a reference to Clay's comment on the anti-Soviet representation of his reparations halt in the American press and for his statement that "I could be praised on the front pages of American newspapers any day. All I'd have to do would be let loose a blast against the Russians."

32. U.S. Dept. of State, Policy and Information Statement, Germany, Aug. 5, 1946, 53 pp. Copy in Byrnes Papers, Clemson University Library; AmEmbassy, Brussels, from Dorr to SecState, Sept. 6, 1946, RG 59, file 740.00119 EW, Box C-249, NA; Clayton to Dorr, Sept. 6, 1946, *ibid.* Interestingly, Dorr referred to the cable of June 11, 1946, which Murphy had objected to and which led to Acheson's concurrence with Murphy.

33. Dept. of State *Bulletin*, 16 (March 30, 1947), 563.

34. Dept. of State *Bulletin*, 14 (June 2, 1946), 953–54. Also printed in U.S. Dept. of State, *Making the Peace Treaties, 1941–1947* (Washington, 1947), appendix 4, p. 94.

35. U.S. Dept. of State, *Making the Peace Treaties*, pp. 24–25.

36. U.S. Dept. of State, *Germany, 1947–1949*, pp. 57–63, esp. p. 59; George F. Kennan, *Memoirs, 1925–1950* (Boston, 1967), pp. 333–35; Edward S. Mason, "Reflections on the Moscow Conference," *International Organization*, 1 (1947), 475–87, esp. 481; Dept. of State *Bulletin*, 17 (Sept. 14, 1947), 530–31; *Washington Post*, Sept. 7, 1947, [by Raymond J. Blair], in DNC Clippings, Box 157, Truman Library.

37. U.S. Congress, House, Committee on Foreign Affairs, 80th Cong., 1st Sess., *Hearings . . . Emergency Foreign Aid*, Nov. 10, 1947, p. 3.

38. U.S. Congress, Senate, *Congressional Record*, 80th Cong., 1st Sess., Dec. 19, 1947, pp. 11680, 11682.

39. Dept. of State *Bulletin*, 18 (Jan. 18, 1948), 78–82, esp. 79; Marshall, "The Stake of the Businessman in the European Recovery Program," Jan. 15, 1948, Holland Papers (Marshall Plan), Truman Library; U.S. Congress, Senate, Committee on Foreign Relations, 80th Cong., 2d Sess., *Hearings . . . European Economic Recovery*, Jan. 14, 1948, p. 445; Dept. of State *Bulletin*, 18 (Feb. 29, 1948), 286; (April 4, 1948), 457–59; (March 14, 1948), 354.

40. U.S. Congress, House, Committee on Appropriations, 80th Cong., 2d Sess., *Hearings Before the Subcommittee . . . on First Deficiency Appropriation Bill for 1948*, Jan. 22, 1948, p. 573.

Chapter Eleven

1. Ulrich Drobnig, "Soviet Corporations in Eastern Germany," *Journal of Central European Affairs*, XVII (July 1957), 150–65.

2. James P. Warburg, "Report on Germany," *The New Statesman and Nation*, XXXII (Aug. 10, 1946), 92–93.

3. See Drobnig, pp. 150–65; Erich W. Gniffke, *Jahre mit Ulbricht* (Köln, 1966), p. 199 and *passim*; Draft memorandum from Haraldson to Murphy, filed 7/17/46, RG 59, file 740.00119 EW, Box 3867, NA; C. P. Kindleberger to Clayton and Thorp, Nov. 1, 1946, RG 59, file 740.00119 Control (Germany), Box C-146, NA; Memorandum, C. R. Coleman to James S. Martin, OMGUS, Oct. 18, 1946, with attached report, "The Soviet Stock Company and 'The Combination System.' Instruments of Reparation Removals from the German Eastern Zone," RG 46, SEN 79A–F30, OP-58, Box 994, NA; Vladimir Rudolph, in Robert Slusser, ed., *Soviet Economic Policy in Postwar Germany: A Collection of Papers by Former Soviet Officials* (New York, 1953), pp. 56–61; Peter Nettl, "German Reparations in the Soviet Empire," *Foreign Affairs*, XXIX (Jan. 1951), 300–307; Nettl, "Inside the Russian Zone, 1945–1947," *The Political Quarterly*, XIX (July 1948), 201–33; Horst Duhnke, *Stalinismus in Deutschland: Die Geschichte der sowjetischen Besatzungszone* (Verlag für Politik und Wirtschaft, 1955), pp. 78–84; and Nicolas Spulber, "Soviet Undertakings and Soviet Mixed Companies in Eastern Europe," *Journal of Central European Affairs*, 14 (July 1954), 154–73.

4. Murphy to SecState, May 7, 1946, RG 59, file 740.00119 EW, Box 3863, NA; Hilldring to Echols, June 20, 1946, RG 165, file WDSCA 387.6, Sec. II, Box 351,

NA; OMGUS to War Dept., July 5, 1946, *ibid.*; OMGUS to War Dept., Aug. 6, 1946, *ibid.*; OMGUS to War Dept., Sept. 13, 1946, *ibid.*; OMGUS to War Dept., Dec. 10, 1946, RG 165, file WDSCA 387.6, Sec. VI, Box 352, NA; OMGUS to War Dept., Dec. 17, 1946, *ibid.*

5. See Harriman to SecState, June 6, 1946, *FRUS*, 1946, V, 565–66; Murphy to SecState, Nov. 2, 1946, RG 165, file WDSCA 387.6, Sec. V, Box 352, NA; and the British *Aide-Mémoire* of Dec. 27, 1947, *FRUS*, 1947, II, 1137–40, in which the British reported that Bevin had made it clear to Marshall in London on Dec. 17, 1947, that "he had never been happy when action had been taken in the Control Council which had prevented allocations being made over a long period."

6. AmEmbassy, Brussels, from Dorr to SecState, Sept. 13, 1946, RG 59, file 740.00119 EW, Box C-249, NA; Byrnes to USPOLAD, Nov. 14, 1946, *ibid.*, Box 3882; Draper to Sir Cecil Weir, British Control Commission, Nov. 30, 1946, RG 165, file WDSCA 387.6, Sec. VI, Box 352, NA; War Dept. to OMGUS, Dec. 19, 1946, *ibid.*; AmEmbassy, Brussels, from Kirk to SecState, March 10, 1947, RG 165, file WDSCA 387.6, Sec. X, Box 355, NA; Inter-Allied Reparations Agency, *First Report of the Secretary General for the Year 1946* (Brussels, 1947), p. 7.

7. Acheson to AmEmbassy, Brussels, for Dorr, April 2, 1946, RG 59, file 740.00119 EW, Box C-246, NA; Acheson to SecState, June 20, 1946, *FRUS*, 1946, V, 570–71; War Dept. to OMGUS, Dec. 19, 1946, RG 165, file WDSCA 387.6, Sec. VI, Box 352, NA.

8. AmEmbassy, Brussels, from Dorr to SecState, May 3, 1946, RG 59, file 740.00119 EW, Box C-247, NA; OMGUS from Clay to War Dept., May 4, 1946, RG 165, file WDSCA 387.6, Sec. II, Box 351, NA; Byrnes to AmEmbassy, Brussels, for Dorr, May 29, 1946, RG 59, file 740.00119 EW, Box C-248, NA.

9. Kindleberger to UnderSecState, Office Memorandum, June 13, 1946, RG 59, file 740.00119 EW, Box 3865, NA; OMGUS to War Dept., June 18, 1946, RG 165, file WDSCA 387.6, Sec. II, Box 351, NA; Hilldring to Echols, June 24, 1946, RG 59, file 740.00119 Control (Germany), Box 3736, NA; War Dept. to OMGUS, June 24, 1946, *ibid.*; War Dept. to OMGUS, June 29, 1946, RG 165, file WDSCA 387.6, Sec. II, Box 351, NA.

10. Acheson to AmEmbassy, Brussels, for Dorr, March 26, 1946, RG 59, file 740.00119 EW, Box 3858, NA.

11. Clay to Echols, Oct. 4, 1946, RG 165, file WDSCA 387.6, Sec. IV, Box 351, NA.

12. Clarence G. Lasby, *Project Paperclip: German Scientists and the Cold War* (New York, 1971).

13. Sparks to Meader, Memorandum, Subj: Military Government, Oct. 31, 1946, RG 46, SEN 79A–F30, OP-58, Box 1010, NA.

14. J. C. Green, Office of Technical Services, to Echols, War Dept., Oct. 30, 1946, RG 165, file WDSCA 014 Germany, Sec. XV, Box 235, NA; Sparks to Meader, Memorandum, Subj: Military Government, Oct. 31, 1946, RG 46, SEN 79A–F30, OP-58, Box 1010, NA.

15. *Science News Letter*, 49 (May 4, 1946), 279. See also *Washington Post*, April 8, 1946, p. 2, in DNC Clippings, Box 145, Truman Library.

16. *New York Times*, Feb. 21, 1947, p. 27L.

17. OMGUS, Economics, to OMGBavaria, Dec. 10, 1946, Subj: Possibility of War Research and Production in Steinhaeil Optische Werke, OMGUS Papers, file AG 004, Box 33-2/1, NA; OMGUS to AGWAR, May 6, 1947, *ibid.*

18. Clay to Echols, Oct. 4, 1946, RG 165, file WDSCA 387.6, Sec. IV, Box 351, NA.

19. Hilldring to John L. Sullivan, UnderSecNavy, July 16, 1946, RG 59, file 740.00119 EW, Box 3867, NA.

20. H. S. Aurand, Director of Research and Development, War Dept., to Clay, Oct. 16, 1946, RG 165, file WDSCA 387.6, Sec. IV, Box 351, NA.

21. Byrnes to AmEmbassy, Brussels, for Dorr, Oct. 22, 1946, RG 59, file 740.00119 EW, Box C-251, NA. The Army file, WDSCA 387.6, Sec. IV, RG 165, Box 351, NA, shows that USFET sent a report, but it contained no valuations. The file also contains a message discussing the difficulties of preparing a list with valuations. Finally the file shows that the United States had made little progress on compiling a report or an evaluation at the time the issue was discussed by Marshall in March 1947, during the Moscow CFM.

22. OMGUS, from Clay, to War Dept., for Noce, Jan. 22, 1947, RG 165, file WDSCA 387.6, Sec. XV, Box 354, NA.

23. OMGUS, from Clay, to War Dept., for Noce, Jan. 30, 1947, RG 165, file WDSCA 387.6, Sec. VIII, Box 354, NA.

24. John L. Kent, "Manufacturing Advances in Wartime Germany: Machines and Processes Which Were Developed in Competition with Allied Engineering Brains Are Now Available to U.S. Industry," *Scientific American*, 178 (April 1948), 164.

25. War Dept. to OMGUS, June 7, 1947, RG 165, file WDSCA 387.6, Sec. XIII, Box 356, NA; War Dept. to CINCEUR, June 21, 1947, RG 165, file WDSCA 014 Germany, Sec. XXIII, Box 239, NA.

26. OMGUS, from Clay, to AGWAR, for Petersen, RG 165, file WDSCA 014 Germany, Sec. XXIII, Box 239, NA.

27. Inter-Allied Reparations Agency, *Report of the Secretary General for the Year 1947* (Brussels, 1948), esp. pp. 6–7, 14–15; AmEmbassy, Brussels, from Dorr to SecState, Jan. 23, 1947, RG 165, file WDSCA 387.6, Sec. VIII, Box 354, NA; SecState to Dorr, Jan. 24, 1947, *ibid.*

28. U.S. Delegation Minutes, CFM, March 18, 1947, *FRUS*, 1947, II, 259. Interestingly, during the discussion that followed, Molotov referred to statements by John C. Green, apparently the ones reported in the *New York Times*, Feb. 21, 1947, p. 27L.

29. U.S. Delegation Minutes, CFM, March 18, 1947, *FRUS*, 1947, II, 260–61.

30. U.S. Dept. of State, *Germany, 1947–1949*, Pub. 3556 (Washington, 1950), pp. 371–72, 372–73; State Dept. Press Release, March 26, 1947, in Dept. of State *Bulletin*, 16 (April 6, 1947), 609.

31. War Dept. to USFET, Oct. 8, 1946, RG 165, file WDSCA 014 Germany, Sec. IV, Box 234, NA; USFET, from McNarney, to OMGUS, Oct. 10, 1946, *ibid.*;

Sparks to Meader, Memorandum, Subj: Military Government, Oct. 31, 1946, RG 46, SEN 79A–F30, OP-58, Box 1010, NA.

32. OMGUS to War Dept., Sept. 18, 1946, RG 165, file WDSCA 387.6, Sec. II, Box 351, NA; Clay to Echols, Oct. 4, 1946, *ibid.*, Sec. IV; OMGUS, from Clay, to War Dept., for Noce, Jan. 22, 1947, *ibid.*, Sec. XV; OMGUS, from Draper, to War Dept., Dec. 23, 1946, *ibid.*, Sec. VI.

33. OMGUS, from Clay, to War Dept., for Noce, Jan. 22, 1947, RG 165, file WDSCA 387.6, Sec. XV, Box 351, NA.

34. SWNCC, Decision on SWNCC 328/5, Unilateral Removals from Germany to Be Accounted For as Reparation, RG 218, file CCS 007 (3/13/45), Sec. 7, NA.

35. War Dept., from Noce, to Hilldring, Aug. 11, 1947, RG 165, file WDSCA 387.6, Sec. VIII, Box 354, NA. The Army also tried to collect reports from its own services and branches. See SecWar to addressees, Subj: U.S. Army Unilateral Removals from Germany, Reports Control Symbol WDGSP-(OT)-152, Sept. 15, 1947, RG 165, file WDSCA 387.6, Sec. XVI, Box 357, NA, which referred to the SWNCC paper of Aug. 8, 1947, provided forms and guidance, and stated: "In order that the United States may be in a secure position before the Council of Foreign Ministers and the Interallied Reparations Agency, it is necessary that the Department of State have a definitive list of all material, subject to being classed as reparations, removed by the United States from Germany."

36. Charles E. Saltzman, to War Dept., for Noce, Aug. 29, 1947, RG 165, file WDSCA 387.6, Sec. XV, Box 357, NA.

37. War Dept. to Clay, Sept. 17, 1947, RG 165, file WDSCA 387.6, Sec. VI, Box 357, NA; Clay to Noce, Oct. 2, 1947, *ibid.*, Sec. XV.

Chapter Twelve

1. Murphy to SecState, Oct. 23, 1945, *FRUS*, 1945, III, 1536; Murphy to Actg-SecState, July 7, 1945, *FRUS*, 1945, Potsdam I, 630–33; USFET, from Clay, to AGWAR, July 9, 1945, *ibid.*, 633–34; War Dept. to Clay, July 10, 1945, *ibid.*, 635–36.

2. Memorandum of Bidault-Byrnes Conversation, Aug. 23, 1945, *FRUS*, 1945, IV, 711–15; Report on Franco-American Conversations, Nov. 13–20, 1945, *FRUS*, 1945, III, 896–906; SecWar to SecState, Feb. 13, 1946, *FRUS*, 1946, V, 501–3; Memorandum by French Delegation, CFM, April 25, 1946, *FRUS*, 1946, II, 109–12; Memorandum of Bidault-Byrnes Conversation, Sept. 24, 1946, *FRUS*, 1946, V, 607–10; James F. Byrnes, *Speaking Frankly* (New York, 1947), pp. 169–71.

3. Acheson to Murphy, Dec. 6, 1946, RG 59, file 740.00119 Control (Germany), Box C-147, NA (see also *FRUS*, 1946, V, 649, note 12). Ernest Bevin had said in a foreign policy speech on the Paris Peace Conference, House of Commons, Oct. 22, 1946 (*Vital Speeches*, XIII [Nov. 15, 1946], 91), that the British were ready to accept the French proposals on the Saar.

4. U.S. Delegation Record, CFM, Dec. 9, 1946, *FRUS*, 1946, II, 1482–83;

Murphy to SecState, Dec. 27, 1946, *FRUS*, 1946, V, 656–57; SecState to Clay, Dec. 30, 1946, *ibid.*, 657–58; War Dept. to OMGUS, Feb. 20, 1947, RG 165, file WDSCA 014 Germany, Sec. XIX, Box 237, NA.

5. OMGUS, Monthly Report of the Military Governor, Coal, No. 1, Aug. 20, 1945, p. 1. See F. S. V. Donnison, *Civil Affairs and Military Government: North-West Europe* (London, 1961), p. 411, for the information that the Nov. 1945 production, which had increased five times since June 1945, was still only 10 percent of the 1943 annual monthly average. See Fred H. Sanderson, "Germany's Economic Situation and Prospects," in Gabriel A. Almond, ed., *The Struggle for Democracy in Germany* (Chapel Hill, N.C., 1949), p. 133ff, for figures that production at the time of Germany's surrender was 10 percent of 1938, in February 1946 it was about 40 percent, and in March 1947 it was about 50 percent.

6. Murphy to SecState, April 28, 1946, *FRUS*, 1946, V, 776–77.

7. Winant to SecState, Nov. 8, 1945, *FRUS*, 1945, III, 1541–44.

8. SecState to Murphy, Feb. 11, 1946, *FRUS*, 1946, V, 767; SecState to French Ambassador, March 13, 1946, *ibid.*, 768, and note 60, *ibid.*, p. 768 (emphasis added).

9. Memorandum of Blum-Byrnes Conversation, March 19, 1946, *FRUS*, 1946, V, 418–20.

10. SecState to Caffery, April 10, 1946, *FRUS*, 1946, V, 426–27. See also Edgar Beigel, "France Moves Toward National Planning," *Political Science Quarterly*, LXII (Sept. 1947), 381–97.

11. Minutes ... National Advisory Council on International Monetary and Financial Problems, April 25, 1946, *FRUS*, 1946, V, 433; May 6, 1946, *ibid.*, 444; OMGUS from Clay to War Dept., for Echols, July 16, 1946, RG 165, file WDSCA 463.3, Sec. III, Box 390, NA.

12. Charles P. Kindleberger, "Germany and the Economic Recovery of Europe," *Proceedings of the Academy of Political Science*, XXIII (May 1949), 288–301, esp. 296.

13. Clayton to McCloy, June 30, 1945, *FRUS*, 1945, Potsdam I, 477–78.

14. Winant to SecState, Nov. 8, 1945, *FRUS*, 1945, III, 1541–44; "Pooling of Past Proceeds of Exports from the British and U.S. Zones. Synopsis of the Problem," GEP/SEC/41, Nov. 18, 1946, attached to Dept. of State, Memorandum of Conversation, Subj: Financial Aspects of Bizonal Unity in Germany, Nov. 19, 1946, RG 59, file 740.00119 Control (Germany), Box C-146, NA; Donnison, p. 415.

15. OMGUS, from Clay, to War Dept., for Echols, July 16, 1946, RG 165, file WDSCA 463.3, Sec. III, Box 390, NA; Murphy to SecState, Sept. 23, 1945, *FRUS*, 1945, III, 1529–30; Kindleberger, p. 296.

16. U.S. Delegation Record, CFM, July 11, 1946, *FRUS*, 1946, II, 896.

17. Murphy to SecState, March 20, 1946, *FRUS*, 1946, V, 768–69; ACC, Minutes of 23d Meeting, March 20, 1946, CONL/M(46)8, RG 59, file 740.00119 Control (Germany), Box C-136, NA.

18. Murphy to SecState, April 4, 1946, *FRUS*, 1946, V, 536–37.

19. War Dept., from Echols, to Clay, April 26, 1946, RG 165, file WDSCA

463.3, Sec. II, Box 222, NA; Minutes . . . National Advisory Council on International Monetary and Financial Problems, May 6, 1946, *FRUS*, 1946, V, 444.

20. Draft Resolution by the French Delegation, CFM, July 11, 1946, *FRUS*, 1946, II, 901–2; Record of Decisions, CFM, July 12, 1946, *ibid.*, 938.

21. OMGUS, from Clay, to War Dept., for Echols, July 16, 1946, RG 165, file WDSCA 463.3, Sec. III, Box 390, NA.

22. OMGUS, from Clay, to USFET, July 19, 1946, RG 316, Clay Papers, Box 3, NA.

23. Murphy to SecState, for Riddleberger, Aug. 8, 1946, RG 59, file 740.00119 Control (Germany), Box 3738, NA.

24. OMGUS to War Dept., Jan. 3, 1947, RG 165, file CAD 100, Sec. VII, Box 286, NA.

25. Sir Cecil Weir, "Economic Development in Western Germany," *International Affairs*, 25 (July 1949), 250.

26. Murphy to SecState, Jan. 14, 1947, RG 165, file WDSCA 091.31, Sec. XV, Box 267, NA.

27. Byrnes to Patterson, July 26, 1946, RG 165, file WDSCA 091.31, Sec. V, Box 263, NA.

28. OMGUS to War Dept., Nov. 6, 1946, RG 165, file WDSCA 091.31, Sec. XI, Box 265, NA.

29. OMGUS to AGWAR, Jan. 28, 1947, CC 7826, RG 316, Clay Papers, Box 3, NA.

30. Austria-Bizone Coal and Power Agreement, July 7, 1947, in RG 165, file WDSCA 463.1, Sec. I, Box 389, NA; ComGenUSFA, Vienna, to SecState, Dec. 29, 1947, RG 165, file WDSCA 463.3, Sec. VI, Box 391, NA.

31. OMGUS, Monthly Report of the Military Governor, No. 28, Oct. 1947, Report of the Military Governor, p. 21.

32. Minutes, Meeting of SecState, SecWar, and SecNavy, July 3, 1947, War Dept. Papers, SecWar, Office of Special Assistant, file 334, Committee of Three, Jan. 1947– , NA; AsstSecWar to OMGUS, July 10, 1947, RG 107, file ASW 091 Germany, Book 2, Box 26, NA.

33. JCS 1779, V, 16c, and V, 18c, in U.S. Dept. of State, *Germany, 1947–1949*, Pub. 3556 (Washington, 1950), pp. 37, 38.

34. OMGUS, Monthly Report of the Military Governor, No. 29, Nov. 1947, Report of the Military Governor, p. 28.

Chapter Thirteen

1. Murphy to SecState, Sept. 10, 1945, *FRUS*, 1945, III, 1527–28; SecState to Diplomatic Representatives, Nov. 8, 1945, *ibid.*, 1539–40; JCS to McNarney, Nov. 24, 1945, *ibid.*, 1547–49.

2. Acheson to AmEmbassy, Brussels, for Dorr, June 18, 1946, RG 59, file 740.00119 EW, Box 3860, NA.

3. *Aide-Mémoire*, Czech Ambassador to SecState, May 16, 1946, RG 59, file 740.00119 EW, Box 3864, NA.

4. Acheson to AmEmbassy, Prague, June 20, 1946, RG 59, file 740.00119 EW,

Box C-247, NA; Acheson to AmEmbassy, Brussels, for Dorr, June 18, 1946, RG 59, *ibid.*, Box 3860; Dorr to DeWilde, July 29, 1946, RG 59, *ibid.*, Box 3868; War Dept., Memorandum for the Record, Aug. 13, 1946, RG 165, file CAD 500, Sec. II, Box 392, NA.

5. Byrnes to Dorr, Oct. 13, 1946, RG 59, file 740.00119 EW, Box C-251, NA. Byrnes's cancellation was in pique at the behavior of Czechoslovakian representatives at the Paris Peace Conference. According to Byrnes, the Czech delegation had applauded a Russian reference to dollar imperialism. See James F. Byrnes, *Speaking Frankly* (New York, 1947), pp. 143–44.

6. OMGUS, Monthly Report of the Military Governor, No. 28, Oct. 1947, Finance (Sept.–Oct. 1947), p. 15.

7. OMGUS to War Dept., Feb. 14, 1947, RG 165, file WDSCA 091.31, Sec. XVII, Box 268, NA.

8. AmEmbassy, Prague, to SecState, Feb. 14, 1947, RG 165, file WDSCA 014 Germany, Sec. XIX, Box 237, NA; SecState to Murphy, Feb. 14, 1947, RG 165, file WDSCA 091.31, Sec. XVII, Box 268, NA.

9. War Dept. to OMGUS, Feb. 21, 1947, RG 165, file WDSCA 387.6, Sec. IX, Box 354, NA.

10. OMGUS to War Dept., March 5, 1947, RG 165, file WDSCA 091.31, Sec. XIX, Box 269, NA; OMGUS to War Dept., March 9, 1947, *ibid.*; Murphy to SecState, March 10, 1947, *ibid.*

11. Acheson to Murphy, March 25, 1947, RG 165, file WDSCA 091.31, Sec. XIX, Box 269, NA; Patterson to Acheson, March 29, 1947, RG 59, file 740.00119 Control (Germany)/3-2947, NA. See also Steinhardt to SecState, April 8, 1947, RG 165, file WDSCA 091.31, Sec. XXI, Box 271, NA, and OMGUS, Monthly Report of the Military Governor, No. 29, Nov. 1947, Trade and Commerce, p. 21.

12. OMGUS, Monthly Report of the Military Governor, No. 26, Aug. 1–31, 1947, Finance (July–Aug. 1947), p. 17.

13. JCS 1779, V, 18c, in U.S. Dept. of State, *Germany, 1947–1949*, Pub. 3556 (Washington, 1950), p. 38.

14. "Recapitulation of Action with Respect to the Routing of Civil Affairs Supplies Imported into Germany via Rotterdam and Antwerp," appendix "A" of SWNCC 363, RG 218, JCS 1946–48, file CCS 091.31 Germany (11/16/45), NA.

15. War Dept. to OMGUS, July 2, 1946, RG 59, file 740.00119 Control (Germany), Box 3736, NA.

16. OMGUS, from Clay, to USFET, July 19, 1946, RG 316, Clay Papers, Box 3, NA.

17. Murphy to Matthews, May 31, 1946, RG 59, file 740.00119 Control (Germany), Box 3735, NA; Murphy to SecState, Sept. 18, 1946, RG 165, file WDSCA 091.31, Box 264, NA; OMGUS to War Dept., Oct. 10, 1946, RG 165, file CAD 500, Sec. II, Box 392, NA.

18. War Dept. to OMGUS, May 19, 1947, RG 218, JCS 1946–1948, file CCS 091.31 Germany (11/16/45), NA.

19. OMGUS to AGWAR, June 11, 1947, RG 165, file CAD 500, Sec. II, Box 392, NA.

20. OMGUS to War Dept., for Noce, July 30, 1947, RG 165, file CAD 500, Sec. II, Box 392, NA; Petersen to Clay, July 8, 1947, RG 107, file ASW 091 Germany, Book 2, Box 26, NA.

21. Caffery to SecState, Aug. 20, 1947, RG 165, file WDSCA 334 EECE, Sec. II, Box 319, NA.

22. War Dept. to OMGUS, Sept. 12, 1947, RG 165, file CAD 500, Sec. II, Box 392, NA; OMGUS to AGWAR, for Noce, Sept. 17, 1947, *ibid.*

23. Noce to C/S, War Dept., Sept. 18, 1947, RG 165, file CAD 500, Sec. II, Box 392, NA; Frederick Winant to Harold H. Neff, Nov. 14, 1947, War Dept. Papers, file ASA 091 Germany, Box 187, NA; Memorandum of Conversation by ActgSecState Lovett, Nov. 26, 1947, *FRUS*, 1947, II, 772–74.

24. L. Wilkinson, OMGUS, to Dept. of Army, Dec. 9, 1948, RG 165, file CSCAD 500, Sec. I, Box 500, NA.

25. Clayton to Blaisdell, July 4, 1945, *FRUS*, 1945, Potsdam I, 626–28.

Chapter Fourteen

1. Marshall, "The Stake of the Businessman in the European Recovery Program," speech to Pittsburgh Chamber of Commerce, Jan. 15, 1948, Holland Papers (Marshall Plan), Truman Library.

2. Dept. of State, Memorandum of Press and Radio News Conference, Oct. 31, 1946, Byrnes Papers, folder 565, Clemson University Library.

3. Patterson to Hoover, Nov. 5, 1946, RG 107, file ASW 430, Book I, Box 76, NA.

4. Clay and Murphy had been in the U.S. since Nov. 8, 1946. See Felix Belair in the *New York Times*, Jan. 23, 1947, p. 1, for a report that Hoover's visit was Clay's idea.

5. Tracy S. Voorhees, Memorandum for the Secretary, Dec. 21, 1946, RG 107, file ASW 430, Book I, Box 76, NA.

6. Patterson, Memorandum for the Files, "Telephone Talk with Mr. Herbert Hoover," Dec. 22, 1946, RG 335, Sec/Army (Patterson), Subj. file, Box 4, NA; Petersen to SecWar, Subj: Hoover's Trip, Dec. 24, 1946, RG 107, file ASW 430, Book I, Box 76, NA; Patterson to Forrest Davis, OMGUS, Dec. 27, 1946, SecWar Patterson Papers, file Germany (OSW 091 Germany 12/27/46), NA.

7. Patterson to Truman, Jan. 16, 1947, OF 950-B (Economic Mission as to Food and Its Collateral Problems), Truman Library.

8. Truman to Hoover, Jan. 18, 1947, OF 950-B (Economic Mission as to Food and Its Collateral Problems), Truman Library; Hoover to Truman, Jan. 19, 1947, *ibid.*

9. Patterson to Truman, Jan. 20, 1947, RG 335, file OSA 430, 1946–47 (Patterson's Safe File), Box 7, NA.

10. See OF 950-B (Economic Mission as to Food and Its Collateral Problems), Truman Library.

11. Petersen to USFET for McNarney and Clay, Jan. 30, 1947, RG 107, file ASW 430, Book I, Box 76, NA. See also Patterson to OMGUS, Jan. 22, 1947, *ibid.*

12. Louis P. Lochner, *Herbert Hoover and Germany* (New York, 1960), esp. p. 179ff; Toni Stolper, *Ein Leben in Brennpunkten unserer Zeit* (Tübingen, 1960), esp. p. 448ff.

13. The President's Economic Mission to Germany and Austria, "Report No. 3—The Necessary Steps for Promotion of German Exports, so as to Relieve American Taxpayers of the Burdens of Relief and for Economic Recovery of Europe," March 18, 1947, OF 950-B (Economic Mission as to Food and Its Collateral Problems), Truman Library. See also *New York Times*, March 24, 1947, p. 4.

14. Hickerson to Lightner, April 3, 1947, RG 59, Hickerson files, Box 3, Memoranda by JDH, 1947, NA.

15. Acheson to SecState, March 20, 1947, *FRUS*, 1947, II, 394–95; Acheson to Hilldring, May 2, 1947, RG 59, file 740.00119 Control (Germany)/5-247, NA; Norman T. Ness to C. H. Humelsine, July 8, 1947, RG 59, file 840.50 Recovery/7-847, NA.

16. Pauley to Truman, April 15, 1947, OF 383 (Edwin W. Pauley), Truman Library.

17. John R. Steelman, Memorandum for the President, Subj: Hoover and Pauley Recommendations on Germany, n.d., but "noted May 21, 1947," by John W. Snyder, Snyder Papers, Box 15 (Germany—General, 1936–51), Truman Library. See also Pauley to Truman, June 9, 1947, *FRUS*, 1947, II, 1106–8.

18. Washington/Berlin Teleconference: Noce, Clay, and Draper, March 5, 1947, RG 107, file ASW 430, Book II, Box 76, NA.

19. Voorhees, Memorandum for SecWar and Others, Subj: Notes as to Mr. Hoover's Present Activities in Completion of His Mission, March 8, 1947, RG 107, file ASW 430, Book I, Box 76, NA.

20. Voorhees, Memorandum for . . . Noce, March 20, 1947, RG 107, file ASW 430, Book II, Box 76, NA.

21. Acheson to SecState, March 20, 1947, *FRUS*, 1947, II, 394–95.

22. Harry B. Price, Notes of an Interview with George F. Kennan, Feb. 19, 1953, Truman Library.

23. Joseph M. Jones, *The Fifteen Weeks* (New York, 1955), pp. 223–24.

24. U.S. Delegation Record, CFM, July 11, 1946, *FRUS,* 1946, II, 896; Murphy to SecState, March 22, 1946, *FRUS*, 1946, V, 530; F. S. V. Donnison, *Civil Affairs and Military Government: North-West Europe* (London, 1961), p. 415.

25. OMGUS to War Dept., Nov. 6, 1946, RG 165, file WDSCA 387.6, Sec. V, Box 352, NA; Dept. of State, Memorandum of Conversation, Subj: US-UK Meeting on Food Supplies for the Bizonal Area of Germany, Nov. 22, 1946, RG 59, file 740.00119 Control (Germany), Box C-146, NA.

26. *Neue Zeitung*, Nov. 25, 1946, p. 1.

27. *New York Times*, Jan. 3, 1947, p. 12L; *Neue Zeitung*, Jan. 20, 1947, p. 1; Jan. 24, 1947, p. 2.

28. See especially SecState to the President, March 19, 1947, *FRUS*, 1947, II, 263–65, and Memorandum of Bevin-Marshall Conversation, March 22, 1947, *ibid.*, 273–74.

29. Marshall's Statement at CFM, March 18, 1947, in U.S. Dept. of State, *Germany, 1947–1949*, Pub. 3556 (Washington, 1950), p. 372.

30. Memorandum of Bevin-Marshall Conversation, March 22, 1947, *FRUS*, 1947, II, 273–74.

31. Acheson to SecState, March 20, 1947, *FRUS*, 1947, II, 394–95.

32. See Truman to SecState, April 1, 1947, *FRUS*, 1947, II, 301–3, for the rigid position that Truman maintained on the first-charge principle, current-production reparations, and the coal needs of "other countries."

33. SecState to the President, March 19, 1947, *FRUS*, 1947, II, 263–65.

34. Murphy to Matthews, Feb. 4, 1947, *FRUS*, 1947, II, 23; Minutes of Marshall-Auriol Conversation, March 6, 1947, *ibid.*, 190–95; SecState to the President, March 19, 1947, *ibid.*, 263–65; March 20, 1947, *ibid.*, 265–66.

35. Memorandum of Bevin-Marshall Conversation, March 22, 1947, *FRUS*, 1947, II, 274; SecState to the President, March 20, 1947, *ibid.*, 265.

36. Memorandum of Bevin-Marshall Conversation, April 5, 1947, *FRUS*, 1947, II, 309.

37. Memorandum of Bevin-Marshall Conversation, April 8, 1947, *FRUS*, 1947, II, 315–17, and note 21.

38. Draper to Clay, April 11, 1947, *FRUS*, 1947, II, 473–75; Clay to Draper, April 11, 1947, *ibid.*, 472–73.

39. Clay to Draper, April 11, 1947, *FRUS*, 1947, II, 472–73; Clay to Draper, n.d. (response to Draper to Clay, April 11), *ibid.*, 476.

40. Bevin to Marshall, April 4, 1947, *FRUS*, 1947, II, 475.

41. Memorandum for the SecState [by Draper and E. S. Mason], April 17, 1947, *FRUS*, 1947, II, 483–84.

42. Memorandum by the British Military Governor, April 17, 1947, *FRUS*, 1947, II, 479–82. See *ibid.*, 482–83, for Draper's comments on the British memorandum.

43. SecState to ActgSecState, April 19, 1947, *FRUS*, 1947, II, 357–58.

44. *Ibid.*, 356–57.

45. Marshall, Radio Report on CFM, Moscow, April 28, 1947, in U.S. Dept. of State, *Germany, 1947–1949*, p. 59.

46. Clay to Walter Brown, April 21, 1947, Byrnes Papers, folder 646(1), Clemson University Library; Clay to Byrnes, May 11, 1947, *ibid.*, folder 651(2).

Chapter Fifteen

1. Lucius D. Clay, *Decision in Germany* (Garden City, N.Y., 1950), p. 174; *Neue Zeitung*, April 28, 1947, p. 1.

2. OMGUS, from Clay, to Marshall, May 2, 1947, *FRUS*, 1947, II, 915–18.

3. Joseph M. Jones, *The Fifteen Weeks* (New York, 1955), pp. 223–24; George F. Kennan, *Memoirs, 1925–1950* (Boston, 1967), pp. 325–26.

4. Walter Millis, ed., *The Forrestal Diaries* (New York, 1951), p. 266.

5. Edwin W. Pauley to Truman, April 15, 1947, OF 383, Truman Library.

6. OMGUS, Memorandum, March 5, 1947, *FRUS*, 1947, II, esp. 233; Actg-SecState to AmEmbassy in France, March 6, 1947, *ibid.*, 188–89; SecState to the President, March 20, 1947, *ibid.*, 265–66.

7. See Memorandum for SecState (by Draper and E. S. Mason), April 17, 1947, *FRUS*, 1947, II, 485–86; SecState to Bidault, April 19, 1947, *ibid.*, 486–88; Bidault to SecState, April 19, 1947, *ibid.*, 488.

8. Radio Report by Marshall, CFM, Moscow, April 28, 1947, in U.S. Dept. of State, *Germany, 1947–1949*, Pub. 3556 (Washington, 1950), pp. 57–63 *passim* (emphasis added).

9. Kennan, esp. 332–34.

10. Kennan to Acheson, May 23, 1947, *FRUS*, 1947, III, 226 (emphasis added).

11. Memorandum by the Director of the PPS, May 16, 1947, *FRUS*, 1947, III, 222 (first emphasis added).

12. Kennan to Acheson, May 23, 1947, *FRUS*, 1947, III, 226–29.

13. Bevin to SecState, April 24, 1947, *FRUS*, 1947, II, 490–91.

14. Murphy to Matthews, April 27, 1947, *FRUS*, 1947, II, 909–11.

15. Clay to War Dept., April 26, 1947, RG 319, Army CAD Messages, CM-IN's 1947, Box 20, NA (repeated in *FRUS*, 1947, II, 910–11).

16. Clay to War Dept., April 29, 1947, *FRUS*, 1947, II, 911–14. See Lewis W. Douglas, Handwritten Notes of a Conversation with Bevin, May 10, 1947, Douglas Papers, Box 240, folder 1, University of Arizona Library, for the information that Bevin was "very anxious to cooperate in every possible way with us in making a success of the fused zones for we have only a few months & 'time is running out' as he put it."

17. See Petersen, Memorandum to SecWar, June 12, 1947, War Dept. Papers, file ASW 091 Germany, vol. 1, NA, for the judgment that the State Department's position was "that anything goes (presumably even communism) as long as it is the result of the freely expressed will of the German people."

18. War Dept., from Noce, to Clay, May 1, 1947, *FRUS*, 1947, II, 914–15.

19. War Dept. to Clay, May 7, 1947, War Dept. Papers, file WDSCA 014 Germany, Sec. XXII, NA.

20. See my *The American Occupation of Germany* (Stanford, Calif., 1968), pp. 123–28, for a description of Clay's implementation of his instructions in the organization of the bizonal administration.

21. Millis, p. 273.

22. Kennan to Acheson, May 23, 1947, *FRUS*, 1947, III, 226.

23. *FRUS*, 1947, II, 924, note 32; Petersen to OMGUS, June 13, 1947, RG 107, file ASW 463.3, Box 77, NA.

24. According to the *Frankfurter Rundschau*, Jan. 25, 1947, p. 1, Robertson said at the meeting that the record daily production had been 217,488 tons, which had been achieved on Jan. 21, 1947.

25. OMGUS, Industry Branch, Memorandum, Field Trip to Minden . . . Jan. 30, 1947, OMGUS Papers, Box 263-2/17, NA; "Bericht über die Sondersitzung des Verwaltungsrats für Wirtschaft in Minden am 25. Januar 1947," Staat-

skanzlei, Wiesbaden, 1d06-01; *Neue Zeitung*, Jan. 31, 1947, p. 5; *Frankfurter Rundschau*, Jan. 25, 1947, p. 1; *Süddeutsche Zeitung*, Jan. 30, 1947, p. 1.

26. See Murphy to Matthews, April 27, 1947, *FRUS*, 1947, II, 909–11, for a repeat of Clay's message to the War Department.

27. See my *The American Occupation of Germany*, pp. 96–100, 118–20, 124–27, for a discussion of the negotiations in Berlin.

28. Nordrhein-Westfalen Landtag, *Stenographischer Bericht* . . . June 16, 1947, pp. 8–15. The German reads: "Das kapitalistische Wirtschaftssystem hat sich an seinen eigenen Gesetzen totgelaufen."

29. According to Murphy, Pakenham agreed that that was the British position. Murphy to SecState, May 10, 1947, *FRUS*, 1947, II, 919.

Chapter Sixteen

1. Clayton to McCloy, June 18, 1945, *FRUS*, 1945, Potsdam I, 468–70; Matthews to McCloy, June 15, 1945, RG 59, H. Freeman Matthews files, Box 1, folder M, NA.

2. Memorandum of Marshall-Clayton Conversation, June 20, 1947, *FRUS*, 1947, II, 929.

3. SecState to Clay, June 24, 1947, *FRUS*, 1947, II, 931.

4. Petersen, Memorandum for the SecWar, June 12, 1947, War Dept. Papers, file ASW 091 Germany, vol. 1, NA.

5. Patterson to Marshall, June 13, 1947, War Dept. Papers, S/A Patterson Subject File, Box 4, NA.

6. Murphy to SecState, June 17, 1947, *FRUS*, 1947, II, 924–25.

7. Minutes of a Meeting of the Secretaries of State, War, and Navy, June 19, 1947, *FRUS*, 1947, II, 927–28.

8. Memorandum of Marshall-Clayton Conversation, June 20, 1947, *FRUS*, 1947, II, 929; Memorandum of Clayton-Bevin Conversation, June 24, 1947, *FRUS*, 1947, III, 268–73; Clayton to SecState, June 25, 1947, *FRUS*, 1947, II, 932–33.

9. Clay to AGWAR, for Petersen, June 24, 1947, War Dept. Papers, file ASW 091 Germany, NA.

10. Murphy to SecState, June 24, 1947, *FRUS*, 1947, II, 929–31.

11. Petersen to Clay, June 24, 1947, War Dept. Papers, file ASW 091 Germany, vol. 1, NA; Petersen to Clay, June 25, 1947, *ibid.*; SecState to AmEmbassy, London, June 27, 1947, *FRUS*, 1947, II, 933.

12. Clay to AGWAR, for Petersen, June 28, 1947, War Dept. Papers, file ASW 091 Germany, vol. 1, NA; Petersen to Clay, July 1, 1947, *ibid.*

13. Petersen to Clay, July 8, 1947, War Dept. Papers, file ASW 091 Germany, Book 2, NA.

14. See the story by Felix Blair, *New York Times*, Aug. 12, 1947, DNC Clippings, Box 198, Truman Library.

15. SecState to AmEmbassy, London, July 8, 1947, *FRUS*, 1947, II, 934, and note 46; July 10, 1947, *ibid.*, 935–36.

16. SecState to AmEmbassy, London, July 15, 1947, *FRUS*, 1947, II, 939.

17. SecState to AmEmbassy, London, July 17, 1947, *FRUS*, 1947, II, 944–45; Marshall to Douglas, July 17, 1947, RG 59, file 840.50 Recovery/7-1747, NA.

18. Douglas to Lovett, July 25, 1947, *FRUS*, 1947, II, 945–46, and note 62.

19. Draper to Clay, July 26, 1947, War Dept. Papers, file ASW 091 Germany, NA; AmEmbassy, London, to SecState, July 26, 1947, RG 165, file WDSCA 014 Germany, Sec. XXIV, Box 239, NA.

20. Report on Anglo-American Coal Conference, Sept. 22, 1947, *FRUS*, 1947, II, 964.

21. German Coal Organization, July 16, 1947, *FRUS*, 1947, II, 940–42; Interim Agreement for Internal US/UK Use on German Coal Organization, July 16, 1947, *ibid.*, 943–44; Summary Minutes, . . . Anglo-American Conversations Regarding German Coal Production, Aug. 21, 1947, *ibid.*, 946–49; ActgSecState to AmEmbassy, London, Aug. 22, 1947, *ibid.*, 950–52; Aug. 24, 1947, *ibid.*, 952; Aug. 26, 1947, *ibid.*, 954–55.

22. Clay to AGWAR, for Noce, Aug. 30, 1947, War Dept. Papers, file WDSCA 014 Germany, Sec. XXV, NA. See also *FRUS*, 1947, II, 956, note 78.

23. Douglas to ActgSecState, Sept. 8, 1947, *FRUS*, 1947, II, 956–57; Memorandum of Stillwell-Douglas Telephone Conversation, Sept. 8, 1947, *ibid.*, 957–58, 959, note 82. See State Dept. *Bulletin*, 17 (Sept. 21, 1947), 576–84, for the "Report on the Anglo-American Talks on Coal Production."

24. Memorandum, Nov. 14, 1947, *FRUS*, 1947, II, 971–75, and Editorial Note, pp. 976–77.

25. Draper to Clay, July 26, 1947, War Dept. Papers, file ASW 091 Germany, NA; ActgSecState to AmEmbassy, London, Aug. 22, 1947, *FRUS*, 1947, II, 950–52.

26. Minutes of a Meeting of the Secretaries of State, War, and Navy, June 19, 1947, *FRUS*, 1947, II, 927.

27. Riddleberger, Memorandum, Subj: Germany: Revision of Directive Regarding Military Government in Germany, June 26, 1947, RG 59, Records of the Office of European Affairs, folder: Memoranda for Secretary Marshall, Box 16, NA. Riddleberger, Memorandum to Hilldring, Subj: Memorandum on Paragraph 21c (Public Ownership), Revised JCS 1067 . . . , July 8, 1947, RG 107, ASW files, Box 26, NA; OMGUS to AGWAR, July 12, 1947, RG 107, file ASW 463.3, Box 77, NA; U.S. Dept. of State, *Germany, 1947–1949*, Pub. 3556 (Washington, 1950), p. 40, for JCS 1779, V, 21c.

28. Clay to Draper, Oct. 20, 1947; Draper to Royall, Oct. 22, 1947; Draper to Forrestal, Oct. 27, 1947, RG 335, file OSA 004 Germany, Box 72, NA.

29. OMGUS, from Clay, to AGWAR, for Noce, July 12, 1947, RG 107, file ASW 463.3, Box 77, NA.

30. Clay to War Dept., Aug. 25, 1947, *FRUS*, 1947, II, 1059–63.

31. Regional Government Coordinating Office (RGCO), "Speech of General Lucius D. Clay . . . 9 Sept. 1947," in file 1g06/01, Staatskanzlei, Wiesbaden.

32. Hickerson to Matthews, June 25, 1947, RG 59, Hickerson Papers, Memoranda, Jan. to June 1947 folder, Box 3, NA.

33. OMGUS to AGWAR, July 3, 1947, RG 165, file CAD 463.3, Sec. V, Box 391, NA; July 5, 1947, *ibid.*

34. War Dept. to OMGUS, July 16, 1947, RG 165, file WDSCA 463.3, Sec. V, Box 391, NA; Patterson to Marshall, July 22, 1947, RG 59, file 740.00119 Control (Germany)/7-2247, NA.

35. Clay to Petersen, July 15, 1947, War Dept. Papers, file ASW 091 Germany, NA.

36. War Dept. to OMGUS, July 16, 1947, RG 165, file WDSCA 463.3, Sec. V, Box 391, NA.

37. Draper to OMGUS, for Clay, July 19, 1947, RG 165, file WDSCA 014 Germany, Sec. XXIV, Box 239, NA; *New York Times*, July 19, 1947, p. 1.

38. Patterson to Marshall, July 22, 1947, RG 59, file 740.00119 Control (Germany)/7-2247, NA.

39. War Dept. to Clay, July 28, 1947, *FRUS*, 1947, II, 1010–1011; Frank A. Southard to Secretary Snyder, Subj: Summary of Anglo-American Talks on Ruhr Coal Production (Based on the Minutes and Papers Covering Meetings Through August 23, 1947), n.d., Snyder Papers, Box 15 (Germany—General, 1946–51), Truman Library.

40. U.S. Dept. of State, *Germany, 1947–1949*, p. 38, for JCS 1779, 18c.

41. Lovett to AmEmbassy, London, Sept. 26, 1947, *FRUS*, 1947, II, 966–68; War Dept. to OMGUS, Sept. 30, 1947, RG 165, file WDSCA 463.3, Sec. VI, Box 391, NA; OMGUS to War Dept., Oct. 10, 1947, *ibid.*

Chapter Seventeen

1. Clay to Draper, April 11, 1947, *FRUS*, 1947, II, 472–73.

2. Riddleberger, Memorandum, Subj: Possible Questions on Germany, May 28, 1947, RG 59, H. Freeman Matthews files, Box 9, Press Conference Memoranda for Secretary, 1947, NA.

3. Petersen to AGWAR, June 2, 1947, RG 107, file ASW 091 Germany, Box 26, NA.

4. SecState to ActgSecState, April 19, 1947, *FRUS*, 1947, II, 357–58. See *ibid.*, 356–57, for an indication of Marshall's confusion on the issue.

5. Memorandum for the Record, JJG, July 2, 1947, RG 165, file WDSCA 014 Germany, Sec. XXIII, Box 239, NA; Patterson to Petersen, June 27, 1947, RG 107, file ASW 387, Book 4, Box 67, NA; Petersen to Clay, July 8, 1947, War Dept. Papers, file ASW 091 Germany, Book 2, NA; Walter Millis, ed., *The Forrestal Diaries* (New York, 1951), pp. 287–88.

6. Petersen to Clay, July 8, 1947, War Dept. Papers, file ASW 091 Germany, Book 2, NA; War Dept. to OMGUS, July 2, 1947, *ibid.*

7. Clay to AGWAR, for Petersen, July 6, 1947, War Dept. Papers, file WDSCA 014 Germany, Sec. XXIV, NA. See also SecState to Dorr, July 10, 1947, *FRUS*, 1947, II, 1108–9.

8. Petersen to Clay, July 8, 1947, RG 107, file ASW 091 Germany, Book 2, Box 26, NA.

9. Notes and Memoranda attached to War Dept. cable 81734 to OMGUS, July 10, 1947, RG 107, file ASW 091 Germany, Book 2, Box 26, NA.

10. Acheson to Riddleberger, Galbraith, Leverich, and Mason, July 31, 1946, RG 59, file 740.00119 Control (Germany), Box 3737, NA; Harris to Matthews, Sept. 17, 1946, RG 59, Records of the Office of European Affairs, Box 14, folder Germany, NA; War Dept. to USFET, Sept. 13, 1946, RG 218, JCS 1946–48, file CCS 383.21 Germany (2/22/44), Sec. 15, NA; OMGUS to War Dept., Sept. 16, 1946, RG 165, file WDSCA 008, Sec. II, Box 230, NA; War Dept. to OMGUS, Sept. 21, 1946, *ibid.*; War Dept. to OMGUS, Oct. 21, 1946, *ibid.*; OMGUS to War Dept., Nov. 2, 1946, *ibid.*; War Dept. to Clay, Dec. 9, 1946, *ibid.*; Claxton to Hilldring, Subj: Comments on Substance of Report of Committee on Policy Toward Germany, Oct. 4, 1946, RG 59, file 740.00119 Control (Germany), Box 3742, NA; War Dept., CAD, Memorandum, Subj: JCS 1067/6—Progress Report on Revision, Dec. 4, 1946, RG 165, Box 316, NA; Fritz E. Oppenheimer to Mr. Fahy, Oct. 22, 1946, RG 59, file 740.00119 Control (Germany), Box C-145, NA; Clay to SecState, Nov. 29, 1946, OMGUS Papers, Box 166-1/3 and 177-3/3, NA.

11. Memorandum, K. W. Hamilton to Mr. Transtrum, April 17, 1947, RG 59, file 740.00119 Control (Germany)/4-747, NA; Riddleberger to Murphy, May 23, 1947, *ibid.*,/5-2347, NA.

12. Draft of JCS 1779, May 19, 1947, RG 218, file CCAC 014 Germany, Sec. 11, Box 125, NA.

13. Petersen to Clay, July 10, 1947, RG 107, file ASW 091 Germany, Book 2, Box 26, NA.

14. See Petersen to Clay, July 8, 1947, RG 107, file ASW 091 Germany, Book 2, Box 26, NA.

15. Memorandum, H. R. Labouisse to Kindleberger, Subj: European Recovery Proposals, July 11, 1947, RG 59, file 840.50 Recovery/7-447, NA. Labouisse's memorandum originated out of a discussion in the first meeting of the State Department's informal committee on European recovery. See Minutes, Committee on European Recovery Program, June 25, 1947, *ibid.*,/8-2547, NA.

16. Murphy to SecState, July 16, 1947, *FRUS*, 1947, II, 988–90.

17. Clay to AGWAR, July 12, 1947, War Dept. Papers, file WDSCA 014 Germany, Sec. XXIV, NA.

18. Memorandum, Matthews to Lovett, July 11, 1947, *FRUS*, 1947, III, 717–22.

19. Caffery to SecState, July 11, 1947, *FRUS*, 1947, III, 328–30.

20. Caffery to SecState, July 11, 1947, *FRUS*, 1947, II, 983–86 (emphasis added).

21. Memorandum, Noce to Petersen, July 15, 1947, RG 165, file WDSCA 387.6, Sec. XIV, Box 356, NA.

22. SecState to Caffery, July 15, 1947, *FRUS*, 1947, II, 986–87, and note 16.

23. Petersen to Clay, July 15, 1947, War Dept. Papers, file ASW 091 Germany, Book 2, NA.

24. Petersen to Hilldring, July 15, 1947, War Dept. Papers, file ASW 091 Germany, Book 2, NA.

25. SecState to Caffery, July 15, 1947, *FRUS*, 1947, II, 987–88; Caffery to SecState, July 18, 1947, *ibid.*, 993–96 (emphasis added).

26. Balfour to SecState, July 24, 1947, *FRUS*, 1947, II, 1005–6.

27. Caffery to SecState, July 17, 1947, *FRUS*, 1947, II, 997, note 29.

28. Caffery to SecState, July 20, 1947, *FRUS*, 1947, II, 997–99.

29. Communication by Bidault, July 17, 1947, *FRUS*, 1947, II, 992–93; Bidault to SecState, July 17, 1947, *ibid.*, 991–92.

30. Caffery to SecState, July 18, 1947, *FRUS*, 1947, II, 996.

31. Clayton to SecState, for Lovett, July 21, 1947, RG 59, file 840.50 Recovery/7-2147, NA.

32. Caffery to SecState, July 18, 1947, *FRUS*, 1947, III, 722–24 (emphasis added).

33. Draper to Clay, July 18, 1947, RG 165, file WDSCA 014 Germany, Sec. XXIV, NA; July 19, 1947, *ibid.*

34. Memorandum of Bonnet-Lovett Conversation, July 18, 1947, RG 59, Hickerson files, Box 3, Memoranda, July to Dec. 1947, NA.

35. Kennan, Memorandum, July 18?, 1947, *FRUS*, 1947, III, 332–33.

36. SecState to Bevin, July 19, 1947, *FRUS*, 1947, II, 997.

37. Bevin to Marshall (July 20, 1947), *FRUS*, 1947, II, 999–1000.

38. Clayton to SecState, for Lovett, July 21, 1947, RG 59, file 840.50 Recovery/7-2147, NA.

39. Memorandum of Marshall-Bonnet-Matthews Conversation, July 21, 1947, *FRUS*, 1947, II, 1000–1003.

Chapter Eighteen

1. Petersen to Hilldring, July 15, 1947, War Dept. Papers, file ASW 091 Germany, Book 2, NA.

2. Balfour to SecState, July 24, 1947, *FRUS*, 1947, II, 1105–6. See also *ibid.*, 1007, note 44, referring to a message from Bevin to Marshall, July 24, 1947.

3. Memorandum of Balfour-Lovett Conversation, July 24, 1947, *FRUS*, 1947, II, 1006–8. Lovett had heard the French complaints from Ambassador Bonnet on July 18. See *ibid.*, 1001, note 34.

4. See *FRUS*, 1947, II, 1007, note 46.

5. Hilldring to SecState, July 24, 1947, *FRUS*, 1947, II, 1004–5.

6. Teleconference, Clay and Petersen, July 24, 1947, TT 8362, RG 316, Clay Papers, Box 2, NA. See also Murphy to SecState, July 25, 1947, *FRUS*, 1947, II, 1008–9.

7. Eisenhower to Clay, July 25, 1947, RG 316, Clay Papers, Box 4, NA; Clay to AGWAR, for Noce, July 26, 1947, *ibid.*

8. Royall (and Marshall) to Clay (and Murphy), July 26, 1947, *FRUS*, 1947, II, 1009–10.

9. Clay to AGWAR, for Royall, July 28, 1947, RG 316, Clay Papers, Box 4, NA.

10. Royall (and Marshall) to Clay (and Murphy), July 28, 1947, *FRUS*, 1947, II, 1010–11.

11. Petersen to Clay, July 29, 1947, RG 316, Clay Papers, Box 4, NA.

12. Memorandum, Lovett to Marshall, Aug. 3, 1947, *FRUS*, 1947, II, 1014–16; Caffery to SecState, Aug. 3, 1947, RG 59, file 840.50 Recovery/8-347, Box 3087, NA. See *New York Times*, Aug. 3, 1947, p. 31, for Jack Raymond's story that Royall's press conference created confusion among the reporters in Berlin.

13. Memorandum, Lovett to SecState, Aug. 5, 1947, *FRUS*, 1947, II, 1017–20.

14. Memorandum of Reber-Penson Conversation, July 30, 1947, *FRUS*, 1947, II, 1013–14.

15. Caffery to Bidault, August 4, 1947, *FRUS*, 1947, II, 1017.

16. Teletype Conversation Between Lovett and Clayton, Aug. 4, 1947, RG 59, file 711.51/8-447, NA; Memorandum, Lovett to SecState, Aug. 5, 1947, *FRUS*, 1947, II, 1017–20. See also David Schoenbrun, "The French and the Ruhr," *The New Republic*, 117 (Aug. 4, 1947), 7.

17. SecState to AmEmbassy, London, Aug. 8, 1947, *FRUS*, 1947, II, 1024–25; Douglas to Marshall, Aug. 11, 1947, as noted in *ibid.*, 1026, note 73; Caffery to SecState, Aug. 9, 1947, as noted in *ibid.*, 1024, note 71.

18. Teletype Conversation Between Lovett and Clayton, Aug. 4, 1947, RG 59, file 711.51/8-447, NA.

19. Memorandum, Lovett for SecState, Aug. 3, 1947, *FRUS*, 1947, II, 1014–16.

20. Memorandum of Marshall-Bonnet Conversation, Aug. 5, 1947, *FRUS*, 1947, II, 1021–22.

21. Clayton to Lovett, July 30, 1947, *FRUS*, 1947, II, 1011–12; Clayton to SecState, Aug. 7, 1947, *ibid.*, 1022–24.

22. Memorandum, Subj: The Bizonal Level of Industry Plan, Aug. 8, 1947, attached to De Wilde to Wood and Saltzman, Aug. 18, 1947, RG 59, file 740.00119 Control (Germany)/8-1847, NA; Caffery to SecState, Aug. 8, 1947, RG 59, file 840.50 Recovery/8-847, NA.

23. See *FRUS*, 1947, II, 1025, note 72.

24. Clay to Byrnes, May 11, 1947, Byrnes Papers, folder 651(2), Clemson University Library.

25. Murphy to SecState, Aug. 9, 1947, *FRUS*, 1947, II, 1026–27.

26. *FRUS*, 1947, II, 1027, note 75; Douglas to Clay, Aug. 16, 1947, Douglas Papers, Box 240, folder 10, University of Arizona Library; Royall to Clay, Aug. 19, 1947, RG 316, Clay Papers, Box 4, NA.

27. Marshall to Patterson, May 23, 1947, RG 165, file WDSCA 321 CAD, Sec. IV, Box 317, NA.

28. Memorandum, Frank to Hilldring, May 29, 1947, Subj: Administrative Responsibility for the Non-Military Aspects of the Occupation of Korea, Japan and Germany When Transferred from the War Department to the State Department, RG 59, file 740.00119 Control (Korea)/5-2947, NA. Clayton, Hilldring, and Peurifoy to SecState, June 20, 1947, Subj: Proposed Reorganization for Administration of Foreign Programs, RG 59, file 840.50 Recovery/6-2047, NA; Saltzman to Lovett, Aug. 25, 1947, RG 59, file 740.00119 Control (Germany)/8-2547, NA.

29. Matthews to Hilldring, May 15, 1947, RG 59, H. Freeman Matthews files,

folder: Memoranda 1947, Box 10, NA. Minutes, Committee on European Recovery Program, June 25, 1947, RG 59, file 840.50 Recovery/8-2547, NA. Memorandum, H. R. Labouisse to Kindleberger, Subj: European Recovery Proposals, July 11, 1947, *ibid.*,/7-447, NA.

30. James A. Stillwell to Saltzman, Subj: Basic Directive to General Clay, Aug. 25, 1947, RG 59, file 740.00119 Control (Germany)/8-2547, NA.

31. Royall to Lovett, Sept. 3, 1947, with attached "Outline Plan for Transfer from War Department to State Department . . . ," War Dept. Papers, file SAOUS 014.1 Germany/State, NA; Royall to Lovett, Sept. 9, 1947, RG 59, file 110.721/9-947, NA, and other materials in the same file.

32. Memorandum of Lovett-Saltzman-Draper-Clay-Gordon Gray Conversation, Oct. 18, 1947, RG 59, file 740.00119 Control (Germany)/10-1847, NA.

33. State Dept. Press Release, Oct. 20, 1947, War Dept. Papers, file SAOUS 014.1 Germany/State, NA.

34. Murphy reported to Lovett and Saltzman on Oct. 25, 1947, that Clay had told him he would announce his retirement for "some time next year" at his next press conference in Berlin, and that he gave as his reason the unwillingness of Royall and Eisenhower to assign him sufficient authority as military governor. Murphy to SecState, for Lovett and Saltzman, Oct. 25, 1947, RG 59, file 740.00119 Control (Germany)/10-2547, NA.

35. Royall to Marshall, Nov. 5, 1947, RG 59, file 110.721/11-1047, NA.

36. Hilldring to Saltzman, Nov. 10, 1947, RG 59, file 110.721/11-1047, NA.

37. T. N. Dupuy, Memorandum for the Record, Subj: Meeting Between Secretary Marshall and Secretary Royall, Jan. 19, 1948, War Dept. Papers, file SAOUS 014.1 Germany/State, NA; Clay to Draper, Jan. 8, 1948, *ibid.*; War Dept., CSCAD, to Clay, Subj: State Takeover of Occupied Areas, Jan. 15, 1948, *ibid.*; Draper to Clay, Jan. 27, 1948, *ibid.*; OMGUS, Public Information Office Release, Jan. 28, 1948, OMGUS Papers, Box 1-2/4, NA; Noce to Draper, repeating White House Release, March 23, 1948, War Dept. Papers, file SAOUS 014.1 Germany, NA.

38. See my *The American Occupation of Germany* (Stanford, Calif., 1968), esp. chs. 11–14.

Chapter Nineteen

1. See Lucius D. Clay, *Decision in Germany* (Garden City, N.Y., 1950), p. 109, for a comment on the lingering sentiment in the United States for a "scorched earth" policy.

2. James W. Riddleberger, "United States Policy on the Treatment of Germany," State Dept. *Bulletin*, XIII (Nov. 25, 1945), 841–49.

3. Kennan to Acheson, May 23, 1947, *FRUS*, 1947, III, 223–30.

4. See Memorandum of Conversation, Ernest Lindley (*Newsweek*) and Mr. Williamson and Mr. Fuller, Aug. 11, 1947, RG 59, file 740.00119 Control (Germany)/8-1147, NA, for the statement that "the Department was confronted with the necessity of rebuilding [the] German economy in such a manner as not to jeopardize the interests of European and world security."

5. War Dept., from SecWar, SecState, and SecNavy, to Clay, June 19, 1947, RG 107, file ASW 091 Germany, Book 2, Box 26, NA.

6. War Dept. to OMGUS, July 2, 1947, RG 107, file ASW 091 Germany, Book 2, Box 26, NA.

7. Minutes, Meeting of SecState, SecWar, and SecNavy, July 3, 1947, War Dept. Papers, SecWar, Office of Special Assistant, 334, Committee of Three, Jan. 1947- , NA.

8. Petersen to Clay, July 10, 1947, RG 107, file ASW 091 Germany, Book 2, Box 26, NA.

9. See JCS 1779, V, 18c and V, 16c, in U.S. Dept. of State, *Germany, 1947–1949*, Pub. 3556 (Washington, 1950), pp. 37–38.

10. Memorandum, Matthews to Lovett, July 11, 1947, *FRUS*, 1947, III, 717–22.

11. Caffery to SecState, July 11, 1947, *FRUS*, 1947, II, 983–86.

12. BrEmbassy to SecState, *Aide-Mémoire*, July 15, 1947, *FRUS*, 1947, II, 986–87, and note 16; Petersen to Clay, July 15, 1947, RG 107, file ASW 091 Germany, Book 2, Box 26, NA; Caffery to SecState, July 17, 1947, as noted in *FRUS*, 1947, II, 997, note 29; Caffery to SecState, July 20, 1947, *ibid.*, 997–99.

13. SecState to Bidault, July 21, 1947, *FRUS*, 1947, II, 1003–4.

14. Memorandum, by Director of PPS (Kennan), July 18?, 1947, *FRUS*, 1947, III, 332–33.

15. Clinton Anderson to Truman, July 18, 1947, Anderson Files (Germany Trip), Box 8, Truman Library; Marshall to Anderson, July 22, 1947, *FRUS*, 1947, II, 1154, note 56, 1156–57.

16. Marshall to Douglas, Aug. 12, 1947, *FRUS*, 1947, II, 1027–29.

17. Douglas to Lovett, Aug. 22, 1947, *FRUS*, 1947, II, 1047–49.

18. ActgSecState to AmEmbassy, London, Aug. 27, 1947, *FRUS*, 1947, II, 1063–64; Douglas to SecState, Aug. 27, 1947, *ibid.*, 1064–66. The record shows, however, that Douglas advised the French delegate (Massigli) informally of the U.S. position, which Douglas and his colleagues had passed on to Bidault in Paris on Aug. 19, 1947.

19. See Memorandum, Hickerson to Lovett, Aug. 23, 1947, *FRUS*, 1947, II, 1050–54, for a judgment that the American and British unwillingness to discuss with the French an international board for the Ruhr was a "negative policy," and a prediction that "a serious crisis will be precipitated if we insist on the ... negative position."

20. Caffery to SecState, Aug. 19, 1947, *FRUS*, 1947, II, 1041–42. But see Memorandum of Bonnet-Lovett Conversation, Aug. 21, 1947, *ibid.*, 1046–47, for the record of Bonnet's efforts to get a commitment on a Ruhr authority from Lovett.

21. The communiqué is in U.S. Dept. of State, *Germany, 1947–1949*, pp. 356–59. See also AmEmbassy, London, to SecState, Aug. 27, 1947, War Dept. Papers, file WDSCA 014 Germany, Sec. XXV, NA, and Hickerson to James C. H. Bonbright, Aug. 30, 1947, RG 59, Hickerson Papers, folder B, Box 4, NA, for

the observation that "your clients [the French] behaved badly but I suppose no more badly than usual."

22. Murphy to Douglas, Sept. 5, 1947, *FRUS*, 1947, II, 1089–90; Murphy to Hickerson, Oct. 1, 1947, *ibid.*, 1096–98; OMGUS, from Clay, to TAG, for Noce, Sept. 30, 1947, RG 165, file WDSCA 463.3, Sec. VI, NA; OMGUS, from Wilkinson, to C/S, U.S. Army, for Clay, Oct. 10, 1947, *ibid.*; Draper to Clay, Nov. 22, 1947, *FRUS*, 1947, II, 725–26; OMGUS, from Hays, to Draper, CC 2392, Nov. 24, 1947, War Dept. Papers, file SAOUS 463.3 Germany, NA; CC 2510, Dec. 6, 1947, *ibid.*; Memorandum, William C. Baker, CAD, to Chief, CAD, Dec. 10, 1947, War Dept. Papers, file CSCAD 014 Germany, Sec. 29, NA.

23. See Douglas to Lovett, Sept. 2, 1947, *FRUS*, 1947, II, 1068–69; Caffery to SecState, Sept. 16, 1947, *ibid.*, 1072, and note 40; Memorandum of Marshall-Bidault Conversation, Nov. 28, 1947, *ibid.*, 739, note 74; *ibid.*, 1097; and John Gimbel, *The American Occupation of Germany* (Stanford, Calif., 1968), pp. 198ff, 208–9.

24. Marshall, Report on Moscow CFM, April 28, 1947, U.S. Dept. of State, *Germany, 1947–1949*, pp. 57–63; Dulles, Report on Moscow Conference, April 30, 1947, *Vital Speeches*, XIII (May 15, 1947), 450–53. Dulles said that "as we studied the problem of Germany in its European setting, we became more and more convinced that there is no economic solution along purely national lines."

25. War Dept., from SecWar, SecState, SecNavy, to Clay, June 19, 1947, RG 107, file ASW 091 Germany, Book 2, Box 26, NA; Clayton to SecState, June 25, 1947, *FRUS*, 1947, II, 932–33; Minutes, Meeting of SecState, SecWar, and SecNavy, July 3, 1947, War Dept. Papers, SecWar, Office of Special Assistant, file 334, Committee of Three, Jan. 1947– , NA.

26. Clayton, "The European Crisis," *FRUS*, 1947, III, 230–32; Caffery to SecState, June 28, 1947, *ibid.*, 297–99; Douglas to Marshall, June 28, 1947, RG 59, file 840.50 Recovery/6-2847, NA.

27. Caffery to SecState, July 20, 1947, *FRUS*, 1947, III, 333–35. See Caffery to SecState, July 27, 1947, *ibid.*, 338–39; July 29, 1947, *ibid.*, 339–41, for further reports of French objection to German recovery.

28. Hickerson, Memorandum, Aug. 11, 1947, *FRUS*, 1947, III, 351–55, said: "The United States must present a united front when talking to other powers. It would be undesirable to have two independent groups of U.S. representatives, one representing our interests in the over-all European recovery and the other representing our interests in Germany alone." Naturally, Hickerson thought the State Department should do it. See also SecState to AmEmbassy, Paris, Aug. 11, 1947, *ibid.*, 350–51; Caffery to SecState, Aug. 12, 1947, *ibid.*, 355–56; Memorandum Prepared by PPS, Aug. 14, 1947, *ibid.*, 360–63.

29. Lovett to Clayton and Caffery, Aug. 14, 1947, *FRUS*, 1947, III, 356–60.

30. Caffery to SecState, Aug. 20, 1947, *FRUS*, 1947, III, 364–67.

31. Douglas to SecState, Aug. 21, 1947, *FRUS*, 1947, III, 368–69.

32. Minutes of Meeting on Marshall "Plan," Aug. 22, 1947, *FRUS*, 1947, III, 369–72; Lovett to SecState, Aug. 24, 1947, *ibid.*, 372–75.

33. The President's Committee on Foreign Aid, *European Recovery and American Aid* (Washington, 1947), pp. 22–23 (emphasis added). For statistics on the comparative lag in German production see *ibid.*, p. 117; U.S. Congress, Senate, Committee on Foreign Relations, 80th Cong., 2d Sess., *Hearings ... on United States Assistance to European Economic Recovery* (Washington, 1948), pp. 249–50; and Bert F. Hoselitz, "Four Reports on Economic Aid to Europe," *The Journal of Political Economy*, LVI (April 1948), 112–13.

34. Marshall, "Problems of European Revival and German and Austrian Peace Settlements," Nov. 18, 1947, in U.S. Dept. of State, *Germany, 1947–1949*, p. 13.

35. *FRUS*, 1947, III, 375, note 5; Lovett to Clayton and Caffery, Aug. 26, 1947, *ibid.*, 383–91; Clayton to SecState, Aug. 31, 1947, *ibid.*, 391–96.

36. C. H. Bonesteel to Lovett, Subj: Discussion of Bizonal Economic Plans at Paris Conference, Aug. 27, 1947, RG 59, file 740.00119 Control (Germany)/8-2747, NA.

37. War Dept., from Noce, to OMGUS, Sept. 3, 1947, RG 165, file WDSCA 334 EECE, Sec. II, Box 319, NA; SecState to Douglas, Sept. 5, 1947, *FRUS*, 1947, III, 409–10; Memorandum of Conversation, Lovett, Saltzman, Draper, Clay, and Gordon Gray, Oct. 18, 1947, RG 59, file 740.00119 Control (Germany)/10-1847, NA.

38. ActgSecState to SecState, March 20, 1947, *FRUS*, 1947, II, 394–95; Meeting of the Non-Partisan Committee of Nineteen Distinguished Citizens, July 23, 1947, Records of the President's Committee on Foreign Aid, 1947, file PCFA—Minutes & Meetings, Box 1, Truman Library.

39. Minutes of the Meeting of the Subcommittee on Economic and Financial Analysis in Hanover, N.H., Aug. 15, 1947, Records of the President's Committee on Foreign Aid, 1947, file Subcommittee—Economic and Financial Analysis, Box 6, Truman Library. Calvin Hoover, it will be recalled, had been the Chairman of the OMGUS German Standard-of-Living Board in 1945 and had left Germany disappointed and unhappy with existing policy and with Germany's economic prospects for the future.

40. Minutes of the President's Committee of Nineteen on Foreign Aid, Sept. 10–11, 1947, Records of the PCFA, 1947, file PCFA—Minutes & Meetings, Box 1, Truman Library; Notes for Press Conference, 9/11/47, *ibid.*; Interdepartmental Committee on Marshall Plan, Minutes, Sept. 9, 1947, Clifford Papers, file ERP—ECA Miscellaneous, Truman Library.

41. Owen D. Young to Harriman, Sept. 12, 1947, Records of the PCFA, 1947, file Member—Owen D. Young, Box 2, Truman Library.

42. The President's Committee on Foreign Aid, *European Recovery and American Aid*, pp. 3, 7, 33–34, 117–22, and *passim*.

43. SecState to Douglas, Sept. 5, 1947, *FRUS*, 1947, III, 409–10; Sept. 8, 1947, *ibid.*, 410, note 2, and 418–19.

44. SecState to Douglas, Sept. 8, 1947, *FRUS*, 1947, III, 418–19.

45. Douglas to SecState, cable number 4950, Sept. 12, 1947, *FRUS*, 1947, III, 428–29; cable number 4951, Sept. 12, 1947, *ibid.*, 429–30.

46. Douglas to SecState, Sept. 17, 1947, RG 59, file 840.50 Recovery/9-1747, NA.

47. Clayton to Lovett, Aug. 25, 1947, *FRUS*, 1947, III, 377–79.

48. Lovett to Clayton and Caffery, Aug. 26, 1947, *FRUS*, 1947, III, 383–89.

49. Clayton to Lovett, Aug. 31, 1947, *FRUS*, 1947, III, 391–96.

50. Lovett to Marshall, Aug. 31, 1947, *FRUS*, 1947, III, 396–97.

51. Kennan, Situation with Respect to European Recovery Program, Sept. 4, 1947, *FRUS*, 1947, III, 397–405.

52. Caffery, from Dept. Economic Advisers, to Lovett and others, Sept. 5, 1947, *FRUS*, 1947, III, 405–8; ActgSecState, Circular Telegram to Representatives Accredited to CEEC Nations and Murphy, Sept. 7, 1947, *ibid.*, 412–15.

53. *FRUS*, 1947, III, 415, note 3; Douglas to SecState, Sept. 9, 1947, *ibid.*, 420.

54. Caffery to SecState, Sept. 11, 1947, *FRUS*, 1947, III, 421–23.

55. Caffery to SecState, Sept. 12, 1947, *FRUS*, 1947, III, 425–28; Douglas to SecState, cable number 4950, Sept. 12, 1947, *ibid.*, 428–29; cable number 4951, Sept. 12, 1947, *ibid.*, 429–30. See also Douglas to SecState, Sept. 17, 1947, *ibid.*, 435, for a repetition of the advice to press for inclusion of the bizone *only after* the first report had been received.

56. Editorial Note, *FRUS*, 1947, III, 439–41; SecState to AmEmbassy, London, Nov. 5, 1947, RG 59, file 840.50 Recovery/11-547, NA; Frank A. Southard to Secretary Snyder, Oct. 3, 1947, Snyder Papers, file Congress—Interim Aid Program, 1947–48, folder 1, Truman Library; U.S. Congress, Senate, *Congressional Record*, 80th Cong., 2d Sess., March 11, 1948, pp. 2528–31.

57. Record of a Meeting Between Members of the Advisory Steering Committee and the CEEC Delegation, Nov. 4, 1947, *FRUS*, 1947, III, 463–70.

58. Ernst H. Van Der Beugel, *From Marshall Aid to Atlantic Partnership: European Integration as a Concern of American Foreign Policy* (Amsterdam, 1966), esp. pp. 77–93. See also Arthur Krock, in *New York Times*, Oct. 5, 1947, DNC Clippings, Box 24, Truman Library; Sir Hubert Henderson, "The European Economic Report," *International Affairs*, XXIV (Jan. 1948), 19–29; and Michael Straight, "The Betrayal of the Original Concept," *The New Republic*, 118 (Jan. 12, 1948), 9–11.

59. U.S. Congress, Senate, Committee on Foreign Relations, 80th Cong., 2d Sess., *Hearings . . . on . . . European Economic Recovery*, Jan. 8, 1948, pp. 11–12.

Chapter Twenty

1. See, for example, U.S. Congress, House, Committee on Foreign Affairs, 80th Cong., 1st Sess., *Hearings . . . on European Interim Aid . . .* (Washington, 1947), pp. 121–22, for a discussion on Nov. 13, 1947, about using an economic pistol on the Russians and forcing a change in the Soviet Union, as well as the prospects of a successful program to roll back Communism behind the iron curtain.

2. Kennan to Acheson, May 23, 1947, *FRUS*, 1947, III, 223–30.

3. George F. Kennan [Mr. X], "The Sources of Soviet Conduct," *Foreign Affairs*, XXV (July 1947), 566–82.

4. Joseph M. Jones, *The Fifteen Weeks* (New York, 1955), esp. pp. 138–40, 150–51, 175–76.

5. See George F. Kennan, *Memoirs, 1925–1950* (Boston, 1967), pp. 325–26; Jones, pp. 223–24.

6. William A. Williams, *The Tragedy of American Diplomacy*, rev. & enlarged ed. (New York, 1962), p. 268.

7. See, for example, Thomas C. Blaisdell, "The Foreign Aid Program and United States Commercial Policy," *Proceedings of the Academy of Political Science*, XXIII (Jan. 1950), 397–407.

8. Caffery to SecState, Aug. 31, 1947, *FRUS*, 1947, III, 391–96.

9. See Williams, pp. 271–76, for the scriptural text and, for commentaries thereon, Bruce Kuklick, *American Policy and the Division of Germany* (Ithaca, N.Y., 1972); Barton J. Bernstein, "American Foreign Policy and the Origins of the Cold War," in Bernstein, ed., *Politics and Policies of the Truman Administration* (Chicago, 1970); Joyce and Gabriel Kolko, *The Limits of Power: The World and United States Foreign Policy, 1945–1954* (New York, 1972); and Lloyd C. Gardner, *Architects of Illusion: Men and Ideas in American Foreign Policy, 1941–1949* (Chicago, 1970).

10. Freda Kirchwey, "Marketing the Plan," *The Nation*, 164 (June 28, 1947), 759; John H. Williams, "Economic Lessons of Two World Wars," *Foreign Affairs*, XXVI (Oct. 1947), 134–54, esp. 137ff; Lewis H. Brown, "American Economic Policy Relating to Germany and Western Europe," *Proceedings of the Academy of Political Science*, XXII (Jan. 1948), 441.

11. U.S. Congress, House, Committee on Foreign Affairs, 80th Cong., 1st Sess., *Hearings . . . on European Interim Aid . . .*, p. 88.

12. The President's Committee on Foreign Aid, *European Recovery and American Aid*, pp. 11, 17–22, and *passim*.

13. Harry S. Truman, "Program of United States Support for European Recovery," Dec. 19, 1947, in House Document 478, 80th Cong., in Committee on Foreign Affairs Records, file HR 80A-R7.6, Box 18825, NA.

14. U.S. Congress, Senate, *Congressional Record*, 80th Cong., 2d Sess., March 4, 1948, p. 2127.

15. Harry B. Price, *The Marshall Plan and Its Meaning* (Ithaca, N.Y., 1955), p. 85. See Barbara Ward, *The West at Bay* (New York, 1948), p. 171, for comments on the Harriman Committee's deliberations as almost a comic rebuttal of the capitalist, imperialist view of the Marshall Plan.

16. Hoover to Marshall, July 28, 1947, in Records of the PCFA, 1947 (Member—Hoover, Calvin B.), Box 2, Truman Library.

17. U.S. Congress, Senate, Committee on Foreign Relations, 80th Cong., 2d Sess., *Hearings . . . on . . . European Economic Recovery*, Jan. 23, 1948, pp. 843–44 (emphasis added).

18. See U.S. Congress, Senate, *Congressional Record*, 80th Cong., 1st Sess., Extension of Remarks of Kenneth S. Wherry, Nov. 20, 1947, p. A4251.

19. See U.S. Congress, Senate, *Congressional Record*, 80th Cong., 2d Sess., Jan. 21, 1948, p. 392.

20. Ernest H. Van Der Beugel, *From Marshall Aid to Atlantic Partnership* (Amsterdam, 1966), p. 93.

21. U.S. Congress, House, *Congressional Record*, 80th Cong., 2d Sess., Feb. 9, 1948, p. 1252. For additional materials on the same theme, see Harold L. Hitchens, "Influences on the Congressional Decision to Pass the Marshall Plan," *The Western Political Quarterly*, XXI (March 1968), 51–68; Quentin L. Quade, "The Truman Administration and the Separation of Powers: The Case of the Marshall Plan," *The Review of Politics*, XXVII (Jan. 1965), 58–77; Frank McNaughton to Don Bermingham, "The Marshall Plan," July 10, 1947, Frank McNaughton Papers, Truman Library; July 11, 1947, *ibid.*; Oct. 3, 1947, *ibid.*; George M. Elsey to Clark Clifford, Subj: The Marshall Plan, Sept. 22, 1947, Clifford Papers (Economic Cooperation Administration, Miscellaneous), Box 4, *ibid.*; Kimball Young, with collaboration of Helen Porowski and William Brown, "Content Analysis of the Treatment of the Marshall Plan in Certain Representative American Newspapers," *The Journal of Social Psychology*, 33 (1951), 163–85; Frank A. Southard to Secretary Snyder, Oct. 3, 1947, Snyder Papers (Congress—Interim Aid Program, 1947–48), folder 1, Truman Library; White House Conference on Foreign Aid, Oct. 27, 1947, Agenda and Program, OF 426, Box 1279, Truman Library; Remarks by John R. Steelman, Oct. 27, 1947, OF 426, *ibid.*; Memorandum of Lovett-Russell Conversation, Aug. 11, 1947, RG 59, file 840.50 Recovery/19-847, NA; F. B. Lyon to Lovett, Subj: Brief Report of Observations Made While Accompanying the Herter Committee on Trip Abroad, Oct. 20, 1947, *ibid.*/10-2047, NA; Freda Kirchwey, "Marketing the Plan," *The Nation*, 164 (June 28, 1947), 758–59.

22. Minutes of Meeting on Marshall "Plan," Aug. 22, 1947, *FRUS*, 1947, III, 370.

23. Lovett to Clayton and Caffery, Aug. 26, 1947, *FRUS*, 1947, III, 383–89.

24. U.S. Congress, Senate, Committee on Foreign Relations, 80th Cong., 2d Sess., *Hearings . . . on . . . European Economic Recovery*, Jan. 8, 1948, esp. p. 4.

25. See, for example, Marshall's and Lovett's remarks, respectively, in U.S. Congress, House, Committee on Foreign Affairs, 80th Cong., 1st Sess., *Emergency Foreign Aid. Hearings . . .*, Nov. 10, 1947, esp. p. 3; Nov. 12, 1947, esp. p. 44.

26. C. H. Bonesteel to Lovett, Memorandum, Subj: Discussion of Bizonal Economic Plans at Paris Conference, Aug. 27, 1947, RG 59, file 740.00119 Control (Germany)/8-2747, NA.

INDEX

Index